Vertical
Aid ┼

Vertical Aid +

ESSENTIAL WILDERNESS MEDICINE FOR CLIMBERS, TREKKERS, AND MOUNTAINEERS

Seth C. Hawkins, MD
R. Bryan Simon, RN
J. Pearce Beissinger, MS, PA-C
Deb Simon, RN

Illustrations by Mark Quire, quiregraphics.com
Medical illustrations by Samantha Zimmerman

The Countryman Press
A division of W. W. Norton & Company
Independent Publishers Since 1923

For information about permission to reproduce selections from this book, write to
Permissions, The Countryman Press, 500 Fifth Avenue, New York, NY 10110

For information about special discounts for bulk purchases, please contact
W. W. Norton Special Sales at specialsales@wwnorton.com or 800-233-4830

Manufacturing by LSC Communications, Harrisonburg
Book design by Anna Reich
Production manager: Devon Zahn

The Countryman Press
www.countrymanpress.com

A division of W. W. Norton & Company, Inc.
500 Fifth Avenue, New York, NY 10110
www.wwnorton.com

978-1-58157-444-9 (pbk.)

10 9 8 7 6 5 4 3 2 1

SCH: To my parents Anne and Sherman Hawkins,
the original writers of my life.

RBS: In memory of Bruce Turnbull. An inspiration to live
the uncommon life.

JPB: To the glory of God, to the love of my life and best friend, Heather,
our children, and all my friends and family who share in this adventure
called life. Thank you for your support and love, both in the valleys and
high places of this world. Jaimashi.

DAS: Voor mijn ouders met liefde. Jullie hebben me dit fantastische
leven gegeven door hard werken en leiding geven. Dankjewel!

CONTENTS

Introduction   ix

I. LIFE   1

1. Assessment of the Patient   3
2. Life-Threatening Emergencies   18
3. Injury Prevention   33

II. MEDICAL   57

4. Orthopedics   59
5. Spinal Injuries   117
6. Head Injuries   123
7. Abdominal and Gastrointestinal Issues   131
8. Chest and Respiratory Issues   154
9. Wounds and Burns   163
10. Skin Injuries and Care   182

III. ENVIRONMENTAL   191

11. Altitude Illness   193
12. Cold Injuries   202
13. Heat Injuries   215
14. Solar-Related Injuries   227
15. Lightning   235
16. Weather Identification   244
17. Avalanche Awareness   251

IV. RESCUE   255

18. Extrication Decisions and Spinal Motion Restriction   257
19. Carries and Litters   265
20. Rescue Communication   271

V. APPENDICES 279

A. First Aid Kit Contents for Mountain Travel   281

B. How to Communicate with Helicopters, and
Preparations for Helicopter Evacuation   286

C. Conversion Tables   292

D. Frostbite and Windchill Table   294

E. Water Purification Methods   296

F. Recommended Medications for Mountain Travel   307

G. Improvised Shelters   313

H. Vertical Medicine Resources Assessment Sheet   317

Glossary   319

References and Additional Resources   327

Index   349

Author Biographies   368

INTRODUCTION

Climbing is a rapidly growing sport with many specializations. Climbing activities range from the cutting-edge athleticism of sport climbing (which in 2020 will become an Olympic event) to the ancient pursuit of climbing mountains, one of the most traditional of human activities.

This text discusses the medical concepts relevant to all the various climbing activities available to enthusiasts today. These range from urban climbing centers to remote alpine peaks, and from long-distance trekking alpinists for whom a single vertical endeavor may last months to sport climbers for whom it may last minutes. Common among all these concepts is a need for quality education and information about prevention and treatment of common climbing illnesses and injuries.

Our perspective is that this quality is best delivered through the tools of evidence-based medicine. We believe the best medical science available, and the most up-to-date and authoritative consensus guidelines, should drive the training and practices of climbers engaging in medical care, whether it be first aid or formal healthcare delivery in the field. When appropriate, we share the recommendation grade of formal consensus recommendations from professional societies to convey the strength of a recommendation (Figure I-1).

In addition, we include references to source material and studies more often than many other texts of this sort. In this way, we encourage you to access the primary material when it interests you, or when the position we are taking challenges other teachings you have read or received. We, the authors of this text, are all healthcare providers ourselves as well as avid climbers, and this is exactly the approach we take when analyzing conflicting medical information. Furthermore, we each have a different niche in the healthcare profession, as well as different backgrounds in

**FIGURE I-1. GRADING RECOMMENDATIONS
(AMERICAN COLLEGE OF CHEST PHYSICIANS)**

Grade of recommendation/ description	Benefit vs risk and burdens	Methodological quality of supporting evidence	Implications
1A. Strong recommendation, high-quality evidence	Benefits clearly outweigh risk and burdens, or vice versa	RCTs* without important limitations or overwhelming evidence from observational studies	Strong recommendation, can apply to most patients in most circumstances without reservation
1B. Strong recommendation, moderate quality evidence	Benefits clearly outweigh risk and burdens, or vice versa	RCTs with important limitations (inconsistent results, methodological flaws, indirect, or imprecise) or exceptionally strong evidence from observational studies	Strong recommendation, can apply to most patients in most circumstances without reservation
1C. Strong recommendation, low-quality or very low-quality evidence	Benefits clearly outweigh risk and burdens, or vice versa	Observational studies or case series	Strong recommendation but may change when higher quality evidence becomes available

* RCT: randomized control trials

terms of climbing that we bring to bear in writing this text. Together, we strive to make this text your single most important and useful guide for navigating medical issues during your climbing adventures.

The text is divided into four sections:

Life—addressing life threats, initial management of all conditions, and prevention/lifestyle topics;

Medical—addressing the management of specific medical and trauma conditions, divided by body systems and injury types;

Environmental—addressing the prevention and treatment of conditions arising from particular environmental conditions; and

Rescue—addressing skills and steps necessary to move from initial

Grade of recommendation/ description	Benefit vs risk and burdens	Methodological quality of supporting evidence	Implications
2A. Weak recommendation, high-quality evidence	Benefits closely balanced with risks and burden	RCTs without important limitations or overwhelming evidence from observational studies	Weak recommendation, best action may differ depending on circumstances or patients' or societal values
2B. Weak recommendation, moderate-quality evidence	Benefits closely balanced with risks and burden	RCTs with important limitations (inconsistent results, methodological flaws, indirect, or imprecise) or exceptionally strong evidence from observational studies	Weak recommendation, best action may differ depending on circumstances or patients' or societal values
2C. Weak recommendation, low-quality or very low-quality evidence	Uncertainty in the estimates of benefits, risks, and burden; benefits, risk, and burden may be closely balanced	Observational studies or case series	Very weak recommendations; other alternatives may be equally reasonable

Source: Guyatt G, Gutterman D, Baumann MH, et al. "Grading strength of recommendations and quality of evidence in clinical guidelines: report from an American College of Chest Physicians task force." Chest. 2006 Jan; 129 (1): 174–81.

management of illness/injury to communication with external resources, extrication, and evacuation.

One challenge in a text like this is the depth in which to discuss medical conditions. We hope this will be a useful text for both healthcare providers and those without any formal healthcare training. Often, terms and language from the healthcare vocabulary are the most useful way to communicate concepts. In these cases, we define such terms the first time they are used, and include a glossary which can be easily referenced whenever such terms appear later in the text. In addition, a basic understanding of anatomical terminology is necessary to facilitate discussions of climber

FIGURE I-2. RELATIVE ANATOMICAL TERMINOLOGY
(SEE GLOSSARY ON PAGE 319 FOR ADDITIONAL TERMINOLOGY)

Anterior: front of the body or a body part

Posterior: back of the body or a body part

Distal: further from the trunk on an extremity

Proximal: closer to the trunk on an extremity

Superior: higher

Inferior: lower

Abduction: movement away from the torso

Adduction: movement towards the torso

External rotation: rotation away from the midline

Internal rotation: rotation toward the midline

Palmar: on the palm side of the hand

Ventral: on the front side of a body part; in the hand, synonym
                            with palmar

Dorsal: on the back side of a body part; in the hand, opposite to
                            the palm

Flexion: movement of a joint towards or into a bent position

Extension: movement of a joint towards or into a straight position

Medial: on the inside and towards the midline of a body por-
                            tion with two sides

Lateral: on the outside and away from the midline of a body
                            portion with two sides

Pronation: in the hand, turning the hand so the palm is facing
                            downwards

Supination: in the hand, turning the hand so the palm is facing
                            upwards

Prone: lying face down

Supine: lying face up

evaluation and treatment. Figure I-2 describes basic anatomical terminology and can serve as a resource for you when reading later chapters.

On the other hand, we've worked hard to eliminate medical jargon or medical terms when they aren't necessary to convey a concept. We feel that orthopedic injuries in particular are an area of great interest for climbers, so in our discussion of them in Chapter 4, we go in great depth into the medical terms and sometimes hospital-based management of these conditions. In these cases, such depth is necessary, as climbers may often be navigating long courses of hospital, clinic, and rehabilitation management of complex orthopedic conditions, and having this depth of information in one text may prove very helpful.

No text can replicate hands-on training. Multiple times in this book, we encourage you, the reader, to obtain specific certificates or enroll in hands-on training courses to become more adept with the skills needed to manage conditions in a vertical environment. We, the authors, collectively make up Vertical Medicine Resources™, a medical guiding and consulting company. VMR is dedicated to providing training and support for clients in a vertical environment in a unique medical guide format. In addition to this book, we offer certification courses, specialty training, on-site medical support, and consulting services. Numerous other high quality wilderness medicine schools, degree programs, and training opportunities exist. Some are discussed in this book. We strongly recommend you use this book as a launching pad for ideas about further training or a reference source to confirm and enhance the training you have already received. Either way, it is most effective when accompanied by hands-on training.

Most importantly, climb hard, climb safe, and we hope this text offers you aid for those times when injury, illness, or preparatory challenges threaten your enjoyment of this activity we all love so much.

I.
LIFE

CHAPTER 1

ASSESSMENT OF THE PATIENT

All patient care begins with an assessment of the patient and their situation. In the vertical environment, efforts to assess a patient can be complicated by situational hazards. Particularly in small climbing teams with limited human resources, it is important to recognize and identify these hazards. For this reason, evaluating and mitigating situational risk factors prior to formal patient assessment may be necessary. This is often known as a "scene safety" check, and is done prior to entering the scene of the injury or beginning any assessment of the patient.

Mitigating risk at a scene of patient care may be accomplished by expedited removal of the victim from the specific hazards of the environment (e.g., impending rockfall and icefall), or at the very least, creating a barrier to further injury while more formal patient assessment can be undertaken (e.g., placement of helmet, insulating from the cold). It may be possible, or even necessary, to remove the injured victim completely from the environmental hazards prior to assessment; for example, removing someone from a river before formal patient assessment begins. More often, hazard mitigation in mountainous terrain is managed while patient assessment is ongoing.

Situational awareness of the changing dynamics of both patient injury and the surrounding environment is critical. Assessing the dangers of the environment goes beyond simply an initial assessment of scene safety, as the environment may be constantly changing, and so requires equally continuous vigilance for change in situational risk. Some potential changes to the scene include:

+ Other parties moving above your route, creating fall hazards
+ Snow and ice melt changing the entire route above and below your position

+ Impending weather (snow, rain, lightning, heat, cold, etc.)
+ Decreasing daylight, resulting in complications to route-finding, patient care, or visibility to rescue services

In addition to changes in the environment, patient condition may often change. At a minimum, reassessing for possible changes in vital signs and the status of any injuries or illnesses initially identified is important when patient care will be prolonged.

A final important part of beginning care, after scene safety has been determined but before a primary survey is initiated, is identifying yourself, your medical background (if any), and asking a prospective patient if they would like your help. This is an imperative legal and ethical step to be taken prior to initiating evaluation and medical care, including first aid. Note that an unconscious person is presumed to agree to medical care under the legal principle of implied consent.

PRIMARY SURVEY

Initial patient assessment is divided into a primary survey, identifying life threats and situations that must be immediately addressed, and a secondary survey, identifying more subtle or less time-limited conditions and providing more comprehensive information. This formula ensures that immediate life threats are handled first (primary survey), and then that no medical threats or issues are missed during the period of care (secondary survey).

The concept of a primary and secondary survey is a consistent teaching throughout medical care, including backcountry, frontcountry, and even hospital-based care. For climbers and other backcountry providers, the prioritization in patient assessment is particularly driven by the limited availability of resources in the wilderness environment. So, for example, the mnemonic ABC as a primary survey guideline may be familiar to many readers with first aid or medical training. In this term, "A" stands for *airway*, "B" for *breathing*, and "C" for *circulation*, dictating the sequence of checks to be completed to ensure that a patient is breathing and has a pulse before proceeding further.

Recently, certifying organizations like the American Heart Association have changed this mnemonic to CAB, reflecting changing teaching that a pulse should be checked before breathing. This approach prioritizes airway or circulation at the forefront of the assessment goal, which is appropriate for frontcountry care.

An important principle of this book, however, is that not all frontcountry or traditional medical care can be indiscriminately applied to the backcountry. In the case of patient assessment, we feel a different algorithm is needed. We recommend the MARCH mnemonic. This mnemonic was originally developed by the United States military to direct initial patient assessment during combat operations. It has since been endorsed and adapted to a wilderness environment by various wilderness medical training programs, including the the American Alpine Club (Simon 2016) and the Advanced Wilderness Life Support curriculum (Della-Giustina 2013), itself endorsed by the Wilderness Medical Society. We have made further adaptions in this book for the climbing environment.

M = **M**assive hemorrhage
A = **A**irway with cervical spine assessment
R = **R**espiration
C = **C**irculation
H = **H**ypothermia/**H**yperthermia/**H**anging AND **H**unker down/
    Hike out/**H**elicopter out

In this method of assessment, priority is given to those patient needs that must be rapidly identified and addressed in climbing and alpine terrain.

Massive Hemorrhage

Management of a massive hemorrhage includes immediate direct pressure over any heavily bleeding site. This step may also require tourniquet application to an extremity with heavy or pulsatile bleeding (bleeding that spurts out with great force upon each heartbeat, indicating an arterial bleed). The placement of tourniquets has historically been met with skepticism in civilian care, and considered to be an option of last resort. However, it has proven effective in combat and tactical medical care, and this experience has been successfully translated to the wilderness environment. The privileging of hemorrhage control to the very first step of patient assessment, in contradiction to traditional medical assessment algorithms, reflects the reality that blood cannot be replaced in a wilderness setting. Most immediate, medical and trauma care is based on the ultimate goal of protecting oxygen flow to body tissues. Adequate breathing (collecting oxygen) and heartbeat (distributing oxygenated blood) is irrelevant if there is no blood to carry that oxygen. Needless to say, it would be challenging to replace lost blood on pitch number four of a seven-pitch climb with a twenty-four-hour walk-out back to the nearest road, making it a critically important goal to keep that blood in the body in the first place! More specific techniques for managing and controlling massive hemorrhages are discussed in Chapters 2 and 9.

Airway with Cervical Spine Assessment

This step directs the rescuer to determine if a patient has a functioning airway and if consideration needs to be made to reduce motion to *cervical vertebra* (neck bones) in case of trauma.

Respiration, Circulation

These steps evaluate the patient's breathing and pulse. Evaluating, establishing, and protecting airway patency, in addition to evaluating breathing and pulse rates and characters, are skills taught in most first aid and medical certification classes at the CPR or first aid level. We encourage climbers to enroll in a formal training class of this sort to gain those practical skills, but then to migrate them to the MARCH format for patient assessments in the climbing environment.

Hypothermia/Hyperthermia/Hanging; Hunker Down/ Hike Out/Helicopter Out

Hypothermia/Hyperthermia/Hanging is an adaptation to more traditional patient assessments that is unique to the wilderness environment. In a frontcountry or hospital environment where professional medical care may be available in fifteen minutes or less, assessing a patient's status as far as excessive heat or cold may not be critically important or worth positioning in the primary survey. However, in remote settings where care may be significantly delayed, rapid intervention to identify and begin managing extreme cold (hypothermia) or extreme heat (hyperthermia) may make the difference between life or death for a patient. A further innovation we introduce to this algorithm for climbers is the addition of "Hanging." This addresses the time-sensitive step of addressing possible suspension syndrome in a hanging climber, which most regulatory agencies agree must be identified and managed within minutes of beginning patient care. The details of suspension syndrome, and its management, are addressed in Chapter 2.

Hunker down/Hike out/Helicopter out as the final step in patient assessment reflects the need in wilderness care to rapidly, even as part of the primary survey, begin assessing for evacuation need. This would include, for critical patients, ensuring a call for help has been made and activating any available formal EMS system. "Hunker down" prompts a consideration of whether, after a primary survey, a patient will need to be promptly evacuated, or whether they might be observed or released to continue with the outdoor activity. Early decision-making regarding evacuation is critical, as it can be one of the most complex, time-demanding components of the medical care delivered. If evacuation is needed, a significant differentiation is whether this patient can be extricated in a slower, less technical fashion (represented by "hike out") or whether more urgent extrication is needed (represented by "helicopter out"). Bear in mind that these are mnemonic representations for a more general sense of urgency, not necessarily specific modes of extrication. Helicopters may not be appropriate or available in a given environment, and selecting this category could represent all-terrain vehicle extrication or simply a very rapid carry-out. Hiking might not be appropriate, and might instead represent continued travel down a river in a raft or a slower and more careful carry-out. This step in evaluation also addresses a number of other primary considerations:

+ the degree to which a patient might be able to participate in their own extrication
+ an initial evaluation of the available resources to the would-be rescuers
+ potential need to activate outside external resources early, including a call for more help or activation of 911 (in the United States) or another formal EMS response.

SECONDARY SURVEY

Much like linking the various pitches of a climbing route together in order to successfully top-out, there are multiple components to patient assessment necessary to adequately care for the injured climber. A "hasty assessment" primary survey mitigates the risk of preventable death in a climbing environment. Once these life threats and critical management steps have been addressed by a MARCH survey, a more thorough assessment must be made. This is termed a secondary survey, and includes further investigation of the victim's history and a more thorough physical exam.

Due to the drama or severity of the injury/illness, acquisition of patient history is often rushed by both patients and clinicians. In the context of care in mountainous environments, it is likely that this issue may be even more magnified. Some patients' level of consciousness will limit their ability to communicate. For these reasons, a systematic approach (facilitated by mnemonics) is important to ensure that nothing is missed.

Beginning the secondary survey, it is critical to recognize the injured climber's level of responsiveness. This will dictate how capable they are to participate sufficiently in the remainder of the secondary survey, will dictate future levels of care and needs for evacuation, and will provide a baseline sense of responsiveness which can be used to track changes in mental status during further care. The mnemonic AVPU provides a basis for establishing and monitoring level of responsiveness.

A = **A**lert and oriented: Responds and converses appropriately
V = **V**erbal: Responds to verbal prompts when spoken to, but is not alert (e.g., awakens or responds to direct questions but is otherwise sluggish, severely confused, or unconscious)
P = **P**ain: Responds only to painful physical prompts (e.g., withdraws or moans when pinched or other unpleasant stimuli are applied)
U = **U**nresponsive: No response to stimuli; however, other vital signs may appear stable

Neurological injuries, while often evaluated with expensive testing in frontcountry and hospital-based care, can very effectively be understood through the process of history and physical examination—even on the side of a mountain. The AVPU responsiveness survey, along with an assessment of vital signs, is an excellent first step in the process and serves as another component of hasty assessment. It can also be utilized during an evacuation process to assess improvement or worsening of an injured climber's condition. Other initial and ongoing assessment tools, such as distal neurovascular examination and evaluation of cranial nerves, will be addressed later in this text.

Assuming an adequate baseline cognitive level of function in the patient, the process of gathering further history is one of the most effective diagnostic tools available. A history serves as the route "beta" that will dictate further components of the treatment plan. It is important to document this information in some format for future reference and to monitor any clinical changes during the evolution of the patient condition. In the absence of writing utensils or computers, a camera may document the appearance of an injury. Furthermore, many smartphones, often readily available, offer the ability to type or dictate spoken text for future reference. At least one wilderness medicine school (NOLS Wilderness Medicine) has developed a smartphone application specifically for wilderness medicine care and documentation to facilitate this. As mentioned earlier, the severity of a situation or a patient's condition may prohibit acquisition of a thorough history from a patient. At the start of patient assessment, a brief history will suffice to initiate a treatment plan. From the EMS world and the training of EMTs and paramedics, the use of a SAMPLE history has proven its worth in initial history taking.

S = **S**ymptoms: What is the chief complaint?

A = **A**llergies: Does the injured climber have medication allergies (e.g., penicillin) or environmental allergies (e.g., bee stings)?

M = **M**edications: Does the climber take any medications, performance-enhancing agents, or herbal supplements? If so, when was the last dose?

P = **P**ast medical and surgical history.

L = **L**ast food and fluid intake: Evaluates nutrition and hydration status.

E = **E**vents of the injury/illness: What happened leading up to the chief complaint?

Failure to acquire the above components in the history process can inhibit thoughtful and effective development of treatment goals. For example, a member of the rope team admits to headache, nausea, and feeling weak. A thorough history reveals that the climber is a diabetic who took his normal morning medication and did not account for the increased metabolic demand of climbing, thereby causing a state of mild hypoglycemia (low blood sugar). This is a potentially easily correctable issue that would not necessarily mean an end of climbing for that individual, but in the absence of a thorough historical assessment, might otherwise result in lowering off and heading back to the car. Conversely, in a different scenario, a climbing partner reveals they have epilepsy, which in their case is well controlled with medication. Solicitation of more history from the patient uncovers that their medication is back at the trailhead, a day's hike from the four-pitch trad climb of the day. In this situation, climbing might be ill-advised, particularly if this member of the team is going to be responsible for the belaying of other climbers.

In the cases of an acute injury or complaint from the climber, provision of an adequate history is a major component to developing the treatment plan and making decisions regarding summit goals versus retreat initiatives. The other component that cannot be neglected is a thorough physical exam. In a hospital or other frontcountry environment, many diagnostic tools (e.g., stethoscope or blood pressure cuff) are present to facilitate the exam process. When an injury happens at the roadside crag, these resources may only be a phone call away. Issues of resources and diagnostic tool availability arise when climbers and alpinists find themselves further immersed in a mountainous environment, where the carrying of these tools is impractical. Additionally, such diagnostic tools may not adequately function or prove equally useful when in the rugged environment of alpine and rock terrain. This may be due to battery consumption, tolerance of temperature variability, or weight limitations. The human body, with its five senses and the interpretive functioning of the brain to which they supply information, is an amazing diagnostic tool. Much like examining the surface of a rock, the hands are quite sensitive in determining abnormalities and configurations of significance. Also, when palpating (touching) a paired body part during exam, the body part in question can be compared to its "normal" pair on the other side of the body. In other words, a possible elbow deformity on the right can be compared to a "normal" elbow for that patient on the left. Furthermore, the sight, smell, and sound of a presenting symptom may provide additional feedback in determining the significance of an injury or complaint. Entering into the physical exam process with a climbing partner poses an interesting dynamic to the already unique relationship, moving it from one of friendship and shared adventure to a caregiver-patient relationship. If a patient is conscious, it is important to consider this issue and ask for permission to conduct a physical examination.

During the examination process, having a baseline level of medical knowledge will assist in developing possible diagnoses (in medicine a list of possible diagnoses is known as the "differential diagnosis"). The remainder of this text is designed to help provide some of that knowledge. Not only will an expanded knowledge base and thorough history facilitate diagnosis, it will also direct the physical exam. For example, suspicion of appendicitis will direct the examiner to the abdominal right lower quadrant rather than the left foot. This patient assessment chapter will outline the general principles of the examination process, followed by a discussion of those portions of the physical exam that address more emergent situations, possibly leading to death or significant compromise of a climbing adventure.

A reasonable approach to a physical exam can be remembered by recalling that fine beverage familiar to many climbers worldwide: the India pale ale, or IPA. While drinking IPA is not recommended while actually climbing, it serves as an excellent facilitator of post-climb celebrations. In the case of the physical exam portion of patient assessment, IPA provides a useful mnemonic:

I = **I**nspection: The act of visual identification. Look for grossly significant issues such as bony/soft tissue deformities, hemorrhage, and behavioral/neurological changes. This can quickly bring to light those issues requiring immediate attention.

P = **P**alpation: The act of hands-on examination. Here, physical abnormalities can be further identified or assessed and, where possible, comparison can be made to the contralateral (opposite) side for further identification of severity or significance. It also frequently helps determine the severity of an injury or illness.

A = **A**uscultation: The act of listening. In healthcare, this is typically thought to represent listening to internal body parts through a stethoscope or with the unassisted ear. This is true here as well, although a stethoscope will rarely be available and may not be crucial. For example, internal sounds can also be heard by placing the ear directly to the affected area of an injured climber's body; for example, listening to breath sounds through the chest wall. More broadly, this step serves as a reminder to listen to the history of the patient (see secondary survey section above).

Prior to expanding the diagnostic processes of patient assessment, it is important to address acute injuries promptly. For example, the fact that the injured climber has a poison ivy rash from that bushy ledge of the second pitch should not distract the partner from helping to address the lower extremity fracture that he suffered when taking a whipper at the crux of the climb. A hasty assessment following the MARCH mnemonic and quickly ascertaining AVPU status will lead to the remaining portion of an initial physical exam, identifying the more emergent issues of the injured climber's health. As stated above, the IPA technique (inspection, palpation, auscultation) will serve as a foundation from which to expand the diagnostic focus, but will also quickly allow the more urgent issues to be addressed.

An important component of an initial primary and secondary survey is to recognize signs of shock. In classic medical terminology, shock represents the inadequate delivery of oxygen to body tissue, and is usually (but not always) represented on exam by a low blood pressure. We would also note that psychological shock, while different from the strict medical definition of shock, is equally real, can be equally dangerous in a mountainous environment where maintaining functional capability is critical, and should be addressed during care. Hypotension associated with medical shock is usually defined as a *systolic blood pressure* (the blood pressure during full heart contraction) of less than 90 mmHg. In a climbing area, the patient's actual blood pressure can rarely be assessed, as a *sphygmomanometer* (blood pressure cuff) is needed and is rarely available. In the absence of such tools, a rough guideline has been proposed, suggesting that a *carotid* (neck artery) pulse ensures a systolic blood pressure of 60 mmHg, a *femoral* (groin artery) pulse ensures a pressure of 70 mmHg, and a radial (wrist) pulse ensures a blood pressure of 80 mmHg. While the exact numbers here have been challenged by further research, the underlying principle is sound: A patient will progressively lose pulses in their wrist, then their groin, and finally their neck as blood pressure drops. A patient without a radial pulse (and without another reason, like trauma to that arm or atypical body morphology) should be considered to already have a critically low blood pressure and to be in shock. A patient without a carotid pulse is felt to have such a low blood pressure that they are functionally or in reality "pulseless," and CPR should be initiated. (Obviously, a talking patient without a carotid pulse is unlikely, and examiners should not initiate CPR; instead they should check their diagnostic skills, and question whether they have had one too many IPAs.) Shock can be assessed by other physical exam findings, including dizziness, pale skin, confusion, and light-headedness when standing (indicating the blood pressure is insufficient to fully get oxygen to the brain when gravity is acting most strongly against brain blood flow).

Any time signs of medical shock are identified, a source should be considered. Usually, the source is from a failure in one of three parts of the cardiovascular system, likened to a plumbing system: the pump (heart, like a heart attack), the pipes (blood vessels, like loss of vessel tone seen in life-threatening allergic reactions), or the fluid (blood volume, like loss of blood from massive hemorrhage or the effects of severe dehydration). In the case of climbing trauma, if another source is not known and massive hemorrhage was not appreciated during MARCH, it is important to consider that blood may be lost into "hidden" (not immediately visible) spaces. We have found the CAMS mnemonic to be helpful in identifying places where blood can be secretly lost, resulting in shock.

C = **C**hest
A = **A**bdomen (front and back)
M = **M**eat
S = **S**kin, Slab, Snow

An initial focus to these areas during the physical exam will identify those issues that pose a threat to the patient's circulation and direct hemorrhage management as necessary.

Chest
A substantial amount of blood loss can accumulate inside the patient's chest. Eventually, death will take place either from lack of blood, inability to breathe sufficiently, or compression of the heart (inhibiting ade-

quate heartbeat). Inspection of the chest wall may reveal bruising, unequal chest movements within the chest or in comparing one side of the chest to the other, or penetrating trauma. Auscultation may reveal muffled heart sounds or absent breath sounds unilaterally or bilaterally. Finally, palpation may identify a bony or chest wall deformity not appreciated upon inspection. Palpation may also reveal *subcutaneous emphysema* (air under the skin—feels like Rice Krispies) indicative of lung collapse.

Abdomen (Front and Back)

The abdominal compartment is divided into two separate cavities: anterior and posterior (front and back). Upon inspection, scars might identify previous surgeries, suggesting more thorough interviewing of the patient may be helpful. In the acute setting, distention (swelling) of the abdomen or the visualization of a hematoma (bruising) may be indicative of bleeding. This may be present anteriorly or posteriorly. Furthermore, for examination purposes, the abdomen has four anterior compartments (Figure 1-1). Knowing their contents will aid the

FIGURE 1-1. THE FOUR ANTERIOR COMPARTMENTS OF THE ABDOMEN

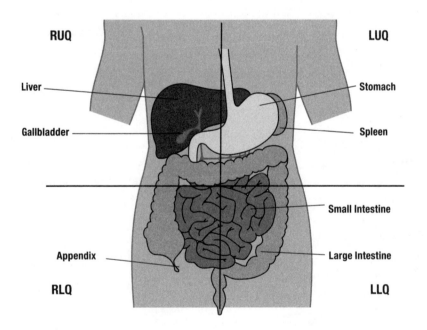

RUQ

LUQ

Liver

Stomach

Gallbladder

Spleen

Small Intestine

Appendix

Large Intestine

RLQ

LLQ

examiner in diagnosis. The discussion of these areas will be detailed in forthcoming chapters. Mere inspection is often inadequate to convey a diagnosis, and auscultation, percussion, and palpation may be needed to establish a final diagnosis.

Meat

As the name implies, attention must be given to the "meaty" areas of the body, those regions containing the vast amount of bony surface and soft tissue coverage. While a fleshy wound to the hand sustained during crack climbing may produce significant pain and soft tissue injury that challenges the climbing season, it does not pose the same threat to life that a fracture to the pelvis, femur, or damage to major vessels in those regions would. A substantial loss of blood, and subsequent threat to life, can be witnessed with fractures in these areas. Care must be given to thoroughly evaluate complaints to this region with the understanding that mere inspection may not reveal injuries deep within the skeletal muscle tissue. Obvious deformity may be evident.

Skin, Slab, Snow

This area is placed last in the mnemonic because it is often the easiest to assess and is heavily focused on inspection, but not necessarily palpation and auscultation. Many people stop here without looking further. The distraction of bloody snow or the smear of bloody tissue across a rock slab represents an injury requiring attention, and it is important to inspect the area underneath the climber during the examination process. Rolling the injured victim may yield appreciation of further injury both to the posterior chest and abdomen as well as identifying soft tissue injuries bleeding posteriorly. As discussed in Chapter 18, the necessity of formal "log rolling" typically taught in field medicine classes is being challenged by medical research (Singh 2016, Gill 2013, Radecki 2013), and the Wilderness Medical Society has favored the BEAM technique (discussed in detail in Chapter 18) over log rolling for these evaluations (Quinn 2014). Furthermore, a consideration of burns needs to be addressed in the process of hasty assessment. A substantial amount of circulatory volume can be lost through the skin surface of a burn. It stands to reason that with the increased surface area of large body burns, this fluid loss could be a significant threat to life even if no actual blood is lost.

EXPANDED ASSESSMENT EFFORTS AND REASSESSMENTS

If the summit were akin to finalizing a diagnosis, the expanded history and physical exam components of patient assessment would be known as "the final pitch." It is here that the implications of injury, the risk of further deterioration, and the ability to carry on climbing are further revealed. Continued reassessment is critical. The initial psychological impact of the event may now be overcome, and further information can be communicated, or an unconscious patient may now be awake and able to relate more relevant history. Similarly, the condition may be worsening. The illumination of various traits and character of the patient's complaint will help further establish a diagnosis.

Furthermore, attention to the smaller details of the physical exam can yield additional information. COLDER, again adapted from the Advanced Wilderness Life Support curriculum, represents an effective mnemonic to capture further information about the complaint. It is especially useful for complaints involving pain.

C = **C**haracter: Is the pain sharp? Dull? Pulsating? What does it feel like? Is it changing?

O = **O**nset: When did the symptoms start? What brought them on?

L = **L**ocation: Where is the pain located? Does it travel or radiate to another area?

D = **D**uration: How long does the pain last?

E = **E**xacerbation: Does something make the pain worse?

R = **R**elief/Radiation: Does something make the pain better? Does it move to any other body part (e.g., pain primarily in the chest that radiates to the jaw)?

These questions should be considered for each of the patient's complaints (e.g., "my head hurts" or "I can't feel my little finger").

For climbers, further attention to each extremity and evaluation of the circulation, sensation, and motor function (CSM) will be particularly important. Bear in mind that, like many elements of the physical exam, these findings are dynamic and may be evolving as a condition worsens.

The fundamental question of patient assessment is answered by establishing the diagnosis and disposition (ultimate plan to transfer or finish care) for the patient. While many factors go into formulating these concepts, it is not as complicated as it may seem. For example, it is not necessary to classify a broken ankle on the side of the mountain as a "Weber type B ankle fracture." It would be more relevant to identify "right ankle pain with inability to bear weight and absent pulse in foot." While understanding the significance of assessment findings is important, using plain language is helpful.

The communication element of the assessment starts with recording findings in a thoughtful way so that they can be communicated across the care medium to other providers as well as to the patient. It may be that this is accomplished through pencil and paper or more advanced technologies, as described earlier. In discussing patient care, sensitivity needs to be maintained to protect the health care information of the injured climber. The patient may not want additional information, pictures, or confidential health data shared with authorities, media, or the public at large. In these days of social media and widespread personal use of cameras, it is particularly important to be mindful of these privacy concerns.

In reviewing the evolving diagnosis and establishing a treatment plan, the rescuer must also address how the information obtained from the patient assessment points to the need for rescue or continued recreation. This refers back to the initial portion of the patient assessment: answering and managing each element of the MARCH mnemonic. Specifically, looking at the H component and answering the question: "Can we care for this patient here, or do we need to work on immediate evacuation?" is an evolving process as further details of both the history and physical exam components of assessment are obtained.

CHAPTER 2

LIFE-THREATENING EMERGENCIES

Climbing and mountaineering can present many threats to climbers' lives. This chapter will address those that may be reversible but require time-sensitive treatments. Conditions where survival depends on interventions within minutes (thus requiring on-site climber intervention rather than dependence on EMS or professional responders) include cardiac arrest, respiratory arrest, massive hemorrhage, anaphylaxis, choking, and suspension syndrome.

CARDIAC AND RESPIRATORY ARREST

Cardiac arrest occurs when the heart stops or is not beating sufficiently to maintain blood pressure at a life-preserving level. *Respiratory arrest* occurs when breathing stops or is insufficient to remove carbon dioxide from the body (a process known as *ventilation*) or absorb oxygen into the body (a process known as *oxygenation*). The heart may beat for a time while in respiratory arrest, similar to the situation when one simply holds one's breath, but invariably fails as oxygen levels drop. In the reverse situation, and in even less time, anyone in cardiac arrest will rapidly go into respiratory arrest. *Cardiopulmonary arrest* is a state of inadequate or absent breathing and blood pressure/pulse. *Cardiopulmonary resuscitation* (CPR, a systematic technique of chest compressions and rescue breathing for patients without a pulse or spontaneous breathing) has been developed to enable a rescuer to maintain basic life signs and to oxygenate key organs.

Happily, CPR, though it requires training, does not require any additional equipment, and so is an ideal intervention for a climber caring for an individual in cardiac arrest. Multiple organizations develop CPR curricula and offer certification courses, and all climbers are encouraged to enroll in such a course. Recurring certification is important here, as CPR techniques and methodology continue to evolve as our understanding of resuscitation science improves. In fact, something of a renaissance has occurred in cardiac arrest resuscitation since significant changes in CPR and field medical interventions for cardiac arrest have produced remarkable improvements in patient outcomes. While in the past survival from cardiac arrest hovered around 5% or less, now some systems are seeing survival rates exceeding 50%, with those patients being discharged from hospitals in a highly functional state. Many of these improvements are directly related to changes in CPR techniques, such as depth and frequency of compressions and the frequency—or even elimination—of ventilations. Because this is such a rapidly evolving skill, and outcomes significantly differ when the most up-to-date techniques are used, continued training and recertification as well as initial training is recommended for all climbers.

One existing school of thought holds that resuscitation should not be started in wilderness settings. This theory proposes that CPR and cardiac or respiratory resuscitation will inevitably be futile if transport units, definitive care facilities, or even just advanced cardiac interventions by EMS personnel are hours or days away. This represents a critical misunderstanding of our modern conception of cardiopulmonary resuscitation.

First, it is increasingly apparent that advanced interventions offered by EMS personnel such as *intubation* (placing a breathing tube in a patient) or advanced life support (ALS) drugs do not make the most significant difference in patient survival—or perhaps don't make any significant difference at all. Increasingly, we recognize that rapid and high-quality CPR is the most important determinant to patient outcome.

Second, many of the most impressive outcomes occur in cardiac arrest patients whose lethal heart rhythms can be shocked back into a normal rhythm. This realization has driven the movement in recent years to place automated external defibrillators (AEDs) in many public areas. These tools require no specific training. They talk a user through the steps of the procedure, and can automatically analyze heart rhythms and apply a potentially life-saving shock when required. Such units are becoming increasingly miniaturized. It is a very real possibility that popular climbing areas, outdoor recreational sites, and climbing gyms could have fixed AEDs present during a cardiac arrest. Similarly, AEDs may become more prevalent on expeditions such as mountaineering or mixed river and climbing trips, where the mountaineer does not necessarily carry all the equipment. The International Commission for Mountain Emergency Medicine (ICAR MEDCOM) suggests that AEDs be installed in ski areas and mountain huts near hiking trails (Elsenohn 2006). They also state that a defibrillator should be in the pack of every advanced healthcare provider, noting that, according to their research, 50% of physicians on mountain rescue teams already carry an AED (Elsenohn 2011). However, our perspective is that the utility of these units is limited, in that they need to be applied as soon as possible after a cardiac arrest. If a shockable rhythm does exist, mortality increases by 10% for every minute of delay in shock application. Therefore, it is clear that climbing groups carrying such units may be much more effective than if the units are carried solely by rescue teams, unless the unit is used on rescue team members themselves (and there are case studies of this).

Third, many of the statistics surrounding cardiac arrest outcomes and the potential futility of treatment are derived from patients whose hearts have failed due to *dysrhythmia* (a spontaneous rhythm problem) or, even more commonly, a *heart attack* (a heart muscle failure). Climbers, however, may be much healthier than the overall population to begin with. They may be more likely to experience cardiopulmonary arrest from traumatic sources like lightning strikes (Chapter 15), drowning (see "Drowning" sidebar), or asphyxiation—death due to not breathing—during avalanche burial (Chapter 17). In each of these cases, the heart muscle is not primarily impaired, and lightning strikes and drowning have much higher rates of recovery from CPR alone than many cases in which primary heart disease or other medical conditions have caused the cardiopulmonary arrest.

In general, CPR entails sequential rotations of rescue breathing and chest compression. In some circumstances only rescue breathing is needed, while in other circumstances compression-only CPR may be appropriate. AED analysis is now always included if an AED is available, as well as mandatory points in the CPR process where the rescuer calls for more help. Not only is complete CPR training beyond the scope of this text, but—as noted earlier—alterations are continuously being made in its technique. Hence, we advise enrollment in a formal course and maintenance of current certification to get the most up-to-date information on ventilation and compression ratios and other details of CPR. Acute coronary syndrome, heart attacks, and sudden cardiac death are discussed in more detail in Chapter 8.

+DROWNING+

Drowning represents a special form of respiratory or cardiopulmonary arrest. Climbers may drown either during *deep-water soloing* (DWS, climbing without a rope on rocks overlying bodies of water that can cushion a fall), during water-based recreational activities on a climbing trip, or during water crossings to reach or return from a climbing site.

Key points for climbers to understand about drowning:

- The modern definition of drowning changed following the Second World Congress on Drowning in 2002. *Drowning* is now defined as "a process of respiratory impairment from submersion in a liquid medium" (van Beek 2014). It can result in three outcomes: drowning without injury, drowning with injury, and drowning with death. By this definition, some (in fact, most) patients who drown actually survive—a reality unfamiliar to many in the lay public. The duty of the first aider or healthcare provider is to interrupt or even reverse the drowning process before significant injury or death results. Note also that with this definitional change, modifier terms such "near-drowning," "delayed" drowning, "wet" or "dry" drowning, "secondary" drowning, or "active" versus "passive" versus "silent" drowning are no longer meaningful or acceptable (van Beek 2014, International Life Saving Federation 2014, Sempsrott 2015, Schmidt 2016).

- Unlike heart-related sources of cardiopulmonary arrest, drowning that does not result from heart attack or other heart illness is caused by a lung failure. Because of this, rescue breathing is critical for any drowning patient in cardiac arrest. Compression-only CPR is never appropriate for drowning patients without a heart-related reason for their collapse (International Life Saving Federation 2008, Morrison 2010, Nolan 2010, Vanden 2010, Schmidt 2016). When possible, drowning patients without a pulse should be removed from the water and placed on a firm surface before beginning CPR, even if this means delay, as chest compressions are ineffective in water (Schmidt 2016). But if the delay will be longer than 15 to 20 seconds, multiple societies and consensus statements confirm in-water resuscitation (IWR, consisting ONLY of rescue breathing) may be appropriate if rescuers are trained in this difficult skill (International Life Saving Federation 2001, United States Lifeguard Standards Coalition 2011, Schmidt 2016).

- A startling number of drownings are caused by submerging vehicles. This can be a risk in driving to or from climbing sites. It is important not to attempt to drive your vehicle through any standing or moving water that is not a routine four-wheel-drive crossing point with a routine water level. If you do find yourself in a submerging vehicle in a body of water, you have about 60 seconds to get out (McDonald 2013). In contradiction to the teaching from many survival authorities, do not call for help on a phone or wait for the vehicle to

continues

submerge so you can open a door. A formulaic sequence of actions to escape a submerging vehicle has been developed: Seatbelt, Windows, Children, Out. This sequence dictates the appropriate steps to take in sequence: removing one's seatbelt and anyone else's in the vehicle requiring assistance, opening or breaking windows, releasing children (oldest to youngest), and everyone immediately exiting the windows for safe escape. All must be done in the first 60 seconds of initial entry into water (McDonald 2013, Hawkins 2015).

- As with CPR, courses in lifeguarding and even wilderness lifeguarding (Landmark Learning 2016) are available, and are recommended for climbers whose work or recreation places them near aquatic environments. This is particularly true for DWS climbers. Such courses teach specific techniques for prevention, rescue, and resuscitation of victims in aquatic emergencies.

- Note that, except for clearing out large foreign bodies that could cause choking (by methods described later in this chapter) or initial positioning to empty large amounts of water in the upper airway, no water removal techniques are needed in drowning management. Foam often appears in the airway but it can be forced back into the airway during rescue breathing and does not need to be cleared. Unless a swallowed object is a part of the drowning (see the section about choking later in this chapter), the Heimlich maneuver and abdominal compressions are *not* an accepted part of any drowning treatment (International Life Saving Federation 1998, Schmidt 2016).

HEMORRHAGE CONTROL

Life-threatening bleeding must be arrested immediately. Direct pressure to any bleeding site is an appropriate initial intervention. If specialized equipment is available—such as gauze or *hemostatic agents* (specialized clotting bandages or pads)—it can be used. But any clean material is suitable for direct pressure. If no material is available, apply direct pressure with a body part (finger, hand, knee, etc.). The danger of *blood-borne pathogens* (diseases that can be transmitted by blood exposure) must always be considered, however, so gloves or some sort of barrier is preferable to direct skin-to-skin contact.

Hemostatic agents (tools applied directly to a wound that stops bleeding through chemical action) are being increasingly marketed directly to outdoor consumers like climbers. It is our opinion that they may form an important element of a hemorrhage control plan, but usually they are more beneficial with additional training. We encourage such training if hemostatic agents are carried. In many cases, understanding how to correctly pack a wound is crucial to the additional effectiveness potentially offered by such products.

Bleeding of an extremity wound that cannot be controlled by direct pressure or is obviously arterial (as indicated by bright red pulsatile bleeding) should be immediately controlled with a tourniquet. Historically, tourniquets have been considered to be a last-resort intervention. However, with increasing understanding of this tool—and particularly given military experiences in the Vietnam War and following—we now know that tourniquets to address life-threatening bleeding can be placed without significant danger to a limb. If they remain in place for more than two hours, limb loss may occur, so once life-threatening bleeding is controlled and a patient is otherwise fully assessed, a tourniquet can be carefully "taken down" (pressure mechanism removed) to see if arterial bleeding is still present. If so, the tourniquet should remain in place even if this extends tourniquet use beyond a threshold where limb loss might occur. If not, the pressure mechanism of the tourniquet can be taken down, but the actual tourniquet should be left in place around the limb so that it can be rapidly retightened if bleeding abruptly returns. Tourniquets should be placed at least two inches *proximal* (closer to the torso on a limb) to the bleeding wound, and should not cross over any joint. Because arteries retract into wounds and because it is sometimes difficult to identify the precise source of bleeding with life-threatening arterial hemorrhage, an acceptable alternative is to put an initial limb tourniquet as proximal as possible on the limb. Commercial tourniquets, often based on military models, are available, and ad hoc tourniquets can be fashioned and applied. Particularly useful is the insertion of a carabiner into an ad hoc tourniquet (Figure 2-1), as it is equipment typically carried by climbers that lends functionality and ease of use to improvised tourniquets. Traditional tourniquets cannot be applied to the torso, neck, or head. Direct pressure should be used to control significant external bleeding from these areas, and significant internal hemorrhage from these areas is discussed in later chapters.

FIGURE 2-1: CARABINER TOURNIQUET

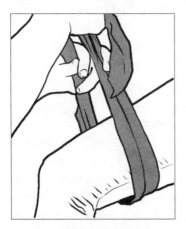

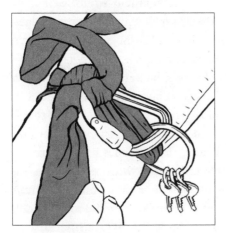

ANAPHYLAXIS

Anaphylaxis is a life-threatening allergic reaction to an *allergen* (a material that triggers an allergic reaction in a specific individual). It is a form of *shock* (inadequate supply of oxygen to body tissue, often caused by low blood pressure). A simple allergic reaction is present when someone experiences a local skin reaction to an allergen (e.g., poison ivy reaction) or cold-like symptoms of runny nose and congestion (e.g., seasonal allergies or hay fever). Anaphylaxis is present when the reaction becomes systemic and life-threatening, and is specifically defined by any one of the three criteria in Figure 2-2 being met (Sampson 2006).

Note that, if unable to measure blood pressure, signs of low blood pressure include confusion, light-headedness, and vision changes.

Common sources of anaphylaxis are animal bites and stings (particularly the *Hymenoptera* order, which includes bees, wasps, and fire ants), medications (particularly antibiotics), or foods (particularly nuts and shellfish).

The *only* definitive treatment for anaphylaxis is epinephrine, a medication that mimics the action of adrenaline in the body. In the United States this medication is currently only available by prescription. However, it is felt to be so important to wilderness medicine that a standard of care now encourages prescribing it to anyone potentially susceptible to an allergic reaction, and considers it to be a medical necessity for wilderness programs (Gaudio 2014, Curtis 2015). Many outdoor organizations now train their guides or leaders in the use of this medication on anaphylactic patients. Sometimes this is technically not a legal practice, and local legal counsel should be sought if this practice is implemented. However, there are many deaths every year from untreated or inadequately treated anaphylaxis, and no case law exists of individuals being successfully held liable for administering epinephrine to someone showing signs or symptoms of anaphylaxis. Hence, many organizations have come to feel the risk-benefit analysis favors carrying epinephrine despite its uncertain legal status. In addition, every year more governmental bodies approve legislation expanding the legal use of epinephrine, either through special delegated practice laws allowing individuals not otherwise healthcare providers to be trained and certified in its use (many states in the United States), or allowing it to be sold over the counter without a prescription (Canada, Australia, and many other countries).

The fact that not all allergies are known before exposure is an additional reason that it may be crucial for climbers to carry epinephrine. Although, medically speaking, one cannot develop anaphylaxis from the first exposure to an antigen (as anaphylaxis is an inappropriate bodily re-reaction to a material previously encountered by the body), this can lead to a false sense of security. Individuals may have been exposed to trace elements of an antigen in the past without their knowledge, or to a material chemically close enough to the antigen to cause a cross-reaction. Nor does a history of non-allergy indicate protection, since by definition all anaphylaxis occurs at a re-exposure to an agent. For example, of the more than 50 fatal sting reactions that

FIGURE 2-2. ANAPHYLAXIS DEFINITION

According to the National Institute of Allergy and Infectious Disease, a person is likely experiencing anaphylaxis when **one** of the following occurs following ingestion of a food allergen:

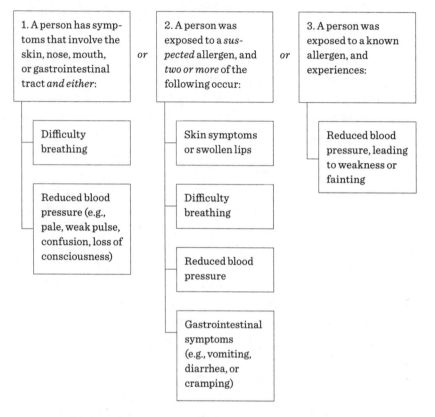

occur annually in the United States due to anaphylaxis, half show no history of previous sting reaction (Golden 2007). Because of this, neither a history of nonreactivity nor a history of never having been exposed to a given material can rule out the possibility of that anaphylaxis. In addition, during climbing expeditions and other trips, individuals are often exposed to foods and environmental materials that are outside their normal patterns. For all these reasons, epinephrine is often included as a critical element of first aid kits—even for those without known allergies or anaphylactic history, and despite being a prescription-only medication in many parts of the world.

Epinephrine for anaphylaxis should be administered by intramuscular (IM) injection, and the thigh is the preferred site, followed by the deltoid (shoulder) muscle (Simons 2001). Prior teachings have endorsed subcutaneous injection as the preferred route and deltoid muscle as the preferred site, but this ignores the fact that epinephrine absorption is fastest after IM injection in the thigh with no clear general benefit to using alternate sites. In specific cases where deltoid must be used it is an appropriate alternate site. Similarly, while IM injection should be the preferred goal, in some large patients or if using a short needle relative to patient body size, an intended intramuscular injection may end up unavoidably being subcutaneous. Injection can be accomplished by needle-and-syringe when the epinephrine is carried in a vial or ampule. In addition, auto-injectors of many different types are available, the most familiar in the United States being the EpiPen®. While multiple dosing is possible with needle-and-syringe techniques, most auto-injectors are single-dose only. However, a team lead by Hawkins and Weil have published a wilderness medicine technique (not endorsed by the FDA or the manufacturer) showing how to obtain up to four additional doses from a single-use auto-injector (Hawkins 2013). This technique can be reviewed via descriptions and videos online.* Multiple doses of epinephrine may be required for anaphylaxis, although the oft-quoted statistic that two or more doses are needed greater than 30% of the time appears overstated based on analysis of the evidence actually available. Recent meta-analysis of these studies completed by Penney et al. suggest the incidence of anaphylaxis requiring multiple doses may be closer to 1-5% (Penney 2015). Nonetheless, many authorities still suggest that one should be prepared to administer multiple doses, and many auto-injectors can now only be purchased in pairs for this reason. The key point is that at least a single dose of epinephrine should always be available to climbers, even during the climb. First aid kits are now available that are built into chalk bags and contain a sleeve for an epinephrine auto-injector,† an elegant solution for a climber to have epinephrine available, even during a climb when nothing is carried but a gear sling and chalk bag.

Adjunct medications such as antihistamines (e.g., diphenhydramine or Benadryl®) or steroids (e.g., prednisone) can be used. But it is import-

---

* Online version (with videos) is available here: http://www.wemjournal.org/article/S1080
-6032(13)00094-X/fulltext. A graphically more appealing PDF, but lacking videos, is available here:
http://www.wemjournal.org/article/S1080-6032(13)00094-X/PDF.
† Vertical Medicine Resources High & Dry medical kit, www.vertical-medicine.com/products-services
/the-cache-vmr-s-online-store.

ant to recognize that these treat the allergic reaction and will not reverse anaphylaxis, for which epinephrine is specifically and exclusively needed. Unfortunately, some wilderness medicine programs teach that antihistamines and steroids are more "definitive" or last longer, implying that these would be more important to carry or use first in cases of anaphylaxis. Their use as supplements is not inappropriate, but the first and most important medication to administer in known cases of anaphylaxis is always epinephrine.

CHOKING

Choking can become a life-threatening emergency if oxygen supply is cut off. Individuals able to move air at all or speak should be encouraged to continue trying to cough up the obstructing material or clear the airway on their own. If the patient is conscious but unable to breath effectively, the Heimlich maneuver can be applied (Figure 2-3). If patients become unconscious, the climber should be laid on their back and immediate chest compressions (CPR) should occur (no pulse check required). After 30 compressions, open the airway, and remove foreign body if visualized. Attempt two breaths and continue cycles of chest compressions and ventilation until object is expelled. Choking infants with inadequate breathing may benefit from back blows and chest thrusts. If the infant becomes unconscious, begin immediate chest compressions (CPR). All of these techniques are typically taught in CPR classes and—as noted earlier—climbers are encouraged to formally certify in CPR for practical training and to ensure the use of the most up-to-date techniques.

SUSPENSION SYNDROME

Suspension syndrome is a state of shock caused by passive hanging—in the case of climbers, most often in a harness.

In normal physiology, blood moves from the feet and lower extremities by way of *venous pumps*, a one-way valve system. When legs are moved or flexed, the muscular contraction forces blood in the veins upward toward the torso. These one-way valves in the veins prevent that blood

FIGURE 2-3. HEIMLICH MANEUVER

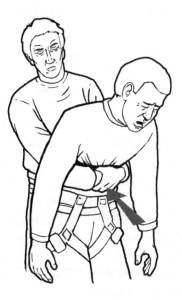

from flowing back down toward the feet between contractions—like a friction hitch when ascending a rope. The next muscular movement continues to force the blood up the leg, resulting eventually in blood being "pumped" passively from the feet back up to the torso, despite there obviously being no pump in the feet pushing upward.

If one remains vertical and does not move the lower extremities at all, this passive venous pump system fails and blood can pool in the lower extremities. Although no actual blood is lost, this causes a relative low-volume state in the core that mimics shock from bleeding. As much as 60% of the body's blood can collect in the lower extremities, removed from central circulation and oxygen/waste exchange.

This problem can be seen in soldiers standing at attention. They are trained to make tiny flexing motions of their lower extremities, or even stamp periodically, to prevent passing out from low blood circulation to the brain. However, if they pass out for this reason, they collapse into a horizontal position and the trapped blood is allowed to travel back to the core, including the heart and brain, returning them to consciousness. But if a climber is hanging suspended vertically and immobile in a harness, the danger is that nothing, including unconsciousness, will change the vertical position unless the climber is actively repositioned. Both case studies and formal tilt testing demonstrate that more than half the population will pass out within minutes if suspended in an immobile state. In the short term this can cause unconsciousness, with consequent possible loss of breathing and death from asphyxiation, or other consequences of shock, such as low oxygenation of the brain or other vital organs due to the amount of blood taken out of functional circulation. Numerous safety and standard-setting organizations have recognized this syndrome, which can occur within five to thirty minutes of being trapped in a vertical position. For industries using harnesses similar to climbing harnesses, the Occupational Safety and Health Administration (OSHA) in the United States requires "prompt" rescue "as quickly as possible," noting that death can occur within thirty minutes (Occupational Safety & Health Administration 2011). Manufacturers of industrial personal protective equipment harnesses, citing suspension syndrome, recommend rescue within fifteen minutes, and the American National Standards Institute (ANSI) recommends patient contact within four to six minutes and "prompt" rescue to follow (Nardo 2014, Roco 2011). Similarly, in climbing environments, climbers trapped in a vertical suspended position should use an etrier to periodically reposition themselves or a cordelette or other rope system to suspend the lower extremities. At the very least, periodic movements of the legs should be made when possible to stimulate the venous pump system in the lower extremity and ensure adequate blood return to the core.

However, coupled with this very real physiological danger, a mythical teaching has evolved among rescue personnel, born out of the climbing and mountain medicine community. The recent dispelling of this myth in the 2009 to 2012 era represents one of the great success stories of evidence-based medicine (EBM) in wilderness medicine, and the critical role of medical science and EBM in climbing rescue teaching and operations.

The story behind the evolution of rescue personnel's misunderstanding of suspension syndrome begins in 1972 at the 2nd International Conference of Mountain Rescue Doctors meeting in Innsbruck, Austria (Mortimer 2011). There, a series of cases where patients died after being taken off rope after prolonged suspension was analyzed. Particularly puzzling were two otherwise unrelated cases—one caving and one mountaineering—in which the individuals were suspended for four hours but died within minutes of being taken off rope. It was hypothesized that this "rescue death" was either caused by blood returning too quickly to the core or that blood in the periphery collected toxic contents which proved lethal when recirculated back to the heart after the patient was placed supine. This hypothesis prompted a recommendation that a slow, gradual process be used to move suspended patients to a supine position and that harnesses be removed slowly, due to the belief that they contributed to the risk of death.

This supposed situation was variously termed "rescue death," "reperfusion syndrome," "harness death," "harness pathology," or it was added to the very real suspension syndrome described earlier. It prompted decades of teaching in climbing and mountain rescue communities that directly contraindicated commonsensical and standard practices in treating patients who are in shock and require urgent resuscitation: to lay them flat. Unfortunately, implementing practices based on hypothesis alone is not how medical science is supposed to work. The next step—testing the hypothesis—should be done before changes to practice are made. In subsequent testing, including by the presenters of the original hypothesis, no evidence could be found that this concept was valid. Nonetheless, the teaching persisted for years.

Mortimer, in a landmark 2011 publication in *Wilderness & Environmental Medicine*, wrote the most compelling and comprehensive analysis of this error. He concluded that "this suggestion is not supported by the original series that demonstrated sudden deaths after rescue nor by modern understandings of physiology. Search and rescue teams and party members assisting a colleague suspended unconscious on rope should follow standard resuscitation measures to restore circulation to vital organs immediately" (Mortimer 2011). Numerous other review articles have come to similar conclusions (Thomassen 2009, Adisesh 2009, Adisesh 2011, Pasquier 2011). Although scattered recommendations that repositioning a suspended climber into a supine position must be gradual still exist, and were still appearing in the *Journal of Emergency Medical Services* as late as 2009 (Raynovich 2009), they are not based on present-day evidence and are steadily becoming increasingly rare or have corrected themselves, as the *Journal of Emergency Medical Services* did in 2015 (Kolb 2015).

Frequently, suspension syndrome is referred to as "suspension trauma," despite the fact that no real blunt or penetrating trauma occurs. We believe this terminology confuses the situation and perpetuates the concept that harnesses are somehow responsible for a crush injury (obviously not the case) or that the unexplained cases of rapid death after rope removal are due to some type of mechanical trauma induced by rescuers. For this reason, we promote the use of the term "suspension syndrome" or "suspension shock," which both more accurately describe the combination of factors that can cause injury to climbers trapped in a suspended state.

Suspension syndrome is a perfect case study for two risks in climbing: first, the danger of divorcing out-of-hospital medical/rescue operations from a research and medical science underpinning; and second, the way medical myths can perpetuate in the climbing and outdoors community.

CHAPTER 3

INJURY PREVENTION

To prevent injuries and maximize climbing ability, all climbers need to consume the correct amount of calories from nutritional food sources at the right time. Additionally, a focus on hydration, proper body composition, training, rest, sleep cycles, mental fortitude, and good technique are key components for climbing, regardless of discipline.

NUTRITION

Nutritional content and timing can affect climbing potential. Nutritional goals vary by type of climbing and the climbing environment. Sport climbers working on a difficult project will focus on maintaining or reaching a very specific lean body profile and weight, while an alpinist, burning 10,000 calories per day, will be most concerned with consumption of calorie-dense and easily digestible foods. No matter the goal, proper nutrition is obtained from a diet consisting of a variety of fruits, vegetables, whole grains, and lean protein.

Meals and snacks should consist of foods that are ideally natural, organic, locally grown, and of free-range protein sources. Purchasing local foods increases the likelihood of freshness and maintains more nutritional content. When choosing a protein source, free-range animals that have not been treated with steroids or antibiotics are generally considered a better nutritional choice. A healthy diet for climbers consists of daily calories containing 50% carbohydrates, 25% fats, and 25% protein. This is not always possible, especially during expeditions with limited food sources or when duration or intensity of activity requires greater amounts of calories to meet increased demand.

Preparation and selection of food types is also an important aspect to consider. Baking, broiling, or grilling are preferred preparation techniques, and the removal of skin and trimming of excess fat from animal protein are helpful when attempting to maintain a lean body composition. To maximize and conserve nutritional content, food should not be overcooked. When considering carbohydrates, products made of whole grains contain more vitamins, minerals, and fiber than processed alternatives. For climbers concerned about maintaining a specific body composition, sauces, dressings, condiments, and other sides such as butter, sour cream, or cheese can add unnecessary calories that they may wish to avoid. For alpinists, these items help create high-calorie meals that are more appealing and edible and assist in maintenance of weight and energy. Again, nutritional goals must coincide with the demands and needs of climbing goals. Many foods can sabotage nutritional diets for climbers and include refined sugars and trans fats, two items readily found in most processed or fast foods. Junk foods filled with simple sugars provide "empty calories" that can trigger a rapid sugar spike followed by a crash and craving for more. These are generally not beneficial to performance and should be avoided.

Protein

Protein is necessary for growth, maintenance, and repair of cells. It is also used to produce enzymes, hormones, neurotransmitters, and hemoglobin, which are all vital for normal bodily functions. Protein contains four calories per gram and is broken down into amino acids used by the body. Climbers require a minimum of 0.8 grams of protein per kilogram of body weight, and during intense periods of training this amount can increase to 1.2 to 1.4 grams of protein per kilogram of body weight. Protein requirements can be met with a proper diet and must be timed appropriately. There are differing views pertaining to the appropriate protein needs, and climbers must select the one that is most appropriate to their climbing goals. Currently, there are no peer-reviewed studies of high-protein, low-carbohydrate diets that indicate performance enhancement for an athlete (House 2014). Nutritional protein sources include eggs, low-fat dairy, seafood, lean, skinless poultry, and limited amounts of lean red meat.

For vegetarians and vegans, meeting the required daily protein requirements is more challenging, but with knowledge and planning, a healthy diet is possible. There are many professional climbers who are vegetarian or vegan, such as Alex Honnold and Steph Davis. It is important to ensure adequate daily intake of vitamins A, B-12, C, iron, and zinc, as these can be lacking in a vegetarian diet. Vitamin B-12 is best obtained in a sublingual liquid form. Seeds, nuts, legumes, beans, and soy products are all excellent sources of protein that can be included within a vegetarian or vegan climber's diet.

Carbohydrates

Carbohydrates are used for energy and are the preferred fuel for the brain, nervous system, and musculature. Each gram contains four calories and is divided into simple or complex carbohydrates, which are broken down into fuel through a process known as glycolysis. This can occur with or without oxygen and is processed twice as fast as energy derived from fats. The body stores carbohydrates in the liver and muscles in the form of glycogen. For a normal eater, this glycogen reserve (or store) is enough to complete an hour of moderate to high intensity climbing.

Individuals require a minimum of one gram of carbohydrate per pound of body weight daily to avoid *ketosis* (the use of fat as an alternative energy source), which is a less efficient method of fueling the body. Low-carbohydrate diets can lead to depleted glycogen stores and reduced performance in exercise lasting longer than 30 minutes.

Refined simple carbohydrates include table sugar, candy, chocolate, soft drinks, white breads, cakes, and jelly, and are heavily processed. These carbohydrates enter the bloodstream quickly, raising and then dropping blood sugar levels, which can lead to food cravings, fatigue, nausea, and headaches. They are helpful for a quick energy boost, to counteract hypoglycemia, and to improve morale. Honey and some fruits are healthy, natural sources of simple carbohydrates and can be consumed for quick energy with nutritional value and are preferable to processed carbohydrates. Combining simple carbohydrates with fats or protein can prevent the drop in blood glucose levels and its associated effects.

Complex carbohydrates are found in whole grains, pasta, cereals, beans, fruits, and vegetables. These carbohydrates enter the bloodstream more slowly than simple carbohydrates, and are not followed by a dramatic drop in blood sugar levels, thus providing a longer-lasting source of energy. Fiber is included in complex carbohydrates and delays digestion, prolonging the feeling of being satisfied. Complex carbohydrates should take preference over simple carbohydrates and comprise a larger portion of the daily total of carbohydrates consumed.

Artificial sweeteners are not considered simple or complex carbohydrates, as they function and are metabolized differently. Many sweeteners are much sweeter than regular table sugar and should be consumed in moderation.

Fats

Fat is essential because the body cannot produce it and cannot function without it. It keeps skin and hair healthy, aids in the absorption of vitamins A, D, E, and K, insulates the body, is essential for brain development, helps control inflammation, assists in blood clotting, and is a source of energy. Fat contains nine calories per gram. In conditioned athletes, fat supplies most of the fuel for low-intensity activities over a long duration. Fat is categorized as saturated, monounsaturated, polyunsaturated, and trans fatty acids (trans fats). Fat is necessary in a healthy diet; the best sources are monounsaturated and polyunsaturated fats. Saturated fat should be limited, and hydrogenated (trans) fats should be avoided. Daily fat requirements can be met through a varied diet.

Saturated fats are found in animal sources and dairy products, and are required to build certain hormones. Intake should be limited due to their influence on blood cholesterol levels, arterial plaque formation, and development of heart disease. Monounsaturated fats are found in olive oil, peanut oil, canola oil, nuts, and avocados, and are good sources of fat—they should comprise the majority of fat calories. These fats are known to reduce blood cholesterol levels, heart disease, and stroke risk (Kris-Etherton 1999). Polyunsaturated fatty acids, particularly omega-3, are important for nutrition and can be found in fish, some nuts (walnuts, among others), flaxseed, fish oil, cod liver oil, and vegetable oils such as flaxseed, sunflower, canola, and soybean oils. These fats have been associated with improvement of a variety of disease processes such as heart health, cancer, and other conditions (GISSI 1999, Koralek 2006, Leaf 2007). Trans fats, commonly found in processed and fast foods and often labeled as hydrogenated oil, should be limited to less than two grams daily or, if possible, avoided.

Alcohol and Caffeine

Alcohol contains seven calories per gram. While some health benefits of moderate alcohol intake have been proposed, alcohol calories are usually considered otherwise non-nutritional. Daily consumption of more than one alcoholic drink for women or two for men has negative effects on health. Alcohol has been shown to reduce sleep quality, decrease testosterone levels for men, increase cortisol levels, suppress the immune system, and enhance appetite. A standard portion consists of 12 ounces (oz.) of regular beer (5% alcohol), 8 to 9 oz. of malt liquor, 5 oz. of wine (12% alcohol), or 1.5 oz. (40% alcohol) of distilled spirits.

Consuming caffeine by drinking a regular cup of coffee or tea can have health benefits when consumed in moderation, meaning no more than three cups daily. Caffeine is a known antioxidant and has been linked to a reduced risk of diabetes, heart disease, Alzheimer's, Parkinson's, and cancer (Butt 2011). Moderate caffeine consumption (3 to 6 mg per kilogram of body weight) has no diuretic effect.

Supplements

The best source of vitamins and minerals is real food. While consuming supplements is unnecessary when consuming a complete and balanced diet, this is not always realistic, especially at altitude or during lengthy expeditions when food sources can be limited in scope. In situations where resources are limited or a balanced diet is difficult to attain, taking a daily multivitamin can be helpful. Vitamins C and E are recommended for mountaineers at altitude. Choose a vitamin that is United States Pharmacopeia (USP)-approved.

Creatine is a natural substance occurring in meat and fish, but can also be purchased as a supplement. It can be useful for short, explosive strength, and many bodybuilders rely on creatine to improve their workout. The primary negative aspect of creatine for climbers is the associated weight gain from water retention.

Iron is essential, and climbers need to ensure adequate intake. Iron is used in the formation of hemoglobin, the oxygen-carrying component of the red blood cells. Women are at higher risk of being iron deficient, due to menstruation, as are vegetarians and vegans, due to dietary restrictions. A feeling of being tired or weak is a sign of iron deficiency. The best method to confirm an iron deficiency is by having your blood tested.

Eating red meat a few times a week or consuming fortified foods (breads and cereals), leafy greens, or cooking with an iron skillet are excellent methods to meet iron requirements. Overconsumption of iron is not beneficial and can affect calcium and zinc absorption. Menstruating women can include 15 mg of iron from a multivitamin in their diets, but other climbers should not rely on vitamins unless a lab result indicates a low iron level.

Protein powder is an alternative and convenient source of protein. Daily requirements can be supplemented with powders, especially during high-intensity training periods or strength training. Protein intake can be increased to 1.5 to 2 grams per kilogram of body weight daily to support recovery during these activities. There are different kinds of proteins, and choosing the most appropriate depends on the timing of consumption.

Whey protein is a protein isolated from the liquid by-product of cheese production, and is available in isolate or concentrated form. The isolate is at least 90% protein and in the purest form contains little fat, lactose, or cholesterol. Non-isolate whey protein is cheaper, has less protein (usually 89% or less, and sometimes as low as 29%), is usually of lower quality, and contains higher amounts of fat and lactose. Whey is considered a fast protein source with rapid muscle absorption, peaking between 60 and 90 minutes after ingestion. It is excellent as a recovery beverage and aids muscle repair and synthesis.

Casein is derived from cow's milk and is a slower-digesting protein that can result in elevated levels seven hours after ingestion. Less of the casein protein is oxidized or wasted, and it produces a greater overall protein balance compared to whey, making it an ideal nighttime protein source.

Soy protein isolate or concentrate is a vegan-friendly protein source. It is digested more gradually than whey protein and consumption should be timed similarly to casein protein.

Branched chain amino acids (BCAAs) are protein supplements primarily composed of leucine products that have the nine essential amino acids for muscle proteins. These supplements stimulate protein synthesis, are fast acting, and can be useful when consumed within an hour after training. Glucosamine and chondroitin are supplements that have been advertised to relieve joint pain. However, current research of these claims is inconclusive.

Body Composition

Calories are important for daily bodily function, weight maintenance, and activity. The number of calories consumed by a climber should be based upon their ideal weight and activity intensity. A climber working bouldering problems in a climbing gym will require far less calories on a daily basis to maintain a healthy body composition than an alpinist traversing a desolate ridgeline in freezing conditions. The body mass index (BMI) scale is the standard formula to determine ideal weight.

FIGURE 3-1. BODY MASS INDEX

BMI	Classification
Below 18.5	Underweight
18.5–24.9	Normal
25–30	Overweight
Above 30	Obese

(Soles 2008)

However, this scale is not well-suited for climbers. No specific weight is optimal for every climber at a specific height. Ideal weight is the weight at which a person's body performs at its climbing best, whether on rock, ice, or snow. Individual climbers can realistically and accurately calculate their ideal body weight by paying close attention to performance at particular weights and body composition. A better, more rock climber-focused approximation of weight uses the following calculation:

FIGURE 3-2. BMI SCALE ADAPTED FOR CLIMBERS

Men	106 lbs. + 6 lbs. per each inch over 5 ft.
Women	100 lbs. + 6 lbs. per each inch over 5 ft.

(Allow 10% range to compensate for bone structure and density)
Example: 5 ft. 11 in. male: 106 lbs. + 66 lbs. = 172 lbs. ideal weight

(Soles 2008)

To achieve performance goals, climbers should not be fixated on weight, but rather on body composition, and in particular on percentage of body fat. Current research illustrates that body fat percentage can have a dramatic effect on performance (Sheel 2004). Striving for a body fat in the range of 6–13% (for men) and 14–20% (for women) can optimize climbing performance. Individual climbers must determine their best ideal weight and body composition to maximize performance in their climbing environment. The "ideal" may vary greatly between a sport climber and a high-altitude mountaineer.

Body fat can be calculated using a variety of techniques. Regardless of the method, consistency is key, and assessing the trend over weeks and months is more accurate and useful than doing so at any given point in time. There are many ways to alter body composition and achieve an ideal fat percentage. Fad or excessively low-calorie diets are not recommended. These promote unhealthy and unsustainable dieting tactics and include diets that advertise more than a couple of pounds of weight loss in a week. In many cases, the majority of rapid weight loss comes from water, muscle, glycogen, and lean muscle mass and not fat. This is the exact opposite of the desired outcome. Lost muscle and rigid calorie restrictions lead to a reduced resting metabolic rate (RMR), triggering the body to use calories more efficiently and storing fat more readily. This makes it even more difficult to lose body fat and is counterproductive.

A baseline calorie intake of eight calories per pound provides enough fuel for daily bodily function without using muscle as an energy source. This is a minimum baseline and is most appropriate for a completely sedentary individual. It is not applicable for a climber who utilizes much more energy on a daily basis. Figure 3-3 shows a more accurate representation of calorie requirements for the climber or alpinist.

If weight loss is the goal, focusing on a realistic reduction in calories, increased cardiovascular training, and improved RMR from increased muscle mass or through high-intensity interval training (HIIT) is key. On average, a climber must burn 3,500 calories to lose 1 pound of weight. Limiting carbohydrates so that the body dips into stored fat as the source of energy can be a good short-term weight loss strategy but should not be a long-term method, as ketosis is not a healthy way for the body to obtain energy. Rigid calorie restriction is not a realistic fat reduction method. Consumption of a balanced nutritional diet comprising less calories than those burned during exercise in conjunction with strength training

FIGURE 3-3. CALORIE REQUIREMENTS FOR CLIMBERS

Activity level	Exercise per day	Calorie requirement per lb. per day
Low	None	14–15
Moderate	45–60 minutes moderate intensity	16–20
High	60–120 minutes moderate intensity	21–25
Extreme	>120 minutes moderate intensity	25–30

(Soles 2008)

and HIIT training to reduce RMR is the best method to reduce weight (House 2014).

If focusing on body composition rather than weight loss, daily calories should not be reduced. Resistance training along with aerobic exercises including HIIT sessions should be incorporated into a training routine. Resistance training can increase RMR, decrease body fat, increase strength-to-weight ratio, and aid in climbing performance. Once an ideal body composition is achieved, maintenance exercises should be incorporated regularly.

Nutrition Tips for Performance

Consuming the right nutrients at appropriate times enables a climber to stay stronger longer and recover more quickly. There are a few important points for climbers to consider. After ingesting carbohydrates or protein, a hormone known as insulin is secreted. Insulin aids in the conversion of glucose into energy, signaling the body to build new protein structures, and controls how glycogen and fats are stored in the muscles and liver. During exercise, insulin output is suppressed, allowing the body to retrieve fat or glycogen for fuel. Not consuming a simple carbohydrate immediately before high-intensity exercise puts digestion temporarily on hold, stimulating fat oxidation as the fuel-producing pathway and thus decreasing stored fat. This can be beneficial for weight reduction or to improve the body's ability to utilize fat stores more easily. Low-intensity exercise lasting more than one hour requires a limited amount of carbohydrates to derive fuel from fat calories. Consuming a small snack that contains complex carbohydrates and a small amount of fat is the best choice prior to low-intensity exercise (e.g., fruit and nut mix).

Consuming carbohydrates before exercise stimulates the release of insulin into the bloodstream, thus turning off fat oxidation. This reduces the use of fat as a primary fuel source and relies on glucose from dietary intake or from glucose stored as glycogen in the body to fuel the exercise. If carbohydrates are not replaced, energy reserves are depleted and the climber "bonks."

Dividing daily intake into three regular meals, with snacks or grazing every few hours from food sources that contain a balance of carbohydrates, protein, and a small amount of healthy fat is the best way to properly nourish the body. Consuming foods that have a positive impact on energy level and performance is important. Adequate meal sizes and grazing on healthy snacks throughout the day prevents an overfull stomach, can be conducive to exercise, maintains energy levels, and prevents overeating.

Starting the day by eating a breakfast that is rich in carbohydrates, protein, and some fat reduces calories consumed over the remainder of the day. If a climber has not eaten a meal within two hours, consuming a simple carbohydrate 20 minutes prior to a session prevents depletion of glycogen stores. Eating during a climbing session helps to provide constant energy and consuming calories after climbing aids recovery.

Consuming 40 to 65 grams of carbohydrates per hour while climbing at moderate intensity will provide adequate energy, preserve glycogen stores, and extend muscle endurance. During more intense climbing, consumed carbohydrate totals may need to be doubled or even tripled to keep up with demand. The best method to avoid depletion of reserves is to ingest some food at least a half hour before feeling tired, and consuming small snacks every 15 to 20 minutes. Keeping the snacks small prevents blood from being diverted from muscles to the intestines for digestion. This should amount to 100 to 280 calories per hour, depending on the intensity of climbing. Gels and bars are convenient options; however, real food such as honey or fruit can be just as effective and easily digested. When consuming energy bars or gels, be sure to drink plain water, as these draw water from the blood to the digestive tract. This can be even more pronounced by consuming extra carbohydrates and sodium from sports drinks.

Consuming protein along with carbohydrates reduces muscle damage and can delay fatigue. After a hard climbing session, and ideally within an hour, a climber should consume 125 calories of a 4:1 carbohydrate-to-protein ratio for every 30 minutes of climbing to support recovery.

Climbing in an alpine environment can make eating anything challenging, but it is essential for the mountaineer to consume adequate calories. Adding 30 to 35 calories per pound per day is a good baseline to consider when planning diets. In the mountains, especially in cold temperatures (0°C and below), basic energy requirements increase by about 1000 calories daily. Above 23,000 feet (7,000 meters), ingesting energy strictly from non-processed carbohydrates is the best fueling option and easier to digest. Eating every 1 to 2 hours is ideal, and choosing foods that are appetizing to alpinists is important.

HYDRATION

Water is essential, and has a significant and often-ignored effect on climbing performance. The standard recommendation of eight glasses of water per day is not a logical hydration technique, nor is relying on urine color alone. Urine becomes darker from an increased concentration of urochrome, a pigment produced from the breakdown of hemoglobin. Additionally, certain vitamins or foods can turn urine a bright yellow or orange color regardless of hydration status. Proper hydration can be determined by normal urination patterns and drinking accordingly can help prevent dehydration. The best recommendation is to drink water like you would place trad gear: early and when needed. Drinking 5 to 7 milliliters (mL) of water per kilogram (0.17 to 0.24 oz. per 2.2 lb.) of body weight in the four hours prior to climbing promotes hydration. During climbing sessions, continue sipping water throughout the day, and take into account overly hot and humid weather. Following fixed hydration regimens based on arbitrary hydration goals during hot or high-exertion exercise can lead to exercise-associated hyponatremia (EAH, discussed in Chapter 13). EAH has become increasingly common in the outdoor sports world, possibly due to recommendations to drink based on a fixed regimen or copiously and not based on thirst. The Wilderness Medical Society practice guidelines recommend that drinking frequency should be based on perceived thirst (Bennett 2014). In addition, drinking excess amounts of water without any sodium content or food can also cause hyponatremia. Climbers participating in long multi-pitch, big wall, or alpine days and consuming only plain water are particularly at risk. See Chapter 13 for a more complete discussion of hyponatremia.

Quickly drinking large amounts of water to make up for lost fluids and time is not an effective method for hydration, as only 800 to 1000 mL (27 to 34 oz.) of fluid can be absorbed by the gastrointestinal tract within an hour. Additionally, having a stomach full of fluid can cause discomfort and increase the difficulty of climbing. Cold fluids are absorbed more rapidly than warm beverages.

Water loss from sweat varies according to gender, work intensity, temperature, and humidity. This type of water loss should be considered when packing water for a climbing trip. Men tend to sweat more than women, although women have more sweat glands. Men are generally composed of around 60–65% water while women are 50–55% water, so even a small deficit has a significant effect on performance.

Losing a liter of fluid in an hour is typical, but losing up to three liters is not unheard of in extreme climbing conditions. A climber must drink enough fluids to prevent a 2% total body weight of fluid loss during activity to stay healthy. It is important for alpinists in cold weather and at altitude to factor in the fluid lost from increased respiration in dry conditions. This can easily add up to 1.5 liters to the normal water loss totals, and high winds can increase this amount. A minimum of three liters of water per person per day should be taken for each climber in cool weather and at least another liter during sunny conditions or heavy exercise days. Melting snow is always an option but the extra weight of a stove and fuel may not be worth the effort compared to carrying the extra fluid.

TRAINING

A climber can boost their performance and reach their full potential with proper training. Training should be focused, well-planned, and designed to meet the individual needs of the climber. Determining climbing goals and making them specific and measurable, both in the long and short term, form the foundation for a training program. It is important to be realistic, and climbers must remember that achieving one's highest fitness level multiple times a year for more than a few weeks at a time is unrealistic. Every training routine should begin by identifying goals and weaknesses. To optimize ability, create a plan that develops base fitness and incorporates skill development, strength, power, and power endurance. Technical climbing is made up of physical, mental, and technical abilities and can be enhanced through gym and outdoor climbing.

Fitness tests should be completed early in the process to determine a base fitness level and form a measure to compare any improvements. Figure 3-4 shows an example of a basic fitness test published by Steve House and Scott Johnston in their text *Training for the New Alpinism* (House 2014). It is easily reproducible and can be used to monitor progress.

FIGURE 3-4. BASIC FITNESS TEST

Basic fitness test	Poor	Good	Excellent
Box step, 1000′ with 20% of body weight in pack	40–60+ min.	20–40 min.	<20 min.
Dips in 60 sec.	<10	10–30	>30
Sit-ups in 60 sec.	<30	30–50	>50
Pull-ups in 60 sec.	<15	15–25	>25
Box jumps in 60 sec.	<30	30–40	>45
Push-ups in 60 sec.	<15	15–40	>40

(House 2014)

It is important to keep a training log, and there are many examples available on the Internet. Climbing multi-pitch, single pitch, traditional, sport, alpine, mountaineering, ice, or bouldering impacts the training style and regimen, as each discipline requires different levels of strength, power, aerobic ability, and muscular endurance of different muscle groups. Conditioning the proper muscles for the particular climbing discipline through aerobic conditioning and strength training allows the climber to handle different levels and intensities of climbing that improve muscular efficiency and optimize climbing performance. Muscle pump, resulting from occluded blood flow, limited fuel, altered pH, and waste removal is often the limiting factor in elite climbing performance (Giles 2006).

Through training, energy pathways utilized by the body while climbing can be sustained longer by the muscles and delay muscle pump. Training both cardiovascular fitness and strength can improve aerobic and anaerobic thresholds. Increased mitochondrial density raises the exertion level at which the climber can rely primarily on fat as a fuel source and preserve the glycogen stores, thus improving muscle endurance.

Aerobic conditioning helps a climber increase cardiac output, oxygen uptake, blood flow within muscles, breathing efficiency, and buffering capacity. This improves aerobic endurance. Aerobic fitness improves overall stamina and assists in weight control. With improved aerobic fitness, the body develops a higher anaerobic threshold, allowing harder climbing for longer periods with faster recovery. This improves the body's ability to use fat as the primary energy source, sparing the use of the limited glycogen reserves in the muscles and liver. Energy derived from the fat reserves is nearly infinite. This is extremely beneficial to alpinists, as fat can provide a vast source of energy to sustain moderate power outputs for hours on long climbing days. Other benefits include better overall heart health, a slower resting heart rate and improved pump volume, new capillary growth in muscles, increased muscle mitochondria, and increased oxygen-carrying capacity of the blood. It allows for better temperature regulation, delivery of oxygen and nutrients, and removal of waste. With improved circulation, body temperature is more appropriately regulated, and in cooler temperatures, extremities are perfused better, remain warmer, and the risk of frostnip or frostbite is reduced. Aerobic exercise also enhances ligament and tendon repair, a particular concern for climbers, as injuries are common to these structures.

For aerobic training to be effective, the climber must be able to calculate a maximum heart rate and a resting heart rate to set a baseline for determining proper training zones. Resting heart rate (RHR) can be calculated by counting how many times the heart beats for one minute while resting. To identify a maximum heart rate (MHR), a commonly used calculation is to subtract a person's age from 220. While this is a useful tool for the average population, climbers can calculate a more accurate number by using the following test.

To accurately calculate MHR:
1. Warm up for 15 minutes. Progressively increase intensity to moderate breathing/sweating.

2. Run hard for two minutes at a 6–10° incline with no rest.
3. For last 20 seconds (of two minutes), run as fast as possible.
4. Immediately check heart rate for a more precise MHR.
(House 2014)

Training zones are defined as percentages of maximum heart rate ranging from Zone 1 to Zone 5. Climbers can also use other methods such as how they feel or breathing effort to calculate aerobic intensity. Figure 3-5 shows an example of various zones to aim for while training (House 2014).

FIGURE 3-5. TRAINING ZONES

	By % of maximum heart rate (MHR)	Feeling	Ventilation
Recovery	<55%	Very light	Conversational
Zone 1 Recovery (aerobic)	55–75%	Easy breathing	Nose breathing
Zone 2 Endurance (aerobic)	75–80%	Medium	Deep and steady
Zone 3 Stamina (aerobic + anaerobic)	80–90%	Fun hard	Short sentences
Zone 4 Economy (aerobic + anaerobic)	90–95%	Hard	No talking
Zone 5 Speed (anaerobic)	>95%	Maximum	N/A

A climber must elevate their heart rate to at least 70% of their maximum for a minimum of three times a week for thirty minutes or more for aerobic conditioning. The higher the intensity, the more calories burned. HIIT is an efficient training method that increases the excess post-exercise oxygen consumption (EPOC). This translates into an increased metabolic rate post-workout because the body is consuming fuel to replenish energy stores, repair tissue, and build muscle. This results in greater fat-burning for hours after completing the workout. There are many different forms of interval training. *Fartleks* (blend of continuous training with interval training) and hill/stair repeats are two excellent examples useful for climbers. Other aerobic activities can include interval training by increasing the speed for a certain number of minutes followed by slowing down for a period and repeating this process. Interval training is very effective but should not be considered a shortcut or complete method of training. This type of training should be limited to one or two sessions a week.

There are many different types of aerobic exercises, and climbers should choose an activity that is enjoyable. Once aerobic conditioning is developed, the climber can progress into a maintenance phase. Hard aerobic training a couple of times per week is adequate. Adding additional aerobic sessions prior to a climbing trip or expedition is all that is needed to improve aerobic conditioning to meet a goal. For alpinists, greater priority and focus on rigorous aerobic training is necessary in comparison to other climbing disciplines, as longer periods of intense activity are required in high altitudes.

Strength training helps climbers to maximize their strength-to-mass ratio, boost power output and speed, increase metabolism, support body composition, strengthen supporting *ligaments* (fibrous cords attaching bone to bone) and *tendons* (fibrous cords attaching muscle to bone), improve overall fitness, increase endurance, reduce the risk of injury, and ultimately improve performance. Muscle growth, increased response of the muscle, increased mitochondria, and increased number and size of capillaries transporting blood and nutrients and removing waste from the muscle all occur due to strength training and improve the muscle's ability to function longer.

Anaerobic metabolism is an energy source used for quick and dynamic muscle contraction during climbing. Unfortunately, this system can only be used for short periods. Through training, anaerobic metabolism can be delayed, preventing "pump," and allowing the climber to utilize the aerobic energy system. This allows the climber to continue climbing at a high level for sustained periods (Watts 2004).

By controlling the level of intensity during training, the climber controls the energy pathways and muscle fibers being trained. There are various energy systems that can be altered to provide more sustained energy for climbing. Oxidative metabolism (aerobic) requires oxygen and primarily breaks down fat (lipolysis) to produce energy that can last for hours and is most suitable for endurance activities. The lactic acid system, also known as the glycolytic system (lasting up to 60 seconds), and the ATP creatine phosphate system (lasting up to 10 seconds), occur without oxygen (anaerobic) and produce energy from the breakdown of glycogen (glycolysis) stored in the liver and the muscles and creatine phosphate from the muscles, respectively. This is used for climbing activities that require short bursts of energy (e.g., bouldering or sport climbing). However, these systems also produce lactic acid, which increases blood acidity. If lactic acid is not cleared by the body efficiently enough, fatigue sets in (Sheel 2004).

Muscle fibers can be categorized as slow twitch fibers (STF) or fast twitch fibers (FTF), and when trained can be converted from one type to another. It is essential that the climber focus on training at a level that is high enough to achieve FTF stimulation. This requires many hours of consistent training. The FTF are responsible for higher muscle power but the length of time the FTF can be powerful is dependent on the aerobic capacity of the STF.

FIGURE 3-6. TRAINING FOR SPECIFIC MUSCLE FIBERS

Fiber type	Type	Mitochondria	Activity	Energy source
Slow twitch fibers (STF)	Type 1 Low threshold (easily stimulated)	High density	Endurance Alpine climbing lasting ≥2 hrs	Oxidative metabolism Fat is the primary fuel source
Fast twitch fibers (FTF)	Type 2a High threshold (not as easily stimulated)	High density	Power Like STF but more forceful, lasting only 20 seconds	Glycolytic metabolism Glycogen is the fuel source; training can convert and aid endurance
Fast twitch fibers (FTF)	Type 2b	Low density	Best for power Fatigue quickly	Beneficial for bouldering and sport climbing

To improve aerobic muscle power, the climber must train for long durations at low intensity (below their aerobic threshold). Ultimately, this will improve the aerobic power of the STF and aerobic threshold. Training at moderate intensities will increase the power of the STF and aerobic capacities of the FTF for higher power. These changes make the muscle more resistant to fatigue and improve mitochondrial function and climbing ability. Linked bouldering or climbing route intervals are helpful training regimens that should be incorporated to accomplish this goal for rock climbers.

Another benefit to strength training is the increase in strength and power through motor neural adaptations that allow the central nervous system to contract the muscle more effectively by recruiting more muscle neurons simultaneously, resulting in a more powerful muscle. This optimizes strength and power with limited hypertrophy, which is important for climbing disciplines like sport climbers who don't want the extra weight but benefit from the extra strength and power. Body weight, free weights, dumbbells, barbells, and kettlebells are great for strength training. There are many different resistance exercises that train the entire body. Choose exercises that use the upper and lower body muscle groups with a focus on the primary climbing muscles. Core training should be included in any plan. Type of climbing, identified weaknesses, and climbing goals determine the specific muscles that should be included in a training routine.

For examples of upper and lower body muscle exercises and proper form, consult weight lifting manuals or work with a personal fitness trainer. All resistance training sessions should start with a warm-up. This should last for five to ten minutes and will increase circulation, warm muscles, and lubricate the joints, thus decreasing the risk of injury. Proper form is extremely important. Frequency, intensity, and volume are all factors to consider when designing a training plan, and the muscles used during climbing should be trained in the same way they are going to be used.

At least two days per week should be set aside for resistance training, except during prime climbing season, when only maintenance sessions should be included. Choosing the number of repetitions, sets, and interval times affects how the muscle will transform. Progressive overload and recovery is a great method to increase strength. Depending upon goals, sets and repetitions performed should be altered appropriately.

For rock climbers, it is important to train in a way that improves strength without hypertrophy, as this leads to increased muscle mass and added weight. Improved weight-to-strength ratio and not weight gain is the goal for most climbers. Power is improved from exercises that target FTF, which enhance the ability to produce greater strength and speed. This is very beneficial for sport climbers and boulderers. Endurance is the ability of the muscle to sustain an activity for a certain length of time and is critical for traditional climbers, mountaineers, and alpinists. Figure 3-7 is a review of how to alter the repetitions, sets, rests, and frequency to obtain improved power, strength, and endurance.

For increased power and strength, completing five or six sets is necessary. Rests are important to allow sufficient recovery for a better workout, and during this time energy sources are replenished. A total of three sets per exercise is ideal for muscle development. Adding more sets does not produce superior results and after each set the returns are reduced unless the goal is to improve power.

If time is limited, it is better to do less sets of all the exercises in a routine than to leave some out in favor of more sets. This is the foundation for working on muscle growth. Super-setting—performing two exercises in a row with no rest—is a time-efficient method to work out and increase endurance.

The main focus should always be to reach fatigue. Two to six exercises should be used and include the back, chest, arm, shoulder, leg, and core muscles. Isometric finger strength, often a limiting factor in climbing, can also be trained. Although there is no scientific research supporting the use of a hang board for training, many skilled climbers use these devices. *Plyometric training*—a form of training emphasizing quick, maximal moves over short periods—is regarded as a good method for improving explosive power because it increases muscle fiber recruitment and aids in muscle fiber contraction. Linking bouldering routes together into a longer routine and campus board sessions improve speed and accuracy for dynamic movement. Many climbers use CrossFit programs as a method to improve fitness. Some studies have indicated a high risk of acute injury from many CrossFit exercises (Weisenthal 2014, Hak 2013). As with all types of training, maintaining proper form is key to injury prevention.

Periodization (breaking training into segments, altering intensity, volume, rest, and frequency over weeks, months, and a year) is linked to

FIGURE 3-7. ALTERNATE TRAINING REGIMES FOR SPECIFIC RESULTS

Desired adaptation	Repetitions with maximum load	Rest time in minutes	Sets
Power	3–5 (fast)	3–5	1–3
Strength	3–6	3–5	3–4
Strength and high-intensity power endurance	6–8	3–5	3–4
High-intensity power endurance	8–12	1–3	3–4
Muscle endurance	12–20	30–60 seconds	2–4

(Soles 2008)

improved climbing performance and should be incorporated into training programs. There are many different terms used to define different segments. Each segment builds from the prior and there should always be an included rest segment. A cycle can run from six weeks to four months. The break or recovery segment of at least one to three weeks is absolutely necessary to refresh the body and mind before beginning the next cycle. Periodization routines vary depending upon climbing type and may not work for every climber. The rigid nature of the training can cause overtraining or undertraining and a lack of motivation to continue the program.

Research has shown that static stretching prior to a workout decreases the ability of muscles to fire as quickly or forcefully and it does not reduce or prevent injuries (Page 2012). Warming up the mus-

Training effect	Growth	Result
Maximum muscular recruitment and neural training	No change in muscle growth or endurance	Explosive power for short, intense problems
Maximum muscular recruitment and neural training	No change in muscle growth or endurance	Improves strength without adding bulk
Moderate recruitment	Moderate muscle growth and power gains	Can add some mass but increases time muscle can be used
Maximum muscle growth	Strength, power, and low-intensity endurance gains	Good overall training range when combined with aerobic conditioning but can add some muscle mass
Modest muscle growth	Minimal strength and power gains	Great starting point for new resistance program or improving low-strength muscle endurance

cles (dynamic stretching) with light exercise is more injury preventative than static stretching and should always be done prior to more intense climbing. Static stretching after exercise is encouraged and provides increased flexibility, which is beneficial to climbing performance. A stretch should never be forced and should be performed during exhalation. Relaxing and sinking deeper into the stretch is valuable for improvement. To increase flexibility even more, contract the muscles for a few seconds followed by relaxing, which will allow even more of a stretch and improved flexibility.

Yoga and Pilates are both practices that can increase strength and flexibility for climbers, which can also help prevent injury. Yoga tends to focus more on flexibility, stress release, focused breathing, and mind/

body connection, whereas Pilates focuses more on core development and flexibility. Balance should not be overlooked, and practicing on a slackline, wobble board, or balance boards can aid in improving balance.

Rest is a time for the body to recover and get stronger. Sleep is essential for recovery and optimal performance. The amount of sleep needed depends on the individual; seven to eight hours is not necessary for everyone. Quality of rest is the most important factor.

Climbers should monitor for overtraining. A common sign of overtraining is repeated shortcomings in performance. Keeping a training log and recording energy levels or feelings after a workout can help to identify a pattern of feeling tired or fatigued and is a simple way to monitor if overtraining is occurring. Common symptoms of overtraining include persistent fatigue, irritability, depression, weight loss, absence of menstruation, insomnia, lowered libido, or loss of enthusiasm and motivation.

Making a Plan

Every workout should be considered an opportunity to improve climbing ability and should begin with a warm-up. Warming up with easy cardio, climbing a few easy routes, or anything that increases circulation will decrease the flash pump that occurs when starting on a hard route too soon. Training plans should be tailored to climbing discipline and should be routinely altered to challenge the muscles and nervous system and prevent a plateau. Sport climbing and bouldering are mostly power-focused, while traditional climbing requires power and endurance. Training for alpine, mountaineering, and big wall climbing should focus on endurance.

Novice climbers can build their climbing-specific muscles and establish a base of climbing fitness through high climbing volume. It is important to remember that training should not occur while lead climbing, but rather on top rope, in order to focus on climbing on more difficult and challenging terrain. Indoor climbing gyms are ideal to train for sport climbing and bouldering. Climbing is a year-round sport and one of the most efficient places to train is in a gym, where the routes and protection are set and the weather is constant. Training for ice climbing can be accomplished with holds that accept picks and are made for ice tools. Cross-training and including other fun activities can help a climber maintain fitness and prevent overtraining.

Muscular endurance is often a weakness in climbers and commonly overlooked, but will allow a climber to hang on for extended periods using only a fraction of their power. Climbing is the best method to improve endurance, rather than weight training. Climbing laps for up to thirty minutes after warming up is a great way to improve endurance. The key to this type of training is continuous movement. Endurance running and hiking uphill are great methods for alpinists to improve endurance. Adding weight with a backpack can increase difficulty.

Bouldering or using a campus board are useful methods to train for power. These types of workouts should be limited to a few per week. Only experienced climbers with established fitness should incorporate a campus board in their training regimen, to prevent injuries to fingers and wrists.

Power endurance involves combining power and endurance together and should simulate actual climbing situations as much as possible. Training for power and endurance assists in a climber's ability to onsight and redpoint more difficult climbs. Choosing a sport route or linking up several difficult boulder problems are methods to accomplish this training. Selecting climbs that are close to the climber's on-sight ability and taking multiple laps on these routes builds power endurance. After a short rest, the climber should repeat this process. For improvement in redpointing climbs, a climber needs to prevent fatigue through high-intensity interval workouts composed of climbing highly difficult routes on top rope for sustained periods, followed by rest, and continued climbing for multiple iterations.

All climbers reach performance plateaus, and rest periods, rest phases, or tapers should be taken to allow the body to heal and ready the mind for performing in the following peak or performance period. Overtraining is worse than undertraining, and it is important for climbers to listen to their bodies and rest when needed. In-session recovery is also important to maximize a training session. A recent study noted that climbers recover better between attempting routes by climbing a nearby easier route rather than by merely walking at the base of a wall or cliff. Climbers were able to go higher on repeated attempts and the study measured lower lactate levels for those climbing easy routes as a recovery versus merely resting or walking (Valenzuela 2015).

For traditional and big wall climbers, indoor gym training is not as beneficial, as it is not as specific to these disciplines. Outdoor climbing in these environments is more useful, as it builds needed stamina. Recommended training methods include added cardiovascular sessions in preparation for the extra work involved in big wall climbing. Traditional climbing should focus on outdoor skill practice, climbing, increasing base fitness, and strength training.

Bouldering training should focus on strength, power, and dynamic movement. Campus and hang board training is extremely beneficial to the boulderer, and sessions should include low repetitions and longer rests. Supplemental strength training that focuses on the shoulders, upper arms, and core is helpful.

Training for alpine pursuits including ice, mixed climbing, mountaineering, and altitude all require endurance and power endurance. Aerobic fitness is the foundation of alpine climbing. The less technical the climbing goal, the greater the focus on aerobic fitness.

Technique and Mental Strength

Good technique and mental fortitude remain two of the most important training aspects for improved climbing. Combining physical ability with refined technique is the key to greater climbing ability. Identification of the different types of climbing moves and practicing the use of each in easy terrain is the best method to develop a larger repertoire. With time and application of these moves, a climber will develop the ability to integrate each at the appropriate time. Watching other climbers or reading about technique are great methods to identify various moves.

Mental strength and confidence during climbing is gained through experience and involves factors such as determination, confidence, and the management of stress and emotions. Fear of falling or injury is an ever-present part of climbing, and the importance of an ability to manage this fear cannot be overstated. There are multiple books available that discuss the mental aspects of climbing and can be useful to identify techniques. Some common techniques include breath control, visualization, concentration, and elimination of distractions. Everyone reacts to and controls stress in different ways, and identifying those techniques that are most effective can assist in developing the mental fortitude to climb harder and safer.

II.
MEDICAL

CHAPTER 4

ORTHOPEDICS

Orthopedic injuries to the extremities are a common problem in both general wilderness activities and specifically in climbing. Early climbing medicine research suggested traumatic lower extremity injuries were more common than upper extremity injuries for climbers and mountaineers in general, but more recent studies have shown that this is not the case for traditional climbers, sport climbers, or boulderers, where upper extremities are in fact more prone to injury. These early studies relied on data gathered from rescue teams, the National Park Service (NPS), and emergency departments, while newer studies utilized surveys to identify common injuries within the climbing community. Due to the less life-threatening nature of upper extremity injuries, these upper body acute and chronic (overuse) injuries were underreported in the early studies, as they usually did not require emergency medical care.

A recent study of ground fall accidents in climbing examined climbing injury research over the last two decades and identified this trend. Upper extremity chronic injuries constituted the majority of climbing injuries, and measured between 71% and 93% of all injuries identified (Simon 2016). Based upon these studies, chronic overuse injuries of the upper extremity are now recognized as being far more prevalent than acute injuries to the lower extremities for traditional climbers, sport climbers, and boulderers. Lower extremity injuries, both chronic and acute, still tend to be more common for alpinists. This chapter will discuss both chronic and acute injuries of the upper and lower extremities within the familiar outline of identify, treat, and evacuate. As with all injuries, a thorough assessment (see Chapter 1) is essential to providing care to an injured climber and should begin with a focus on life-threatening injuries.

According to Auerbach's *Field Guide to Wilderness Medicine* (Auerbach 2013), the general principles of musculoskeletal guidelines that mandate evacuation from the wilderness environment include:

+ Suspected spine injury
+ Suspected pelvic injury
+ Open fracture
+ Suspected compartment syndrome
+ Hip or knee dislocation
+ *Vascular* (blood vessel) compromise to an extremity
+ Laceration with tendon or nerve injury
+ Uncertainty of injury severity

While this list serves as a foundation for evacuation principles, the demands of the mountainous environment require a more strict investigation of the isolated components of the injured extremity and what functional capacity may be required to safely participate in such regions.

When an injury to an upper or lower extremity occurs, the impact of this impairment may have greater repercussions when considering the nature of demands placed on the climber to continue their participation in climbing activities. In comparison to hiking on level terrain, cycling on a suburban roadway, or being in an otherwise frontcountry environment where treatment is more easily facilitated, climbers and alpinists often find themselves farther removed from comprehensive care and management of an injury. Furthermore, the demands of the climbing environment leave little room for compromised function. A lower extremity injury may impair movement with crampons or standing on a belay ledge. Likewise, an injury to the upper extremity can impede the ability to grip a handhold, an ice axe, or the rope during a rappel or belay. As this presents an issue of safety both to the patient and the partner or group, strict consideration must be given to the ability of the climber to continue to participate in climbing activities.

Compartment syndrome must be considered with injuries to an extremity. This is characterized by dangerously increased pressure within the muscle fascia layers, causing potential tissue death as pressures rise above blood pressure, preventing oxygenated blood from reaching tissue. Signs of compartment syndrome include severe pain, paleness to the skin, loss of distal pulses, and a pins-and-needles sensation around and distal to the site, with rigidity externally to compartment tissues that normally would not be firm. In such a case, expeditious evacuation is recommended.

As with all injuries, a thorough assessment is essential to providing care to an injured climber and should begin with a focus on life-threatening injuries (see Chapter 1). This chapter will address upper body orthopedic injuries (Chapter 4A) followed by lower body orthopedic injuries (Chapter 4B). Types of injuries are divided by area of the body and then subdivided by the type of injury (acute or chronic) in parentheses. Each section discusses how to identify and treat each condition as well as evacuation considerations. These general categories are helpful for all types of lower body injuries and should be considered whatever the injury.

IDENTIFY

A thorough assessment and examination should identify any injuries. Note any obvious deformities or loss of circulation, sensation, or movement of an extremity.

TREAT

The acronym RICE (rest, ice, compression, elevation) is helpful during care of orthopedic lower body injuries (see "RICE" sidebar on page 76). Resting an injured extremity prevents further damage, while ice, snow, or cold water (such as from a stream) can help reduce swelling and pain. Compression can help to reduce swelling for some injuries and provide support for others, while elevation of the extremity above the heart can also assist in reducing swelling.

EVACUATE

While every injury is unique in circumstance and severity, the following types of extremity injury should always be evacuated:

+ Injuries to the pelvis
+ Hip dislocations
+ Any open fractures
+ Any nerve or vascular injury
+ Any other injury that causes special concern

UPPER BODY ORTHOPEDIC INJURIES

Neck
Belayer's Neck (Acute)
IDENTIFY

Belayer's Neck is a common condition for climbers caused by the extension of the neck while belaying a partner. It is primarily a muscle issue affecting the splenius and levator scapulae muscles of the neck and the trapezius and erector spinae of the upper back. In extreme cases, it can cause irritation to the facets of the cervical vertebrae and the spinal cord.

TREAT

The best treatment is prevention. Changing position, whether in a standing or hanging belay, allows for release of muscle tension while belaying. Stretching the muscles described above, between belays, is also helpful. Multiple companies have created "belay glasses" that use mirrors to allow the belayer to maintain normal forward neck positioning while still being able to visualize the climber above.

EVACUATE

Evacuation is not needed for this condition.

Shoulder

The shoulder is a remarkable joint, with an extremely wide multidirectional range of motion and a very limited attachment to the axial skeleton of the trunk. Its primary union to the trunk is muscular, with the clavicle providing the most significant bony attachment. The glenohumeral joint (ball and socket component) is a shallow surface that does not lend itself to inherent stability but does contribute to the joint's excellent mobility, allowing vertical use of the arm and hand in climbing. The soft tissue architecture of the joint lends itself to the complex ability of the joint but also exposes the joint to injury. In any given year, the average US resident has a 1 in 88 chance of presenting to the emergency department with an upper extremity injury (Ootes 2012). Injury at the shoulder joint represents approximately 17% of these patient visits, with 50% of those being due to dislocation. Given the exposure to possible injury required in certain climbing maneuvers, the potential incidence is felt by the authors to be even more prevalent in the climbing community.

Acromioclavicular (AC) Separation and Clavicle Fracture (Acute)

IDENTIFY

The AC joint represents the ligamentous interface between the clavicle (collarbone) and the acromion (a bony process located at the superior and lateral aspect of the shoulder blade). AC separation is most often the result of direct trauma during a ground fall either by axial loading the arm or direct trauma to the shoulder during a fall. Injury at this location is graded based upon the severity of damage to the ligamentous structures.

Following an injury to this joint, the patient may demonstrate swelling or bruising over the area with tenderness to palpation. A step-off deformity may be felt at the distal end of the clavicle where it interfaces with the acromion. Pain may also be experienced with overhead activity, and be particularly worsened with movements involving the arm extended away from the skeleton or crossing in front of the skeleton (e.g., bouldering traverse). Rehearsing various arm motions with a focus on motions similar to stemming or the performance of a mantel can identify AC separation—its pain is exacerbated by these types of motions. Physical exam findings of a clavicle fracture include tenderness, bruising, or deformity. Examine the junction of the clavicle and sternum (breastbone), which may be separated. Although rare, injury to the soft tissues and organs beneath the clavicle must be considered. Examine extremity CSM distal to the injury. Injury to the lung pleura with possible pneumothorax (lung collapse) must be considered. Pneumothorax signs include absent breath sounds and palpable air (resembling Rice Krispies) under the skin.

TREAT

Depending upon the severity of the injury, continued participation may be possible; however, it may be necessary to isolate and support the extremity. This may be performed quite simply with the formation of a sling and swath utilizing a T-shirt or jacket sleeve (Figure 4-1), or a 48-inch nylon runner tied around the wrist of the injured extremity and suspended from the neck (Figure 4-2, and consider additional neck padding depending on clothing). In such a situation, an assisted belay or lowering may be necessary.

EVACUATE

Further climbing activities will be difficult, but evacuation can be done without urgency.

FIGURE 4-1. IMPROVISED SLING WITH SHIRT

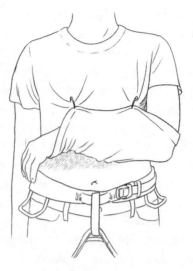

Glenohumeral (Shoulder) Dislocation and Proximal Humerus Fractures (Acute)

Often described as a "ball and socket" joint, this joint is more aptly described as a coffee cup sitting on a saucer or a golf ball sitting on a tee. The joint is primarily stabilized by surrounding muscular and ligamentous structures, making it very mobile but also relatively weak and prone to injury.

IDENTIFY

More than 90% of the time, dislocations occur when the humerus (upper arm bone) tears through the anterior joint capsule and remains dislocated. This is called an "anterior dislocation" because the humeral head lies anterior to the joint. Occasionally, an injury like this will return to the anatomical position within a few seconds, which is a *subluxation* (a partial or incomplete dislocation) rather than a dislocation. The most common arm position leading to a dislocation is an abducted (outstretched) and externally rotated upper extremity (shown in this anatomical positioning in Figure 4-3). One must also consider the presence of a proximal humerus fracture instead of dislocation. While shoulder girdle and muscular development may hide anatomical findings in more robust climbers, an area of deformity can often be seen in the upper arm

FIGURE 4-2. WEBBING SLING

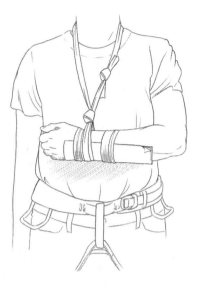

in cases of upper humerus fracture. Other times, a proximal humerus fracture will have *crepitus* (crackling or rattling sound made by a part of the body) to palpation. With both injuries, the climber will cradle the extremity and avoid further use. Certain individuals are more prone to injury such as subluxation or dislocation at the shoulder joint based on inherited disorders such as Ehlers-Danlos syndrome. These individuals may have a history of such injuries and may be prone to unusual dislocation types, such as a posterior or inferior dislocation, due to their inherited traits of ligamentous laxity. Victims of lightning strike and seizure disorders may also present with posterior dislocation injuries due to extreme muscular contraction in anatomically unusual directions. Careful evaluation of CSM must be made. Pay particular attention to the *regimental patch area* (side of shoulder over deltoid muscle), an area that can have reduced sensation with this injury.

TREAT

Dislocation reduction should be considered if a trained provider is present. If training in dislocation reduction is desired, we recommend enrolling in a quality wilderness medical training program that teaches the maneuvers and practices them under controlled circumstances.

FIGURE 4-3. GUTTER SPLINT

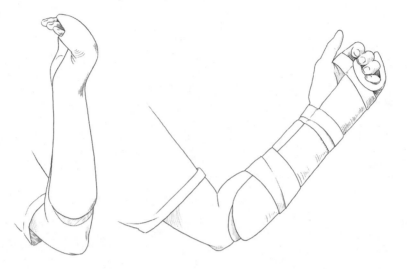

These procedures would be difficult to learn exclusively from a book without other hands-on training. Following reduction, the injured climber should be placed in an improvised sling. Attempts at reduction of shoulder dislocations should be followed by repeat neuromuscular exams—specifically, distal CSM should be assessed before and after any intervention. The definition of a "trained provider" is controversial. This is considered an advanced medical skill, and in EMS care, is outside of the scope of practice even of paramedics in most American states (Hawkins 2018). However, it is frequently part of wilderness medicine training, even at levels below that of a paramedic. For example, both the Boy Scouts of America (BSA 2010) and the American Red Cross (ARC 2014) categorize certain dislocation reduction techniques as first aid. Ditty demonstrated that non-healthcare provider paddlers were able to successfully reduce shoulders 72% of the time, with a mean time to reduction of 5 minutes, compared to 135 minutes for those seeking more formal medical care (Ditty 2010). We believe training should be obtained before reduction attempts are made. We advise those not credentialed to perform this skill (but trained in it) to consider performing emergency attempts at reduction only in three situations: 1) distal CSM is disrupted; 2) if evacuation safety would be significantly impaired by leaving the dislocation in place; or 3) evacuation to a healthcare provider will take more than two to three hours. If reduction is not achieved, splint the extremity in a position of comfort with a sling.

EVACUATE

With or without reduction, patients with a dislocation should be promptly evacuated. Persistent dislocation is time-sensitive, as reduction complexity and chance of nerve damage increases with the duration of dislocation. Reduced dislocation evacuation is not time-sensitive. Subluxations are treated as severe sprains and do not require evacuation, but may limit further climbing depending on pain and degree of sprain.

SLAP Lesion (Acute or Chronic)

These tears in the labrum (a fibrocartilaginous lip to the encasing sheath around the shoulder joint) are commonly encountered in "throwing athletes," including baseball, football, and volleyball players, as well as swimmers. A similar mechanism is common among climbers who repetitively move their shoulders through an overhead arc. The occasional dynamic loading of the shoulder joint during abrupt bouldering moves contributes to these injuries in the climbing population. In this maneuver, climbers find their shoulder abducted and often externally rotated, stretching the biceps muscle. This muscle originates in two locations, the coracoid process of the scapula and the superior portion of the labrum within the joint. At the position of risk, the long head of the biceps tethers the superior portion of the labrum, which places it in a position that increases the rate of injury for climbers (see Figure 4-4). Another possible mechanism of injury includes chronic grinding of the labrum at the joint leading to labral derangement.

IDENTIFY

There is occasionally a distinct point of injury and even an audible pop or click to the joint. This leads to continued discomfort with climbing activity, often with crepitus in the joint during overhead or reaching activities. While evidence has shown a chronic degenerative component to labral tears of the shoulder within the general population, with some not even symptomatic, these are more often acute and symptomatic for the overhead athlete (De Palma 1949, Wilk 2013). SLAP lesions may produce discomfort at the time of injury but are rarely severe enough to abandon a climb or order evacuation. Indeed, the diagnosis of SLAP lesion is often difficult and may be missed by the untrained eye. For those trained in these modalities, certain physical exam findings may be suggestive of a SLAP lesion, however, the definitive diagnosis is identified with MRI.

TREAT

Field treatment should be symptomatic, with a goal of pain relief and restoration of function. Definitive management in a hospital setting has historically included surgical repair, resection, and conservative care, all of which have been suggested in the literature. A climber's actual treatment plan must be tailored to the individual athlete, their climbing activity, and long-term goals.

EVACUATE

Evacuation is not needed unless functionality is impaired and a safety issue on a climb results. Surgical repair is indicated based on the location, type, and degree of injury to the labral complex and involves a balanced rehabilitation program.

FIGURE 4-4. ANTERIOR SHOULDER

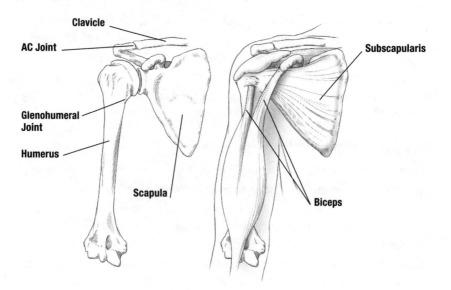

Impingement Syndrome and Rotator Cuff Tears (Acute or Chronic)

These two diagnoses coexist as a progressive cascade of injury and derangement of the soft tissue structures in the shoulder. Impingement syndrome is characterized by pain within the shoulder that is particularly worsened during maneuvers of shoulder abduction (lateral raising of the arm) and internal rotation of the arm. The source has been felt to be due to either structural or functional cause. Continued overhead and cross-body maneuvers cause irritation of the soft tissue—the *bursa* (fluid-filled sac found at points of friction) is irritated as it rubs at the underside of the acromion and coracoacromial ligament, leading to a condition called *bursitis*. Further irritation and trauma can lead to injury to one of the four rotator muscles, the supraspinatus (Figure 4-5). Rotator cuff tears appear in about 25% of the general population, and risk increases with age (Tempelhof 1999). However, the extent and significance of the tear must be considered. Partial thickness tears are fairly common, in which case continued shoulder use, albeit painful, is possible. While structural causes, as described earlier, are a contributing factor, a significant portion of impingement and rotator cuff pathology has a functional etiology rooted in muscular and postural imbalance, scapulothoracic instability, and capsular tightness of the joint. Many of these factors can be corrected through diligent physiotherapy.

IDENTIFY

There are multiple physical exam findings including pain and/or weakness with abduction AND pain with the shoulder moving through the overhead impingement arc. Impingement syndrome can mimic a rotator cuff tear, requiring diagnostic imaging (i.e., MRI or ultrasound) not present in the wilderness to confirm the presence or absence of an actual tear. For those with proper training, lidocaine along with a corticosteroid may be injected into the subacromial space. Following this, climbers with bursitis and/or partial thickness rotator cuff tears will recover some functional motion in shoulder abduction and internal rotation, while those with a full thickness rotator cuff tear will have pain relief but no improvement in function.

TREAT

Ice should be applied and NSAIDs (nonsteroidal anti-inflammatory drugs) used to reduce inflammation. Overhead activity, including climb-

FIGURE 4-5. POSTERIOR SHOULDER

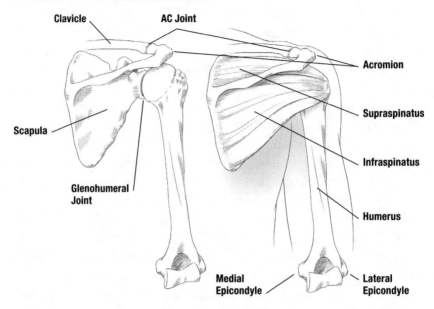

ing, should be limited. Post-trip treatment includes physical therapy, possibly steroid injections, and consideration of surgery for full thickness tears. While the recovery process of shoulder surgery can be quite laborious, climbers with full thickness rotator cuff tears, especially younger climbers, should consider surgical repair, as the tear can progress and subsequent further injury to the joint may result over time (Tashjian 2012).

Elbow

Elbow Dislocations (Acute)

The elbow functions to stabilize the hand in place to allow completion of fine motor tasks. Despite the appearance of stability in this "hinge" joint, it is the second most commonly dislocated joint (the shoulder being first).

Stability of the elbow is maintained by both bony and ligamentous structures. Of the elbow ligaments, four are notable: the radial and ulna collateral ligaments, the anterior capsule, and the annular ligament. Compromise of these structures during high-energy trauma or with repeated abuse can lead to elbow instability.

The *olecranon* (proximal portion of the ulna) is frequently injured

FIGURE 4-6. DERMATOME MAP/NERVE ANATOMY

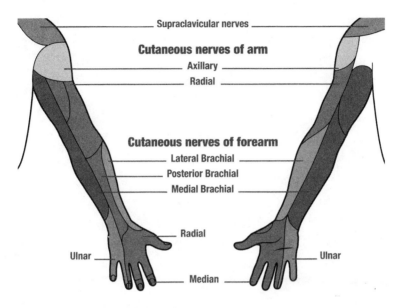

Supraclavicular nerves

Cutaneous nerves of arm

Axillary

Radial

Cutaneous nerves of forearm

Lateral Brachial

Posterior Brachial

Medial Brachial

Radial

Ulnar

Ulnar

Radial

Median

with falls on outstretched arms. While such a mechanism may not be common in top-rope climbing, it is quite possible for such a force to be generated in a leader fall, during the down-climb portion of a mountaineering trip, or from a missed attempt at a hold when bouldering. Dislocations are most often posterior (90%) and are often associated with fractures at either the proximal ulna, proximal radius, or distal humerus.

IDENTIFY

It may be difficult to examine the elbow joint following acute injury due to swelling. Indeed, swelling can be so significant that compartment syndrome (discussed earlier in this chapter) can become a concern. Injuries to the brachial artery and, more frequently, the ulna nerve, are seen with posterior dislocations as often as 21% of the time. Distal CSM examination must be completed, including evaluation of the median, radial, and ulnar nerves (Figure 4-6).

TREAT

Compromise to any function distal to an elbow dislocation should increase the motivation to promptly evacuate or provide field reduction

FIGURE 4-7. IMPROVISED GUTTER SPLINT

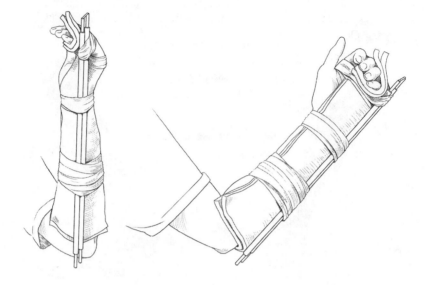

if trained in this skill. Consideration of the distance from definitive care should drive decision-making toward management in the field. Repeated CSM exam should be made before and after attempts of reduction in any joint. Placement of the extremity in a dorsal "gutter"-type splint (Figure 4-3) at the elbow can facilitate stabilization, and gutter splints can be improvised—an example is provided in Figure 4-7. In the absence of suitable splint material, a sling may be made with the climber's shirt and a safety pin (Figure 4-1) or, even more simply, with the use of climbing slings or webbing (Figure 4-2). Compartment syndrome remains a risk even after adequate reduction has been made.

EVACUATE
Elbow injuries suspected to be dislocations or fractures should be evacuated.

Lateral Epicondylitis or Tennis Elbow (Chronic)
It is interesting that tennis generated the name of this source of elbow pain, as it is quite prevalent in many other populations, including climbers and alpinists. Roughly 14% of surveyed sport climbers report lateral epicondylitis (Hochholzer 2006). In the general population, most elbow

FIGURE 4-8. FOREARM ANATOMY

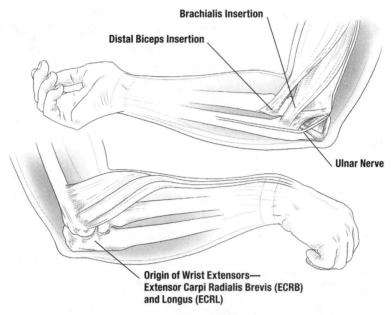

Brachialis Insertion

Distal Biceps Insertion

Ulnar Nerve

Origin of Wrist Extensors—
Extensor Carpi Radialis Brevis (ECRB)
and Longus (ECRL)

pain is in the lateral elbow, and lateral epicondylitis is the most frequently identified source.

In a "position of utility," wrist extensors originating at the lateral epicondyle must maintain a wrist posture that is either neutral or slightly extended to facilitate gripping. Thus, heavy gripping maneuvers such as climbing, whether crimping small edge lips, holding large slopers, or grasping ice tools, requires firing of the wrist extensors. In lateral epicondylitis, it is the extensor carpi radialis brevis (ECRB) that is commonly the culprit of pain, although other muscular tendinous origins can be involved at this shared point of origin (see Figure 4-8). This is thought to be a mechanism of initial inflammation coupled with repetitive trauma and degenerative changes of the tissue—often as the result or rapid progression of intensity and duration in gripping maneuvers. From a histological perspective, the tissue involved at the lateral epicondyle will demonstrate increased collagen deposition and microtears of the ECRB and/or other wrist extensors. Additionally, periostitis (inflammation of the periosteum) and microavulsion fractures at the lateral epicondyle may be identified.

IDENTIFY

Pain in the lateral epicondyle is gradual in onset, perhaps the day after hard climbing, and will worsen with continued climbing attempts. Pain with resisted wrist or middle finger extension or with gripping will be identified on exam. It is often seen at transitional times during a climbing season, such as going "big" at the beginning of the rock season, increasing frequency and intensity of gym climbing in the off-season, or transitioning from rock to ice climbing before ice tool grip has been retrained.

TREAT

Cessation from climbing activities with a gradual return is the best approach to management. Other therapeutic modalities to consider include rest, ice massage, cross-frictional massage, elbow bands, NSAIDs and/or acetaminophen, and, if available, corticosteroid injection. More recently, platelet-rich plasma injections to the area of the lateral epicondyle have been suggested as an additional non-operative treatment (Jindal 2013). Symptoms may persist unless otherwise properly addressed; it is not uncommon for this condition to plague climbers with pain for several months. Eventual surgery (debridement and release of the inflamed tissue at the lateral epicondyle) may be necessary if conservative measures fail to reduce pain or improve function.

EVACUATE

Evacuation is not necessary, but follow-up care and establishment of a treatment plan is recommended. Continued climbing may exacerbate symptoms.

Anterior Elbow Pain or Climber's Elbow (Chronic)

While multiple causes of anterior and medial elbow pain exist, the most common among climbers is "climber's elbow." Described as a strain or partial tear of the distal portion of the brachialis tendon, this condition is characterized by progressively worsening anterior and medial elbow pain without distal neurological compromise (Figure 4-8). Occasionally, a crackling or crepitus can be felt over the anterior and medial portion of the elbow with elbow flexion or extension. Warmth and tenderness to palpation over the affected area is also common. Elbow flexion against resistance can elicit pain, and it is not rare for slight elbow flexion contracture (fixed positioning) to be present depending on the duration and severity of symptoms.

Climber's elbow is often mistaken for medial epicondylitis or biceps tendinitis. Often, a remote history of traumatic distraction injury or fall may be reported. A hypothesis of overuse has been put forward as a culprit as well (Peters 2001). The proposed mechanism is linked to the fact that the brachialis is the primary and strongest flexor of the elbow. When the climber repetitively engages the elbow in a position of flexion and pronation (e.g., locking off), the brachialis is isolated to perform even more of the workload as the biceps is less engaged. Symptoms of pain may present weeks to months later, following the injury, making the initial diagnosis difficult. Traumatic myositis ossificans, or inappropriate deposition of bony material, may be seen on lateral X-rays, demonstrating *ossification* (bone formation) within the distal brachialis muscular and tendinous insertion. This is related to continued inflammation from "climbing through" or repetitive inflammation causing excessive bone formation in muscular tissue. Other complications include the previously mentioned loss in range of motion, chronic pain at rest, and potential (rare) rupture of the brachialis.

IDENTIFY

Climber's elbow can occur with low-grade trauma such as dynamic loading of the extended elbow sustained through loss of footing and absorption of a fall by an extended arm, or in a leader fall with injury of the extended arm. Pain with palpation over the distal insertion site of the brachialis (medial to biceps insertion) should raise suspicion to this ailment as the culprit of the elbow pain. Additionally, pain with resisted elbow flexion (with or without palpation) should also prompt further consideration. It is worthy to note that pain with supination points to a different diagnosis more likely involving the distal biceps; however, it is conceivable that both could be injured simultaneously.

TREAT

Prevention is the key to resolution, and includes proper warm-up with stretching, range of motion exercises, and dedicated recovery intervals between climbing sessions. RICE (rest, ice, compression, and elevation; see sidebar below) and NSAIDs are appropriate. While not life threatening, cessation from climbing activities may be required to allow

+RICE ACRONYM AND CREATING ICE CUPS/PACKS+

R REST: Take weight and stress off of injured areas

I ICE: Ice, snow, or cold water assists in reducing swelling and inflammation

C COMPRESSION: Light pressure, such as from an ACE wrap, that does not cut off blood suypply can reduce swelling and provide support.

E ELEVATION: Place injured area above the heart to reduce swelling

CREATING ICE CUPS AND REUSABLE ICE PACKS

Using the RICE acronym is not just a field treatment, but can also be continued once you return from climbing. The information below includes two ways of continuing the "I" portion of the RICE regimen to help lessen inflammation and swelling. Remember, you should limit icing to about 20 minutes or until the site is numb.

ICE CUPS

Ice massages help fight inflammation and swelling, and are easy to make. Purchase foam or paper cups and fill them with water. Place in the freezer. To use, merely tear away the foam or paper, apply the ice to the injury and gently rub the area.

REUSABLE ICE PACKS

Building reusable and malleable ice packs is cost effective and simple to create.
Items needed:

1 container of rubbing alcohol (ideally 80-90%)
Tap water
2 quart or gallon sized Ziploc bags

Instructions: Mix two parts water with one part alcohol. Pour into Ziploc bag, remove as much air as possible, and seal. Place the filled bag inside a second, remove as much air as possible, and place in the freezer.

---

healing. Thereafter, once pain-free range of motion is obtained at the elbow, strengthening and a gradual return to activity may be entertained. In conjunction with a structured rehabilitation program, most climbers are able to recover without further intervention. Occasionally, persistent pain or the development of ossification may lead to surgical intervention.

EVACUATE

Urgent evacuation is not needed. The prognosis of this injury is fairly good with a brief period of RICE and NSAID therapy in association with rehabilitation as described above.

Medial Epicondylitis or Golfer's Elbow (Chronic)

While not as common as climber's elbow, pain involving the wrist flexors and pronators is frequently seen in rock and ice climbers. Of the two epicondylar tendinopathies, lateral epicondylitis is much more common (80%) than medial (almost 20%) in the general population (Shiri 2006). That said, medial epicondylitis does effect a large number of climbers, specifically ice climbers where there is an increased incidence of these symptoms for those using "leashless" tools, and rock climbers utilizing a pronated, locked-off positioning of the wrist/elbow (as seen in a horizontal cross-body traverse) or in the side-pull maneuvers of crack climbing. In all of these scenarios, there is increased pull of the flexor carpi ulnaris (the primary wrist flexor) from its common flexor origin at the medial epicondyle, while the wrist is both flexed and pronated (Figure 4-8). To date, there have been no known randomized or large number observational studies to confirm this mechanism in climbing; however, it matches the pathophysiological pattern observed in the golfing community.

IDENTIFY

Pain will be present at the medial epicondyle. Pronation and wrist flexion maneuvers, especially against resistance, will elicit increased pain. Ulnar nerve function should be examined to rule out alternative diagnosis (Figure 4-6).

TREAT

As with lateral epicondylitis, symptoms can be persistent and slow to resolve with continued climbing.

EVACUATE

Urgent evacuation is not needed. Prevention, counterforce bracing, and therapy are mainstays of treatment. Surgery is rarely pursued but may be helpful in persistent symptoms.

Ulnar Collateral Ligament Stress

Other causes of medial elbow discomfort may be seen as chronic or progressively worsening symptoms of pain due to stressing of the ulnar collateral ligament (UCL) during climbing maneuvers (Figure 4-8).

IDENTIFY

Cross-body adduction of the arm often seen with bouldering or traverses across a route can lead to stressing of the UCL. This stress, over time, can lead to increased ligamentous laxity or tearing that contributes to elbow joint instability and potentially painful conditions. The ulnar nerve traverses superficially along the medial aspect of the elbow and is susceptible to injury from *valgus* stressors (stressors pushing the joint outward). Ulnar neuritis and radiation of pain distally may be present along with weakness and clumsiness in the hand. These findings will be best appreciated in the ulnar nerve distribution (Figure 4-6). Other conditions at this location include cubital tunnel syndrome (entrapment of the ulnar nerve) and "snapping elbow syndrome" (subluxation of the ulnar nerve from its normal location in the cubital tunnel), both seen in the climber population.

TREAT

Modification of climbing technique (reduction of valgus stressing) can be made to facilitate reduction in symptoms; however, temporary cessation of climbing is often required for relief of symptoms. A "heel-bow" type sleeve providing padding to the posterior and medial aspect of the elbow can provide daytime relief. Rotation of this sleeve into a backwards position (padding in anterior position) may be helpful for reduction of nocturnal symptoms of pain or numbness associated with prolonged elbow flexion while sleeping.

EVACUATE

Urgent evacuation is not needed. Further orthopedic and neurologic consultation is warranted when conservative measures fail, and may include additional studies such as electromyogram (EMG) and nerve conduction velocity (NCV) assessment. Chronic instability, severe cubital tunnel syndrome, or persistent snapping may require surgical reconstruction of the UCL or release of the cubital tunnel.

Wrist and Hand

Motion of the wrist and hand is one of the most intricate processes in the human body. More than thirty muscles contribute to the ability of the hand to accomplish the necessary movement of daily life and a climber's ability to grip rock, rope, and ice tools.

Distal Radius/Ulna Fracture (Acute)

Not every venture into the mountains entails going upward and, in fact, many injuries occur during the approach or departure from the vertical portion of a climbing trip. As such, considering a fall on the outstretched extremity, the distal radius has been reported as the most common site of upper extremity injuries, accounting for 17% of upper extremity fractures. For those familiar with distal radial fracture types, Colles' fracture patterns predominate in the general population, characterized by dorsal angulation and displacement. But within the climbing community, this fracture pattern is likely no more common than the other variants of distal radius fractures, including Barton's and Smith's fracture patterns.

IDENTIFY

Understanding how a fall occurred will help identify possible injuries. A typical scenario would be a fall onto an outstretched extremity. Volar angulation and displacement results from the force mechanism pushing the fracture segment from the back of the hand toward the palm side, causing dorsal angulation and displacement. A thorough examination of the neurovascular status must be done. Median nerve injury (Figure 4-6) and compartment syndrome (1% simultaneous occurrence) should be considered.

TREAT

Splint distal radius/ulna fractures in a position of comfort with the arm secured to the torso, and with the elbow and wrist included in the splint. Acetaminophen can be used for pain and is preferred over NSAIDs due to the likelihood of impending surgical intervention and the inherent inhibition of platelet function associated with NSAIDs. Fabrication of a splint can be improvised by multiple components including rigid (but padded) tent poles, webbing, and clothing. Commercially available

FIGURE 4-9. IMPROVISED ELBOW SPLINT

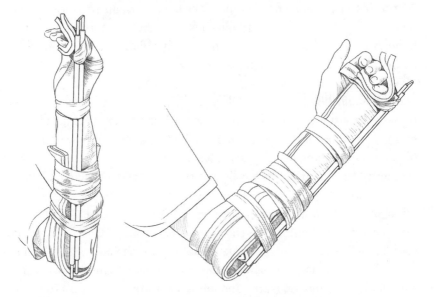

products such as padded aluminum splints (e.g., SAM splint device) are helpful. Securing the injured extremity to the patient's torso will help minimize pain or propensity for entanglement. This can be accomplished by a safety pin attachment or securing with miscellaneous clothing articles such as T-shirts or jackets (Figures 4-1 and 4-2). See Figures 4-3, 4-7, 4-9, 4-10, and 4-11 for examples of fixation and splinting stabilization. Careful attention to the distal circulation, sensation, and motor function should be made with repeated exams throughout care.

EVACUATE

Fractures of the upper extremity, particularly at the wrist, will eliminate use of the affected side for climbing or rope management. With the exception of the most simple Colles' fractures, prompt and definitive management of these injuries by an orthopedic surgeon is required. This may be accomplished by closed reduction and casting under fluoroscopy, but often requires open reduction and internal fixation with plate/screw hardware. Alternatively, external fixation devices may be applied percutaneously. Despite the best care, long-term outcomes often include complications from these fractures. This may include nonunion or malunion at the fracture site, post-traumatic arthritis at the distal radioul-

FIGURE 4-10. SUGAR TONG SPLINT

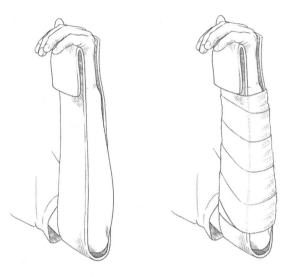

nar joint (DRUJ), or rupture of the extensor pollicis longus tendon. With these factors in mind, prompt delivery of the injured patient to definitive care is indicated.

Other Wrist Fractures (Acute)

Unfortunately, the *distal* (further away from the torso on an extremity) radius and ulna are not the only ways for a climber to suffer a wrist injury. With eight carpal bones present in the wrist, it would be a difficult undertaking to address each of the many types of fractures that may occur in climbers. There are also a host of possible ligamentous disruptions. The carpal bones are configured in two rows of four (Figure 4-12). Viewed from thumb to small finger, the proximal row includes the scaphoid, lunate, triquetrum, and pisiform; the distal row includes the trapezium, trapezoid, capitate, and hamate.

Scaphoid Fracture (Acute)

IDENTIFY

The most frequently fractured carpal bone is the scaphoid (Figure 4-12). Typically, the mechanism of injury involves a fall to the outstretched extremity, such as a glissading accident. This mechanism is similar to the cause of a distal radius fracture, but typically involves a more

FIGURE 4-11. ULNAR/SPICA SPLINT

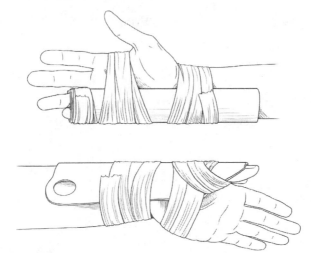

FIGURE 4-12. CARPAL BONES

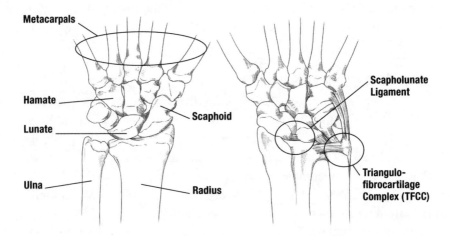

extreme angle of wrist extension. With its multiple ligamentous attachments and integral position extending from the proximal row to the distal row of the carpal bones, the scaphoid serves as a "connecting strut" for the wrist, allowing for complex and multidirectional articulations. Patients often have persistent pain, crepitus, and mild swelling. Side-to-side motion of the wrist causes pain on the thumb side of the wrist. Occasionally, however, symptoms can be quite mild and may represent only a mild ache or tenderness in the two regions of palpation—the dorsally located anatomical snuff box or the palmar located, proximal portion of the scaphoid tubercle (Figure 4-12).

TREAT

Field management includes splinting as previously described in the management of distal radius fractures (see above), but with a specific additional isolation of the thumb along with the wrist splint. Such an apparatus is called a thumb spica splint (Figure 4-11). Acetaminophen can be used for pain.

EVACUATE

Evacuation is necessary due to functional impairment, but need not be urgent. Unfortunately, due to the way the blood flows to the bone, frequent *avascular necrosis* (dead bone) of the proximal section occurs if scrupulous attention is not given to anatomical reduction. For this reason, surgery is indicated for more than 1 mm of fracture displacement. Both surgical and nonsurgical recovery from this fracture often requires prolonged immobilization for adequate fracture healing (six to twelve weeks). A nearly equal amount of time should be allowed for rehabilitation efforts of strength and mobility. X-rays may be inconclusive, requiring further diagnostic imagery such as computed tomography (CT). Continued pursuit of climbing without proper evaluation can have deleterious effects to the long-term prognosis of not only the scaphoid, but also the remaining wrist structures. Suspicion of ligamentous injury should also be considered with referral to a hand specialist for assessment of the scapholunate ligament. Injuries at this location, even in the absence of fractures, can lead to advanced arthritis of the carpal structures years following the injury.

Lunate Fracture (Acute)

Though it is less commonly injured than the scaphoid, the high energy encountered during falls (e.g., ski mountaineering or bouldering falls to the ground) will still occasionally fracture the lunate (Figure 4-12).

IDENTIFY

In such an injury, the lunate may be dislocated, with either palmar or dorsal misalignment. Signs and symptoms associated with this type of injury vary broadly due to the multidirectional aspects of displacement, but will often include swelling and deformity in the central aspect of the wrist on either the palmar or dorsal sides. Pressure of the lunate dislocation may affect the median nerve on the palmar aspect of the wrist, resulting in numbness and tingling in median nerve distribution, as shown in Figure 4-6. Pain with movement at the wrist and reduced grip strength may also be present. An injury to the lunate is a prime example in which careful evaluation is warranted, as delayed onset or persistent pain may indicate avascular necrosis of the lunate or advancement of arthritic conditions due to ligamentous injury.

TREAT

The injury should be splinted in a position of comfort; the splint should include the wrist, forearm, and metacarpals. Figures 4-3 (a gutter splint), 4-7 (an improvised gutter splint), and 4-10 (a sugar tong splint) demonstrate wrist splinting that may be applied to distal radius fractures, wrist sprains, and suspected injuries at the lunate or scapholunate ligament. The arm should be secured to the torso, and the splint configured to immobilize the joint above and below the point of bony injury. Acetaminophen can be used for pain.

EVACUATE

As the climber suffering this type of injury will likely have difficulty in carrying on to belay, climb, or grip ice tools, evacuation is needed, but need not be urgent.

Hamate Fracture (Acute)

The hamate is often the last bone injured in the injury pathway after the energy of the trauma has traveled through the scaphoid and lunate bones (Figure 4-12). Additionally, the hamate can suffer a specific injury along its palmar surface with a direct blow during climbing, as pointed out in *Rock and Ice* (Saunders 2015). At this location, the bony structure of the hamate forms a hook (known as the "hook of the hamate"), which covers the most distal aspect of the ulnar nerve. Traditionally, injuries at this location have been characterized to occur in golfers. The gripping position of a golf club exposes this bony prominence to injury when the golf swing misses the ball and hits a divot at the ground surface. Similarly, other athletes like ice climbers using hammers and hand tools may

+SPLINTING THE WRIST (AND OTHER EXTREMITIES)+

Wrist splints vary in their indication and purpose. A good splint should reduce pain, prevent further movement of a fracture, and prevent further damage to muscles, nerves, and blood vessels. Placement in the field dictates that the affected limb cannot be effectively used to climb, belay, or rappel. While it may seem that "any old splint will do" in the context of a local crag where definitive care at the local emergency department is just a short car ride away, care should be made to place purpose-driven splints. Because of the nature of related swelling in acute injuries, providers must ensure that a well-supporting splint (of any type) does not later become an effective tourniquet and limit the vascular supply to the tissue past the splint. This can be ascertained in the field by checking CSM of the digits or the portion of the extremity just past the splint. In such a case, reapplication of the splint to accommodate swelling must be promptly made. Excessive immobilization from continuous use of a cast or splint can lead to chronic pain, joint stiffness, muscle atrophy, or more severe complications. Other potential complications include ischemia, heat or cold injury, pressure sores, skin breakdown, infection, neurologic injury, and compartment syndrome.

The techniques of application and formation of splints from improvised materials is as much an art as the proper placement of rock/ice protection. Learning and practicing techniques during a wilderness medicine class is helpful to gain the necessary knowledge. General principles of splint placement include addressing the joint or bone above and below the site of injury. For example:

1. If the suspected site of injury is the wrist, the splint would in most cases extend from the forearm to the end of the metacarpals but not completely into the fingers (e.g., joint injury—splint bone above and bone below).
2. If the suspected injury was thought to involve a bone, a well-applied splint would immobilize the joints above and below the site of injury (e.g., forearm fracture [bone injury] would immobilize elbow and wrist—splint joint above and below).

encounter such an injury. The authors have specific experience where such an injury was the result of an inadvertent ice tool striking rock instead of ice.

IDENTIFY

Symptoms include dull pain on the palmar surface and ulnar side of the wrist. Pain may be exacerbated with further gripping and associated compression of the fracture fragment upon the ulnar nerve. This may produce numbness and tingling in the ring and small fingers. Delayed rupture of finger and wrist flexor tendons can occur.

TREAT

Field management includes splinting and cessation of climbing. Splinting should follow principles described above for other carpal bones, but in particular should include the wrist, ring, and small fingers with the fingers in a slightly relaxed posture (Figure 4-11). Continued CSM reassessment is necessary due to potential swelling. Acetaminophen can be used for pain.

EVACUATE

Evacuation will be necessary due to functional impairment, but does not need to be urgent. Follow-up care often requires six weeks of splinting, followed by extended physical therapy. Displaced fractures often require surgical intervention. Advanced diagnostic imaging including a CT scan or X-ray of the wrist may be required to identify the fracture site.

Metacarpal and Phalangeal (Finger) Fractures (Acute)

There are five metacarpal bones in each hand. They are the bony extensions that separate the wrist carpals and finger phalanges. Each of the metacarpals is surrounded and held in configuration by the tendinous attachments of two large muscle groups (extrinsic and intrinsic muscles), which affects fracture injury patterns. Fractures of the metacarpals and the phalanges result from various types of trauma and account for 10% of all types of fractures, with 50% of these fractures being work-related. The border digits and metacarpals (thumb, index, small fingers) appear to have a higher propensity for injury.

IDENTIFY

Mechanisms of injury include crushing, avulsing, shearing, splitting, and torque/rotational/angular forces. Torqued, rotational, and angular forces are often present in a dynamic (dyno) move, or from a foot slip with resultant force landing upon the affected digit. A finger lodged in a crack/pocket, entrapped by belay device, or even crushed by a rock can produce these same mechanisms. Other sources include animal bites and mechanical injuries from cutting instruments like a crampon, for which wound contamination becomes a factor. Open fractures, fractures above or near a joint, hand fractures with distal neurovascular compromise, or hand/finger fractures with obvious deformity (displacement or angulation) should be considered unstable in a wilderness context.

TREAT

A trained climbing partner may facilitate reduction of a displaced finger fracture or a finger dislocation by providing axial (in-line) traction, but care should be taken to not compromise a digit that has intact neuromuscular status. Stable fractures of the digits may be adequately managed in the field with buddy taping, using climbing tape. Continued climbing may not be possible until more definitive evaluation and X-rays can be made. With regard to fractures of the metacarpals, the intrinsic and extrinsic forces applied to fracture fragments may contribute to further displacement, rotational, and angular deformity. This deformity can not only affect activities of daily living but also impact future climbing ability, as the subsequent misalignment may make various grip positions more challenging or impossible. Maintain good splinting principles as discussed earlier and incorporate the digits past the metacarpal fracture to leverage any malrotation. See Figure 4-11 for multiple examples of improvised splinting to the hand and wrist. In the case of avulsed (missing) tissue or finger amputation, hemorrhage control is a priority, using direct pressure directly over or just proximal to the wound. Once bleeding is controlled, the amputated tissue should be gently rinsed with clean water and transported in a sealed bag wrapped in damp gauze or cloth. The amputated portion may survive if reattached within four to six hours; the addition of cooling via ice (over the bag, not directly to the tissue) can extend this time to nearly 18 hours (Krzyzaniak 2017). An open fracture or amputation represents an increased risk for infection and debridement. Irrigation and antibiotic prophylaxis may be needed.

EVACUATE

Evacuation will be needed due to functional impairment, and should be urgent if there is a chance the digit can be reattached given the parameters discussed above.

Tendon and Pulley Ruptures (Acute)

Prior to the introduction of sport climbing to the United States in the early 1980s, traditional climbers saw injury patterns predominantly to the lower body from injuries due to a fall on rock or rockfall. A different distribution of injury is seen in the modern climber population, where injury to the hand is the most common (Pegoli 2015). While relatively rare in the general population, soft tissue injuries of the hand are commonly identi-

FIGURE 4-13. PULLEYS & FINGER TENDONS

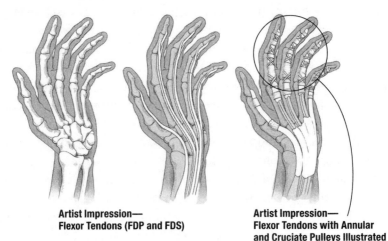

Artist Impression—
Flexor Tendons (FDP and FDS)

Artist Impression—
Flexor Tendons with Annular
and Cruciate Pulleys Illustrated

fied in sport climbers and primarily occur along the pathway and insertions of the flexor tendons (Crowley 2012). In addition to bony trauma, the dynamic forces placed upon the upper extremity during climbing exposes the climber to multiple types of soft tissue disruption. As the muscles travel from their origins at the elbow to their insertion points in the digits, they transition to tendons. On the palmar side, these nine flexor tendons are housed within a circumferential synovial sheath, which traverses through the carpal tunnel and then inserts onto the finger digits. Looking at two tendons specifically, each flexor digitorum superficialis tendon inserts on the middle phalanx of the digits, while the flexor digitorum profundus travels farther and terminates in the distal phalanx (Figure 4-13).

The tendinous sheath has multiple attachment points (fibrous pulleys) along its course in the fingers. These attachment pulleys help facilitate the unique functions of the hand. In climbing, the biomechanics and grip techniques, coupled with frequent dynamic loading of the fingers, places a burden of force upon the tendons and tendon pulleys, often resulting in injury. The extensor tendons have a similar course on the dorsum of the hand. While some of the digits have individual extensors, these digits often extend in conjunction with each other though their shared attachment points—the juncturae tendinum. While extensor tendon (more superficial and exposed) injuries are significantly more common in the general population, this section will attempt to bring additional focus to the palmar side of the hand (Figure 4-13), where climber-specific injuries are known to occur more commonly (Simon 2001).

Flexor tendon injuries in the general population are common, and the result of occupational trauma such as open lacerations. In the climbing community, there is a 20–40% prevalence of flexor tendon pulley injuries. Additional injuries include flexor tendon injuries, joint capsule injuries, tenovaginitis, and tenosynovitis (Hochholzer 2006). As the flexor unit is composed of many units working in synchrony, multiple injuries may exist simultaneously.

Isolated Flexor Tendon Injuries (Acute)

Flexor tendon injuries are often the result of laceration, as it would otherwise require a substantial force to rupture the tendon alone and, typically, this force is strong enough to cause additional injury in the form of pulley disruption or fracture of a phalangeal bone.

IDENTIFY

These types of lacerations take place on the palm or the flexor side of the digits and could conceivably occur in an alpine environment, where crampons, ice tools, knives, or other instruments may lacerate the flexor tendons. Rock climbers expose their hands to cracks and finger pockets, which under significant dynamic loading such as a slipped foot may cause an injury to the digit. In the case of a *degloving* (total skin loss) injury, further trauma to the neurovascular bundle may occur. Inspection of the isolated laceration wound is often not helpful to identify the extent of an injury. Examination of the hand function by a trained medical provider may be required to identify the culprit lesion within the laceration.

TREAT

Field treatment includes: 1) control of bleeding, 2) examination of the finger function, 3) inspection of the wound for debris, 4) careful irrigation of the wound with clean water, and 5) bandaging.

EVACUATE

Self-evacuation from the climbing area to definite care for a thorough exam, cleaning, and a full injury assessment is needed. On the flexor side of the hand, significant retraction of the lacerated tendons into the

FIGURE 4-14. CRIMPING TEAR

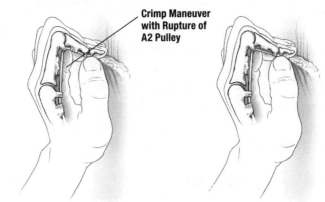

Crimp Maneuver
with Rupture of
A2 Pulley

palm can make repair challenging. The regions of injury on the palmar surface of the hand are divided into different zones with surgical and rehabilitation protocols established to identify the feasibility of repair. Recovery time can extend beyond weeks to months.

Flexor Pulley Injuries (Acute)

Pulley injury (Figure 4-14) is one of the most common ailments for climbers today and queries regarding injured fingers fill page after page of the various rock climbing forums online. Within the hand, each finger is comprised of three phalangeal bones (proximal, middle, and distal) under which the flexor tendons are positioned. The two previously mentioned, flexor digitorum superficialis and flexor digitorum profundus, travel from their origin near the elbow to insert on the middle phalanx (in the case of flexor digitorum superficialis) and distal phalanx (flexor digitorum profundus) (Figure 4-13).

IDENTIFY

The flexor tendons are held close to the fingers on the underside (palmar) surface of the hand through a series of fibrosseus bands. In this group are five annular bands referred to as the flexor tendon pulleys. Along with the four smaller cruciform pulleys, these bands of tissue facilitate the intricate process of finger flexion. For climbers, the two pulleys of primary concern are the A2 and A4 pulleys, which have been found to rupture with increasing frequency in the climber population with an incidence between 19 and 26% in four focused studies (Klauser 2002,

Schöffl 2003, Schöffl 2006a, Schöffl 2006b). Rather than having soft tissue insertion, these two pulleys have a bony insertion at the proximal and middle phalanx respectively. Pulley disruptions for climbers occur more often in the ring and middle fingers, due to the positioning and use of those digits during climbing.

Common climbing grip positions of the hand cause increased strain at the pulley sites. Primarily, the dynamic addition of the climber's weight upon the digits when in the crimp position (Figure 4-14) is believed to be the primary culprit that exposes the excessive loading and subsequent flexor tendon pulley tear (Crowley 2012). Without pulley integrity, the flexor tendons lack in grip strength and function with a resultant bowstringing between their origin and tether to the phalangeal insertions. Trauma-related bowstringing is less commonly noted than originally postulated, and it has been described that multiple (more than two in the same finger) pulley ruptures would need to be present for bowstringing to be visualized. Symptoms of pulley disruption are more likely associated with a "popping sensation or sound," swelling, pain, bruising, and weakness of finger flexion in the affected finger. The severity and type of disruption (partial versus full thickness or A2, A4 versus both) also affects the presenting clinical symptoms. Injuries to the cruciate pulleys have not been observed with great prevalence (Schöffl 2010). While often a safe belay can be maintained with the unaffected fingers after a pulley injury, climbing on the digits injured by pulley disruption will not only be uncomfortable, but an obvious loss of functional hand strength may be apparent. With the previously cited bowstringing being less common than originally thought, a more thorough evaluation tool such as a dynamic ultrasound or MRI is indicated to confirm the diagnosis (El-Sheikh 2006). The measurement of separation (>2 mm) between bone and tendon, as determined by ultrasound or MRI, identifies the possibility of a pulley rupture. Establishing the number of pulleys involved has become the model for assigning a treatment algorithm (Schöffl 2006b). Finally, juvenile climbers may exhibit similar symptoms of a flexor tendon pulley injury when in fact they have an *epiphyseal* (growth plate) fracture just distal to the A2 pulley, near the base of the middle phalanx.

TREAT

Within the medical literature there has been a diversity of opinion regarding the management and rehabilitation of pulley injuries with new recommendations showing great promise in the functional outcome for injured climbers. While traditionally repaired with surgery where 80% of climbers return to a functional capacity equal or greater than their baseline, there is growing consensus that many singular A2, A3, or A4 pulley injuries can be managed non-operatively, with taping, ring splints, hand therapy, and a six- to eight-week climbing cessation (Gnecchi 2015). While risks and complications must be considered, in the situation where complete or partial rupture of multiple pulleys are involved, surgery remains an option. This has been described by multiple methods and techniques involving the use grafting material (flexor retinaculum or palmaris longus—if available). Following this, a short period of splinting followed by early mobility, and protective taping is often employed for an additional three months during a gradual return to climbing. Recovery and return to function may require several months. Finally, the chronicity and location of the injury, goals of the climber, current functional state, and previous management strategies must all be considered as the climber works in partnership with their healthcare provider to achieve the best outcomes.

For uninjured climbers at the gym or crag, taping of the proximal or middle phalanx has not been shown to reduce rupture occurrence and may actually reduce the strength of the pulleys by hindering the natural physiologic conditioning that occurs during climbing (Warme 2000, Schöffl 2007). Taping to protect the injured finger can be useful to prevent unintended re-injury. Surgery should be considered if return of function and strength does not occur.

EVACUATE

Evacuation is not needed, but climbing may be impaired, and follow-up attention is needed after climbing.

Trigger Finger or Flexor Tenosynovitis (Acute or Chronic)

IDENTIFY

Trigger finger may occur abruptly or gradually. It is frequently observed following an extended climbing session or in conjunction with a rapid increase in climbing frequency or intensity. Symptoms include pain at the palmar surface of the hand just proximal to the junction of the palm of the affected finger. In addition to tenderness at the affected area, a palpable lump may be identified. With active flexion/extension of the affected finger, increased pain and "popping" is felt as the trigger finger goes through its range of motion. While this does not involve disruption of a finger pulley, the described symptoms are related to a swelling of the flexor tendon sheath and difficulty for it to slide through the A1 finger pulley near the base of the finger. As swelling increases, symptoms increase to the point of the finger "catching" or "triggering" during flexion and extension maneuvers. Predominantly, trigger finger is an activity-associated diagnosis (e.g., increased climbing) but occasionally, these symptoms are due to an underlying flexor tendon infection that has developed an abscess traveling within the flexor tendon sheath.

TREAT
Symptom relief can often be achieved with decreased climbing intensity or frequency to allow for recovery from inflammation. This approach, however, may not resolve the condition. An ice bath to the hand during the acute phase of symptoms can be helpful, as may moist heat or paraffin wax therapy during continued recovery. Topical or systemic use of NSAID medications assist recovery.

EVACUATE
While climbing may be impaired, evacuation is not necessary. After climbing, an orthopedic or hand specialist may be needed for possible steroid injection to the flexor tendon sheath or surgical release of the A1 pulley. Formal hand therapy exercises may be prescribed.

Dupuytren's Contracture (Chronic)
Originally described by the French military surgeon Baron Guillaume Dupuytren, this condition is a progressive flexion contracture of the fingers with a thickening of the palmar fascia. Bouldering, sport, and traditional climbing rely more heavily on upper extremity usage, and prevalence in this subset of climbers is more evident (Logan 2005).

IDENTIFY
Initially, the presence of occasionally tender nodules or thickening of fascia can be felt along the palmar surface of the hand (O'Donovan 2010). These are often described as "cords" which with continued time result in a tethering of the fingers to the point where they can be no longer fully extended and a flexion contracture is present. A survey of British climb-

ers in 2005 identified a prevalence in the climbing community that was linked to earlier onset than seen in the general population (Logan 2005). Additionally, experience level and technical climbing ability seemed linked to onset and severity of disease.

TREAT
Field treatment would include pain control and reduction in use as much as possible. The surgical cure for this ailment involves Z-plasty incisions (jagged lines) over the Dupuytren's cords with careful dissection of the fibrous tissue away from the tendon sheath and digital neurovascular bundles. Recurrence of the disease is possible and the potential of scar formation mimicking the disease make this a moderately successful solution. Until recently, once the onset of Dupuytren's contracture began, there were very few treatment options available outside of surgery for effective improvement or limitation of progression.

Recently, new pharmaceutical developments have made available an injection series of collagenase clostridium histolyticum (Xiaflex®), which, after repeated treatment, has shown great promise and potential surgical avoidance (Gilpin 2010).

EVACUATE
While climbing may be impaired, evacuation is not needed. Routine follow-up may be necessary after climbing.

Carpal Tunnel Syndrome (Chronic)
Carpal tunnel syndrome is the most common nerve compression syndrome. It occurs in roughly 50 people per 1,000 patients in the general population and is more common in certain subpopulations. In addition to being more common with some medical diagnoses, it is also more prevalent in the female population and with certain occupational and recreational activities. Rock climbers, ice climbers, and alpinists often find themselves performing heavy gripping maneuvers that may predispose them to develop this syndrome.

IDENTIFY
Typical symptoms are night pain and numbness and tingling in the digits innervated by the median nerve (Figure 4-6). Due to repetitive injury and localized strain or exertion, the subsynovial tissues at the palmar

side of the wrist and flexor tendons proliferate over time and become thickened. Increased compressive pressure is exerted upon the median nerve. Physical examination by a trained hand specialist can establish the diagnosis with additional EMG and nerve conduction studies being used for confirmation. In addition to the above-mentioned symptoms, climbers may have difficulty with fine motor function in the affected hand, such as clumsiness in dropping cams or weakness in pinching their rope.

TREAT
Treatment includes rest, splinting, and, if available, steroid injections to the carpal tunnel.

EVACUATE
While climbing may be impaired, evacuation is not necessary. Follow-up medical attention should be obtained. Although injections add a diagnostic value in confirming the diagnosis, definitive relief is seen in surgical carpal tunnel release. Following surgery and in conjunction with physical therapy, normal return to activity usually occurs within four to six weeks and a return to climbing at eight to twelve weeks.

Ganglion Cyst (Chronic)
IDENTIFY
Often the result of a "forgotten blow," these soft tissue benign tumors are commonly seen on the palmar or dorsal sides of the wrist and are occasionally mildly tender to touch. Pain and tenderness can worsen with additional activity. The size of the ganglion may fluctuate (2–5 cm at wrist). The most common hypothesis to their formation includes a weakening of the wrist joint connective tissue synovium, leading to an outpouching into a fluid-filled sac.

TREAT
No field treatment is needed.

EVACUATE
No evacuation is needed. Historically, the most effective non-wilderness treatments included two options: aspiration or removal. Needle aspiration (with or without steroid injection) has been shown to be temporarily

effective, but there is a higher incidence of recurrence when compared with surgical excision. Removal is not necessary unless the ganglion is painful or contributing to weakness of the hand.

DeQuervain's Tenosynovitis (Chronic)

DeQuervain's tenosynovitis is an interesting phenomenon of increased friction involving the tendons at the back of the thumb.

IDENTIFY

The two tendons involved are the extensor pollicis brevis (EPB) and abductor pollicis longus (APL), which both lie in the first dorsal compartment along the back of the wrist. While there are six compartments which host the wrist and finger extensors, this particular compartment becomes aggravated with the use of gaming consoles and texting on smartphones, with an increase seen in this condition corresponding with the increase in those activities in our society (Ali 2014). Additionally, climbers have been known to irritate these two tendons with increased exertion on routes comprised pinches and sloper hand holds. Alpinists or ice climbers may feel discomfort in this region due to gripping ice tools for long periods. The process of hammering mimics one of the more well-known tests for this diagnosis, called the Finkelstein test. Along with the above-mentioned pain, which is localized to the base of the thumb and thumb side of the wrist, climbers will often describe a gritty or "creaking" sensation with movement of the thumb or as the wrist deviates side-to-side.

TREAT

Multiple treatment options are available, with varying levels of efficacy. Avoidance of pain-causing maneuvers and varying climbing style and technique are helpful for resolution. RICE therapy (see "RICE" sidebar on page 76) is helpful for mild cases with limited effectiveness of steroid creams, ultrasound therapy, and splints.

EVACUATE

No evacuation is needed. During follow-up care, injections of a long-acting steroid to the first dorsal compartment have been found to provide permanent relief to 50% of individuals with the first attempt of injection. An additional injection in those patients with persistent or recurring pain provided permanent relief in 45% of patients. For those with recurrence or resistance to injection therapy, surgical release of the first dorsal compartment is an option, which may provide a relatively quick return to climbing.

LOWER BODY ORTHOPEDIC INJURIES

As noted in the upper body portion of this chapter, some early research reported higher incidence of lower body injuries for climbers and mountaineers in general, but more recent studies have shown that this is not the case for traditional climbers, sport climbers, or boulderers. Within these climbing disciplines, chronic overuse injuries of the upper body far exceed that of the lower extremities. Lower extremity injuries, usually due to a fall, tend to be more severe, result in visits to hospitals and medical centers, and are one of the leading causes for evacuation from the backcountry for non-mountaineers. For mountaineers, studies suggest that lower body injuries continue to be among the most common areas of any type of injury.

Indoor climbers are also susceptible to lower body injury, even in the highly controlled and safety-conscious setting of a climbing gym. Schöffl et al., in their detailed study "Acute Injury Risk and Severity in Indoor Climbing—A Prospective Analysis of 515,337 Indoor Climbing Wall Visits in 5 Years," found that, while acute injuries are rare (only 32 in those five years), a full 50% involved the lower body, with 40% being injuries to the ankle or foot (Schöffl 2011).

Most reported chronic rock climbing injuries affect the upper extremities, while most traumatic injuries occur in the lower extremities. One interesting study, conducted by Nelson and McKenzie, focused on 17 years of emergency department data within the United States and noted that 46.3% of all visits by climbers and mountaineers resulted from injuries to the lower extremities (Nelson 2009). This study found much smaller percentages of serious injuries in other areas of the body (upper extremity: 29.2%, head: 12.2%, and torso: 10.5%). This and other studies indicate that the most common lower body injuries are those of the ankle and foot, with percentages ranging between 12.6% and 29.5%.

This section will discuss both chronic and acute injuries of the lower extremities.

Pelvis/Hip

Hip Dislocation (Acute)

Hip dislocations most often affect the posterior (back) of the hip and can be caused by a fall. A fall severe enough to cause this type of dislocation is usually associated with multiple instances of trauma and a full assessment should be conducted.

IDENTIFY

The chief signs and symptoms will be intense pain and an obvious deformity since the affected leg will be shorter, flexed, internally rotated, and adducted (leg/foot turned inward).

TREAT

A climber suffering a fall significant enough to cause a hip dislocation often has other life-threatening injuries. Complete a thorough assessment and address any of these injuries. Check the patient for circulation, sensation, and movement distal to the dislocation (somewhere along the leg). The definitive treatment for a hip dislocation is relocation, but this is not possible in the backcountry without training. Femoral neck fractures are a real possibility with hip dislocations and attempts to reduce the dislocation in the field risk additional damage to the hip and underlying structures.

EVACUATE

Evacuation should be immediate, as hip dislocation is an orthopedic emergency and delay can lead to neurovascular compromise, particularly of the peroneal branch of the sciatic nerve, which supplies movement and sensation to the lower leg, foot, and toes.

Pelvis Fracture (Acute)

One of the most potentially deadly injuries of the lower body is a fracture of the pelvis. Significant falls ending in seated impact or long cartwheeling falls often result in a pelvic fracture along with other serious injuries to other parts of the body. Significant hemorrhage within the pelvis from veins in the posterior pelvis and the internal iliac arteries is of the utmost concern.

IDENTIFY

A thorough assessment should be completed for any climber who sustains a serious fall, and all life-threatening issues should be addressed. A fractured posterior pelvic ring fits within this category because of the significant blood loss that can accompany such a fracture. Low blood pressure (hypotension) with a weak pulse is indicative of blood loss. It is difficult to ascertain blood loss in the pelvis due to its internal nature, but the flank, scrotum, and urethral meatus (opening of the penis) should be examined for blood. Lacerations of the buttocks, vagina, or rectum are signs of a fracture. Rescuers should look for a difference in leg length or for a rotational deformity of the leg without obvious signs of a fracture, since these may be signs of a possible pelvic fracture. Light downward pressure on a supine patient should be exerted on the iliac crests (bony portions of hip at the front of the body) to test pelvic stability. If there is any "give," a pelvic fracture should be assumed and evacuation should be initiated immediately. Other signs that indicate a fracture include bruising (ecchymosis), swelling, and pain in the *sacrum* (a large triangular bone that intersects with the hip bones to form the pelvis) and/or the buttocks region.

TREAT

Efforts to resuscitate a climber with life-threatening injuries should begin immediately. Specific treatment for a pelvic fracture is the placement of a field-expedient pelvic binder. This will stabilize the fracture, slow bleeding, and assist in clot formation, allowing time for evacuation to a medical center and surgery.

A pelvic binder can be made of any item that can be placed around the pelvis. Other than boulderers, all climbers will be wearing the best expedient binder available—their climbing harness. Simply loosen and shift the harness waist loop down from the waist to the greater trochanter of the femur and tighten to stabilize it.

If a harness is not available, a tent fly, long articles of clothing, or even an inflatable sleeping mat can be used. To create a binder, carefully slip the fly or clothing below the patient's pelvis and wrap remaining material to the front. Remove anything in the patient's pant pockets. Tie the material snugly to the pelvis with an overhand knot. Place a stick, tent stake, tent pole, or any similar item on this knot and tie another overhand knot on top. This item will act as a "windlass." Twist the improvised windlass to create a tight binding and secure it to the patient. Place padding between the patient's legs for stability and tie the upper and lower legs together to prevent additional movement. Place the patient on a litter or other evacuation device and begin evacuation. If using an inflatable sleeping mat, wrap the deflated mat and as tightly as possible around the pelvis and secure with large amounts of climbing tape. Inflate the mat to provide more padding and greater tension.

EVACUATE
Immediate evacuation limiting movement of the back, torso, and legs is needed to prevent death. This is a true emergency.

Thigh/Femur

Femur Fracture (Acute)
Another serious injury caused by significant falls is a femur fracture. Although fairly rare, these fractures are one of the more serious injuries to the lower body that a climber or mountaineer can sustain. The femur is the long bone that originates within the hip and extends to the knee, where it interacts with the patella (knee cap) and the bones of the lower leg (tibia and fibula).

IDENTIFY
A femur fracture usually occurs in one of three areas: the "neck" below the "head" at the top of the femur (commonly thought of as a hip fracture), mid-shaft, or just above the knee (commonly thought of as a knee fracture). Injured climbers will complain of significant pain in the thigh, and there will be swelling and leg deformity in the fracture area. This type of fracture can result in severe blood loss and impingement of nerves. Because the muscles of the leg are the largest and most powerful within the body, when a break in the femur occurs, the bones are often pulled by muscle spasms into and over each other, increasing the risk of impingement of nerves or laceration of blood vessels. A detailed check of CSM should be completed distal to the injury. This check should be repeated every 30 minutes during evacuation because compartment syndrome can develop after an injury of this type. See sidebar below for a detailed description of how to check for CSM.

Checking climbers for circulation, sensation, and movement (CSM) in an injured extremity is essential to identify injury and prevent long-term negative outcomes. It is most easily done at the foot because the arteries in the feet are the most superficial and easiest to palpate (feel). Are the pulses present? Pulses in the dorsalis pedis artery and the posterior tibial artery may be difficult to locate, especially with swelling. The dorsalis pedis artery is located on the top and outside of the most prominent ridge of the foot (tibial/inner side of the dorsum of the foot). The posterior tibial artery is located behind and below the bone that sticks out on the inside of the ankle (medial malleolus). A good technique for finding these pulses is to press hard into the skin along these areas and slowly release pressure. If neither of these pulses are palpable, pinch the patient's toe. This will remove blood from beneath the nail (making it white). If normal color returns with three seconds, this is indicative of normal blood flow. Next check for sensation. This is checked in two ways—dull and sharp. Using the pad of your thumb or finger is an easy way to check for dull touch, while the use of a pine needle or a sharp twig is adequate for sharp touch. Finally, ask the injured climber to wiggle the toes to check for the movement portion of CSM. If the patient fails any of these checks, the leg/ankle/foot injury is serious and they require evacuation.

TREAT

Stabilizing the femur to prevent additional movement is the best treatment for climbers with little or no medical experience. Multiple studies have found the incidence of femur fracture in climbers to be rare. One possible field treatment is the creation and application of a femoral traction splint, although among wilderness medicine authorities and even within the formal EMS community itself this tool is becoming more controversial (Bledsoe 2004, Johnson 2011, Gandy 2014). It is outside the scope of this text to teach climbers and mountaineers with limited resources and experience how to create such a device. If you have training and *know* that you can create a traction splint, this may be a useful treatment. Otherwise, stabilize and splint the injured leg and evacuate the injured climber as soon as possible. A fractured femur can produce compartment syndrome through swelling and blood loss in the closed portion of the femur. This is extremely painful and will result in loss of pulses distal to the injury.

EVACUATE

Climbers with a femur fracture should be evacuated as soon as possible. If present, compartment syndrome is a time-sensitive medical emergency.

Knee

Anterior Cruciate Ligament (ACL) and Medial Collateral Ligament (MCL) Sprains/Tears (Acute)

The anterior cruciate ligament is one of four main ligaments that connect the femur with the tibia (the others are the medial collateral, lateral collateral, and posterior cruciate ligaments). It is the most commonly injured ligament in the knee, and though usually associated with team sports, can occur with climbers. Drop knees, climbing in severe overhangs, or uneven falls onto bouldering pads can trigger an ACL sprain or tear. Many professional climbers and boulderers—including Chris Sharma, Alex Puccio, Steph Davis, and Jason Kehl—have suffered ACL tears during their climbing careers. While not as common as ACL tears, a tear of the medial collateral ligament is still a concern for climbers. Located on the inside of the knee, this ligament attaches the femur to the tibia and provides stability on the inside of the knee, preventing it from bending inward. The most common cause of an MCL injury for climbers is a poor landing that forces the knee inward or from the drop knee movement.

IDENTIFY

The first indication of an ACL or MCL tear is a pop or snap sound in the knee, which will immediately become unstable and begin to swell. A meniscal tear often also occurs with an ACL injury. An in-depth assessment should be conducted to ensure that the knee damage is ligamentous rather than a fracture. Sprains are not as destructive as full tears, but the extent of the damage is not as easy to assess in the field.

TREAT

The best treatment is prevention. Strong and balanced leg muscles are key, as is careful movement while climbing, and controlled, prepared falls. RICE (see "RICE" sidebar on page 76) is the best field treatment. Medical attention should be sought, and surgery is often the treatment of choice to repair ACL injuries, although it is less often necessary for MCL injuries.

EVACUATE

Injured climbers should be able to walk out with assistance.

Lateral Collateral Ligament (LCL) and Posterior Cruciate Ligament (PCL) Injuries (Acute)

For most athletes, including climbers, tears or sprains of the lateral collateral ligament (LCL) and the posterior cruciate ligament (PCL) are not as common as an ACL or MCL tear. The signs and symptoms of injury are similar to those described in the ACL and MCL, though pain is localized either to the outside of the knee (LCL) or the back of the knee (PCL).

Meniscal Tears (Acute)

The meniscus is a layer of cartilage that acts as a shock absorber within the knee between the femur, tibia, and patella. While meniscus tears are fairly common in athletes, they do not occur as frequently among climbers, even though some common moves put undue strain on the meniscus.

The heel hook, drop knee (Egyptian), and the frog position are all stances commonly used in climbing. They also exert strain on the outside portions of the knee and edges of the meniscus. All of these moves place considerable force on the medial meniscus and can cause damage when the leg bones pinch the meniscus, sometimes causing fraying of its edges.

IDENTIFY

Pain is the primary symptom and can vary in intensity at the time of injury depending upon its severity. Pain usually occurs on the inside (medial) or outside (lateral) portion of the knee. Sometimes there is little or no pain from the initial tear, or even over subsequent small tears, but over time these will grow and cause more considerable pain and damage. Swelling does occur, usually on the following day, but it can sometimes be hard to see due to the size and nature of the knee joint. As this condition worsens, climbers may feel their knee momentarily "lock" or move with a "hitch." A complete assessment should be performed by a medical provider to make a definitive diagnosis. If pain continues after the initial insult, climbing should be discontinued for the session.

TREAT

Field treatment consists of RICE (see "RICE" sidebar on page 76) along with NSAIDs. A medical professional will be able to assess the damage to the meniscus and suggest further interventions. These can range from continuing RICE and NSAIDs to an invasive surgical treatment (knee arthroscopy).

EVACUATE

Evacuation should not be needed unless the injured climber is unable to walk out.

Patella Fracture (Acute)

The patella is a sesamoid bone, and its fracture is usually the result of direct trauma. A fractured patella is a painful experience and easily diagnosed due to the very superficial location of the kneecap below the skin.

IDENTIFY

Pain is the chief complaint, together with swelling and often an inability to bend or straighten the affected leg without increasing pain. There may be a laceration at the site of the break, since little tissue covers the patella.

TREAT

Treatment for a patella fracture is to assess, irrigate, and dress the overlying laceration (see Chapter 9). A detailed CSM check (see "CSM" sidebar on page 101) should be conducted distal to the injury, and the leg should be aligned in a straight position (which will relieve tension on the patella fracture). Splint the leg from the hip to the ankle, preventing movement of the knee joint (this is accomplished by ensuring the back portion of the splint is sufficiently strong).

EVACUATE

Evacuation to a medical facility is required for definitive treatment.

Patella Dislocation (Acute)

A patella dislocation is painful but can be relieved easily in the field. It is usually caused by climbers making a twisting movement, or by the quadriceps muscles contracting asymmetrically during a fall.

IDENTIFY

Pain and deformity are the two symptoms of a patella dislocation. The patella usually dislocates to the lateral (outside) portion of the knee.

TREAT

A patella dislocation is easily reduced by applying gentle pressure on the outside of the patella while straightening the injured climber's leg. The rescuer should check CSM before and after this intervention (see "CSM" sidebar on page 101). A splint should be applied and the patient should be able to walk, though with stiff legs.

EVACUATE

The climber can probably self-evacuate but should seek medical attention to ensure that no underlying fracture exists.

Tibia/Fibula

Tibia/Fibula Fracture (Acute)

The most common lower extremity fracture that a climber will suffer is a tibia and/or fibula fracture, usually the result of a direct high-impact trauma caused by a collision with a rock wall, a ledge, or the ground. A tibial shaft fracture is also the most common open fracture in the wilderness (Switzer 2012).

IDENTIFY

Signs and symptoms of a tibia/fibula fracture are pain, deformity of the lower leg, swelling, tenderness at the fracture site, and crepitus when the leg is moved. Climbers with a tibial fracture will not be able to bear weight. These fractures can occur at any portion of the tibia, including within the knee joint (tibial plateau fracture); just below the knee (proximal tibia fracture); mid-bone (tibial shaft fracture); just above the ankle (distal tibia fracture); and within the ankle itself (pilon fracture). A tibial fracture does not necessarily also imply a fibula fracture and vice versa. A climber with a fibula fracture will still be able to bear weight on the injured leg, though this will be painful.

TREAT

Regardless of the fracture location, a detailed assessment including a CSM check (see "CSM" sidebar on page 101) should be conducted. The CSM check should be repeated every 30 minutes during evacuation, as compartment syndrome can develop after an injury of this type. The patient's leg should be splinted using whatever materials are available, and this splint should run from foot to thigh to stabilize the tibia/fibula.

EVACUATE

A fracture of the tibia or fibula requires evacuation. If pulses are lost, or if there is a numbness or decrease of feeling in the limb, the splint should be adjusted and the evacuation should be hastened—these are potential signs of compartment syndrome and the injured climber needs urgent medical assistance.

General Muscle/Tendon Injuries

Muscle/Tendon Strains and Tears (Acute or Chronic)

Muscle or tendon strains and tears can happen in any muscle in the body, and everyone, at some point in their life, will experience this at least once. For climbers, the hamstring (muscle group located below the buttocks and above the knee) is the most commonly injured muscle in the lower body. This usually occurs when attempting a heel hook or when transitioning to a foothold that is distant and taking extreme weight onto one leg in a flexed position. Additionally, dorsal sided pain, sometimes accompanied by a "snapping sound" to the pelvis, hamstring, and posterior knee have been noted in the literature from the use of the heel hook maneuver (Thompson 2011, Schöffl 2016).

IDENTIFY

Whatever the location of a muscle strain or tear, pain will occur at the site. Unlike the pain associated with many of the other injuries described in this chapter, the pain of a strain or tear is moderate and is often characterized as "aching." Other symptoms include swelling, muscle spasms, weakness, inflammation, and sometimes cramping.

TREAT

As with most soft tissue injuries, RICE is the first line of treatment (see "RICE" sidebar on page 76). Light stretching is also helpful. If significant weakness and pain occur, consider seeing a medical professional to diagnose the severity of the tear. Some severe tears require surgical intervention. Patience is also needed with muscle strains and tears, since muscle can take from six to eight weeks to heal. Tendons take even longer (12 to 36 weeks).

EVACUATE

Most injured climbers can walk or limp out under their own power, and this is not a time-sensitive emergency. The decision to stay or evacuate depends on circumstances and continued climbing capacity. In remote areas, evacuation of an injured climber with posterior leg pain indicative of a severe tear of a muscle or tendon may be difficult and lengthy.

Ankle

Achilles Tendon Rupture/Tear (Acute)

An Achilles tendon rupture will bring an immediate end to a climbing trip. This tear of the tendon requires evacuation.

IDENTIFY

Anyone who has suffered a ruptured Achilles tendon will report that the event is unmistakable. This injury is most commonly described as a "pop" with intense pain in the back of the ankle and the immediate inability to bear weight. It is impossible to walk with a full tear and often even with a partial tear. The tendon will retract into the leg near the calf in the case of a complete rupture.

TREAT

Field treatment is limited. Climbers with a complete tear should be splinted to protect the leg and evacuated. With a partial tear, RICE should be implemented (see "RICE" sidebar on page 76), and the climber should be splinted.

EVACUATE

Climbers with a ruptured Achilles tendon should be evacuated immediately to a medical center for definitive treatment.

Achilles Tendinitis (Chronic)

Achilles tendinitis, a common injury among runners, can also happen to climbers and mountaineers. For these athletes, carrying heavy loads uphill elongates the Achilles tendon and can cause inflammation. This often occurs among those new to mountaineering or those who have a typical desk job and decide (without proper preparation) to go climb a mountain. The tendinitis occurs from the elongation of the Achilles tendon beyond normal limits. The change from sedentary lifestyle to highly physical uphill climbing can create the perfect scenario for Achilles pain.

The structure of some climbing shoes can also put pressure on the Achilles tendon and cause pain. The rubberized, close-fitting cup of a climbing shoe heel is designed to keep the calcaneus (heel) from shifting during climbing. The tight fit presses on the Achilles tendon, and with repeated movement and long-term wear can cause inflammation. This can be resolved by changing shoes or by creating a small cut near the heel loop or along the lining of the heel cup to release pressure on the Achilles tendon without destroying the integrity of the shoe.

IDENTIFY

Pain in the heel leading up to the calf is the principal symptom with Achilles tendinitis, especially in the morning or with increased activity. Stiffness sometimes accompanies this morning pain, and some patients complain of pain the day after exercise. Swelling also occurs and often increases throughout the day.

TREAT

Achilles injuries are difficult to treat and often entail months of rehabilitation. The first step in treatment is to decrease or halt the activity that is causing the inflammation. For example, rather than running, try an elliptical machine or stationary bike. Such activities, or others such as swimming, can maintain cardiovascular fitness without exerting strain on the Achilles.

Icing the Achilles tendon with a reusable ice pack or foam ice cup for 20 minutes multiple times throughout the day (see "RICE" sidebar on page 76 for information on how to create these) can aid in inflammation control. NSAIDs can also be beneficial in reducing inflammation but should be used cautiously, and preferably only for a short period after the initial injury.

Stretching with a focus on the calf is key in helping to prevent further injury. Other treatments include physical therapy, *eccentric strengthening exercises* (slow release of lengthening muscles while under load), steroid injections, orthotics, and surgical intervention.

EVACUATE
Evacuation is not needed.

Ankle/Foot Fracture (Acute)

An ankle and/or foot fracture for climbers usually results from a fall, sometimes into the rock wall, but more commonly onto a ledge or from a ground fall. This discussion will include both the ankle and the foot, since aspects of each will often be involved in a fracture. Common fractures for climbers include the talus bone within the interior of the ankle and the calcaneus (heel), both of which include a large amount of spongy tissue.

The talus is a key part of the ankle, since it is located below the tibia and fibula of the lower leg, above the calcaneus, and behind the navicular bone. It is responsible for transferring the weight of the entire body in proportion to the foot. In a fall, it may be overwhelmed by the additional forces, causing a fracture. The calcaneus is the most common bone within the foot to break due to its location and absorption of high-impact forces resulting from a climbing fall. Depending upon the severity and type of break, a climber may need surgery to realign the bones and allow the injury to heal. Other fractures do occur, depending upon the fall; field treatment for all of these is included below.

IDENTIFY
Pain, tenderness, and swelling will be the primary symptoms of an ankle fracture, but this is also the case for an ankle sprain. The Ottawa Ankle Rules, a simple three-step assessment (discussed below), can help differentiate these two.

In order to assess the injury, remove climbing shoes. If the patient is wearing mountaineering boots or approach shoes, remove these, but after quickly performing the assessment, consider putting them back on and integrating them into a splint. Obvious signs of serious injury to the ankle or foot include any deformity or angulation, pain or tenderness, inability to bear weight, bruising, rapid swelling, crepitus, and loss of normal range of motion.

The next step in assessing an ankle injury is applying the Ottawa Ankle Rules themselves. This consists of the following:

1. Check for CSM of the foot, distal to the injury (see "CSM" sidebar on page 101 and Figure 4-15). If the patient fails any of these checks, the ankle/foot injury is serious and they need to be evacuated.
2. Can the climber bear weight on the injured ankle and take five steps? If they can, they likely do not have a fracture.
3. Does the climber feel pain when pressure is placed on the following points? (Figure 4-15)
   + Posterior medial malleolus (the back side of the bone that sticks out of the inner ankle)
   + Posterior lateral malleolus (the back side of the bone that sticks out of the outer ankle)
   + The fifth metatarsal (the bony point at the middle of the outside of the foot)
   + The navicular bone (the point where the leg and foot meet)—for thin patients, this area often looks like a triangle

If the patient has intact CSM (see "CSM" sidebar on page 101), is able to bear weight and walk five paces, and has no pain at any of the four areas listed above in Figure 4-15, the ankle is most likely not broken.

TREAT

If the examination steps above suggest the ankle is most likely not broken, see the "Ankle Sprain" section below for appropriate treatment. If an ankle fracture is suspected, the first step in treatment is RICE (see "RICE" sidebar on page 76). If the patient has a loss of CSM below the injury (see "CSM" sidebar on page 101), this condition must be corrected to prevent permanent nerve damage, hemorrhage, or tissue death. Attempt to identify the reason the climber does not have intact CSM. This is usually due to a deformity caused by the fracture that is impinging nerves or blood vessels. The foot/ankle must be realigned in order to restore normal CSM to the injured foot. This procedure is quite painful and requires great care. If you are a medical provider or feel confident in skills learned during a wilderness medicine course, it may be helpful

FIGURE 4-15. OTTAWA ANKLE RULES

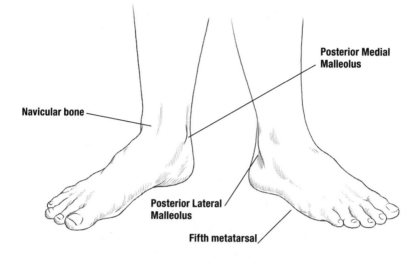

Posterior Medial Malleolus

Navicular bone

Posterior Lateral Malleolus

Fifth metatarsal

to apply light traction away from the body to realign the ankle into normal anatomical position. This should restore normal CSM. If you are not confident in your skills, do not attempt to do this, as additional damage can result if it is performed incorrectly. If CSM cannot be restored, the climber needs to be evacuated as soon as possible.

EVACUATE

Climbers who have suffered an ankle or foot fracture need medical attention and should be evacuated immediately. Because they will be unable to walk, a field-expedient litter can be used for evacuation. Climbing rope can be used in this evacuation to create a one- or two-person rope litter. See Chapter 19 for detailed instruction on how to build and use this litter. Delay in evacuation increases the likelihood of complications.

Ankle Sprain (Acute)

A sprained ankle is the most common injury to the musculoskeletal system for outdoor adventurers. It is also quite common among climbers: One study reports up to 24% of climbers suffer from ankle sprains at some point in their climbing career (Schöffl 2013b). This is often because climbing shoes restrict the foot from spreading and absorbing some of the impact from falls. Sprains occur more frequently for boulderers landing on poorly placed pads or without proper spots. It is important to differentiate between an ankle sprain and an ankle fracture. Most ankle sprains are the result of inversion or eversion injuries (rolling the ankle to the inside or outside) rather than from a significant fall. If a climber has taken a fall onto a ledge or ground, see the "Ankle/Foot Fracture" section above for detailed assessment information.

IDENTIFY

Pain, tenderness, and swelling are the common complaints resulting from an ankle sprain. They are caused by damage to the lateral ligaments, often the anterior talofibular ligament or the medial deltoid ligament (for an eversion sprain).

TREAT

Ankle sprains are graded into three grades based upon severity. Though generally minor, they need to be treated with care to prevent lasting damage. Treatment begins with RICE. Some patients will need added support. A tape or improvised splint provides some support and helps prevent swelling. See "Improvised Splinting Techniques" sidebar on page 113 for additional information about simple splints, improvised using climbing tape and other common climber gear.

EVACUATE

While not a life-threatening emergency, an ankle sprain can severely limit the mobility of a climbing partner and extend the trip. Depending upon severity, the time required to evacuate and the resources needed may be substantial. Luckily, climbers almost always have rope with them. (Sorry, boulderers and free soloists!) An improvised one- or two-person rope litter can be created to simplify evacuation without additional help (see Chapter 19).

Foot

Hallux Rigidus (Chronic)

This is a degenerative arthritis of the first joint of the *hallux* ("big toe"). It can be hereditary, but many people whose jobs require them to squat

+IMPROVISED SPLINTING TECHNIQUES
FOR ANKLE INJURIES+

There are two types of ankle splinting technique that require only gear that a climber carries every day. The first, a U-Splint, uses only clothing and tape, while the second, the Tape Splint, uses only climber tape. A few rules about splinting:

1. Remember when applying any type of splint, whether to the ankle or any other part of the body, it is essential to check CSM distal to the injury (see "CSM" sidebar on page 101). This check should occur prior to placing the splint and every 30 minutes afterward.
2. Always pad the injury and any bony prominences to prevent further injury.
3. "Avoid the void": Fill any open space between the splinting material and the tissue.
4. Get feedback on all of this—Is it secure? Is it padded?

The U-Splint: To create a U-Splint for your partner find any suitable material, ideally a jacket, shirt etc. Roll this into a tight tube. Put the injured foot into the middle of this roll at a 90 degree position and wrap both ends up the outside and inside of the leg. Secure the material with climbing tape at the foot, ankle, and middle of the lower leg.

The Tape Splint: This splint works best on a bare foot and leg that is as clean as possible. Try to align the foot into a 90 degree angle with the lower leg. Start taping to the inside of foot (on top, behind big toe) and wrap under the ball of the foot, around the outside of the foot, and then to the inside of ankle across the top of the foot. Continue taping behind the ankle, angling upward and anchoring the tape strip below the calf on the outside. Repeat this at least three more times for stability. Using 3 to 4 longer strips of tape, attach one end to the interior of the leg (mid-calf) and run directly under the heel and anchor it to exterior of the leg (mid-calf). This will look like the U-Splint. Finish all this taping by anchoring the top of the twisted tape strips and the u-shaped tape strips to the lower leg.

Final Notes: Remember, while you are doing the hard work of carrying injured climbers out of the backcountry, they are doing little physical activity. Make sure they are warm enough, they are eating and drinking, and that the splint is still stable. Take frequent breaks and take care of yourself.

Severe sprains may result in complete ligament tears and require surgical intervention. All sprains should be treated carefully and be seen by a medical professional if necessary.

often or to place pressure on the large toe also develop this condition. For climbers, hallux rigidus often results from tight climbing shoes.

IDENTIFY

Hallux rigidus is characterized by pain and stiffness of the toe and can be accompanied by swelling and inflammation. Severe cases will be painful even when at rest.

TREAT

Early identification of hallux rigidus is helpful in limiting its progression. Wearing shoes with larger toe boxes and taking NSAIDs for pain and inflammation are recommended. If pain continues, see a medical provider for additional options that include orthotics, physical therapy, steroid injections, and surgical intervention.

EVACUATE

Evacuation is not needed.

Hallux Valgus (Chronic)

This condition is caused by the use of tight climbing shoes by climbers to aid their performance. These shoes mold feet into smaller toe boxes, thus pushing all of the toes together. The hallux is most affected and is pushed inward (medially). This inward pressure, over time, causes the hallux valgus deformity to the first toe. Research also points to a hereditary component in the development of this condition.

IDENTIFY

This condition can be identified visually. The hallux will point inward toward the remaining toes and can be painful for some climbers. Callousing of the inner aspect at the ball of the first toe often occurs, along with pain.

TREAT

Conservative treatments are limited. For climbers, choosing a shoe with a larger toe box is most helpful, though with some cost in performance. Surgical treatment is needed to remedy the pain, and there are roughly 130 different procedures that can be performed based upon the severity of the condition.

Evacuation is not needed.

Morton's Neuroma (Chronic)

Climbing shoes are arguably the most important piece of gear climbers own, and are specially designed to help them perform to the best of their ability. Besides the pain normal with such tight-fitting shoes, some climbers suffer from a condition called Morton's neuroma.

IDENTIFY

The significant symptom of this neuroma is pain, usually at the ball of the foot between the third and fourth toes. It sometimes radiates into the toes, and some climbers may also feel numbness or "pins and needles." This pain is caused by swelling and irritation as the nerve passes under the ligaments that connect the metatarsals. Sometimes a mass can be felt at the location of the pain.

TREAT

Changing shoes is the best remedy. Rather than climbing steep sport routes with heavily downturned shoes, switch to comfortable all-day shoes and work some multi-pitch trad routes. Changing shoes should help immediately, along with a course of NSAIDs. If a shoe change does not resolve the pain, custom orthotics that pad and spread the toes can help. For extreme cases, see a medical provider, who may suggest a steroidal injection or perhaps surgical intervention.

EVACUATE

There is no need for evacuation.

Plantar Fasciitis (Chronic)

Plantar fasciitis is inflammation of the fascia (connective tissue) that connects the heel of the foot to the toes. It is a common problem for runners, but can also be troublesome for mountaineers or climbers who routinely hike long approaches to their destinations.

IDENTIFY

Pain rarely occurs during activity, but instead begins afterward, usually in the morning or after prolonged periods of sitting or rest. It emanates near the medial side of the heel. This pain can also be significant when "pushing off" for a step or stride.

TREAT
Rest is most helpful when combined with NSAIDs and stretching of the calf muscles. Orthotic arch supports that cup the heel and support the arch help improve symptoms. Deep tissue massage may also help, while steroid injections and surgery are rarely needed.

EVACUATE
There is no need for evacuation.

Foot Sesamoid Injury (Chronic)

While rarer than other injuries to the foot, sesamoid injury can occur. The sesamoid bones are located at the ball of the first toe, and injuries take the form of "turf toe," sesamoiditis, or a fracture.

IDENTIFY
Sesamoiditis is caused by continually wearing climbing shoes that place pressure on these bones and the surrounding ligaments. Causes of more acute exacerbations include landing hard on this area, either from a boulder problem or a ground fall, and can result in a fracture of these small, pea-sized bones. Crack climbing can place tension on this area of the foot.

TREAT
The best method for treating this injury is padding the joint, using a donut-shaped padded orthotic, together with a course of NSAIDs and resting the foot. If conservative management does not resolve the pain, a medical provider may recommend physical therapy, steroid injections, or in extreme cases, surgical intervention.

EVACUATE
No evacuation is needed.

CHAPTER 5

SPINAL INJURIES

The spine is a series of square or rectangular bones beginning with the first cervical vertebra (spine bone, plural *vertebrae*) at the base of the skull and extending down through the *coccyx* (tailbone) (Figure 5-1). Vertebrae differ from other bones discussed in this book in that they are not long bones, like the *femur* (thigh bone), *humerus* (upper arm bone), or *digits* (finger bones). While the long bones of the body are usually used as fulcrums to promote movement around a joint via ligaments, the bones of the spine permit less movement. While there are joints between these bones and there is motion, the range is substantially less than with other joints, and the primary purpose is as much protection of the spinal cord running along these bones as it is movement.

There are seven cervical vertebrae. The seventh of these has a distinctive bump that can be felt at the bottom of the neck. Following the seventh cervical vertebra, there are twelve thoracic vertebrae that generally correspond to the chest level of the torso. Below this are five lumbar vertebrae that make up the lower back. The fifth lumbar vertebra attaches to the sacrum. The coccyx represents a vestigial tail, and consists of three or more small bones that help anchor the pelvis. These bones in sequence are illustrated in Figure 5-1.

IDENTIFY

Spinal injuries are one of the most feared consequences of a fall or of some object striking a climber. While bony fractures of the spine can be very painful, the greatest fear is of associated injury to the spinal cord, the mechanism by which all nerves communicate with the body below the neck to transmit sensation and motor function. For generations, EMS and climbing medicine authorities have recommended a very conservative approach to identifying spinal injuries and possible threats

FIGURE 5-1. NORMAL SPINE

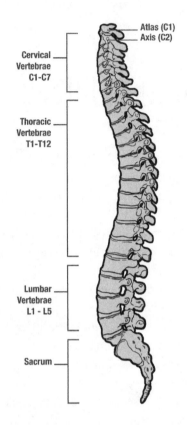

Atlas (C1)
Axis (C2)

Cervical
Vertebrae
C1-C7

Thoracic
Vertebrae
T1-T12

Lumbar
Vertebrae
L1 - L5

Sacrum

to the spinal cord. This included immobilization of patients' spine to prevent causing or exacerbating a spinal cord injury. In many cases, a "mechanism of injury" that might be thought to cause a spinal injury has been enough to warrant immobilization of the spine.

However, in the modern era, emergency medicine and EMS clinical scientists have more extensively explored ways that spinal injuries can best be identified and managed. A major landmark in this research was the publication in 1998—and validation in 2000—of the NEXUS (National Emergency X-Radiography Utilization Study) criteria for cervical spine injury (Hoffman 1998, Hoffman 2000). These criteria identified specific characteristics requiring X-ray imaging of the cervical spine for possible fracture. If none of the findings were present, no X-ray was needed. More than 34,000 patients were enrolled in this study, and only two patients with significant cervical spine injury were missed using the criteria. This meant that the NEXUS criteria were 99.6% effective in ruling out a significant cervical spine injury without the use of any X-ray machinery.

Prior to this, many wilderness medicine schools were teaching techniques to "clear" the spine of injury, but these techniques did not have significant scientific validation. The benefit of the NEXUS Group's study was the proof that if a specific set of scientifically validated criteria were not present, significant cervical spine injury could be excluded in more than 99% of cases. In these cases, prehospital immobilization would not be helpful, since no further testing would be done at the hospital anyway and all immobilization tools would simply be removed. Fortunately, the NEXUS criteria requires no special equipment and can be applied anywhere, including climbing environments. The criteria can be represented by the mnemonic INDIAN (Hawkins 2010).

I = **I**ntoxication (if patients are intoxicated, their expressions of possible pain, tenderness, or neurological deficit described below cannot be trusted)

N = *Neurological deficit* (problems with nerve conduction, i.e., numbness or paralysis or weakness in one body part)

DI = **D**istracting **I**njury (an injury away from the spine so dramatic or painful that it could distract a climber from possible pain, tenderness, or neurological deficit remote from the more significant-appearing injury)

A = **A**ltered level of consciousness (patients whose level of consciousness is altered or who are confused cannot, as described in intoxication above, reliably express possible pain, tenderness, or neurological deficits)

N = **N**eck tenderness or pain (technically, according to the criteria, only tenderness, and only on the midline bony parts of the neck, but to be more conservative we would recommend not only tenderness but also any pain)

Other publications followed the NEXUS criteria in emergency medicine literature, including the Canadian c-spine study in 2004 (CCC Study Group 2004) and its out-of-hospital validation in 2009 (Vaillancourt 2009). Together, they contribute to our current understanding that simple physical examination techniques can exclude the possibility of a clinically significant fracture. The term "clinically significant" is important here. A common misunderstanding is that these criteria exclude neck injuries altogether. In fact, they only exclude bony injuries that would result in a change in management; for example, surgery or further immobilization. Radiological technology has improved to the point where even tiny fractures or disruptions can be seen in bones on advanced generations of CT scanning or magnetic resonance imaging (MRI). However, if these injuries do not alter the management of a patient—or require further immobilization or treatment—they are not considered "clinically significant," and thus also would not require special prehospital precautions. In the opinion of the authors, despite further refinements and suggestions such as algorithms that combine the NEXUS and Canadian C-spine criteria (Weingart 2011), the original NEXUS criteria as embodied in the INDIAN mnemonic remain reliable for the climber to use to determine when a clinically significant spinal fracture can be excluded.

For patients with clinically significant fractures, spinal cord compromise may be present, and this often appears in the form of neurological deficits. Healthcare providers are trained to recognize patterns of various deficits and how they relate to specific injuries. But for climbers without healthcare training, it is enough to know that any new numbness, weakness, or paralysis of a specific body part after a fall or blunt trauma should be presumed to be related to a spinal cord injury unless another source of the deficit is obvious (e.g., numbness in a finger that has a major laceration and no suggestion that the numbness could be from a back or arm injury). Sensory losses may be very specific and subtle, such as isolated loss of ability to tell the position of a body part in space or loss of the ability to sense vibrations.

TREAT
These clinical research milestones, begun around 2000, help identify situations where a clinically significant spinal injury can be ruled out. About a decade later, a further series of clinical research findings also changed our understanding of the treatment of patients who may have a clinically significant spinal injury.

Traditionally, *spinal immobilization* techniques (maneuvers to prevent any spinal movement after a suspected injury) were the accepted field intervention for potential spinal fracture. However, researchers are now demonstrating that these techniques rarely succeed in actually immobilizing the spine, and that when spinal immobilization is in fact achieved, the evidence suggests the patient experiences more harm than benefit. This represents a fundamental paradigm change in our wilderness management of trauma, overturns many of the most long-standing teachings about patient immobilization, and, like suspension syndrome (described in Chapter 2), represents a victory of evidence-based medicine over dogma and traditional practice for its own sake without evidence. Chapter 18 discusses these scientific findings in more detail, along with more modern techniques of *spinal motion restriction* (reducing motion of the spine, usually using pain as a threshold, without specific attempt to completely immobilize). If the identification tools above flag an injury as needing spinal motion restriction, follow the recommendations outlined in Chapter 18.

Any bony injury to the back benefits from *analgesia* (pain control). If patients do not require spinal motion restriction, analgesia may help a climber become more mobile and functional in their own rescue.

Historically, steroidal medications (particularly methylprednisolone) have been considered to be a standard of care for spinal cord injuries. However, in a very recent change in the medical community, most professional consensus guidelines now discourage or minimize their use, including the Congress of Neurological Surgeons, the American Association of Neurological Surgeons, the American College of Surgeons, and the Canadian Association of Emergency Physicians (Hadley 2013, Chin 2016). They should certainly only be used in the out-of-hospital care of a climber if a professional healthcare provider is specifically prescribing and providing them.

In contrast to the growing amount of skepticism over the benefit of early immobilization, there is growing evidence that early mobilization of patients with spinal injuries may be beneficial (Epstein 2014). A fascinating historical footnote to this concept is the story of Hans Kraus (Schwartz 2015). Kraus was simultaneously one of the premier rock climbers of the twentieth century, putting up many of the first ascents in the Shawangunks in the United States, and one of the premier orthopedic back surgeons of his era, serving as the private back doctor for John F. Kennedy and many celebrities of the mid-twentieth century. Though he was featured on the cover of *TIME* magazine and twice identified as "Man of the Year" by that publication, his legacy is now largely forgotten.

But a key element of his back rehabilitation strategies—frequently used for climbers, skiers, and mountaineers—was the concept of early mobilization, often enhanced with ethyl chloride, a topical numbing analgesic spray still available today.*

EVACUATE

A complete discussion of packaging and evacuation of spinally injured patients can be found in Chapter 18. All patients with suspected spinal injuries require evacuation within the context of risk-benefit analysis. Those found to have neurological deficits following a traumatic injury involving the spine need professional medical attention and follow-up. Positive outcomes are often related to the quality of initial surgical/ medical attention; however, professional rehabilitation (and compliance with rehabilitation recommendations and regimens) is often equally important, or perhaps even more important, to successful outcomes and return to outdoor sports, including climbing.

* http://www.gebauer.com/ethylchloride

CHAPTER 6

HEAD INJURIES

Head injuries include a range of traumas to the brain, skull, and associated organs. Traumatic brain injury (TBI), skull fracture, intracranial hemorrhage (ICH), and concussion, along with associated syndromes, are all considered head injuries.

Head injuries are a particularly important concern for climbers for three reasons: first, because, given the physiology of falls, they are a frequent risk for climbers in particular; second, because their consequences can be so dire, including neurological complications and brain damage; and third, because examination of them is not straightforward, since the brain is encased in a solid wall of bone (the skull), limiting direct examination. If direct examination of the brain or intracranial contents is possible during a climbing emergency, it is a very bad day for all involved. More seriously, wilderness medicine practice guidelines identify brain content extrusion from the skull as a sign of obvious death (with resuscitation attempts not indicated), at least in the context of a patient who is simultaneously hypothermic (Zafren 2014).

PREVENT

As with most other medical issues in climbing, prevention is far more effective than treatment. A helmet is the mainstay of prevention for head injuries. For some types of head injuries, there is no clear evidence that climbing helmets currently in use are preventive. However, it is equally rare for helmets to prove dangerous to a climber, and they can be preventive for many other types of head injuries. A survey completed by the British Mountaineering Council in 2007 concluded that wearing a helmet significantly reduces the chances of suffering a severe head injury; in contrast, the absence of helmet use correlated with two times greater chance of suffering such injuries (MacDonald 2013).

Helmet use is far more common than it was decades ago, but is still not as prevalent as it might be. Soleil completed a survey of rock climbers suggesting that 49% of sport leaders, 53% of top-ropers, and 86% of traditional climbers "usualy or always" used helmets (Soleil 2012). These numbers are somewhat discouraging, especially since he did not survey any climbers under 18. His mean age was 36, and—at least anecdotally—younger climbers seem to wear helmets even less often. In 2006, *The Journal of Trauma and Acute Care Surgery* published a survey of 1,887 rock climbers. Among this group, 19% stated they never wore helmets, and only 36% reported wearing helmets "most or all of the time" (Gerdes 2006). Similar results have been reported by Attarian in 2002 (14% never wear helmets, 22% only sometimes, 34% always) and Simon (20% never wear helmets, 44% only sometimes, 23% always) (Attarian 2002, Simon 2016). Given the propensity of survey respondents to exaggerate their own safety compliance, one would expect the actual numbers here to be slightly lower too. Even more troubling, Soleil's data suggests that as climbs get steeper and more difficult, fewer people wear helmets, especially on sport routes. Helmet use is extraordinarily low during bouldering and indoor climbing (probably more due to cultural reasons surrounding these particular niche climbing activities than any other rationale), and is estimated at less than 1% by some authorities (MacDonald 2013).

Clearly, there is significant work still to be done in promoting helmet use in climbing. Other outdoor sports have been more successful in promoting a culture of helmet and brain safety. Cyclists hover around 50% regular helmet use, and ski areas see about 61% helmet use (MacDonald 2013). Other sports may have done a better job at designing sport-specific helmets as well. Climbing helmet certifications and standards (largely designed by the International Mountaineering and Climbing Federation [UIAA] and the European Committee for Standardization [CEN]) are built to provide protection from a falling object striking the head from above, and are quite rigorous in this regard. Less is known about helmet design for climbing falls. However, more than 75% of emergency department visits for climbing injuries come from falls, whereas getting hit by an object is responsible for only 6% (Nelson 2009). Similarly, as Dougald MacDonald points out in his head injury review in *Climbing* magazine, *Accidents in North American Mountaineering* reports seven times as many fall-related injuries as falling object-related injuries over a 60-year period (MacDonald 2013).

It is important, however, to recognize that helmets do not prevent all injuries or deaths from head blows. Large objects striking the helmet, or long falls ending in a blow to the head, can still injure or kill a climber even wearing a helmet. So it is important to keep other preventive measures in mind as well. These include:

+ Avoiding climbing below other parties
+ In trad rock and ice climbing, placing protection at frequent intervals to reduce the length of a potential fall
+ Carrying a knife, accessible on the front of your body (similar to paddling procedures) to cut a helmet chinstrap should it become constrictive in a trapped or dangling position after a fall
+ If you are wearing a helmet, wearing it correctly; it should be secured squarely on top of your head, not allowing the helmet to tilt to one side or off the forehead

IDENTIFY

About 10% of injuries seen in an emergency department from rock climbing are head injuries (Nelson 2009, MacDonald 2014). The most common of these is a TBI, which includes concussions, post-concussion syndromes, and intracerebral hemorrhages. All are caused by the exertion of sudden force on the head and brain, causing an abrupt back-and-forth motion.

Concussions

Concussions are considered a mild TBI (MTBI) and are like brain bruises. However, they are not visible to the eye in any way, and cannot even be seen on advanced imaging like X-rays and CT scans. Therefore, they are identified by the signs and symptoms associated with them. In medicine, this is known as a *clinical diagnosis* (a diagnosis made solely based on exam without any testing), meaning that with training, the injury can be identified as easily in the field as in a clinic or hospital. Because of this, nobody need be sent to a healthcare facility simply to be "screened for concussion" if personnel capable of clinically diagnosing it are available in the field, since no special equipment is used to diagnose concussion. Evacuation and immediate medical care may likely still be necessary in cases of significant head injury, but that is not so much to identify or treat a concussion as it is to test for the more serious conditions below.

Since it is a clinical diagnosis, multiple clinical tools exist to evaluate for the presence of concussion. SCAT3 is a standardized tool designed by the Summary and Agreement Statement of the Second International Symposium on Concussion in Sport, last updated in 2013. It is available online* and is designed for those with healthcare training. For non-healthcare providers, there is a similar "Sport Concussion Recognition Tool,"† which has descriptors used to "suggest" the presence of a concussion.

The formal medical definition of concussion is "a clinical syndrome marked by immediate and time-limited alteration in brain function resulting from mechanical trauma." The American Association of Neurological Surgeons (AANS) defines confusion as a primary alteration, and lists three principal features of confusion (AANS 2016):

+ Inability to maintain a coherent stream of thought
+ A disturbance of awareness with heightened distractibility
+ Inability to carry out a sequence of goal-directed movements

Chapter 1 describes the AVPU scale, which is helpful in assessing a patient's alertness and mental status.

In addition to confusion, AANS lists the following concussion symptoms:

+ Prolonged headache
+ Vision disturbances (including double vision or "fuzzy" vision)
+ Dizziness
+ Nausea or vomiting
+ Impaired balance
+ Memory loss
+ Ringing ears
+ Difficulty concentrating
+ Sensitivity to light
+ Loss of smell or taste

* http://bjsm.bmj.com/content/47/5/259.full.pdf
† http://bjsm.bmj.com/content/47/5/267.full.pdf

The National Collegiate Athletic Association (NCAA) adds the following criteria:

+ Amnesia
+ Headache
+ Loss of consciousness (LOC)*
+ Sensitivity to noise
+ Feeling sluggish
+ Slowed reaction time
+ Unusual irritability

If any of these symptoms occur after a blow to the head, a healthcare professional should be consulted as soon as possible, and a concussion should be suspected.

Intracranial Hemorrhage (ICH) and Severe Traumatic Brain Injury (STBI)

A major reason for seeking further health care after a head injury if any of these concerning signs are present is not to rule in or out concussion, since treatment for concussion is largely supportive, but to evaluate for the more serious conditions of ICH or STBI.

The warning symptoms of a serious brain injury are the following:

+ Pain: Constant or returning headache
+ Motor dysfunction: Inability to control or coordinate motor functions, or balance problems
+ Sensory: Changes in ability to hear, taste, or see; dizziness; increased hypersensitivity to light or sound
+ Cognitive: Shortened attention span; easily distracted; overstimulated by surroundings; difficulty in staying focused on a task, following directions, or understanding information; feeling of disorientation, confusion, and other neuropsychological deficiencies
+ Speech: Difficulty finding the "right" word; difficulty expressing thoughts

---

* It is important to recognize that LOC may be a sign of concussion but is NOT required for such a diagnosis. In other words, absence of LOC does not rule out concussion.

ICHs are particularly dangerous. Bleeding in the brain cannot be treated by any of the standard hemorrhage techniques except perhaps elevation. The fact that the bleeding is occurring in the skull, a closed space incapable of swelling, can eventually suppress the bleeding, but more often means the bleeding occupies more and more room, squeezing the soft brain and damaging it.

Many signs of an STBI are taught in first aid classes, but some of these alleged signs are of dubious value in the field. For example, it is often taught that unequal pupils are a sign of brain injury. This is true in very specific cases, where the swelling described above gets so bad that the brain *herniates* (bulges) out of the skull and through the hole at its base, which is the exit of the spinal cord. In these cases of herniation, one pupil can suddenly become larger than another as a corresponding nerve is compressed. However, in an injury of such severity, there will be multiple other signs of critical injury preceding this—it is a late sign, so of questionable help in clarifying an uncertain diagnosis. Also, since 15% or more of the population have a condition known as *anisocoria* (unequal pupils) all the time, this is not particularly helpful as a sign in itself, without other associated conditions of STBI being present.

More helpful signs of STBI would be sudden "raccoon eyes" (black eyes without direct trauma to the eyes or orbits) and Battle's Sign (bruising behind an ear without direct trauma there). Both of these are potential signs of a skull fracture at the skull's base. Another concerning sign would be clear fluid coming from the nose and ears, which can be *cerebrospinal fluid* (the fluid surrounding the brain and spinal cord) escaping out a skull fracture.

Skull Fracture

Skull fractures may be visible through lacerations to the head or palpable as crepitus or a "step-off." Skull fractures are themselves not particularly dangerous—in fact, they may help prevent the closed-space swelling described above—but they are a cause for concern, as they result from extremely forceful impact to the skull and may indicate a brain injury underlying the fracture.

Laceration

Lacerations to the scalp and other similar external trauma are generally easily identified on physical exam. It is important to remove helmets and hats to evaluate for laceration and potential foreign bodies in wounds. A more complete discussion of lacerations and other skin injuries are in Chapters 9 and 10.

Concussion and MTBI

Climbers should discontinue climbing after a concussion or other MTBI. The use of any tools or products that produce significant visual stimulation ("brain engagement") should be minimized. This includes books, videos, computers (or, more likely in the wilderness, smartphones or GPS tools). In general, "brain rest" is the recommended regimen, until a baseline mental state is reached and often for weeks afterward if this is directed by a healthcare provider. With or without treatment, a *post-concussive syndrome* can develop with persistent neurological problems like headaches, nausea, or other complaints.

ICH, STBI, and Skull Fracture

According to the American Alpine Club, these actions are recommended to help a climber with an STBI (Simon 2015b):

+ If the patient is hanging from a rope or stranded high on a route, lower him or her to the ground or a ledge. The risks of damage to the spine or internal injuries must be balanced with the need to get the patient out of immediate danger.
+ In sloping terrain, keep the patient's head uphill. (This represents "elevation," the only one of the traditional hemorrhage control techniques that may help manage an ICH.)
+ Monitor the patient's airway and breathing; watch for changes in rate and character.
+ Be prepared to "log roll" the patient to one side if he or she vomits. Maintain spinal motion restriction and, as possible, move the body as a unit.*
+ Wake the victim every three to four hours to monitor condition and changes in consciousness.

---

* Note that, at time of publication, AAC used the terminology "spinal immobilization," but we now recommend the more recent terminology of "spinal motion restriction," as discussed in Chapter 18. This is a good example of how quickly medical standards and terminology can change, and why it is important to continue recertifying in medical courses to remain aware of changes as evidence continues to be collected and changes practice and terminology.

Laceration and Fracture

A case of laceration and fracture is a rare instance where diffuse rather than direct pressure is preferable. While direct pressure is more likely to stop the bleeding, it may also plug up a defect in the skull, allowing pressure to be released from a deeper ICH. Diffuse pressure will tend to slow scalp bleeding while not stopping the potential release of underlying pressure. Be aware that bleeding from a scalp wound can be profuse, and direct pressure may ultimately be necessary. Hair strands on either side of a laceration can be used as stitching material to pull together over a wound and knot the wound closure in place. Dermabond or other medical glue (or superglue in a pinch) can be used to further secure the knot. Ice can be used to reduce swelling. More complete discussions of lacerations and other external injuries is in Chapters 9 and 10.

EVACUATE

It will be difficult to evaluate possible ICH in the field, and will likely require a CT scan, so anything more significant than an MTBI should be treated as a potential intracranially bleeding head injury or other STBI. This requires, when feasible, immediate evacuation. In fact, the time to evacuation of a climber with a head injury directly correlates with survivability and better outcomes (Simon 2015a). Patients with minor head injuries such as small lacerations without any other sign of more extensive injury or mechanism for underlying blunt injury to the brain may be monitored in the field. In cases of uncertainty, MTBIs should be evacuated to be conservative, after considering the relative risk of missed injury or injury progression versus risks of evacuation.

CHAPTER 7

ABDOMINAL AND GASTROINTESTINAL ISSUES

Abdominal pain can quickly end a climbing trip or mountaineering expedition no matter the cause. From traumatic injury to a host of bacteria, viruses, or amoebas that cause dysentery and diarrhea, this chapter will discuss the most common issues that climbers face, both within the United States and at common climbing locales worldwide. The issues discussed also include common genitourinary issues that originate in the abdominal region.

Gastrointestinal (GI) issues are frequent during climbing activities. A ten-year study conducted at Everest Base Camp (EBC) from 2003 to 2012 showed that GI diagnoses accounted for almost 16% of patient visits to the Everest ER (Nemethy 2015). Gastrointestinal issues were the second most common medical diagnosis (after pulmonary issues), with acid reflux, diarrhea, and gastroenteritis as the top three. Diarrhea is a common problem among mountaineers, and many medical studies—including one relating a gastroenteritis outbreak on Denali in 2002—have documented this problem (McLaughlin 2005).

While some GI and abdominal problems cannot be solved easily, a few simple points can help prevent a great majority of those most commonly experienced by climbers. These easy measures include:

1. Good hand hygiene
2. Proper food preparation
3. Proper water disinfection (see Appendix E)

This chapter is subdivided into distinct areas focusing in sequence on abdominal pain by location (upper and lower), other medical GI issues without specific location, pain associated with abdominal trauma, and infectious diseases that cause gastrointestinal distress.

UPPER ABDOMINAL PAIN (RIGHT UPPER/LEFT UPPER QUADRANTS)

The following conditions will cause pain in the upper abdominal region (both right and left upper quadrants) emanating above the *umbilicus* (belly button) (Figure 1-1). These are the most common medical ailments for climbers and mountaineers but they do not include every possible abdominal condition. Err on the side of caution and never risk your own or your partners' health and safety by not seeking medical attention.

Gallstone-Related Disease/Cholecystitis

IDENTIFY

The gallbladder's main function is to assist in digestion. It is located in the upper right quadrant just beneath the liver. While gallstone-related problems can range from mild to severe and include biliary colic, acute cholecystitis, ascending cholangitis, and obstructive jaundice, the most common is cholecystitis.

Acute cholecystitis causes right upper quadrant pain and tenderness that can radiate into the right shoulder. This pain increases with deep breathing and is accompanied by nausea and vomiting. Those predisposed to cholecystitis often have flatulent dyspepsia (upset stomach) with intolerance to fatty or fried foods.

It is important to note that symptoms associated with gallbladder problems, if severe, can also represent acute pancreatitis. While uncommon, this condition produces acute pain in the central and right side of the abdomen, sometimes radiating to the back, along with nausea and vomiting, low blood pressure, and high heart rate. Evacuation is necessary for this condition, and supportive measures during evacuation should include pain relief and intake of fluid by mouth or by intravenous (IV) route if available.

TREAT

Treatment of acute cholecystitis includes pain relief, and if the symptoms continue, beginning a course of antibiotics such as ciprofloxacin. Because of the accompanying nausea and vomiting, rehydration is essential and fluids should be administered in small amounts. Fatty foods should be avoided.

EVACUATE
Evacuation is necessary for cholecystitis as well as all of the major differential diagnoses for this condition (acute pancreatitis, ascending cholangitis, and obstructive jaundice).

Gastroesophageal Reflux Disease (GERD)
IDENTIFY
Commonly known as GERD or acid reflux, this problem is caused by the reflux or movement of stomach (gastric) contents into the lower esophagus. The intrusion of gastric contents causes a host of symptoms, of which the most common is heartburn (the feeling of burning or cramping along the center of the chest below the sternum). Other common symptoms include regurgitating small portions of recently eaten food into the upper esophagus and mouth, a sense of fullness, belching, and sometimes difficulty swallowing. The onset of symptoms is usually soon after eating, and they usually ease as food is digested.

TREAT
The best "treatment" is prevention, especially for a person who has experienced these problems in the past. Smaller meals are helpful as is avoiding fatty foods, caffeine, and chocolate. Avoiding food prior to sleeping and sleeping with the upper body slightly inclined can both decrease symptoms.

Antacids, H_2 blockers, and a class of medications known as PPIs (proton pump inhibitors) can help. The most common examples of these drugs are: antacids (TUMS®, Rolaids®, and Maalox®); H_2 blockers (Zantac®, Pepcid®); and PPIs (Prilosec®, Nexium®). Follow manufacturer recommendations for dosing.

EVACUATE
This condition is rarely severe enough to limit climbing activities. Evacuation is not needed. However, substernal (midline) chest pain can also be caused by a host of other factors, including a heart attack, so a climber complaining of chest pain should be thoroughly assessed and monitored.

If there is any question that the pain is heart-related rather than GERD, medical attention should be sought and evacuation considered.

Peptic/Stomach Ulcer

IDENTIFY

A peptic ulcer is an area of stomach lining or intestine that is degraded due to the enzymes and acids of the stomach. It is identified by continual gnawing abdominal pain, usually in the center of the upper abdomen. Many peptic ulcers are caused by *Helicobacter pylori* infection. Risk factors for developing these ulcers include stress, smoking, long-term use of NSAIDs, steroids, and alcohol. Pain is the most common symptom and usually peaks one to four hours after eating.

TREAT

Use of all NSAIDs (including aspirin) should be discontinued immediately due to risk of bleeding. Otherwise, treatment of peptic ulcers is much like that of GERD. Avoid risk factors and use antacids, H_2 blockers, and PPIs to treat. Eating bland foods helps, as does drinking milk. If you are diagnosed with a peptic ulcer prior to a long climbing trip in a remote area or expedition, you should seek medical assistance to treat this condition prior to leaving.

EVACUATE

Peptic ulcers do not usually require evacuation, though a climber experiencing symptoms should see a medical provider upon returning home. Severe cases that do not respond to field treatment should consider evacuation.

LOWER ABDOMINAL PAIN (RIGHT LOWER/LEFT LOWER QUADRANTS)

The medical conditions below are the most common for climbers, but they do not include every possible ailment that could occur in this region of the abdomen. The lower abdomen is considered to be any area below the umbilicus (belly button) and extends downward into the pelvis (Figure 1-1).

Appendicitis

IDENTIFY

Appendicitis is a serious wilderness emergency. There is no widely accepted field remedy, and immediate evacuation is required. Initial symptoms will be general pain in the abdomen with nausea and vomiting. Diarrhea is usually not present. Within six to eight hours, this pain/tenderness will typically localize to the right lower quadrant but can occasionally be referred to the left side. Appendicitis can occur at any age, though it is more common for younger adults and children. Often people with pain associated with appendicitis bend forward or limp as they walk in an attempt to relieve the discomfort. Needless to say, climbers with a history of an appendectomy (appendix removal) are generally unlikely to have appendicitis. Even then, however, a rare condition known as "stump appendicitis" exists, when the stump of the removed appendix becomes infected, mimicking traditional appendicitis. While rare, its incidence is increasing, and surgical authorities feel it is both underreported and underestimated (Kumar 2013). Because of this, appendicitis cannot be completely ruled out even in climbers with a history of appendectomy.

TREAT

Evacuation is needed for anyone believed to have appendicitis. Delay in evacuation could result in a ruptured appendix and the complications it entails (peritonitis). Food should not be given to the patient and drinks should be limited to very small amounts in preparation for surgical intervention. An antibiotic should be started for any patient suspected of having appendicitis. A recent publication (the Non-Operative Treatment for Acute Appendicitis, or NOTA, study) examined whether antibiotics alone could safely and effectively treat uncomplicated appendicitis without surgery. Patients in this study were given amoxicillin/clavulanate (Augmentin®). Results showed that 88% of patients had complete resolution of appendicitis with antibiotics alone. At a two-year re-evaluation, appendicitis had reappeared in 14% of patients, but of these, 64% enjoyed resolution of appendicitis again with another series of antibiotics (Di Saverio 2014). The implication of this study for climbers is that, for extremely remote trips or trips where evacuation may be prolonged, initiation of antibiotics rapidly may temporize or even treat the appendicitis. However, surgery is still the standard of care for appendicitis, and this study only looked at uncomplicated cases of appendicitis, so all cases of possible appendicitis should still prompt as rapid surgical attention as possible.

EVACUATE
Climbers exhibiting symptoms of appendicitis should be evacuated as soon as possible.

Diverticulitis
IDENTIFY
Diverticulitis is an inflammation of a diverticulum (small outpouching) within the colon. It is more common in older climbers and is rarely seen in anyone under 40. It is most commonly located in the left lower quadrant, with symptoms that include nausea, vomiting, abdominal pain, and tenderness. Diarrhea may be present but not profuse as with gastroenteritis. In acute cases there may be a perforation of the intestinal wall, which can result in peritonitis. Signs of peritonitis include abdominal rigidity, high fever, and vomiting. These patients require evacuation. Additionally, blood in the stool is also a sign that the condition may be worsening and will require more immediate attention.

TREAT
Rest, pain relief, and a fluid diet for 24 to 48 hours is recommended. An antibiotic should be given to these patients.

EVACUATE
Evacuation is only necessary if the climber shows signs and symptoms of peritonitis, blood in the stool, or if the patient does not respond to treatment.

Ectopic Pregnancy
IDENTIFY
An ectopic pregnancy occurs when a fertilized egg is implanted in a fallopian tube. Any climbing expedition with women of child-bearing age should carry pregnancy tests, since severe abdominal pain with concern for ectopic pregnancies can easily be ruled out with a negative test. Sudden pain to one side of the lower abdomen is the most common symptom. Other symptoms may include breast tenderness, a menstrual period that is atypical or missing (amenorrhea), pain appearing

in or radiating to the shoulder, and small amounts of vaginal bleeding, usually dark in color.

A female with a ruptured ectopic pregnancy will have the symptoms above as well as weakness, dizziness when standing, high pulse rate, and low blood pressure due to internal blood loss.

TREAT

A ruptured ectopic pregnancy is a medical emergency and evacuation should not be delayed. Sexually active females of childbearing age experiencing any lower abdominal pain should be treated as an ectopic emergency until proven otherwise. IV fluids should be given if available and rescuers should be prepared to start resuscitative procedures en route to definitive medical care.

EVACUATE

This is a medical emergency and evacuation should be expedited, using the fastest means available.

GI Obstruction

IDENTIFY

Obstruction of the intestines causes diffuse, cramping pain across the abdomen. Nausea and vomiting will occur, but may be delayed depending upon the location of the obstruction. Obstruction of the small intestine elicits nausea and vomiting earlier than in the large intestine. The abdomen will be swollen and tender. A complete obstruction will prevent any stool, liquid, or flatulence (gas) passing through the intestinal tract or out the anus. Patients will be dehydrated, have a high heart rate (tachycardia), and low blood pressure (hypotension).

TREAT

There is no effective field treatment to remedy GI obstruction, whatever the cause, but there are many supportive treatments that should be undertaken while evacuation is completed. These include pain relief, rest, hydration by mouth (if vomiting permits), and, if possible, IV hydration.

EVACUATE

Climbers experiencing an intestinal obstruction, whether total or partial, should be evacuated.

Hernia
IDENTIFY

A hernia is defined as the protrusion of a portion of the intestine through a weak area within the abdominal wall. Hernias develop most commonly in the groin (inguinal) area of the lower abdomen and look like a slight abnormal bulge. They also are common at a site of previous abdominal surgery and near the umbilicus. Any climber who suspects a hernia should have it treated prior to leaving on a trip. Most hernias can be reduced (e.g., the intestine can be pushed back into the abdomen), but some become *incarcerated* (trapped). Symptoms of a hernia include swelling or protrusion at the site and general discomfort. Symptoms of an incarcerated hernia are severe pain, vomiting, no passage of stool or flatulence, and abdominal tenderness. The overlying skin is often red and hot to the touch.

TREAT

If the climber is able to reduce the hernia by pushing the intestine back into the abdomen, they should avoid any type of work that might cause them to strain or put tension on their abdomen, such as heavy lifting or carrying a backpack. Analgesia should be given.

EVACUATE

Any climber with an irreducible or incarcerated hernia should be evacuated immediately.

Pelvic Inflammatory Disease (PID)
IDENTIFY

Also known as salpingitis, this genital tract infection can occur in all sexually active females, regardless of age. Roughly 50% of all cases of PID are due to chlamydia. Risk factors for PID include number of sexual partners and the use of an intrauterine contraceptive device (IUD).

Symptoms of an ascending infection include pelvic pain, fever, pain during intercourse, painful menstruation, and GI upset. Sometimes vaginal discharge is apparent and tenderness at the top of the pubic bone may be evident.

TREAT

A combined course of antibiotics is the treatment for PID. The most commonly prescribed combinations include 1) amoxicillin-clavulanic acid or erythromycin and doxycycline, or 2) penicillin, metronidazole, and doxycycline. Analgesia should also be considered for the patient.

EVACUATE

Evacuation is not necessary unless the patient is exhibiting *sepsis* signs and symptoms of systemic infection (discussed further in the sidebar above).

Urinary Tract Infection

IDENTIFY

A urinary tract infection (UTI) is a common problem, especially for female climbers. The most common symptoms include frequent urination and a burning sensation when urinating.

TREAT

The best treatment for a UTI is to increase fluid intake and begin a course of amoxicillin, ciprofloxacin, or trimethoprim-sulfamethoxazole (Bactrim®).

EVACUATE

Evacuation is not needed for this problem unless signs of sepsis are present (see sidebar above).

OTHER ABDOMINAL ISSUES

Constipation
IDENTIFY
Constipation is best described as difficult passage of stool. For climbers, this often occurs due to the change of routine, change in daily foods, lack of adequate water intake, and other dietary changes that occur on trips and expeditions. Constipation can also be a result of "holding" stool rather than defecating, as sometimes occurs on small ledges in roaring storms. Discomfort or feeling of a full or swollen abdomen are the most common symptoms of constipation.

TREAT
The best treatment for constipation is probably to relax a little, increase fluid consumption, and eat fruits, bran-based cereals, and other foods that have high levels of fiber. Severe cases of constipation may lead to fecal impaction—hard stool that is wedged against the rectum. This may require breaking up the stool using a gloved and lubricated finger. No amount of water, laxative, or enema will soften this stool.

EVACUATE
Evacuation is not necessary for constipation or fecal impaction unless the latter cannot be relieved in the field.

GI Bleeding
IDENTIFY
Bleeding from the gastrointestinal tract should be considered a serious problem and addressed immediately. Obvious signs include vomiting or defecating large amounts of red blood, vomit that resembles "coffee grounds," stool that is black or tarry in color, weakness, and signs and symptoms of shock. Patients will exhibit signs and symptoms common to large-volume blood loss such as pale skin, high pulse (tachycardia), low blood pressure (hypotension), confusion, and low urine output. Small amounts of bleeding from the rectum may be related to hemorrhoids or anal fissure (tear of skin at the anus), and these are the only instances where bleeding in the GI tract is not a major concern.

TREAT

The best treatment for GI bleeding is evacuation. Place the patient on their back (supine) with legs elevated, give IV fluids if available, stop any NSAIDs or aspirin, and give H_2 blockers or PPI if available and tolerated.

EVACUATE

Evacuate as soon as possible.

Hemorrhoids

IDENTIFY

Hemorrhoids develop over time but can be exacerbated while on expedition due to the change in routine, food, and prolonged periods of sitting associated with travel. While some can be painful, especially if *prolapsed* (protruding) or *thrombosed* (clotted) outside the anus, generally hemorrhoids are simply an annoyance because of itching and general discomfort. Small amounts of red blood may be seen on toilet paper or outside of stool. If blood is a part of the stool and darker in color, intestinal bleeding may be present.

TREAT

Itching and pain can increase due to hard stool. Staying hydrated by drinking plenty of water is the best treatment in the field and will soften stool. Hemorrhoid creams can help to lessen itching and irritation.

EVACUATE

Evacuation is not needed.

ABDOMINAL TRAUMA

Abdominal trauma comes in two forms: blunt and penetrating. While blunt abdominal injury is most commonly associated with motor vehicle accidents, 9% of all cases are from falls. While abdominal injuries in trauma patients are relatively rare (1%), they do occur, and climbers should understand the signs and symptoms associated with both blunt and penetrating injuries.

Blunt Trauma

IDENTIFY

Although there are no known statistics of blunt abdominal trauma for climbers, statistics from the general population indicate that blunt trauma is more common than penetrating trauma. The major concern for climbers who have suffered abdominal trauma due to a fall is *intra-abdominal hemorrhage* (bleeding within the abdominal cavity). This bleeding is difficult to identify, as a physical exam is often unreliable. Patients with blunt abdominal trauma frequently have other serious and distracting injuries. A "distracting" injury refers to a head injury or other significant injury that can reduce a person's ability to sense pain and tenderness, either directly (e.g., a head injury) or due to pain that is severe and overwhelms other sources of pain (e.g., an open leg fracture distracting the patient from their also-present abdominal pain).

Ninety percent of all blunt abdominal injuries occur to solid organs, namely the liver or spleen (Figure 1-1). There is also the possibility of an abdominal shearing injury related to severe deceleration during climbing injuries. This type of deceleration can cause thrombosis or tearing of the renal artery. Regardless of cause, intra-abdominal hemorrhage is a life-threatening injury.

The most common signs and symptoms of an intra-abdominal hemorrhage are decreased blood pressure, increased pulse, abdominal pain and tenderness, bruising, abrasions, and increasing abdominal size. There are some visible indicators that can assist in identifying the location of intra-abdominal bleeding. These are listed in Figure 7-1.

FIGURE 7-1. CLINICAL INDICATORS OF INTRAPERITONEAL BLEED

Kehr Sign	Pain at left shoulder	Suggestive of splenic rupture
Cullen Sign	Bruising at umbilicus	Retroperitoneal bleed
Turner Sign	Bruising at flank	Retroperitoneal bleed

TREAT

The only field treatment available for patients suffering blunt abdominal injury is to give fluids by IV, stabilize all other life-threatening injuries, and evacuate the patient to advanced medical care as soon as possible.

EVACUATE

Evacuation should be immediate and the process started as soon as possible to prevent death.

Penetrating Trauma

IDENTIFY

There are no statistics related to high-energy penetrating abdominal trauma for climbers. However, there are certainly incidents of penetrating/puncture wounds, as is evidenced by the 54 reported incidents since 1984 in *Accidents in North American Mountaineering* (MacDonald 2015). Most penetrating abdominal trauma in the United States is due to gunshot wounds or stabbings, which are unlikely to occur in the climbing environment. But climbers do use items that can cause low-energy penetrating injuries. These items include ice axes, crampons, ice screws, carabiners, and various other forms of climbing protection.

Seventy percent of deaths from penetrating abdominal trauma occur within the first six hours. Most of the remainder occur within a period of 72 hours. Thus, it is essential to stabilize injured climbers and evacuate them as soon as possible. In addition to intra-abdominal hemorrhage, the other concern with puncture wounds to the abdomen is peritonitis from organ contents or blood spilled into the abdomen.

TREAT

Stabilizing the patient, with a focus on life-threatening injuries, is the first step of treatment. Depending upon the embedded object, it may be best to secure it in place rather than removing it. Irrigation around the penetration site is helpful as long as it does not push organic material deeper into the wound. Control any external bleeding present at the wound site. If a lengthy evacuation is anticipated, consider antibiotic use if available. Patients must be evacuated to a medical center for a complete evaluation.

EVACUATE

Evacuation should occur as soon as possible to prevent death or serious injury.

INFECTIOUS DISEASES AFFECTING THE GASTROINTESTINAL SYSTEM

Gastrointestinal upset, diarrhea, and dysentery account for up to 33% of all medical problems on overseas climbing trips. Like constipation, diarrhea can occur due to changes brought on by travel, including changes in diet, the stress of travel, water consumption from a variety of sources, and of course, infection. Many of the diseases discussed in this section could be avoided through following these rules (mentioned at the beginning of this chapter but repeated here because they are so important):

1. Good hand hygiene
2. Proper food preparation
3. Proper water disinfection (see Appendix E)

FIGURE 7-2. ORGANISMS THAT CAUSE DIARRHEA

The following table divides the organisms discussed within this chapter into four categories based upon the presence (or lack thereof) of blood in stool and accompanying fever.

DIARRHEA— NO BLOOD, NO FEVER	DIARRHEA— NO BLOOD, FEVER
Travelers' Diarrhea *(E. Coli)*	Salmonellosis
Cryptosporidiosis	Cholera
Norovirus	
Giardiasis	
DIARRHEA—BLOOD, NO/OCCASIONAL FEVER	**DIARRHEA— BLOOD, FEVER**
Amebiasis	Shigellosis
	Campylobacter Enteritis

Sources: Hawker J, et al. Communicable Disease Control and Health Protection Handbook. 3rd ed. Chicester, UK. Wiley-Blackwell; 2012.
Johnson C, Anderson S, Dallimore J, et al. Oxford Handbook of Expedition and Wilderness Medicine. Oxford, UK. Oxford University Press; 2010.

Diarrhea and Dysentery

Diarrhea, though easy to prevent and fairly easy to treat, is as likely to stop an expedition in its tracks as an unstable serac above the only available line of advance. Some general rules for both prevention and treatment of gastrointestinal upset and disease will be discussed, followed by detailed information on the most common pathogens that cause diarrhea and dysentery.

IDENTIFY

Diarrhea is defined as four or more loose stools within a 24-hour period. Organisms causing diarrhea are described in Figure 7-2.

Dysentery is severe diarrhea that includes blood or mucus in the stool. Both can be debilitating, but dysentery is considered much more serious. By far the most dangerous element of these conditions is dehydration. Figure 7-3 describes how to identify moderate or severe dehydration.

FIGURE 7-3. SIGNS AND SYMPTOMS OF MODERATE AND SEVERE DEHYDRATION

MODERATE DEHYDRATION	SEVERE DEHYDRATION
Restlessness/irritability	Lethargy/unconsciousness
Dry mouth/tongue	Very dry mouth/tongue
Increased thirst	Weak or absent pulse
Skin returns to normal slowly after pinched	Low blood pressue
Decreased urine	Skin returns to normal slowly (tenting) when pinched
Sunken eyes	Minimal or no urine

Source: Centers for Disease Control and Prevention (CDC) "Rehydration Therapy"

TREAT

Rehydration is the most important thing for diarrhea or dysentery. Oral rehydration solutions (ORS) should be included in all overseas medical kits for climbers. ORS may not be found in small villages or with other climbing parties. Most diarrhea and GI upsets will resolve within 48 hours and the use of antibiotics should only be considered if symptoms persist. Acetaminophen is recommended in general if there is accompanying fever or abdominal pain. Loperamide (Imodium®) is useful to limit diarrhea if needed (e.g., in a bivy during a storm or for a time-sensitive evacuation where stops should be reduced) but can also be associated with significant complications, so should only be used as directed and for as short a period as critically needed (Davis 2018). Generally, rehydration is more important than preventing fluid loss from diarrhea, and in this sense stopping vomiting may be much more important, as most rehydration is done orally. Ondansetron is a prescription medication with relatively minimal side effects that may help reduce vomiting and which can be administered as an oral dissolving tablet (not requiring swallowing and absorption, which can be difficult for a vomiting patient).

EVACUATE

Seek medical attention if diarrhea continues and the patient has the following signs and symptoms: severe dehydration (Figure 7-3), fever greater than 40°C (104°F), high fever lasting more than 48 hours, diarrhea lasting more than four days, inability to drink and keep down fluids, and presence of dysentery.

Included in the following section are some of the more common organisms that affect climbers both in the United States and abroad. This list is not exhaustive, but it includes most of the usual suspects that cause diarrhea and dysentery.

Traveler's Diarrhea

Often caused by a strain of the bacteria *Escherichia coli* (*E. coli*) and referred to as "traveler's diarrhea," this is a common affliction of those traveling in Mexico, Southeast Asia, and South America. Most commonly acquired through contaminated food or water, traveler's diarrhea can also be transmitted through contaminated eating utensils and dishware.

IDENTIFY

Watery, soft diarrhea is the main symptom. Climbers may also experience abdominal cramps/pain, nausea, vomiting, fatigue, and on occasion, fever. These symptoms usually last between two and five days.

TREAT

Traveler's diarrhea is often self-limiting and antibiotics are usually not needed, though a single dose of ciprofloxacin may help. An oral rehydration solution is recommended to prevent dehydration and keep electrolytes in balance.

EVACUATE

There is usually no need for evacuation unless dehydration becomes severe (Figure 7-3).

Cryptosporidiosis

Best known by the nickname "crypto," this is a common enemy of the climber. Often caused by untreated or unfiltered water, the protozoa *Cryptosporidium* cause acute bouts of diarrhea. Cryptosporidiosis can also be acquired from infected individuals or contaminated food. It is especially harmful to climbers who are immunocompromised. Immunocompromise is sometimes a long-term condition if a climber has AIDS, takes routine steroid medications, or for other medical reasons, but climbers may also be temporarily immunocompromised at the end of a long expedition simply because food, drink, and rest have been limited.

IDENTIFY

Symptoms include watery diarrhea, abdominal pain, anorexia, nausea, weight loss, bloating, and in few cases, fever.

TREAT

Crypto is self-limiting, and antibiotics are of no use. Maintaining hydration is key, as is rest and pain relief. It usually resolves within two weeks, but can reoccur for months to years afterwards.

EVACUATE

There is no need to evacuate unless severe dehydration occurs (Figure 7-3).

Norovirus

The genus *Norovirus*, of which the only species is the *Norwalk* virus, is an increasing cause of travel-related diarrhea. Some estimate that it accounts for between 3% and 17% of diarrhea among returning travelers. Media attention has focused on recent outbreaks on cruise ships, but this viral illness often occurs in campsites and other areas where people live close together. Contaminated food and drink are frequently the source of this virus, though contaminated ice, shellfish, and prepared cold foods (sandwiches/salads) have been implicated in outbreaks.

IDENTIFY

Diarrhea and violent vomiting are the signature symptoms of *Norovirus* infection, along with abdominal cramps and, in some cases, a low-grade fever.

TREAT

This illness is self-limiting. Focus should be on hydration status of the patient. *Do not use* antibiotics: They are *not* effective on viruses.

EVACUATE

There is no need to evacuate unless severe dehydration occurs (Figure 7-3).

Giardiasis

Giardia intestinalis is a scourge of climbers both within the United States and overseas. This protozoal parasite infects through fecal contamination of food and water or by contact with infected persons or objects (contaminated clothing or hard surfaces). Nicknamed "backpacker's disease" and "beaver fever," it is common among outdoor enthusiasts in the United States. Of importance for alpinists, *Giardia* is common in Nepal.

IDENTIFY

Most commonly, patients will have persistent pale, greasy diarrhea that has a particularly bad smell and may contain mucus (no blood or pus). Other symptoms include abdominal cramps and pain, bloating, flatulence that smells strongly of sulfur, nausea, fatigue, and anorexia.

TREAT

Treatment is with antibiotics. A ten-day course of metronidazole (Flagyl®) is most effective. Maintain hydration and adequate rest.

EVACUATE

Evacuation is rarely needed unless proper hydration is not maintained and signs or symptoms of dehydration appear (Figure 7-3).

Salmonellosis

This condition is caused by the bacterial genus *Salmonella,* and includes *Salmonella typhi,* discussed in detail later under "Typhoid." The most common forms of *Salmonella* are acquired by eating undercooked poultry and from eggs. This infection occurs worldwide.

IDENTIFY

The most common signs and symptoms of non-typhoid salmonellosis are fever, abdominal cramps and pain, and severe diarrhea that may sometimes contains blood or mucus.

TREAT

Staying hydrated is key. Antibiotics are not usually needed for salmonellosis, and symptoms should resolve in four to seven days. *Salmonella* has become resistant to many antibiotics, but ciprofloxacin and ampicillin are recommended for severe cases that spread beyond the intestines.

EVACUATE

Patients need rest and hydration and will rarely require evacuation unless they are unable to maintain adequate hydration and signs or symptoms of dehydration appear (Figure 7-3).

Cholera

Caused by the organism *Vibrio cholerae,* this disease causes massive amounts of watery diarrhea. It is transmitted through water and food contaminated with fecal material from persons with the active disease. A cholera vaccine is available and offers 60–80% immunity for a period of three months.

IDENTIFY

Patients will have prolific "rice water" diarrhea that is watery and has a "fishy" odor. This diarrhea, along with vomiting, can cause massive fluid and electrolyte loss. Tachycardia, hypotension, and thirst will be present. The large loss of fluid and electrolytes could cause a cascade of effects that include *hypovolemia* (low volume in blood vessels, such as from loss of fluid from bleeding or dehydration), shock, and death.

TREAT

Rehydration is key, both by mouth and by IV solutions. It is important to ensure that the patient receives electrolytes during rehydration treatment. Antibiotics can help shorten the duration of the illness. Tetracycline is the most suitable choice, and doxycycline and ciprofloxacin can also be considered.

EVACUATE

In remote areas, patients should be evacuated to medical care that will provide adequate rehydration and electrolyte replacement.

Amebiasis

Amebiasis (amebic dysentery) can be an acute or chronic protozoal infection of the intestines caused by *Entamoeba histolytica*. While 90% of infected persons show no symptoms, the effects of the disease can be very widespread for some. Amebiasis can occur anywhere in the world but is more common in tropical regions. This infection is usually acquired by eating undercooked meats or drinking contaminated water.

IDENTIFY

Acute amebic dysentery can cause sudden high fever (40°C [104°F]), chills, abdominal cramping/pain/tenderness, diarrhea with blood and mucus, and excessive gas. Chronic amebic dysentery will cause irregular bouts of diarrhea that will recur multiple times within a year. Lesser forms of all the symptoms of acute amebic dysentery accompany it. There can be more advanced complications of amebiasis. Some of these rare complications include hepatic abscess, infection of the lungs, heart, and brain.

TREAT

Examination of stool by a trained medical professional is needed for positive identification. Metronidazole (Flagyl®) is the antibiotic of choice for this infection.

EVACUATE

As only ten percent of infected climbers will show symptoms, evacuation is not necessary; however, these ten percent may need advanced care depending upon the severity of the infection and resulting symptoms.

Shigellosis

Shigellosis is also known as bacillary dysentery and causes severe diarrhea. There are four specific groups of shigellosis, all of which are treated in a similar fashion. The *Shigella* bacterium is transmitted by fecal and oral routes, and usually by direct contact with contaminated items or through eating or drinking from contaminated food or water.

IDENTIFY

Average incubation period from exposure to signs and symptoms is 72 hours. Common signs and symptoms include cramping and sometimes intense abdominal pain, headache, and fever. Diarrhea is often explosive and contains blood, mucus, and pus. Dehydration should be expected with a corresponding decrease in urine output.

TREAT

Care to avoid disease transmission should be taken when treating these patients. Any soiled clothing or bedsheets should be isolated. Replacement of lost fluids is of the utmost importance and may require IV solutions. ORS should be used to counter dehydration. Antibiotic treatment may be useful; ciprofloxacin or trimethoprim-sulfamethoxazole (Bactrim®) are the most useful agents.

EVACUATE

Climbers suffering from shigellosis will require intensive rehydration that may only be accomplished by IV solutions at a medical facility. Evacuation is necessary.

Campylobacter Enteritis (Campylobacteriosis)

Campylobacter is the most common cause of bacterial diarrhea within the United States, and is common in the summer months. It is most often transmitted by contaminated food (particularly raw poultry), fresh produce, water, unpasteurized milk, and through contact with stool from an infected person or animal.

IDENTIFY

Beginning 48 to 96 hours after infection, patients will suffer from diarrhea with blood that can sometimes be severe. Abdominal pain and cramping with nausea, vomiting, and fever also may occur.

TREAT

Unless severe, campylobacteriosis often resolves without treatment. For severe cases, ciprofloxacin or erythromycin should be used. Patients should rest and ensure that they remain hydrated.

EVACUATE

There usually is no need to evacuate patients with campylobacteriosis.

Typhoid

Also known as enteric fever and caused by the bacterium *Salmonella typhi*, this disease affects more than 21 million people worldwide. The risk of typhoid is high in southern Asia (including Nepal and India) and also in Southeast Asia, Africa, the Caribbean, and Central and South America.

Typhoid is often acquired from contaminated food (especially shellfish) or from water contaminated by infected human feces. The best treatment is prevention, and a typhoid vaccine is recommended to prevent infection.

IDENTIFY

Signs and symptoms include fever, malaise, diffuse abdominal pain/tenderness, and constipation. This will usually begin seven to fourteen days after infection, with fever increasing in the evenings of the second week. Sweating, chills, continued weakness, delirium, increasing abdominal pain (with constipation or diarrhea), and a rose-colored abdominal rash will be present in the first two weeks. Symptoms will steadily worsen through the third and fourth weeks.

TREAT

Antibiotics are the first line of treatment. Cefixime (Suprax®) or azithromycin (Zithromax®) are the drugs of choice. NSAIDs or acetaminophen should be used for fever and pain control. Rest and ORS are appropriate.

EVACUATE

Patients suspected of having typhoid should seek medical attention as soon as possible.

CHAPTER 8

CHEST AND RESPIRATORY ISSUES

While we often focus on extremities or orthopedic injuries when considering climbing accidents, a review of climbing data reveals that many accidents are categorized as "other" or include medical diagnoses in addition to traumatic musculoskeletal injuries (Jones 2014, MacDonald 2015, Némethy 2015). Also, many traumatic injuries have a primary medical component such as cardiac or pulmonary disease (National Park Service 2016). This chapter considers such illnesses and injuries in the chest region.

MEDICAL CONDITIONS OF THE CHEST

Coronary Artery Disease (CAD), Acute Coronary Syndrome (ACS), Sudden Cardiac Death (SCD), and Dysrhythmias

CAD, the leading cause of death in the United States, occurs when the arteries that supply blood to the heart muscle develop reduced flow along their inner walls. This process, known as atherosclerosis, occurs over time as cholesterol and other plaque materials continually narrow the myocardial vessels and thus blood flow. Because blood carries oxygen, the decreased flow begins to reduce the oxygen supply to the heart muscle. According to the American Heart Association's National Health and Nutrition Examination survey (2009–2012), the prevalence of CAD is exceedingly rare between the ages of 20 and 39. Between the ages of 40 and 59, however, that risk is multiplied nearly ten times. For men at age 60, that risk has increased at least 30 times (Mozaffarian 2015).

IDENTIFY

Climbers with CAD may develop heart-related chest pain (angina) from exertion. This is due to increased oxygen demand by the heart during these activities. Occasionally, there are no warning symptoms when one of the vessel plaques ruptures and completely blocks flow in the associated coronary artery. Abrupt loss of flow through a vessel results in *myocardial ischemia* (heart muscle damage), which can lead to a full *myocardial infarction* (heart muscle death, popularly known as a *heart attack*). This spectrum, beginning with ischemia and leading to infarction, is called *acute coronary syndrome* (ACS). Climbers and especially alpinists—who more frequently must maintain a continued aerobic exertion—should be wary of angina associated with exertion. If angina is suspected, they should have it evaluated prior to expedition participation. This is especially relevant for aspiring climbers who are relatively untrained and deconditioned, but who have easy access to larger alpine goals near large urban or metropolitan centers (e.g., Mt. Hood, Mt. Rainier). The best strategy for treatment of coronary disease in a mountain setting is prevention and screening. Assessing a climber's risk for coronary disease is something that can be accomplished through their primary care provider (PCP). A PCP will try to identify and correct the most relevant risk factors, including hypertension (elevated blood pressure), hyperlipidemia (elevated cholesterol), obesity, sedentary lifestyle, diabetes, smoking, age, gender, and family history.

ACS is not the only heart problem climbers may face. Although rare, sudden cardiac death (SCD) is well known in the athletic world. The sudden death of otherwise healthy high school and college athletes due to SCD has generated significant public awareness of this condition. It has also prompted the placement of automated external defibrillators (AEDs) in many public areas. Additionally, multiple problems with heart valves exist. The demands of mountaineering activities and potential for dehydration or electrolyte imbalance may place climbers at increased risk for heart failure and fluid accumulation. Finally, these same factors may also play a role in the development of *dysrhythmias* (abnormal heart rates or rhythms).

TREAT

Assuming these issues have been addressed, managing coronary (heart-related) events during climbing requires awareness of ACS symptoms. These symptoms include angina that may wax or wane with activity; radiation of pain to the jaw, back, shoulder blades, stomach, or arms; nausea; vomiting; and sweating. Climbers experiencing ACS may also describe light-headedness. Other signs include abnormal blood pressure (hypertension or hypotension) or obvious breathlessness. The Wilderness Medical Society (WMS), the American Heart Association, and the American College of Cardiology all recommend the following initial medications for treatment of suspected ACS: aspirin, nitrates, beta-blockers, and clopidogrel (Plavix®) (Forgey 2006). A more robust medical kit carried by a large expedition might contain these medications, but none might be available to the average climber. Other NSAIDs do not convey the same effect as aspirin and cannot be substituted in its place. WMS has practice guidelines with recommendations for ACS care that are relevant for climbers (Forgey 2006), described in sidebar above. Recommendation grade for these guidelines is 1B.

If the patient becomes unresponsive and loses pulses or stops breathing, CPR should be started unless circumstances prevent this intervention. CPR is discussed in further detail in Chapter 2. In general, wilderness medical authorities agree that CPR should be discontinued if rescuers are endangered, care is transitioned to a higher level of care such as EMS responders, the patient awakens, or there is no response after 30 minutes of vigorous CPR (Forgey 2006, Johnson 2015).

EVACUATE

If the signs or symptoms described above are present and suspected to be due to ACS, particularly if they are new in onset, immediate evacuation must occur. Evacuation should not be delayed, even if this requires that the patient walk. Exertion should be limited, but the best strategy for a good outcome is to reach definitive care quickly. With regard to dysrhythmias, outside of electrocardiogram (ECG) interpretation, it would be challenging to adequately determine if they are safe or not in the backcountry environment. In the event that palpitations are newly experienced while climbing, especially if they appear together with angina, the climber should be evacuated.

Asthma and Chronic Obstructive Pulmonary Disease (COPD)

Roughly 8% of the United States population suffers from asthma, resulting in missed school and lost workdays. COPD is described by the Global Burden of Disease study as somewhere between the third to fifth leading cause of death worldwide (Mannino 2006). Climbing can be affected by both, particularly when other environmental factors play a role.

IDENTIFY

Asthma is a chronic reactive disease in which the airways become swollen and inflamed when in the presence of certain inhaled substances and stimuli. In response, the muscles surrounding the airways begin to constrict and make breathing more difficult. COPD is a progressive disease in which the air sacs of the lungs become dilated and the airway walls become thick and inflamed with increased mucous production. The presence of cold air in an alpine environment, pollution in the valley below, or allergic reaction can each precipitate a worsening of asthma or COPD symptoms. COPD is also significantly impacted by simultaneous infection such as pneumonia. This could be particularly troublesome in third-world nations where fecal material or other hazardous chemicals are utilized as cooking or heating fuel without proper ventilation.

TREAT

In general, most climbers and alpinists who have these chronic respiratory processes are aware of their limitations and have a specific regimen in place for treatment of symptoms and prevention of a flare-up. In optimizing treatment, both short- and long-term therapies should be employed. Care should be made to protect inhalers from environmental mishaps resulting in decreased function, such as being crushed in the bottom of a pack or frozen in an alpine environment. As asthma symptoms may be affected by an allergic reaction, all climbers should be trained in the use of epinephrine administration. We feel epinephrine should be a mandatory part of any climbing medical kit. In fact, chalk bags are now made with a sleeve that can hold a generic epinephrine auto-injector, such as Vertical Medicine Resource's High & Dry Kit.* Anaphylaxis is addressed more completely in Chapter 2. When dealing with both entities of asthma and allergic reaction, additional treatments in a climbing environment include an inhaled bronchodilator (such as albuterol), an antihistamine (such as diphenhydramine), and corticosteroids (such as oral prednisone and inhaled fluticasone).

Management of these entities in the mountain environment dictates appropriate pre-trip planning through a PCP or pulmonologist. Additional time on expeditions to accommodate teammates during acute exacerbations should be expected. Mitigating risk of exacerbations by proper medication usage and using barriers to filter inhaled materials (e.g., face masks against pollutants or balaclavas to buffer cold air) are of benefit. In the case of acute exacerbations, supplemental oxygen (if available) may be helpful.

EVACUATE

Evacuation must be considered when available resources and medications are exhausted or if the patient appears to become unstable in any way.

Pneumonia

It is not uncommon for climbers, especially those pursuing faraway summits, to find themselves in poor accommodations. Alpinists en route to distant base camps often travel in densely populated public transportation, sleep in areas contaminated with fecal material or fungus, travel to altitude, and are often fatigued and jet-lagged by travel. Upper respiratory infections and pneumonia are common ailments given these circumstances. Pneumonia exists in many forms, including bacterial, viral, and fungal subtypes, but in the climbing environment diagnosis is

---

* http://www.vertical-medicine.com/products-services/the-cache-vmr-s-online-store

made and treatment initiated based on clinical findings rather than test results showing the source of the pneumonia.

IDENTIFY

Signs and symptoms of pneumonia include chest pain with breathing, muscle aches, cough with or without sputum production (but a foul-smelling or thick productive cough is more characteristic of pneumonia), fever, and shortness of breath, particularly with exertion. Listening to the chest wall may reveal abnormal breath sounds in the affected area. Sputum production (if present) may be yellow, green, or streaked with a rusty color (blood-tinged), all of which suggest an ongoing infection. Chronic, pre-existing asthma or COPD may also worsen pneumonia symptoms.

TREAT

Treatment in the climbing environment is supportive. Cough suppressants, medications to break up mucus, and over-the-counter analgesics such as acetaminophen are all appropriate. Antibiotics should be considered in the presence of the above findings, especially fever. An established pre-expedition relationship with a PCP may permit a climber to carry antibiotics. Doxycycline, azithromycin, or levofloxacin would be appropriate choices in the absence of specific bacterial identification.

EVACUATE

If improvement does not occur with treatment, the patient should be evacuated. Partial retreat to the next lower base camp with adequate recovery time may eliminate the need for full evacuation. If exercise tolerance remains diminished, evacuation to more definitive care is indicated.

TRAUMATIC CONDITIONS OF THE CHEST

The very nature of both activity and environment exposes climbers and alpinists to risk of chest trauma. Taking a "whipper" off an extended lead or tumbling down a rock-covered alpine slope are merely two examples where injury to the torso may occur.

Rib fractures

Rib fractures are often the result of chest trauma. Individually, they are not a significant risk to health. However, when combined with multiple rib fractures where they cause flail chest (discussed later) or soft tissue injury to underlying organs, they can be dangerous.

IDENTIFY

Rib fractures result from a direct blow to the chest wall and can be quite painful and limit continued climbing due to pain. They make deep breathing very uncomfortable for both general aerobic maneuvers and particularly with "pressure breathing" necessary as alpinists gain elevation. Furthermore, as the torso is positioned and torqued to accomplish off-width, crack, or chimney maneuvers in rock climbing, the rib fracture sites are often painful.

TREAT

Historically, some have suggested that snug circumferential splinting of the torso may help mitigate pain, but this risks restricting adequate ventilation and may also contribute to pneumonia following the injury, so we do not recommend it. In fact, patients may "splint" a broken rib themselves by not breathing deeply by choice, which can lead to those same complications. The injured climber, although uncomfortable, should be encouraged to take ten deep breaths/hour, and strong analgesia should be administered if available, including NSAIDs (which will also help with inflammation), acetaminophen, and, if available, prescription opioids.

EVACUATE

Climbers with broken ribs should be evacuated. This is non-urgent unless pain control is severely inadequate or complications are present (as described below).

Flail Chest

Flail chest is a complication of multiple rib fractures in which rib segments move inappropriately with breathing.

IDENTIFY

One segment of the chest wall will appear to be "inhaling" or expanding while the rest of the non-injured chest will be "exhaling" or shrinking.

TREAT

Splinting of the chest with non-circumferential padded dressings may help facilitate breathing. Additionally, it may be helpful for the patient to lie on the injured side to assist inspiratory efforts on the uninjured side.

EVACUATE

Injured climbers with this condition must be evacuated.

Pneumothorax

Pneumothorax occurs when the outside layer of the lung has been disrupted due to chest trauma and air leaving the lung partially exits through the trachea (the appropriate route) and partially exits into the chest cavity (an inappropriate route). With continued respiration, the growing air pocket in the chest cavity begins to collapse the affected lung. Eventually this pressure may begin to exert a force across the entire chest, ultimately compressing the heart vessels and causing the heart to stop (cardiac arrest).

IDENTIFY

Classical signs (not always present and often difficult to identify in the field) include absent breath sounds on the affected side, trachea deviation away from the affected lung, and swollen neck veins. The patient will often complain of pain with inspiration, and an asymmetrically expanded chest wall may be present. A variant of this condition is an "open pneumothorax," also known as a "sucking chest wound." In this form, the trauma causes an opening in the chest wall that communicates with the lung cavity and allows air to enter via the opening in addition to the mouth, becoming trapped in the same way as the closed pneumothorax.

TREAT

In the case of a "sucking" open wound in the chest wall, consider a tight, and ideally occlusive, dressing taped to the chest wall on three of its four sides. This will function as a one-way valve to allow air to escape. These types of dressings have been fabricated from sandwich bags and freeze-dried meal packaging in the climbing environment, and can be held in place with climber's tape.

Unless promptly treated with a chest tube or needle decompression (only appropriate for trained healthcare providers, but possible in the field), any type of pneumothorax may progress to shock and death.

EVACUATE

This injury must be rapidly evacuated.

Cardiac Tamponade

Cardiac tamponade occurs when the sac containing the heart fills with blood or other fluid, often as the result of blunt trauma or a rapid deceleration injury (e.g., rappelling off a rope end). Such an injury is often fatal.

IDENTIFY

A slow bleed into the heart sac is often missed even by skilled clinicians in a hospital setting. Eventually, the more classic signs of muffled heart sounds, swollen neck veins, and hypotension may be found.

TREAT

In the field, in situations where cardiac arrest is imminent or has occurred, providers trained in the technique and with a sufficiently long needle can perform an emergency intervention known as pericardiocentesis to drain fluid out of the pericardial sac. Otherwise, the best treatment is rapid evacuation.

EVACUATE

Treatment is evacuation, diagnostic imaging, and rapid surgical intervention.

CHAPTER 9

WOUNDS AND BURNS

While the two most common types of climbing injuries are chronic issues of the upper extremities and traumatic injuries to the lower extremities, wounds such as abrasions and lacerations are also very common. Falls on rock or ice or a self-arrest in ice and snow can cause severe abrasions. Rock fall and impact can cause severe lacerations, and ice axes, tools, carabiners, and branches can cause deep puncture wounds. An understanding of wound management, including methods to stop bleeding, cleanse and bandage injuries, and prevent infection, is a must for today's climbing community.

The American Alpine Club's *Accidents in North American Mountaineering* (now *Accidents in North American Climbing*) has compiled data on climbing accidents annually since 1952. In a recent 30-year period (1984–2014), there have been 822 recorded lacerations, 402 abrasions, and 54 puncture wounds included in the accident descriptions (Simon 2016). Two studies found that lacerations made up between 12 and 19% of total climbing injuries (Gerdes 2006, Nelson 2009). These statistics reflect incidents that occur during actual climbing and do not include approaches to climbing areas. Other studies that focused on a broader scope of outdoor activities (mainly hiking) found that wounds were more common in the outdoor population. The National Outdoor Leadership School (NOLS) gathered data between 1984 and 1989 and again from 1999 and 2002 and found that soft tissue damage accounted for approximately 30% of all outdoor injuries (Leeman 2003). Non-gym climbers spend a large amount of time in the outdoors, specifically hiking to and from crags and on long approaches common for many mountaineering objectives. These studies indicate that basic knowledge regarding wound care is critical.

The most common types of wounds are abrasions, lacerations, punc-

FIGURE 9-1. BASICS OF WOUND CARE

STOP bleeding

IRRIGATE the wound

CLOSE if needed

BANDAGE to protect

EVACUATE if needed

ture wounds, burns, and animal bites and stings. In addition to these common wilderness wounds, climbers often suffer from flappers, split tips, blisters, worn/smooth tips, and callus formation. These specific skin-related injuries are covered in Chapter 10.

Wounds are generally subdivided into three types based upon level of cleanliness: clean, dirty, and contaminated. A clean wound is one that occurs on a relatively clean portion of the body (arm, leg, torso) with a low bacteria count. An example of a clean wound would be a knife cut on the arm. A dirty wound occurs in an area of high bacteria count such as the armpit or groin, or is a wound that is not cleaned for longer than six hours. A contaminated wound is one that contains, or is covered in, dirt or other organic material, or a wound that is already infected. The delineator between these categories is bacteria count. As the potential for bacterial contamination increases, so does the probability of infection.

The primary goals of all wound management are to stop bleeding, cleanse the wound to reduce bacteria count and possibility of infection, reduce the pain or discomfort caused by the wound, minimize loss of function, and mitigate further effects of the wound such as scarring. These steps are discussed in general below and in Figure 9-1, with additional detailed information pertaining to specific types of wounds later in the chapter.

The rescuer should also be aware of the danger of exposure to blood and body fluids while treating an injured climber. Protective gear, specifically some form of barrier gloves (usually made of nitrile or latex), is essential. These protect a rescuer from blood-borne pathogens such as hepatitis and Human Immunodeficiency Virus (HIV). Always dispose of bloody materials in a waterproof sealable container. Wash your hands after removing gloves; use either soap and water or an alcohol-based solution. Always use soap and water if your hands are visibly soiled.

ASSESSMENT

As stated in Chapter 1, a thorough history of both the accident and the patient should be obtained. It is critical to focus on life-threatening injuries first and not allow minor injuries to misdirect focus. For example, only profusely bleeding wounds, especially "spurting" wounds indicative of a severed artery, fit the life-threatening category for bleeding wounds. These should be addressed immediately. The rescuer should continue assessment only once control of bleeding is accomplished and other life-threatening issues are resolved.

Once a complete assessment has been performed and any life-threatening injuries are addressed, a specific examination of the wound should be completed. This includes visualizing the wound to ascertain its depth, structures involved, and amount of organic material located within it. Anatomic locations of concern include involvement of a joint, exposure of tendons or bone, and cuts to the face. CSM should be checked distally from the wound if there is concern of vascular, nerve, or tendon damage.

HEMORRHAGE CONTROL

While most wounds require little in the way of hemorrhage control, some will bleed significantly and require *hemostasis* (bleeding control) to prevent blood loss. The first method to control bleeding is direct pressure. It should be applied for a minimum of five minutes with an intense focus on the site of the bleeding. Recent studies showed that focused direct pressure resulted in 180 mmHg of pressure applied to the wound (WMS recommendation grade 1B) (Quinn 2014). This figure is important as it exceeds the usual range of *systolic blood pressure* (SBP, the top number on a blood pressure reading, representing the force of blood flow during heart contraction). Exceeding SBP is vital for successful hemostasis. This pressure should be applied by placing the cleanest available material over the wound.

If bleeding is controlled using direct pressure, a pressure dressing should be placed over the wound. An adjunct to direct pressure is elevation of the wound, and while there are no studies that validate this technique, no harm will be done to the patient and it may provide some value to hemostasis (WMS recommendation grade 2C) (Quinn 2014). In the past, pressure points have also been taught as a hemostatic adjunct. This is no longer the case, as hemorrhage control using this technique is extremely difficult, requires anatomic knowledge of arterial location, and takes away valuable time from more effective methods.

Hemostatic gauze and bandages are also becoming more prevalent. Some of the most common brands include QuikClot®, HemCon®, Celox®, and Curad BloodStop®. Depending upon the brand, these dressings contain kaolin, chitosan, or cellulose. Care should be taken in patients with shellfish allergies, as chitosan is derived from shellfish. Hemostatic dressings should be used in conjunction with direct pressure, and may require training in wound packing to work properly. The Wilderness Medical Society (WMS) guidelines for wound care utilize a recommendation grade of 1B for hemostatic agent use for hemorrhage control (Quinn 2014).

For severe bleeding or arterial bleeds that cannot be controlled using direct pressure and hemostatic agents and are present in an extremity, a tourniquet should be considered. In cases where bleeding is spurting (suggestive of an arterial bleed) or extremely rapid, a tourniquet should be contemplated within the first 30 seconds if direct pressure is not controlling bleeding, or even be applied prior to other intervention. Great gains in knowledge of tourniquet use have come from military experience in Afghanistan and Iraq. This increase in understanding has saved untold lives and limbs, and has led to a better understanding of the effectiveness and limitations of tourniquets. According to WMS guidelines, the use of a tourniquet is an "effective means to control arterial bleeding and should be considered the primary intervention to control life-threatening arterial bleeds in the extremity" (recommendation grade 1A) (Quinn 2014). There are many tourniquets available for purchase, with the two most common types being the Combat Application Tourniquet (C-A-T®) and the SOF® Tactical Tourniquet (SOF®-T). While these are only moderately expensive ($25–$30, less than the cost of an average single cam), they are not commonly carried by climbers or mountaineers. Therefore, it is useful to know how to apply an improvised tourniquet, whether as a primary intervention or as a stopgap technique to control bleeding and allow for proper placement of a pressure dressing.

While the WMS guidelines mentioned above advocate the "use of appropriate tourniquets by appropriately trained individuals," they do not address the use of improvised tourniquets (Quinn 2014). A review article published in the the *Journal of Trauma and Acute Care Surgery* in January 2015 identified improvised tourniquets as being as capable of occluding arterial bleeding as commercial devices, though the authors conceded that they are recognized as more painful (Stewart 2015). As described in Chapter 1, blood is a finite resource in the wilderness. Based upon the current literature, we advocate the use of improvised tourniquets in order to save lives. See sidebar on next page for a detailed explanation of a field-expedient tourniquet that utilizes a standard climbing harness.

IRRIGATION AND CLEANSING OF WOUNDS

This aspect of wound care is arguably the most important factor for long-term healing and prevention of infection.

Timeliness and pressure of irrigation are central factors in removing potentially infectious materials from wounds. By applying irrigation as soon as possible after the incident, using at least one liter of the cleanest water available under pressure, a rescuer can remove debris much more easily than after the wound has had time to begin to coagulate (WMS recommendation grade 1A/1B). Several studies have shown that using clean, ideally potable, water is as effective as using sterile saline solution in cleansing wounds (Quinn 2014).

There are many field-expedient methods to irrigate wounds using common hiking and climbing gear. If a first aid kit is available, the use of a 30–60 mL syringe with an 18-gauge needle is ideal. Puncturing a corner of a waterproof or plastic bag with a small safety pin, adding water, and squeezing the bag is also a useful technique. The same technique can be used with a soft water bottle if the cap is punctured. The use of a CamelBak® under pressure can also replicate the high pressure needed, though the "bite valve" should be removed before irrigation to prevent introducing bacteria harbored in the valve.

In addition to irrigation, physically removing material from a wound may be necessary. This can be accomplished in a variety of ways while in the backcountry, ideally using clean tweezers or, if necessary, by hand. In this case the rescuer should wear clean protective gloves. Removing all debris from a wound is a must for infection prevention. Care should

+USE OF A CLIMBING HARNESS AS A TOURNIQUET FOR UNCONTROLLED LOWER LIMB HEMORRHAGE+

A climbing harness can be used as an improvised lower extremity tourniquet. When properly applied, this and other improvised windlass tourniquet techniques have been shown to be as effective as commercial devices in occluding arterial flow. This technique enables climbers to render hemostatic aid that is timely, efficient, and effective while allowing continued evacuation in a difficult environment.

This field expedient tourniquet technique can be used with any climbing harness and can be combined with any type of carabiner, though two locking carabiners are preferable. The following is a step-by-step technique for an improvised lower extremity tourniquet using a climbing harness and two carabiners.

1. Position the leg loop at the highest point needed on the upper thigh or groin.
2. Place a carabiner (preferably a pear shape [HMS] locking) by hooking the nose beneath the front of the climbing harness leg loop in an upward movement. Adjust placement so that the carabiner is located at the portion of the leg loop that connects to the lower tie in point. This carabiner acts as the "windlass" within the system.
3. Rotate this carabiner so that the spine of the carabiner is against the patient and the gate faces up. Have a second carabiner ready and within arm's reach.
4. Begin twisting the first carabiner clockwise. This action will pull the narrow portion of the harness (often containing a buckle) away from the patient's skin. Continue to turn the windlass carabiner until enough force is applied to stop bleeding. Placing a block or soft wad of clothing over the area of the femoral artery and under the leg loop usually results in less effort required from the windlass mechanism as well as improved tolerance of associated pain by the patient.
5. To secure the windlass, take the second carabiner (the smallest available), pass the nose through the climbing harness belay loop, harness tie in points, or to the opposite extremity leg loop and then through the 'windlass' carabiner. This carabiner is used to secure the tourniquet in place and to prevent the windlass from loosening. Lock both carabiners.
6. Document the time that the tourniquet is applied and communicate this information upon any transfer of care.

NOTE: Utilization of a leg loop as a lower extremity tourniquet does not negate the use of the climbing harness in the evacuation and continued stabilization of the patient.

be taken if the wound includes impaled large objects such as sticks, branches, ice axes, carabiners or other foreign bodies. If such impaled objects are near vital structures such as large arteries, body cavities, or the face, they should not be removed, but rather stabilized in place and the patient should be evacuated immediately.

BANDAGING AND WOUND CLOSURE

There are many techniques that can be used to bandage a wound. Bandaging a wound promotes healing and protects it from further contamination. Generally, wounds should be bandaged as soon as possible after irrigation with the cleanest material available. While sterile gauze, bandages, and other materials are ideal, often these are not immediately available to a climber. In this case, a clean T-shirt or other clothing is the next best solution. If possible, when using a non-sterile item, apply antibiotic cream to the wound. Not only will this potentially assist in infection prevention, but it will also keep bandaging material from adhering to the wound, and prevent pain when the wound is exposed later (Diehr 2007, Draelos 2011). Generally, bacitracin alone or bacitracin/polymyxin B (Polysporin®) are preferable to "triple antibiotic" ointments (bacitracin/polymyxin B/neomycin, sold as Neosporin®) due to high rates of allergy to neomycin in the general population. Routine use of antibiotic ointments has been challenged recently due to suggestions that they do not reduce infection rates (Draelos 2011); however, the study suggesting this was small in scale, and a larger study appears to confirm effectiveness in reducing infection (Diehr 2007). Routine use of antibiotic ointments has also been implicated in the creation of antibiotic-resistant bacteria, which may be a more compelling reason to avoid use (Suzuki 2011). However, currently, we recommend antibiotic ointment use for wilderness settings due to the high risk of infection in this environment.

There are also a variety of techniques to close wounds. This should be done in a timely manner to lessen the chance of infection. High-risk wounds should be left open. Such wounds include those still open after eight hours, wounds from human or animal bites, puncture wounds, crushing wounds with a large amount of damaged tissue, and deep wounds to the hands and feet. They should be addressed as follows: stop the bleeding, copiously irrigate with potable water, dress and pack wounds with wet sterile dressings to all tissue, cover with sterile or clean bandages, wrap the affected body part, and splint if needed. Climbers with these types of wounds should be evacuated to a medical facility capable of cleaning and adequately dressing and/or closing the wound. Simpler wounds without high-risk criteria present can be closed in the field (if trained personnel are present) or when the climber arrives at a facility capable of caring for them.

IMMUNIZATION

Two types of immunizations should be considered in wound care: tetanus and rabies.

A tetanus booster or vaccine should be given to any climber suffering a traumatic wound and for burned victims. The organism *Clostridium tetani* is found in soil and human/animal waste and can cause the medical condition tetanus. Tetanus can be fatal if the injured person is not immunized or has not had a booster within the last five years. Remember that vaccinations trigger the immune system to fight a future infection and take many weeks to become effective. Anyone with a tetanus-prone wound needs tetanus immunoglobulin to attack the current infection; the vaccination (which should also be given along with it) reduces risk from the current exposure but more importantly prevents infection from future exposure (WMS recommendation grade 1C) (Quinn 2014).

Rabies kills about 55,000 people every year. While rare in the United States and Canada due to the vaccination of dogs, climbers overseas should be knowledgeable about the disease. Ninety-nine percent of all human cases are attributed to dog bites in Central and South America, Africa, and Asia. Climbers should take care around dogs in these areas to prevent exposure from bites or scratches.

In the United States, animals such as bats, raccoons, skunks, and foxes are the most common carriers of rabies. Climbers in the United States should pay special attention to bats, as they are common in areas frequented by climbers. Two bat-related incidents have been described in *Accidents in North American Mountaineering* in 2014 and 2015. A climber in West Virginia and another in Oregon suffered bat bites/scratches and had to undergo the post-exposure prophylaxis (PEP) series of rabies immunizations, as well as receive immunoglobulin (Simon 2015, Simon 2016).

If an animal you suspect has rabies (because it is acting strangely or has foaming at the mouth) bites or scratches you, the best field treatment is to immediately and copiously wash the area with soap and water (WMS recommendation grade 1C) (Quinn 2014). Use a virucidal agent such as povidone-iodine or chlorine dioxide-treated water if available. After washing, the climber should be immediately taken to a nearby hospital for treatment as PEP is time-sensitive and should be initiated within 24–48 hours (Presutti RJ 2001). Call ahead to ensure that the facility has the rabies post-exposure series available. Two vaccination types exist, but the Immunization Action Coalition (in conjunction with the CDC) has confirmed that they can be used interchangeably within the same series to complete the 4-shot series (IAC 2013). Urgent care centers and many smaller hospitals will not have the needed prophylaxis. Rabies, without treatment, will result in death. Seek treatment and PEP if bitten or scratched by an animal you suspect has the rabies virus (WMS recommendation grade 1B) (Quinn 2014). Currently, in the case of bats, the CDC recommends treatment if climbers are merely in proximity to a bat and cannot prove no exposure, for instance waking up in a room with a bat, due to concerning cases of rabies from bat exposure without confirmed physical contact.

ABRASIONS

IDENTIFY
Abrasions, also known as "gobies," are the most common type of wound in the general population and are commonly encountered by climbers. They are caused by tissue being scraped or worn away from shearing forces against the outer layers of skin. Luckily, abrasions usually affect only the superficial layers of skin and infrequently develop infection, although some can affect the underlying structures.

TREAT
Treatment of abrasions is straightforward and usually requires minimal materials. Copious irrigation using the cleanest water available is recommended. Removing all debris and material from the wound will help to prevent infection. Once cleaned, covering the abrasion with an antiseptic and non-adherent gauze completes the treatment, although many abrasions are so superficial in nature that they will not need any dressing.

EVACUATE

There is little cause to evacuate a climber with mild abrasions unless they are located on the bottoms of the feet, the palms of the hands, the genitalia, or if an abrasion begins to show signs of severe infection and cellulitis.

LACERATIONS

IDENTIFY

Lacerations are deep cuts or tears to the skin. They are the most common wound suffered by climbers and can occur due to a wide variety of reasons, from a slip of the knife while preparing food at a cramped bivy to a blow from a sharp rock edge sustained due to a fall. Assessment of the wound is key to determine the best method of care.

TREAT

Wound care should follow the standard outlined earlier. Special attention should be paid to any laceration that involves tendons, ligaments, nerves, vascular structures, or other deeper tissues such as muscle or bone. If the use of an extremity (arm, leg, finger, toes) is impeded by a laceration, after initial first aid care, the person should be evacuated to a medical facility capable of fully assessing and treating this injury.

Most shallow or superficial lacerations can easily be treated in the climbing environment. In addition to the care described in the overview, lacerations will need to be closed. This closure can occur immediately, if the wound is superficial and clean, or can be delayed if it is deeper or grossly contaminated.

A clean and shallow laceration should be irrigated thoroughly with clean, potable water, and can be closed using a variety of techniques, including skin glue (octyl cyanoacrylate), Steri-Strips™ (or butterfly bandages), or sutures or staples if the rescuer is trained to apply them.

Steri-Strips™, with tincture of benzoin applied to the skin prior to placement, are a lightweight and effective approach to close most lacerations. These strips are placed perpendicularly on one side of the laceration, pulled across the wound site, and placed on the opposite portion of skin. Repeat this process by placing additional strips perpendicularly to the wound until the entire laceration has been closed. Remember when placing Steri-Strips™ that the key is to approximate the wound edges without placing the wound under additional or extreme tension, which could cause complications in healing. Cover the entire laceration with sterile or clean dressing.

Scalp lacerations are somewhat more difficult to contain using normal bandaging materials. These lacerations bleed profusely. If the climber has longer hair, small bundles of hair on either side of the cut can be tied together to close the wound, which can be further secured with skin glue or superglue. A sterile or clean dressing should be placed over the wound and Kerlix™, or long strips of clothing, should be wrapped around the head to secure this dressing.

For any deep or grossly contaminated wound, thorough irrigation should be performed as soon as possible and the wound should have wet dressings or gauze applied to keep the exposed underlying tissue moist. The wound should be packed with additional moist gauze until the skin surface is reached. These wet dressings should then be covered by dry dressings and secured. Grossly contaminated lacerations should not be closed, and the injured climber should be evacuated for medical care.

EVACUATE

Any lacerations that involve tendons, ligaments, nerves, or vascular structures (arteries or veins) should be evacuated immediately. Additionally, any lacerations that are complex in nature or structure or that are grossly contaminated should be evacuated. Lacerations, even minor ones, that begin to show signs of infection should be evacuated unless appropriate antibiotics are available.

PUNCTURE WOUNDS

IDENTIFY

A puncture wound is an injury caused by an object that penetrates deeply into the skin. Common items that cause puncture wounds to climbers and mountaineers include ice axes, tools, carabiners, and branches. Over the last approximately three decades there have been 54 reported puncture wound injuries in *Accidents in North American Mountaineering* (MacDonald 2015). Puncture wounds occur often to the feet. They are considered high-risk wounds due to the bacterial load introduction deep into tissue.

TREAT

Puncture wounds are difficult to treat in the field. Standard care should be applied as described in the overview portion of this chapter. The risk for infection is extremely high for puncture wounds. All climbers who experience a puncture wound should consider a tetanus booster and tetanus immunoglobulin if their last tetanus vaccine/booster was more than five years earlier, especially if the wound is due to organic material such as a branch or from an item embedded in the soil (such as a nail).

EVACUATE

The decision to evacuate should be based upon the type and location of the puncture wound. If the penetrating object is organic in nature or covered in soil, evacuation to medical care for deep tissue cleansing is optimal.

BURNS

IDENTIFY

While burns may not seem like a common injury for climbers, there are many cases each year of climbers being burned, with the majority of these occurring during the preparation of food and drink. Also remember that, while we usually think of thermal burns when we use this word, burns can result from friction injuries as well, which may be more common in climbing with rope use. Burns, depending upon severity, may require evacuation, and certainly all but the most minor will require some type of first aid.

There is an additional and significant danger related to fire for climbers in multi-pitch settings and for alpinists tucked away in bivys on snowy ridges. In these situations, climbers are protected from the elements or suspended above a thousand foot drop by a thin sheet of nylon or polyester variant. These materials can easily catch fire as can the rope, slings, and cordelettes used to secure the climbers. Moreover, high-tech fabrics in climbing clothing are extremely combustible. A fire, ten pitches up a climb or on a snowy ledge, can quickly spell disaster for a climbing party.

There are six main types of burns. They are scald burns, flame burns, flash burns, contact burns (including friction), electrical burns, and chemical burns. The most common types of burns for climbers and mountaineers are the first four. Electrical burns during climbing trips most commonly result from lightning strikes, which are discussed in greater detail in Chapter 15. Chemical burns are the least common and are associated with strong acids or alkalis.

There are two areas of focus when assessing a burn. The first is the total body surface area (TBSA) that the burn covers. This is easily quantified by using either the "rule of nines" or "palm method." The rule of nine method measures TBSA burned by estimating the body surface area contained in a particular portion of the body. For example, an arm represents 9% and a leg 18%. See Figure 9-2 for all percentages.

A more accurate and easier assessment is the palm method. The palm of the patient's hand represents approximately 1% TBSA. Circumferential burns (burns that wrap around a limb) are serious and almost always require immediate evacuation.

FIGURE 9-2. RULE OF 9s

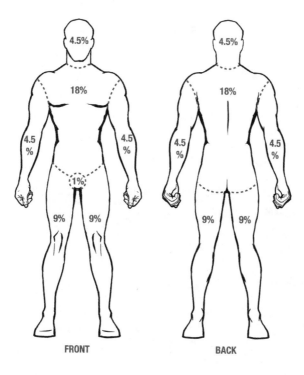

FRONT   BACK

The second area of concern in assessing a burn is the depth of the burned tissue. In the past this categorization was described by degree (first, second, third, fourth) but now burns are described both by degree and by the terms *partial thickness* and *full thickness.*

First Degree

A first-degree burn is exemplified by mild sunburn and involves only the outer portion of the skin (Figure 9-3). It is usually characterized by red, painful skin that is devoid of blisters. Pain resolves in two to three days and the damaged layer of skin cells peels or sloughs off.

Superficial Partial Thickness

This type of burn is painful, and the burned skin will be pink or red and appear wet. It affects all of the epidermis and a portion of the dermis (Figure 9-3). Blisters form at the junction of these two layers. These burns typically heal in two to three weeks without skin grafts and often leave only small scarring.

Deep Partial Thickness

These burns blister, often look pink or white immediately after the burn, and have a dry appearance. Some will appear bright red. Such burns

FIGURE 9-3. SKIN LAYERS

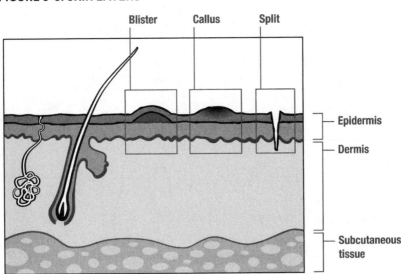

involve all of the epidermis and most of the dermis (Figure 9-3). The burned portion may not be as sensitive as surrounding tissue, and on day two will turn white in appearance. These burns heal within four to nine weeks, but will often require skin grafting and physical therapy to prevent contracture and loss of movement.

Full Thickness

This type of burn involves all of the epidermal and dermal layers (Figure 9-3). The skin will look like leather and is often red, white, or even blackened. The burn patient will feel no pain in the area, and the skin will not whiten when pressure is applied.

Fourth Degree

These burns involve underlying structures including subcutaneous fat, muscles, and bone (Figure 9-3).

TREAT

Extinguishing any fire present on the body is the first step to treatment and is best accomplished by smothering the flames with clothing, blankets, or water, or by the affected person rolling on the ground. Clothes should be removed from the location of the burn—otherwise the blended material common in technical clothing will continue to smolder against the skin. Following the MARCH acronym (Chapter 1), presuming no bleeding, attention should immediately turn to the climber's airway, which is particularly threatened by burns due to potential swelling. If airway involvement is suspected, evacuation should begin without delay. Oxygen should be administered if available.

For less severe burns caused by scald, flame, flash, or contact, cool water may help provide immediate pain relief and limit damage. Cold water, ice, or snow is not recommended. Any constricting clothing or jewelry should be removed. For burns that are less than 5% TBSA and that do not involve the airway, do not extend completely around a limb, and do not involve the face, hand, feet, or genitals, first aid can usually be very effective. Wash the area with soap and clean water and blot dry the affected tissue. Any dead skin should be peeled or cut away. Antibiotic ointment should be spread lightly over the burn. Ideally silver sulfadiazine should be used, but bacitracin or bacitracin/polymyxin B ointment are easier to acquire and more common in first aid kits. Also, silver sulfadiazine should not be used on facial burns even if available. While there are many specialized dressings for burns, common gauze and bandage from a standard first aid kit perform adequately as long as they cover the entire area of the burn, allow the burned tissue to remain moist, and do not prevent movement of the area.

The injured climber should keep the affected tissue elevated to reduce swelling to the region and should move it actively to prevent tightening. Not only will this increase range of motion of the burned area during the healing process, but it will also reduce pain and swelling.

EVACUATE

Any burns that are circumferential on a limb, involve the airway, are greater than 5% TBSA, involve the face, hand, feet, or genitals, or are deeper than partial thickness should be evacuated. All lightning victims, electrical burns, chemical burns, and infected burns should be evacuated. It is always better to err on the side of caution in the evacuation of burn patients. Burns are complex wounds that are easily infected. Waiting even 24 hours can put the burn victim at increased risk for infection, complications, and long-term disability.

ANIMAL BITES AND STINGS

IDENTIFY

Creatures in the wilderness that bite or sting run the gamut from large mammalian predators to snakes to ticks and mosquito bites. Depending upon the region and the animal, care for these bites and stings will vary. Environmental awareness is crucial in preventing these incidents in the first place.

TREAT

Care for animal bites is similar to that for puncture wounds, as these wounds often become infected. Animal bites should be cleaned vigorously with soap and water as soon as possible and a virucidal agent should be used if available. These wounds should be packed (if large) with wet dressings and then covered with dry dressings and bandages. All animal bites should be considered grossly contaminated and the injured climber should be evacuated. Rabies is always a possibility, especially with bat bites in the United States and dog bites overseas. Rabies is nearly one hundred percent fatal if not treated, and a painful way to die.

For snakebites, most climbers carry the one first aid item needed for treatment—car keys. Irrigate the wound with clean water as soon as possible to remove any remaining venom at or near the surface of the skin, calmly walk patients to the nearest form of transportation, and evacuate them to a nearby hospital. Antivenin is not carried routinely in many small medical centers, and urgent care centers do not stock it at all. Call ahead to inquire about availability. Remember to remove all constricting clothing or jewelry near the bite.

If possible, take a photo of the snake from a safe distance. If tissue surrounding the bite begins to turn red and swell, mark the outer edges with a pen or marker and note the time. This will help medical providers better estimate the degree of envenomation.

When treating a snakebite: 1) DO NOT suck the wound or use a suction device, 2) DO NOT make any incisions at the site of the bite, 3) DO NOT apply a tourniquet, 4) DO NOT use any electrical current, 5) DO NOT decapitate the snake and bring it with you. Detached heads can still deliver venom. Remember, the best treatment is to calmly get the climber to the nearest medical facility that is equipped with antivenin.

Bites from mosquitos, bees, spiders, scorpions, and ticks can cause varying degrees of pain and discomfort. The *Hymenoptera* order (specifically wasps, bees, and fire ants) cause more human deaths than any other animal via anaphylaxis. Anaphylaxis treatment is discussed in detail in Chapter 2. Mosquitos can transmit dangerous diseases such as dengue fever, malaria, Zika, and yellow fever, and ticks can transmit other diseases such as Rocky Mountain spotted fever and Lyme disease. Prevention of insect and tick bites begins with proper clothing that includes long-sleeve shirts and long pants, regular checks of exposed skin, and the use of insect repellents. Regional-specific information about mosquito-borne diseases is included in Appendix F. See sidebar below for tick bite prevention and removal guidelines.

EVACUATE

All climbers who are bitten by a wild animal or who develop anaphylaxis from a bite or sting should be evacuated immediately and evaluated by a medical professional.

+TICK BITE PREVENTION AND REMOVAL GUIDELINES+

Prevention:

- The best method to prevent tick bites is a systematic check of clothing and exposed skin at least two times daily. Studies show that the most common sites of tick attachment to humans are the legs, feet, stomach, groin, followed by the chest, shoulders, hips, head, and finally the arms.
- Proper clothing is essential for preventing tick bites. Wearing long pants when outdoors and tucking long sleeve shirts into the belt and pants into socks are outstanding protective measures. Wearing smooth and loose-fitting clothing also is helpful.
- The use of DEET (*N,N*-diethyl-*m*-tolumide/*N,N*-diethyl-3-methylbenzamide) has proven moderately effective in reducing tick bites, especially in conjunction with proper clothing. DEET effectiveness deteriorates at around two hours and reapplication is recommended at that time. Care should be taken using DEET as it can melt some plastic and nylon components of climbing gear.
- Other available but lesser-known repellents include permethrin, IR3535, picaridin, oil of lemon eucalyptus, and BioUD (2-undecanone). Permethrin is approved by the US Environmental Protection Agency (EPA) for use on clothing only.
- IR3535 (3-[N-butyl-N-acetyl]-aminopropopionic aced, ethyl ester) is approved by the US Centers for Disease Control (CDC) and the EPA for use on the skin and is the active ingredient in the Skin-So-Soft line of Avon products. Picaridin is also approved by the CDC and EPA and is the active ingredient in Off!' and Cutter' brand products. The final products, oil of lemon eucalyptus and BioUD, are plant-based products. Oil of lemon eucalyptus is a primary ingredient in the Cutter' brand of repellents. BioUD (2-undecanone) is derived from portions of wild tomato and is the primary ingredient for the BioUD/HOMS products. All of these products are effective against ticks, and, when used in conjunction with twice daily visual checks and proper clothing choices, act as a substantive barrier to tick bites.

Removal:

- Different schools of thought, and standards of care, exist with regards to tick removal. The following are the two most evidence-based and consensus-approved methods of which we are aware in the medical community. We have named them the "American" standard and the "Australasian" standard based on where the sources were primarily derived during our research. The American standard is primarily geared towards reducing chance of disease transmission, where the Australasian standard is more geared towards reducing allergic reaction. Note that these labels are based on where the standards originate, not on geographic appropriateness for each technique—they are just two opinions about the same problem, managing an imbedded tick, although disease and allergy prevalences may vary geographically and drive some of the technique preferences, as discussed further below.

AMERICAN STANDARD (Della-Guistina 2013, Forgey 2017)

1. Hold tweezers parallel to the skin and grasp the tick as close to the skin as possible nearest the site of attachment (Della-Guistina 2013) or, in an alternate version, grasp the skin just next to the tick (Forgey 2017)
2. Apply slow, gentle, and consistent upward pull on the tick.
3. After the tick is safely removed from the skin, disinfect the site with soap and water or alcohol if available.

AUSTRALIAN STANDARD (ASCIA 2016, ANZCOR 2016)

If you find a tick, do *not* forcibly remove the tick, but rather *kill the tick first* by using a product to rapidly freeze the tick to prevent it from injecting more allergen-containing saliva. Ether-containing aerosol sprays are currently recommended for killing the tick. Aerostart® and other similar products have been used extensively to kill ticks in allergic patients. It should be noted that these products are not registered for use in humans and contains benzene but there is long term experience with these products which have been shown to be very effective in treating those with serious tick allergies. The use of other ether-containing sprays (e.g. Wart-Off Freeze , Elastoplast Cold Spray) has also been effective. These products will continue to be studied and advice updated as experience increases. If available, liquid nitrogen applied by a doctor should also (in theory) be effective.

Our opinion? The Australasian approach is entirely expert opinion without clinical evidence (acknowledged by ASCIA), and also relies primarily on chemicals that are not approved for use on humans (also acknowledged by ASCIA). Such chemicals would need to be carried as additional gear, while the American standard requires no additional gear except tweezers likely already in a first aid kit. While allergic reaction to ticks is a concern, we are also very concerned about disease transmission, and therefore feel that ticks should be removed as soon as possible (not left in place, as suggested by ANZCOR for non-allergic patients). In this case, geographic location may be relevant, as Lyme Disease and Rocky Mountain Spotted Fever were originally described in America and their presence of any sort in Australasia is controversial. Also, the ANZCOR protocol, while dated 2016, is referenced from a 1985 pediatrics review, and we feel more modern evidence is available. We understand the concern about squeezing tick body and releasing toxins, so we advocate the American standard with tweezer placement as close to the head attachment as possible, or even including portions of skin as proposed by Forgey. We do, however, await more clinical data and regulatory review which might make the chemicals used in the Australasian approach more defensible, and for a protocol review by ANZCOR using more modern evidence.

CHAPTER 10
SKIN INJURIES AND CARE

The skin is the largest organ of the human body and takes the most punishment of any part of a climber's anatomy. Specifically, the skin on the hands, fingers, and feet is critical to our success in the mountains. Understanding the skin, its structures, and how best to care for it is one of the most important ways we can help our performance as climbers.

The skin is composed of three separate layers: the epidermis (outer), the dermis (middle), and the subcutaneous tissue (inner) (Figure 9-3). The epidermis is the visible portion of the skin, measures around 1 millimeter or less in thickness, and is of the most importance to climbers. The outermost layer, known as the keratin, or cornified layer, is made up of dead cells that are constantly shedding. This "dead" skin layer plays an important role in protecting the body. The living portions of the epidermis replicate themselves and are continuously replaced every three to four weeks, and it is within this layer that blisters form.

The next deeper portion of the skin is the dermis. The dermis is home to many important structures, including the sweat glands, hair follicles, motor and sensory nerves, blood vessels, sebaceous (oil) glands, tiny muscles (responsible for goose bumps), and collagen and elastin fibers. The sweat glands are present throughout the skin surface of the body but are concentrated on the palms, soles, and forehead. Although climbers use chalk specifically to counteract sweat, the glands producing it are essential in the regulation of body temperature. It is also important to note that excessively blocking the action of sweat glands can cause a condition known as miliaria (prickly heat), discussed later in this chapter. The importance of our nerve tissue and vascular network within the dermis cannot be overstated. Without their sensory and motor function and the blood they supply to the skin, our efforts at ascending mountains and scaling vertical rock walls would be futile.

The deepest layer of skin is the subcutaneous tissue. Comprised mostly of adipose tissue, this layer acts as a fat storage depot, insulates the body, and protects internal structures from trauma.

Friction, created by the application of the skin of climbers' hands and feet (or gloves and footwear) to the surface they are climbing (rock, snow, ice), is the foundation of climbing. Because of this, in discussing skin care and injury, we will focus on the skin of the hands and the feet.

BASICS OF SKIN CARE

The following sections discuss common climber skin injuries, ways to prevent them, and methods of treatment. When it comes to climbing and many of the conditions within this chapter, the most important concept is friction. It is the basic principle that allows climbers to pursue our passion. Incorporating the following skin care principles into climbing activities helps maximize performance.

To climb as hard as possible, climbers need to optimize the skin of our hands to allow for the best contact. The ideal is to have dry, smooth skin devoid of dead, hanging tissue that can be easily torn. Smooth, moderate-depth calluses at key points of contact help to prevent skin damage.

Healthy skin starts with a varied diet that meets all daily nutritional needs and includes proper hydration, and while beer is the favored beverage of climbers, water is better for healthy skin. Additional information on nutrition and hydration and their benefits for injury prevention are available in Chapter 3; the particular challenges of hydrating in hot environments is discussed in Chapter 13.

In addition to healthy skin, good hand hygiene is essential. This includes proper hand washing as well as chemicals applied to the skin. Lotions, fragrances, and food affect our skin as do items we come in contact with on the way to the crag (e.g., grease on the gasoline pump). Washing hands with soapy water is the best method of cleaning hands prior to climbing.

Many climbers use hand creams and salves in the evening after a day of climbing or during rest days. Some of the large variety of brands are designed specifically for climbers, while others intended for the greater public are also popular with climbers. Joshua Tree and Climb On® are examples of the first type, while Burt's Bees® Hand Salve and O'Keeffe's

FIGURE 10-1. SKIN CREAMS AND SALVES

CLIMBING SPECIFIC:

Climb On	www.skinourishment.com
Get Giddy	www.getgiddy.com
Joshua Tree Skin Care	www.jrtreelife.com
Metolius	www.metoliusclimbing.com
Sypeland Climber's Balm	www.climbersbalm.com
Tip Juice	www.tipjuice.co.uk

OTHER COMMON BRANDS USED BY CLIMBERS:

Badger Balm	www.badgerbalm.com
Beta Balm	www.bulksoapcompany.com/beta-balm
Burt's Bees Wax	www.burtsbees.com
O'Keeffe's Working Hands	www.okeeffescompany.com
Rocket Pure	www.rocketpure.com

Working Hands® exemplify the second. The skin of different individuals will respond differently to various creams and salves. The purpose of these products is to help repair and rejuvenate skin damaged by the rigors of climbing, not to soften hands. Figure 10-1 lists some skin creams and salves available.

The skin of climbers' feet is also a concern. Healthy diet, good hygiene, and basic care are important. Well-fitting and broken-in approach shoes and mountaineering boots will prevent hot spots and blisters. Cutting toenails short and straight helps prevent subungual hematomas (collections of blood underneath a nail) and associated pain. Washing your feet and keeping your climbing shoes/mountaineering boots clean and "funk free" are the basics of hygiene and will help prevent athlete's foot and various other foot fungi. Fungus likes to grow in damp and dark places, so attempt to dry your shoes and boots daily by exposure to air and sunlight. A useful technique for drying soaked boots is to remove the insoles, prop them to allow the air to dry both sides, and then stuff crumpled newspaper into the boots. Allow this newspaper to remain over a few hours or overnight.

SKIN CARE KIT

In addition to the creams and salves already mentioned, a skin care kit is a necessity for climbers. The kit recommended below is not a "one type fits all." Every climber is different and while some use these items continuously, others may have little need for them. Experiment and find out what works best for you.

+ *Adhesive Bandages*: A few of these in various sizes can help protect any cuts, splits, or flappers. Buy quality bandages, as they will stay on when used in conjunction with tape.
+ *Antibiotic Ointment*: Small packets of bacitracin or bacitracin/polymyxin B antibiotic ointment should be included in your kit. When injuries do occur, applying ointment to the damaged area after cleaning and before bandaging will keep the wound clean and moist and will encourage healing. See Chapter 9 for a more complete discussion of antibiotic ointments.
+ *Athletic Tape*: Two sizes of tape are recommended. One narrow roll (usually ½ inch) is for use on the fingers and one larger roll (usually 2 inches) is for use on the hand and to make gloves. There are endless uses for tape both as a preventive measure and for bandaging and improvisation.
+ *Compound Tincture of Benzoin*: This is a combination of benzoin resin with alcohol. Benzoin has many medical uses. It can toughen skin, increase the adhesive properties of bandages, and treat blisters.
+ *Cuticle Cutters*: These handy additions to nail clippers allow for a straight cut to nails or nasty flappers. They also are useful to cut away rough areas of skin.
+ *Nail Clippers*: For obvious reasons these are a must. Clip fingernails and toenails to keep them manageable. Clippers can also be used to remove flaking skin or small flappers.
+ *Safety Pin/Needle*: The chief use of a safety pin or needle is to assist with blister care, but this item can be useful for subungual hematomas and removing splinters. A safety pin is the better option as it can be used in a variety of ways besides skin care and is safer to carry.
+ *Sanding Block*: Found in any hardware store, these blocks come with various levels of grain. A block with fine grit and one with a

more coarse grain should be included. Some blocks come with two different grains, which saves room and money. An emery board or nail file also works well and is smaller and lighter. Some climbers use small sheets of sand paper. When folded, these allow for a fine tune along small areas.

+ *Skin Glue/Liquid Bandages*: Ranging in cost from approximately $4 to $20, these can be an expensive addition to a skin care kit. Skin glue can be used to seal flappers, split tips, and blisters. In using these glues, it is important to ensure that the wound is clean to prevent trapping any bacteria. Some climbers substitute hardware brand super glue for medical grade glues. Early research indicated that non-medical glues are *histotoxic* (poisonous to tissue), and today some research continues to support this conclusion (Davis 2013). With the cheaper medical grade adhesives such as New-Skin® now available, there is little need for including super glue in this kit.

COMMON CLIMBER SKIN INJURIES

Blisters

Blisters are one of the most common medical problems in the out-doors. While frequently seen on the feet, they can also occur on hands and often form under calluses. In the climbing world, blisters may also appear due to friction caused by a rope, typically during a fall. Blisters are usually preceded by what is commonly known as a "hot spot." This is an area of inflammation of the outer layer of the epidermis that is caused by repeated sliding at a friction point. Such points are often between the skin and a sock. This region of *erythema* (redness, usually from irritation or infection) causes cells in the middle living layer of the epidermis to delaminate and split. With continued friction, the middle stratum of epidermis fills with fluid, thus creating the blister. This fluid is usually clear, but sometimes can be blood-tinged.

Once formed, blisters can be very painful and difficult to heal. If still intact but bulging and greater than 5 mm (0.19 in) in size, a blister should be carefully drained, ensuring that the "roof" or outer skin is left in place (WMS recommendation grade 1C) (Quinn 2014). An "unroofed" blister can be particularly painful. A blister should be drained with a sterilized needle or safety pin. Sterilizing a needle in the backcountry is best done by flaming the needle and allowing it to cool. Alternatively, an alcohol swab can be wiped across the pin and then on and around the blister. Often multiple holes may be needed to ensure drainage. The preferred method is to create pinholes at the lowest point on the blister close to the margin with normal skin, allowing drainage by gravity. It may be necessary to drain the blister several times over the first day after blister formation. Eventually the roof (outer skin flap) will dry. Maintaining its integrity will promote healing and reduce pain.

There are many methods to bandage a blister. The use of paper tape, cut to overlap the edges of the drained blister, soaked with compound tincture of benzoin and covered with an adhesive bandage works well for intact blisters. Unroofed (or open) blisters are more difficult to dress properly. First trim away all dead/loose skin from the edges of the blister. If a Spenco 2nd Skin® or similar dressing is available, place it over the exposed skin and then dress as with a roofed blister. The key points to any blister dressing are to provide adequate padding, and to keep the blister clean, dry, and free of debris.

Prevention of blisters begins with identifying rubbing surfaces. Properly-fitted gear and footwear that is broken-in is the first step in prevention. Additionally, identifying hot spots and treating these will prevent the more dramatic pain associated with a blister.

Calluses

Calluses are merely a thickened portion of the *stratum corneum* (the outer layer of the skin), and develop due to chronic friction at that location. Climbers carefully cultivate these calluses to their advantage, but these areas, when not properly treated, can lead to split tips and flappers. Calluses protect the skin and generally do not need treatment unless a blister forms below the thickened skin. Using a sanding block, emery board, or sandpaper along the edges of thickened calluses to blend them into the surrounding skin helps prevent a flapper from occurring and should be incorporated into routine skin maintenance.

Chafing

Chafing is the mechanical friction between a portion of the body and clothing/gear or between two adjacent parts of the body. For the general population, chafing usually occurs on the upper thighs or in the *axilla* (underarm region), but for climbers it often occurs around the waist belt or leg loops of a climbing harness. The red inflamed skin at the chafing site is best cared for by applying an antibiotic ointment or petroleum jelly to reduce the friction or by substituting clothing that causes less friction. There are also a number of commercially available products specifically designed to decrease chafing, including Body Glide®, Desitin®, and Monistat® Chafing Relief Powder Gel®, or simply generic zinc oxide or talcum powder. When friction occurs around the waist belt or leg loops, smoothing the clothing under these areas or tightening the loops for a more secure fit can help. But a dirty harness may be a contributing factor. Thorough washing of the harness using only water and a scrub brush to the padding of the waist belt and leg loops may remove the sweat and grime that is the cause of chafing.

Flappers

Flappers, or small avulsions of the outer layers of the skin, are a common problem for climbers. Flappers are created when a portion of the skin pulls away, usually due to contact with a sharp hold. They often occur at or near a callus that is thicker than the surrounding skin. The ridge created by this thickened skin can often be caught by rock, creating the tear.

Treatment of a flapper depends upon its severity. If minor and not bleeding, it can be clipped and the rough edges filed to prevent recurrence. But if the wound is bleeding, it should be irrigated, cleaned, and dressed with an antibiotic cream and adhesive bandage/tape. Skin glue may be used after the wound is cleaned. If climbing is to continue, cover the area with climbing tape to maintain the integrity of the dressing and prevent introduction of bacteria to the wound.

Flappers can be prevented by proper skin care using sanding blocks or emery boards to prevent ridges that can get caught on sharp edges of holds.

Split/Cracked Tips

Splits or cracks usually develop on rough, dry hands and can be very difficult to heal. Often these cracks occur on or along calluses. All splits should be thoroughly cleaned and bandaged. Antibiotic ointment is useful to promote healing, prevent infection, and keep the wound moist. If the crack is small, it may be possible to continue climbing, but monitor the split to ensure that it does not grow in size. Keep the injured skin moist and be patient while it heals. If there is obviously dead tissue around the split, attempt to remove this layer as it speeds healing and prevents the split from catching on objects and causing further damage. To treat and to prevent recurrence of splits, use a hand salve to keep the skin soft.

Subungual Hematoma

A *subungual hematoma* is the medical term for pooled blood beneath a toenail or fingernail, often dark red or black in color. This most frequently occurs under the large toenails of mountaineers after a steep descent. If a boot or approach shoe is loose and the toenails come into repeated contact with the climber's toe box, a subungual hematoma may form. Usually painful, the pressure below the nail can be released using a heated safety pin or paperclip. Apply this perpendicularly to the outer portion of the nail until it penetrates to the pool of blood and tissue below. Often the release of pressure will cause the underlying blood to squirt. Prevention of this hematoma is easy. Cutting the large toenail short and straight and purchasing properly fitting shoes or boots with an appropriate toe box usually suffices.

Worn/Smooth Tips

Worn tips are characterized by soft, pink, sensitive skin that results from wearing away the keratin layers of skin and exposing lower layers of the stratum corneum. This can occur on any type of rock, but is common on sandstone. No medical care is needed beyond normal skin care, as these layers of keratinized cells will be replaced over the course of a night, or after a rest day.

USE OF CHALK

The use of chalk by the climbing community is the foundation of skin care and climbing performance today. The kind and quantity of chalk each climber uses is due to a combination of factors and amounts to personal preference. As stated earlier, all skin is different. Some climbers sweat more than others and therefore will use more chalk. Some climbers like to use loose chalk, some prefer liquid/paste chalk, while others swear by chalk balls. Some climbers use antihydral cream, and some use no chalk at all. Wherever you fall on that scale, understand that chalk is primarily used to dry the hands, and too much can be as detrimental as too little.

III.
ENVIRONMENTAL

CHAPTER 11
ALTITUDE ILLNESS

The majority of climbing around the world occurs in areas of moderate elevation and many climbers will never venture on trips to the distant Alps, Andes, or Himalayas. Many may never experience the elevations of the Rockies and Cascades in the United States and Canada, but for all other climbers and alpinists, a knowledge of altitude illness is essential. All of the altitude illnesses discussed within this chapter include prevention and treatment options for those at altitude. Additionally, each option includes a recommendation based upon existing evidence as compiled by the Wilderness Medical Society's practice guidelines in the prevention and treatment of these illnesses.

Originally credited to the writings of Aristotle and then later to St. Augustine, the earliest documented accounts of altitude illness date back to 32 BC, when a Chinese official, Too Kin, described a region as "Big Headache Mountain." Travelers there experienced difficulties moving across the Himalayan Karakoram Pass as they "suffered the effects of high altitude" (Gilbert 1983, West 1998). Since that day travelers, and now climbers, have felt and witnessed the effects of high altitude.

The effects of altitude can vary physiologically between individuals depending on gender, age, body type and size, health status, perceived exertions, and the elevation of permanent residence (Basnyat 2003). The principal factor, however, is the rate of ascent. Furthermore, the geographic latitude of the climbing site may affect atmospheric pressure and the physiologic concentration (partial pressure) of oxygen (Harris 1998). An example of the effect of latitude is the comparison of Denali's latitude in Alaska versus the latitude of Mt. Everest in Nepal. The barometric pressure at Nepal's latitude of 27 degrees and the Everest summit elevation (6200 m) is 253 mmHg, but a similar elevation at the Denali latitude of 62 degrees has a barometric pressure of only 222 mmHg.

Variations in barometric pressure are also affected by season, weather, and temperature.

Taking all these factors into consideration, criteria have been established to classify ranges of altitude by susceptibility to illness in those ranges. Consensus panels have defined high altitude as 1500 to 3500 m, very high altitude as 3500 to 5500 m, and extreme altitude as 5500 m (Auerbach 2013).* However, symptoms of altitude illness can appear even at lower altitudes with studies indicating the incidence of acute mountain sickness (AMS) and high altitude pulmonary edema (HAPE) as low as 2000 m (Luks 2014).

Understanding altitude physiology is necessary to understand altitude illness. The body attempts to minimize the effects of altitude through a process known as acclimatization, which is the adjustment to changes in the amount of oxygen breathed in at higher altitudes. Climbing quickly to altitude increases the chance that a climber will experience altitude illness because the body has no time to adapt and acclimatize to decreased barometric pressure.

Acclimatization occurs through multiple physiologic changes that increase the efficiency of oxygen use and its transport to the cells. The most rapid response of acclimatization is an increase in breathing (respiratory) rate. This is due to peripheral chemoreceptors in the carotid bodies sensing a decrease in inspired oxygen and stimulating the respiratory centers in the brainstem to increase breathing. This process is known as the hypoxic ventilatory response (HVR) (Hackett 2012, Simon 2014). This increased breathing results in a respiratory alkalosis that triggers a braking mechanism within the body, limiting any further increase in rate of breathing. This occurs because the decrease in carbon dioxide in the blood is identified by central chemoreceptors, creating a negative feedback mechanism that suppresses the ability for the body to breath faster (West 2012). At this point, metabolic changes occur and the kidneys compensate for the respiratory alkalosis by excreting additional bicarbonate (HCO_3^-) through increased urination. Eventually, the blood pH becomes more normalized, the ventilation braking mechanism is overcome, and further increases in respiratory rate and arterial oxygen content occur (Simon 2014). This

* See Appendix C for conversions from metric meters to English feet. Internationally, the convention is for high altitudes to be expressed in meters. For these particular thresholds, high altitude is defined as 4,921 to 11,483 ft, very high altitude as 11,483 to 18,045 ft, and extreme altitude as >18,045 ft.

process usually takes four to seven days but can be altered by medications such as acetazolamide (discussed later). An appropriate ascent profile allows the body's compensatory mechanisms to catch up and optimize the climber's oxygenation.

Other physiological changes include an increase in hematocrit concentrations and the alteration of the oxygen binding capacity of hemoglobin (West 2012). These occur within the first month at altitude. The increase in hemoglobin concentration is initially due to loss of plasma volume from increased urination and/or by movement of fluid from blood vessels to cells and tissues (West 2012). Hypoxia causes an increase in production of red blood cells after seven days at altitude that is due to renal erythropoietin production, resulting in erythropoiesis and greater red blood cell mass (Simon 2014). This causes an increase in arterial oxygen content and tissue oxygenation to close to that of sea level for the acclimatized alpinist. Climbers who spend less than seven days at altitude will experience only the increased hematocrit due to initial fluid loss (Simon 2014). For those on longer expeditions at altitude, red blood cells and plasma volume will increase with time. The other physiologic alteration that assists in negating hypoxia is an increase in production of 2,3 diphosphoglycerate, which lessens the affinity of oxygen for hemoglobin and allows easier transfer of oxygen to the cells within the body (Hackett 2012). Exposure to high altitudes also causes an increase in heart rate and the amount of blood pumped by the heart per beat (West 2012). These changes normalize over time once acclimatization has occurred. If a gradual ascent profile is not maintained, these changes will not have time to take effect and there is an increased risk of developing altitude illness.

Acute Mountain Sickness (AMS)

AMS is the most common altitude illness with studies indicating that it affects roughly 27 to 51% of those living or traveling at altitude. Prevention of altitude illness should be the goal of all mountaineers. A controlled, gradual ascent of no more than 500 meters in vertical elevation gain in sleeping altitude should be adhered to as much as possible (Luks 2014). Other modalities of prevention are discussed below.

IDENTIFY

The most accepted definition for AMS was developed in 1991 during the International Hypoxia Symposium in Lake Louise, Alberta, Canada. The Lake Louise Consensus Committee definition of AMS provides an excellent way to identify AMS, and symptoms may begin as early as two hours after arrival to altitude. A headache is required for the diagnosis, plus one or more of the following symptoms: anorexia, gastrointestinal symptoms (anorexia, nausea, or vomiting), insomnia or frequent awakening during sleep, dizziness or light-headedness, and fatigue (Simon 2014).

TREAT
While no treatment plan is perfect and each person will react differently to changes in altitude on any given day, certain preventive measures can be helpful to avoid AMS.

+ *Staged Ascent*: After passing 3,000 meters, climbers should limit their sleeping elevation to no more than 500 vertical meters per day thereafter and include a day of no gain in sleeping elevation every three to four days (WMS recommendation grade 1B) (Luks 2014). In addition, the "climb high, sleep low" technique of staging a cache of resources up high but returning to base camp for sleeping is helpful (Beidleman 2009).
+ *High-Carbohydrate Diet*: The work effort required at increased altitude often leads to a substantial energy deficits. Increased caloric intake (despite anorexia) has been associated with a reduction in AMS occurrence. Further details regarding nutrition at altitude are discussed in Chapter 3.
+ *Reduction in Energy Expenditure*: Exertion is linked to increased incidence of AMS. This can be helped by reducing exercise and exertion efforts to a moderate level until the climber is acclimated.
+ *Hydration*: Many factors can lead to dehydration at altitude. Adequate hydration is essential to stave off dehydration and is a common differential diagnosis to consider when identifying AMS. A balanced approach to hydration at altitude is essential due to insensible loss of fluids from sweat, which evaporates quickly, and respiratory loss in cool, dry air (Simon 2014). Overhydration without adequate food intake may lead to hyponatremia as discussed in Chapter 13.
+ *Pharmaceutical Prophylaxis*: There are many medications and supplements that have been shown to be helpful in the prevention

and treatment of AMS. Alpinists should discuss these options with their PCP prior to trips involving high altitude destinations.

1. *Acetazolamide (Diamox®)*: By far the most significant body of evidence and number of trials point to acetazolamide as an appropriate preventive medication for AMS (Forwand 1968, Luks 2014). Multiple strengths have been investigated, but currently the recommended prophylactic dose is 125 mg twice daily and started the day prior to ascent (WMS recommendation grade 1A) (Low 2012, Luks 2014). Higher doses have been associated with side effects that can be unpleasant and do not have additional benefit to the climber. These include nausea, headache, ringing in the ears, metallic taste, and numb and tingling extremities. Climbers allergic to sulfa are sometimes advised to avoid acetazolamide, but the evidence supporting this recommendation is weak (Kelly 2010, Platt 2012) and this avoidance is only appropriate for those with a history of anaphylaxis to sulfonamide medications (Luks 2014). Prophylactic doses may be discontinued 48 hours after target elevation is reached or descent begins, whichever occurs first. Acetazolamide increases urination and care should be taken to maintain proper hydration.

2. *Dexamethasone (Decadron®)*: This steroid has demonstrated the reduction of AMS symptoms at a dosage of 2 mg every six hours or 4 mg every twelve hours (WMS recommendation grade 1A). It does not facilitate acclimatization, and stopping the medication may lead to rebound AMS symptoms. Steroid toxicity may be encountered if use persists beyond ten days (Hackett 2014). Should the goals of therapy switch from prevention to treatment, the dosage should be adjusted to 4 mg every six hours.

3. *Ibuprofen*: Recently, two trials have supported the use of ibuprofen (600 mg three times daily) in preventing AMS symptoms (WMS recommendation grade 2B) (Luks 2014). Further research is needed to measure its performance in comparison to other available products such as acetazolamide and dexamethasone (Gertsch 2012, Lipman 2012). The likely mode of action for ibuprofen is a decrease in inflammation due to hypoxia at higher altitudes (Zafren 2012).

4. *Ginkgo biloba*: As with many herbal and natural supplements, consistency and potency remain a concern for accurate dosing. There have been multiple studies with results that support and oppose Ginkgo biloba as an effective way to reduce AMS symptoms (WMS recommendation grade 2C).

In treating AMS, descent from elevation is the single best treatment option but may not be required (WMS recommendation grade 1A). If the patient is paired with a climbing partner for continued observation, taking a rest day at the current elevation may be considered with time allowed for acclimatization and treatment of symptoms. Both acetazolamide and dexamethasone are helpful. Note that the *treatment* dose of acetazolamide is 250 mg twice daily and the *treatment* dose of dexamethasone is 4 mg every six hours (WMS recommendation grade 1B).

EVACUATE
Further ascent should be delayed until symptoms resolve. Continued prophylactic doses of either acetazolamide or dexamethasone should be considered. Dexamethasone does help prevent and treat AMS symptoms but does not actually facilitate acclimatization. Therefore, WMS practice guidelines recommend that a climber be asymptomatic and no longer taking dexamethasone before any further climbing (Luks 2014). If a climber does not respond to these treatments or if there is any question whether the climber is suffering from AMS or HACE, they should descend immediately. Other treatments of AMS include the use of oxygen and Gamow bag when descent is not possible (WMS recommendation grade 1C). Evacuation is not needed if symptoms can be resolved with time or by not ascending higher.

HACE (High-Altitude Cerebral Edema)
HACE is far less common than AMS, with a reported occurrence of only 1% in climbers, trekkers, and alpinists (Bärtsch 2013). As with all altitude illnesses, prevention through gradual ascent and appropriate acclimatization is key.

IDENTIFY
HACE is often seen as a progression of AMS. HACE is differentiated from severe AMS by a change in neurological status: chiefly *ataxia*

(inhibited motor function coordination), confusion, and altered mental status (Luks 2014).

TREAT

While AMS victims may occasionally remain at high altitude for further acclimatization, any suspicion of HACE requires immediate descent (WMS recommendation grade 1A). No other potential treatments should delay descent or evacuation. Acetazolamide may aid in acclimatization and prevention of HACE, but it is not an effective treatment strategy for this condition. In accordance with WMS practice guidelines, AMS and HACE may be prevented by acetazolamide with a dosage of 125 mg twice daily (WMS recommendation grade 1A) (Luks 2014). Dexamethasone (2 mg every six hours or 4 mg every twelve hours) is also an option for prevention of HACE, but this dosage does not facilitate acclimatization (WMS recommendation grade 1A). Treatment of HACE should include dexamethasone (initial dose of 8 mg once, then 4 mg every six hours) delivered by mouth, by IM injection, or IV (WMS recommendation grade 1B). In either case, descent should not be delayed. When descent is not immediately possible (such as in white-out conditions), supplemental oxygen and a Gamow bag may be utilized (WMS recommendation grade 1C). As with AMS, once elevation is decreased and symptoms have resolved without any further pharmaceutical therapy, cautious return to elevation may occur with appropriate acclimatization. Several days may be required to allow for resolution of ataxia, mental status deterioration, and loss of coordination.

EVACUATE

Patients with HACE should be evacuated, at a minimum to lower altitude and likely to definitive care.

HAPE (High-Altitude Pulmonary Edema)

HAPE represents a distinct condition that is thought to be separate from AMS and HACE, although the conditions may coexist. HAPE is primarily a pulmonary problem, whereas AMS and HACE primarily manifest as neurological problems. Fifty percent of alpinists suffering from HAPE will not experience AMS symptoms (Hultgren 1996). Despite its relative rarity, with studies indicating its effects between 0.2% and 15% of unacclimatized individuals (Jones 2013), it is still the most common altitude-associated cause of death (Simon 2014).

IDENTIFY

The following signs and symptoms may be observed in HAPE:

1. Persistent and sometimes progressive cough (initially dry, often transitioning to wet, pink, bloody, and frothy in more severe cases).
2. Shortness of breath with exertion may be experienced even with simple activities at camp.
3. Low-grade fever, respiratory crackles, rapid breathing, and tachycardia may all occur.

The Union Internationale des Associations d'Alpinisme (UIAA) cites the following criteria for diagnosing HAPE—chest tightness, shortness of breath at rest, decreased exercise tolerance, *and* two of the following signs: blue discoloration of lips, respiratory crackles, tachycardia, and tachypnea. The patient must exhibit at least two of these symptoms to diagnose HAPE (Basnyat 2016).

Many factors contribute to the onset and progression of HAPE, including rapid ascent to high altitude, resulting in low oxygen levels, and also a maladaptive physiological but non-cardiac response (Stream 2008). Those climbers who have previously suffered from HAPE are more likely to experience it again and should consider prophylaxis. Genetic predisposition, pulmonary hypertension, *alveolar hypoxia* (low oxygen levels in gas-exchanging sacs in lungs), capillary stress failure and leakage, inflammation, infection, or impaired clearance of alveolar sodium and water all may contribute to HAPE appearance (Schoene 2008, Man-kam 2010, Dorma 2002, Bärtsch 2002). Many of these processes form parts of an inflammatory cascade initiated in the low-oxygen environment. Therefore, we make a guarded recommendation for a pocket-size pulse oximetry test. While a single snapshot of oxygen levels can be affected by multiple factors (e.g., compensated hyperventilation, tissue perfusion, etc.), continued and regularly scheduled monitoring may help track the physiologic trends of climbers on an expedition. Our recommendation is guarded because the quality and accuracy of the pulse oximeter must be confirmed, along with its durability, and the user must be trained in interpreting its results. However, in association with clinical findings, this data may provide further insight to a climber's condition (Bachman 1992). Finally, other respiratory ailments discussed in Chapter 8, such as asthma, pneumonia, and pulmonary embolism must be ruled out before making a diagnosis of HAPE. If there is any doubt regarding the onset of HAPE in a climber, descent should be initiated.

As rate of onset of HAPE can vary between individuals, it is unwise to leave tired partners in their tent for dinner so they can "get rest" away from the group. Symptoms can develop precipitously and close observation of suspected patients is necessary.

TREAT

Prevention via staged and gradual ascent is an excellent way to mitigate HAPE, since rapid ascent often produces or worsens symptoms. The Wilderness Medical Society recommends nifedipine (30 mg Extended Release [ER] every 12 hours, WMS recommendation grade 1A), possibly supplemented by salmeterol (WMS recommendation grade 2B), for primary HAPE prevention (Luks 2014). Dexamethasone and tadalafil have been proposed as preventive measures in a single study (Maggiorini 2006), but clinical experience and further research data is lacking, making this a recommendation grade 1C from WMS.

Once symptoms are suspected, descent is the gold standard of treatment (WMS recommendation grade 1A). If retreat is not possible, use supplemental oxygen (WMS recommendation grade 1B), Gamow bags (WMS recommendation grade 1B), and nifedipine (30 mg ER every 12 hours, WMS recommendation grade 1C as an adjunct). While the use of phosphodiesterase inhibitors (tadalafil and sildenafil) to treat HAPE has been described (Fagenholz 2007), these agents have a WMS recommendation grade of 2C, as no systematic studies exist testing their efficacy (Luks 2014). The UIAA Medical Commission has recommended caution in the use of these two drugs due to their potentially dangerous side effects (Donegani 2016).

EVACUATE

Patients with HAPE should be evacuated immediately.

UV Keratitis

Photokeratitis, aka "snow blindness" from ultraviolet radiation in sunlight, is discussed in Chapter 14.

CHAPTER 12

COLD INJURIES

The most common cold-related injuries are hypothermia and frostbite. To prevent and treat these illnesses, it is essential to understand the way heat is lost or gained in the environment. There are four mechanisms of heat exchange (Figure 12-1).

Hypothermia

Normal bodily functions occur when the body's core temperature is between 36.5 and 37.5°C (97.7 to 99.5°F). Normal metabolic processes and working muscles generate heat within the body. When necessary, the body will generate additional heat by shivering and increasing respiratory rate or heart rate to maintain temperature. If these heat-producing mechanisms fail and the core temperature drops, the climber experiences hypothermia (net heat loss from the body) (Zafren 2014).

IDENTIFY

Accidental hypothermia is defined as a drop in core temperature below 35°C (Zafren 2014). However, patients may be cold-stressed and symptomatic before having a body temperature below the hypothermia threshold. Hypothermia can be divided into mild, moderate, and severe (Figure 12-2). Such distinctions are typically made based on rectal body temperature and differ based on different sources. The Wilderness Medical Society defines mild hypothermia as a CBT of 35°C (95°F) to 32°C (90°F); moderate hypothermia between 32°C (90°F) and 28°C (82°F), and severe hypothermia as below 28°C (82°F). Some experts have proposed an additional level of profound hypothermia, representing CBT less than 24°C (75°F) or 20° (68°F) (Zafren 2014). The American Heart Association has published alternate guidelines, most recently updated in 2015, setting mild at >34°C, moderate as 34°C-30°C, and severe as

FIGURE 12-1. METHODS OF ENVIRONMENTAL HEAT TRANSFER

	Heat exchange	Prevention
Radiation	- Heat lost to the environment as infrared radiation, much like the sun radiating heat. - The amount is determined by the temperature difference of the environment and skin.	- Shelter is the primary source of protection against radiant heat losses. Clothing aids in reducing radiative heat loss.
Conduction	- Heat lost by direct contact to objects. The better the conductor the greater the rate of heat lost (cold metal/snow).	- Remove wet clothing, replace with dry, and place an insulating layer such as a mat on snow or rock.
Convection	- Heat loss by movement circulating around the body such as moving air, referred to as the wind chill factor, calculated by the velocity of air. Water current also.	- Layered clothing is the best defense.
Evaporation	- Heat lost through sweat or water evaporating or drying on the skin and during respirations when the inspired air is warmed and moistened.	- Avoid perspiring and layer clothing appropriately. - Always replace wet garments. - Vapor barrier systems are limited and often cause sweat accumulation, however footwear can be effective as long as wet socks are changed. - Using a scarf or facemask helps during high altitude climbing when respiratory rate increases.

<30°C (Kleinman 2015). The AHA guidelines have been criticized as not consistent with more standard classifications, and for over-emphasis on response to defibrillation (which is less likely to be successful below 30°C). Defibrillation is a single criteria unlikely to be meaningful in a climbing environment versus more universal and widely relevant physiologic changes present at each stage (Zafren 2014). Perhaps even more importantly, understanding the signs and symptoms of these stages

FIGURE 12-2. SIGNS/SYMPTOMS AND TREATMENT OF HYPOTHERMIA

Hypothermia	Sign/Symptom	Treatment
Mild	- 35–32°C - Shivering - Unable to care for themselves - Pale and cold - Tachycardia, tachypnea, and hypertensive - Urinary frequency - Alert - Impaired coordination (especially fine motor skills) - Progress to weakness/lethargic - Slow pace - Stumbling/ataxia - Mild confusion - Apathy - Amnesia - Slurred speech - Poor judgment/disoriented	- Protect from further cooling/insulate - Move to shelter - Remove wet clothing - Put on dry clothing - Wrap in sleeping bag, tarps or anything available and insulate from the ground - Huddle to reduce heat loss - Warm fluids and food with added carbs to provide fuel to generate internal heat - No walking or standing for 30 min. - Active warming with heat packs to chest, axilla, back - Evacuation may not be required but monitor and keep warm
Moderate	- 32–28° C - No shivering - Decreased heart rate, respiratory rate, and blood pressure - May not be able to walk - Disorientated - Slurred speech - Confused - Combative	- Protect against further cooling - Shelter - Remove wet clothes - Wrap in sleeping bag, etc. - Use heat packs or water bottles on the axilla, chest, back, and neck (insulate to prevent skin burns) - Keep in a horizontal position

Hypothermia	Sign/Symptom	Treatment
Moderate	- Irrational behavior - Paradoxical undressing - Progress to stupor - Semi-conscious to unconscious - Pupil dilation - Severe muscle rigidity - Slow to undetectable heartbeat and respiration - Dysrhythmias	- Avoid abrupt movements - Place on mat or other insulating material - Heat the air - Limit exercise to avoid post-rescue death (a result of an increase mixing of warm core blood with cold blood from the skin) - Evacuate
Severe/Profound	- < 28° C - Coma - Nonreactive & dilated pupils - Muscle rigidity - Severely low to undetectable blood pressure - Heart rate 10-20 beats a minute - Very irritable heart with the greatest danger for ventricular fibrillation (VF) - Death	- Perform all treatments listed for Moderate and Mild - Active rewarming with skin to skin contact with rescuer - Gentle handling to prevent VF - Begin evacuation arrangements - Consider active warming in a facility

(Zafren 2014)

are more relevant to a climbing environment than knowing the body temperature. Climbers will rarely have access to a rectal thermometer. Furthermore, even if a rectal thermometer were available, the Wilderness Medical Society (with a recommendation grade of 1C) believes rectal temperature should not be measured in the field until the patient is in a warm environment (Zafren 2014). Figure 12-2 describes signs and symptoms which can be used instead of a thermometer to gauge the severity of hypothermia and provide guidance for appropriate treatment.

The climber will appear pale and cold and will experience uncontrollable shivering in an attempt to produce heat. Mental status may become impaired with confusion, ataxia, and disorientation. Urinary frequency increases due to increased kidney blood flow caused by elevated cardiac output and peripheral *vasoconstriction* (constriction [narrowing] of blood vessels), increasing the blood flow to the kidneys.

If cooling continues, respirations and cardiac function slow, and may eventually stop. Cooling dramatically reduces the baseline metabolic rate and oxygen demand, aiding in the protection of the vital organs. Brain function and activity declines at a core temperature of 33 and 34°C (Geisbrecht 1993). These effects sometimes allow the patient to survive for a prolonged period even with a very slow or even undetectable heart rate. Such patients will appear lifeless and if not rewarmed will die. Even after several hours of being hypothermic, climbers have been resuscitated and a severely hypothermic person should not be considered dead until they have been appropriately warmed. In the remote environment where climbing often occurs, it is important to remember that someone suffering from hypothermia is not dead until they are warm and dead.

PREVENT
Hypothermia can occur even when the environmental temperatures are warm. Factors such as wind and rain can have a dramatic effect on the risk of hypothermia even in moderate temperatures. An elevated wind chill factor, constantly blowing warm air away from the climber's body, accelerates the rate of cooling through convection. Perspiration, rain, or other wet conditions enhance the cooling effect through evaporation. Combined conditions create an environment for even more rapid cooling and increased risk of hypothermia. Prevention and preparation is the surest method to avoid hypothermia (see "Cold Injury Prevention" sidebar).

Water, food, and clothing are preparation essentials. Dehydration will impair heat production and cause vasoconstriction. While climbing, fluids must be replenished to maintain a balanced and adequate fluid status. Blood volume and the water lost from the kidneys, skin, and lungs must be taken into consideration when balancing hydration. Food is necessary to fuel physical activity and generate heat. Frequently, consuming small amounts of dense, tasty foods helps to

COLD INJURY PREVENTION
Stay out of the wind, even low winds cause greater cooling
Wear layers of appropriate clothing avoiding perspiration and limiting heat loss
Remove and replace wet clothing, wet clothes encourage faster cooling
Exercise and eat to generate body heat
Hydrate properly and avoid drinks that are diuretics or vasodilators (caffeine or alcohol)
Avoid smoking (increases vasoconstriction)
Avoid vasodilation drugs (heat is lost more quickly)
Maintain good physical condition to aid in the length and amount of heat produced

maintain energy stores and a positive frame of mind. If the climber is drinking water, snacks should contain sodium to prevent hyponatremia (see Chapter 13).

Proper clothing is essential because in cold climates it is difficult to improvise. It is important to have the appropriate materials worn in a layering system. A three-layer approach is effective and common (Figure 12-3).

The base layer is underwear, followed by one or more middle insulating layers, and an outer rainproof or windproof shell. The middle and outer layers can be adjusted when heat production or environmental temperatures increase. It is essential to avoid sweating, as this can moisten the clothing, reduce insulating ability, and increase heat loss through evaporation. Timing when to adjust the various layers is critical. Layers must be opened or removed prior to sweating and closed or replaced as soon as activity ceases prior to getting cold, thus preventing the use of energy to replace heat loss during the transition.

Appropriate clothing helps to maintain a warm core, which is the best way to prevent cold extremities. Wearing suitable hand-, foot-, and headgear can optimize heat retention and comfort of the extremities. To keep the hands and fingers warm, wool mittens with an outer nylon shell are much warmer than gloves. For the feet and toes, the best material for a single-layer boot in moderately cold temperatures continues to be leather. It allows moisture to escape, and is more comfortable as it expands to accommodate swelling while climbing. At altitude, double or

FIGURE 12-3. CLOTHING LAYERS

Inner layer	*Polypropylene* - decreases evaporative heat loss because it wicks moisture from the skin to the fabric surface to evaporate. A disadvantage is the retention of body odors.
	Polyester - has replaced polypropylene but is more expensive.
	Wool - excellent for the base layer and merino wool is the most comfortable.
Insulating layer	*Wool* - oldest and one of the best insulating materials and retains heat even when wet; however, it is heavier than other synthetic materials.
	Fleece - breathes well, and it is light, durable, and fast drying.
	Goose down - the best insulating material but only when it remains dry. *Synthetic* brands are effective even when wet but are more bulky, less compressible, and heavier.
Outer layer	Must be water repellent to protect the underlying layers. Synthetic fibers such as Gore-Tex® possess small pores that allow water vapor to pass through but resist water penetration from the environment.

triple boots are a better option. These are constructed with a soft inner insulating material covered by a protective hard plastic outer shell. Effective headgear to inhibit heat loss from the head can include wool caps, balaclavas covering the neck and face, and hoods worn over caps, along with scarves and neck gaiters, usually made of wool.

TREAT

All hypothermic climbers should be protected from further cooling. This is accomplished by moving the person to a warm location protected from the wind, and when possible, warming the air with a stove to aid the rewarming process. If necessary building a snow cave or group shelter provides insulation from the wind. Change wet clothing for warm dry items and put on additional layers. Wrapping the individual in a sleeping bag or improvising layers such as blankets and insulated pads can help protect against the cold, dampness, and wind (Henriksson 2009, Thomassen 2011). If this is not possible and there is access to plastic, wrap the individual and make sure to seal around the neck to eliminate evaporative heat loss. Place warm water bottles or *large* thermal chemical packets close to the skin at the axilla, chest, and back, and additional heat to the neck, taking care not to place the packets directly on the skin and causing a burn (Lundgren 2009). Note that Wilderness Medical Society practice guidelines, with a recommendation grade of 1B, discourage the use of *small* thermal chemical packets for overall body heating, citing risk of burns and insufficient heat generation to affect core body temperature. They do endorse the use of small thermal chemical packets to prevent local cold injury to hands and feet with a recommendation grade of 1C (Zafren 2014). Position and insulate the climber from the ground or rock by placing the person on a sleeping pad or rucksack. If there are no swallowing concerns, give them warm drinks and food to help generate heat production. If the individual is not shivering uncontrollably, heat can be generated by a gradual increase in exercise, though initially a hypothermic patient should not be allowed to stand or walk (WMS recommendation grade 1C; Zafren 2014). Body-to-body rewarming may be useful for a mildly hypothermic patient but should not be done if it delays evacuation (WMS recommendation grade 1B; Zafren 2014). Extremities should be warmed first to prevent the mixing of cold peripheral blood with the warm core blood, which could cause a drop in the core temperature.

For severely hypothermic individuals, the measures listed above may not be enough to rewarm them due to their slow metabolism. For extreme cases, external heat sources or central rewarming in a medical facility is the only viable option. Severely hypothermic individuals may be susceptible to *ventricular fibrillation* (Giesbrecht 2001, Zafren 2014). With a recommendation grade of 1B, WMS guidelines recommend these climbers should only be moved gently if at all (especially minimizing movements of extremities) and their clothes should be cut off rather than manually removed to prevent ventricular fibrillation. Ventricular fibrillation is a serious heart rhythm disturbance that causes the lower heart chamber to contract in a rapid, unorganized manner and the heart to pump little to no blood to the body. Evacuation must be carried out in the gentlest manner, avoiding any jarring or bouncing over rough terrain. Artificial respirations should be started only if the patient has no respirations. Individuals with a detectable heartbeat should not receive CPR, as ventricular fibrillation, if not already present, may occur. One minute should be spent attempting to detect a pulse at the carotid artery prior to deciding if CPR should be initiated in hypothermic climbers (Zafren 2014).

Anyone suffering from mild hypothermia can remain in the wilderness as long as they are able to stay warm and are not showing any signs of further deterioration. Moderate to severely hypothermic individuals should be evacuated, as they can no longer warm themselves.

Hypothermia is easily preventable and preparation is the most important factor. Being aware of the weather conditions, wearing the proper gear, maintaining hydration, bringing adequate food supplies, and having a contingency plan in the event of condition changes are the essentials for cold illness prevention.

Frostbite

Frostbite is a cold injury caused by the freezing of tissue, occurring most commonly in the hands, feet, ears, and face but can occur on any portion of exposed skin. In cold temperatures, the body shunts blood away from the extremities to preserve a warm core. Initially, this decreases the peripheral circulation in the hands and feet, as they are located the farthest from the heart. Further decrease in circulation results from increased blood viscosity from the damaged endothelial cells that line the blood vessels. The damaged vessels allow blood plasma to leak out, causing the blood to become even more sluggish. When the circulation is slowed in this way, tissues begin to freeze and ice crystals form in and between the cells of the extremities. As the ice crystals form and swell, the cells are depleted of water, causing cell rupture and additional tissue damage. An intense inflammatory response follows. During the thawing process, damaged cells clot and further obstruct circulation. The tissues beyond the thrombosis (clot) are often dark red or black in color and indicate ischemic and necrotic tissue.

IDENTIFY

Frostbite usually occurs in freezing temperatures and is often associated with hypothermia. The degree of frostbite is extremely difficult to identify in the field and not until the tissue is rewarmed do the blisters develop. Blisters are helpful to determine the degree and stage of the injury. Historically, frostbite has been divided into four degrees but recent guidelines suggest dividing the stages into superficial and deep classifications is more useful (Figure 12-4).

If the blisters cover the entire affected tissue and are filled with a clear or milky fluid, the chance of recovery is high and a superficial

FIGURE 12-4. FROSTBITE STAGES

1 (superficial)	2 (superficial)	3 (deep)	4 (deep)
- Pale, yellow	- Pale, white	- Pale, white	- Pale, white
- Numb	- Numb	- Numb	- Numb
- Erythema	- Erythema	- After rewarming skin will be swollen and red with bloody filled blisters	- No capillary refill
- Mild edema	- Edema		- Cyanotic
- White or yellow plaque	- After rewarming skin will be swollen and red with clear or milky filled blisters	- Dermis involvement	- After rewarming, skin will be swollen and red with no blisters or edema
- After rewarming skin will be swollen and red		- Anticipate tissue loss	- Damage into the muscle, tendon, and bone
- Minimal to no tissue loss	- Minimal to no tissue loss		- Anticipate tissue loss

(McIntosh 2014)

injury is suspected. If the blisters are filled with a bloody fluid or the area is free of any blisters, prognosis suggests a deep tissue injury, and much of the underlying tissue may be lost. The most severe injuries have no blisters and retain a deep purple color. After about a week and continuing over many weeks, a black layer known as eschar appears. Individuals who have had frostbite in the past have residual damage and an increased sensitivity to cold temperatures and are more susceptible for future injury.

PREVENT

Appropriate preparation and avoiding risky cold conditions are the best preventative measures to avoid frostbite. Well-layered clothing to include mittens, hat, scarf, or balaclava, and properly fitting footwear that does not constrict circulation is essential in cold temperatures. Any medications that cause vasoconstriction should be avoided if possible. Hydration should be maintained to support a sufficient blood pressure. Proper nutrition to provide energy for normal bodily functions, compensatory mechanisms, and exercise are all essential. Ensure adequate sleep and a proper ascent profile while climbing at increased altitude.

Avoid alcohol, caffeine, and smoking, as all affect the peripheral circulation. Individuals with pre-existing risk factors such as Raynaud's phenomenon or previous frostbite should be extra-cautious and limit cold exposure. Chemical or electrical warmers can be used to keep extremities warm. Maintain a warm core to deter the body from shunting the blood to the core with peripheral vasoconstriction, and avoid direct skin contact with metal or other cold items (WMS recommendation grade 1C) (McIntosh 2014). Additionally, aiding peripheral perfusion through exercise has been shown to be effective in two studies, though continual exercise will obviously lead to exhaustion (WMS recommendation grade 1B) (McIntosh 2014).

TREAT
Treatment of hypothermia should be the priority if present. Rewarming is the best treatment and should occur immediately in the wilderness if the affected tissue can remain thawed (WMS recommendation grade 1C) (McIntosh 2014). The greatest damage occurs when tissue is thawed and then refrozen. If there is a chance of refreezing it is better to delay rewarming. If spontaneous thawing occurs all efforts should be made to keep the tissue thawed. If options are limited, the frozen tissue can be used to aid a self-evacuation and the climber should be encouraged to walk out in order to obtain definitive care. Walking on a frozen foot produces far less damage than allowing the foot to refreeze after thawing. Climbers suffering from frostbite should be evacuated as soon as possible.

The climber should be placed in a shelter and protected from the cold. All restrictive or wet clothing should be removed. Avoid further tissue damage and do not rub frozen skin as this will increase damage. Warming with external heat such as a fire should not occur, as the decreased sensation may allow the tissue to burn, causing more damage. The affected tissue should be submerged in water that is between 37 and 39°C (Cauchy 2016). Water must be added to maintain this temperature and circulated around the tissue, and an antiseptic solution can be added (WMS recommendation 2C) (McIntosh 2014). Without a thermometer, the use of an uninjured hand to judge the temperature is the most ideal option. The tissue should be suspended in the center of the water as feeling is diminished and the tissue must be protected from external damage such as resting against the side or bottom of the basin. Thawing should continue for 30 to 60 minutes or until the skin is red/purple in color (Cauchy 2016). Once this is accomplished, the tissue should be air dried or gently blotted. The application of aloe vera ointment has been shown to be beneficial (WMS recommendation 2C) (McIntosh 2014). Bulky dry sterile gauze should be placed between the fingers or toes to avoid further tissue damage and blisters should not be ruptured (WMS recommendation grade 1C) (McIntosh 2014). The injured tissues should be elevated above the heart to decrease swelling and movement should be restricted. If warm water is not an option but refreezing is avoidable, digits can be rewarmed by placing them on another climber's skin (Cauchy 2016).

Thawing is extremely painful and analgesics should be given. NSAIDs have been shown to decrease the damaging effects of inflammation (WMS recommendation grade 2C) (McIntosh 2014). Aspirin (75 to 81 mg) or ibuprofen (400 to 600 mg) two to three times daily will assist in pain control (Cauchy 2016). The individual should be kept warm. Evacuation should be immediate. Healing requires weeks to months and the need and extent of surgery cannot be determined until demarcation of dead tissue is unmistakable. A tetanus immunization should be up-to-date, as frostbite is a tetanus-prone wound.

Raynaud's Phenomenon
IDENTIFY
Raynaud's phenomenon (RP) is a disorder that is caused by exposure to cold temperature or emotional stress and is precipitated by the constriction of small blood vessels in the fingers and toes. Affected digits become pale, often white in color, and numb. With rewarming, the digits can be painful.

PREVENT
Climbers with RP must be careful in cold temperature situations, but this syndrome does not preclude them from participating in climbing or mountaineering activities. Rather, it requires additional caution while in these environments. Remaining warm through proper clothing and high-quality gear, particularly for the hands and feet, is the best prevention technique. The use of mittens rather than gloves and the use of chemical hand and feet warmers are recommended to prevent this disorder.

TREAT

Field treatment consists of warming the affected body parts using chemical hand warmers or by placing them in warm water. Exercising can be helpful to increase peripheral circulation. Climbers with known RP should discuss this problem with a medical professional. Nifedipine has been found to be helpful, and some with the disorder use ginkgo biloba (Luks 2009).

Frostnip

IDENTIFY

Frostnip is a temporary superficial reversible and nonfreezing cold injury of the skin surface most commonly involving cheeks, nose, and earlobes but sometimes also the chin and the tips of the fingers and toes. Frost-like ice crystals form on the surface of the skin and the affected area is numb, painless, and pale in color. The tissue remains soft and pliable. It resolves quickly once affected tissue is covered, warmed by direct contact, or after moving into shelter. There is no permanent damage though climbers should be aware that weather conditions that cause frostnip can also cause frostbite (McIntosh 2014).

PREVENT

In cold temperatures, make sure to cover all exposed skin and keep a warm core to prevent vasoconstriction.

TREAT

Cover all areas where frostnip is noted. If possible, seek a warm environment to rewarm affected areas. Often, cupping hands over the mouth and nose and breathing out is enough to rewarm the superficial skin where frostnip occurs. Chemical heat packs are beneficial but care must be taken not to burn the skin. Frostnip can cause mild pain when rewarming. Evacuation is not necessary but care should be taken to prevent future occurrences.

CHAPTER 13

HEAT INJURIES

Climbers are exposed to a wide range of temperatures and, regardless of environmental conditions, the human body attempts to maintain a core body temperature between 36.5 and 37.5°C. Maintaining temperature within this range is known as normothermia. With the exception that fever is sometimes an adaptive bodily response to infection, normothermia is essential for proper bodily function of human organs. A shell of tissue surrounds the core organs (the brain, heart, liver, and kidneys). This shell and the hypothalamus (a part of the brain) maintain core homeostasis. Heat is produced in the body by normal metabolism, exercise, and shivering. When the body temperature is elevated, heat is transferred from the core to the environment via compensatory mechanisms. Proper regulation of body temperature prevents heat injury.

When heat must be dispersed, the cardiovascular system stimulates more blood flow to the skin and less blood flow to abdominal organs by increasing the heart rate and cardiac output. This shunts warm core blood to the skin surface for heat dissipation. Respirations increase and result in evaporative cooling from the lungs. There is a release of stimulatory hormones that increase sweat production, another effective method of heat transfer. The hypothalamus inhibits metabolic heat production, decreasing the amount of heat the body has to regulate. Hydration is a key element for these adaptations to occur. When heat gained or produced exceeds heat lost, the individual is at risk of developing hyperthermia (inappropriately elevated body temperature) and heat illness (Lipman 2014). During elevated temperatures body metabolism becomes deranged and enzymes denature, cellular damage occurs, and compensatory mechanisms max out and fail.

The cascade of heat illness can be divided into three phases. In the initial or acute phase, toxins are released and trigger the release of pro-

FIGURE 13-1. PREDISPOSING RISK FACTORS FOR HEAT ILLNESS

Environmental	Individual characteristics	Medications	Pre-existing conditions
Hot ambient temperature	Age	Diuretics	Viral infection
High humidity	Sex	Anti-cholinergics	Inflammation/ fever
Still air	Obesity	Beta blockers	Skin disorders
No shade/shelter	Poor physical fitness	Antihistamines	Cardiovascular disease
No air conditioning	Dehydration	Amphetamines	Diabetes
	Lack of acclimatization	Ergogenic aids	Endocrine disorders
	Sleep deprivation	Phenothiazines	
	Fatigue	Salicylates	Sickle cell trait
	Poor nutrition	Antidepressants to include lithium	Malignant hyperthermia
	Recent air travel	Alcohol	Neurologic disease
		Recreational drugs such as cocaine	Sunburn (reduces thermoregulation)
			Previous heat illness

Sources: Hall B, Hall J. Sauer's Manual of Skin Diseases. 10th ed. Philadelphia, PA: Lippincott Williams & Wilkins; 2010.
Krakowski A, Goldenberg A. Exposure to Radiation from the Sun. In: Auerbach PS, ed. Wilderness Medicine. 7th ed. Philadelphia, PA: Mosby Elsevier; 2017.

inflammatory and anti-inflammatory hormones throughout the body. This reaction—the *systemic inflammatory response syndrome* (SIRS)— marks the second phase, known as the hematologic or enzymatic stage. In the initial acute stage, the gastrointestinal tract is damaged due to low blood flow, allowing bacteria to leak into the bloodstream. In the second phase, blood clotting disturbances called *disseminated intravascular coagulation* (DIC) appear, leading to the final phase of multi-organ system failure. The liver begins to fail, and dehydration and low blood pressure to abdominal organs cause kidney failure. Cerebral edema occurs with bleeding in the brain and degradation of brain tissue. Cardiovascular dysfunction causes blood vessel swelling, followed by constriction. All of these combined contribute to shock, and eventually, if untreated, to death.

Predisposing risk factors that contribute to developing heat illness are broadly categorized as environmental, individual characteristics, medications, and pre-existing conditions. Figure 13-1 lists common components of each.

Clothing, shade, fanning, and air-conditioned shelter are all behavioral actions that complement the body's internal heat regulation mechanisms, but environmental variables such as air temperature, humidity, wind velocity, and radiation have the greatest impact on heat exchange.

As described in Chapter 12 (Figure 12-1), there are four primary methods that allow transfer of body heat to the environment: conduction, convection, radiation, and evaporation.

Conduction occurs through direct contact with an object. The amount of contact surface and conductivity of the object affect the heat lost or gained. The heat exchange ceases when the items in contact reach equilibrium.

Convection consists of heat transferred through the flow of one substance over another. Body exposure to windchill (air flow over the body, discussed in Appendix D) and water current (water flow over the body) are examples, and the amount of exposed skin has a large impact on heat lost or gained. Wearing appropriate clothing when climbing in sun-exposed hot areas can increase the amount of heat transferred.

Radiation is the direct transfer of heat between the body's surface and all other sources of radiant energy. The sun is the main source of radiation in hot environments. By day, the sun can transfer large amounts of heat to the body, while at night heat radiates away from a warm body. Shelter reduces the amount of heat transferred and wearing light-colored clothing while climbing in direct sun will reduce the heat gained.

Evaporation is achieved through vaporized sweat. The conversion of sweat to water vapor from the skin is dependent on the air humidity and wind. With high humidity, the vapor transferred is limited because the air is already saturated, and the sweat that drips from the skin loses its cooling effect, contributing only to dehydration. An environment of dry air and wind is more conducive to heat exchange, and this is the ideal environment for evaporative heat transfer from a climber's body.

When homeostasis is not maintained, mild to fatal heat illness can occur. Assessing the environment for heat illness risks is essential for successful climbing in hot environments. Numerous resources are available to aid in this.

Experts have developed an internationally accepted measure of heat stress, known as the wet bulb globe temperature (WBGT). It is used to estimate the effect of temperature, humidity, wind speed, and visible and infrared radiation on humans and is one of the most useful metrics in determining environmental heat impact (WMS recommendation grade 1A) (Lipman 2014). This can be difficult to calculate without the proper equipment and in mountainous terrain.

AccuWeather produces a "RealFeel" temperature that includes radiation in their calculations, creating an easy and useful reference without the difficult calculations of the wet bulb temperature measure (WBGT).* If the temperature and humidity are extremely high, climbing activities should be scheduled for times of the day that are cooler and less humid. Not only will the decrease in temperature and humidity be helpful in reducing heat illness risk, but it will also improve the dryness and texture of the rock, and result in a better chance of sending a project.

Hydration, adequate rest, proper nutrition, and acclimatization are other measures that help prevent heat illness. Proper choice in clothing and equipment can play a large role in prevention of heat illness with a focus on optimizing all four methods of heat transfer (WMS recommendation grade 1C) (Lipman 2014). To achieve acclimatization after entering a new climate, one must participate in up to 120 minutes of exercise for at least eight days (WMS recommendation grade 1C) (Lipman 2014). Over time, sweat glands will produce more hypotonic sweat, conserving salt and inducing sweat at lower temperatures. The kidneys will conserve sodium and increase the serum sodium level. This allows climbers to maintain lower body temperatures in hot environments. Acclimatization is delayed if much of the day is spent in air-conditioned environments, and it is lost after 20 to 40 days of exposure to normal temperatures. Acclimatization benefits include lower resting heart rate, lower body temperature, decreased sodium loss in sweat, and increased blood flow to the skin. In addition, the kidneys retain more sodium and water, plasma proteins increase in number (improving fluid volume in the body), and exercise tolerance for climbing in a warm environment improves.

* www.accuweather.com

Heat Exhaustion

IDENTIFY

Heat exhaustion consists of a core temperature of 38.5 to 40°C with no neurological deficit—that is, a climber is alert and oriented without signs of confusion. The signs and symptoms of heat exhaustion can include hot skin, dehydration, fatigue, dizziness, headache, nausea, vomiting, hypotension, tachycardia, and malaise ("feeling crummy"). The affected climber may present as cold, clammy, and pale. Heat exhaustion happens more commonly when climbing in hot environments, but it can occur with or without exercise.

PREVENT

Dehydration causes blood vessels in the skin to constrict and limit sweat production. Waiting to feel significantly thirsty is a poor strategy, and thirst is indicative of early dehydration. On the other hand, episodes of *exercise-associated hyponatremia* (EAH, discussed later in this chapter) have occurred because people forced themselves to drink unnecessarily to meet a fluid "goal." This reality has led many wilderness medicine authorities, including the Wilderness Medical Society, to propose a strategy of *ad libitum* hydration (drinking when desired or as dictated by thirst) during wilderness exercise—WMS gives this a recommendation grade of 1B or 1C (Bennett 2014, Lipman 2014). The best practice is likely somewhere between these two approaches. A problem in using urine color alone is that some fluids commonly used by climbers that promote urination (such as caffeine or alcohol) can produce very clear urine despite early dehydration. Similarly, many things, like vitamins, can produce darkly colored urine despite adequate hydration, which runs the risk of prompting over-hydration and hyponatremia, described later in this chapter.

Fluids should be cool beverages containing a maximum of 6% carbohydrates. A higher concentration of sugar delays gastric emptying, and when the solution is cool, the body absorbs it more easily. Salt can be replaced through fluids or dietary intake; salt tablets should be avoided. Choosing crags or climbs that are in the shade also helps prevent heat illness—most guidebooks indicate when crags are sheltered from the sun. Schedule climbing during the morning or evening when the heat is less intense and the sun is low. Climbers should take into account certain medications alter the body's ability to regulate temperature, including antihistamines (which reduce sweat), antihypertensives (which reduce heart rate, blood pressure, and cardiac output), and diuretics (which promote urination, thus altering hydration).

Wear lightweight, light-colored, and loose-fitting clothing for ventilation and heat reflection. The material should be breathable and have water-wicking properties that aid in evaporative cooling. Prior to a big climb day, the athlete should be well-rested and acclimatized.

TREAT

The 'seven Rs' listed in Figure 13-2 help remind a climber of actions that should be taken if someone is suffering from heat exhaustion.

The patient should be moved to a cooler area and placed in a sitting position. One liter of electrolyte-containing fluids should be consumed over an hour, continuing until the climber is rehydrated. Severely dehydrated individuals will require half a liter for approximately every half-kilogram of weight lost. This should be replaced over the next day and a half with oral hydration. Care should be taken when rehydrating as EAH presents in a similar fashion as heat exhaustion (Lipman 2014). All restrictive clothing should be loosened or removed. These passive cooling methods receive a recommendation of grade 1C from the WMS guidelines (Lipman 2014). Active cooling methods should be administered, including exposing skin and misting it with ambient-temperature water, followed by fanning. Current recommendations stress placing cold packs or ice over the entire body, not just the largely vascularized areas such as the groin, axillae, and neck/scalp—WMS gives this a recommendation grade of 1C (Lipman 2014). This is unrealistic in many climbing environments, but an excellent cooling measure if available. Be sure not to place ice directly against the skin, as this could cause tissue damage. Additional cooling measures include wrapping wet sheets around the person or immersion into cool water. Meticulous attention should be paid to any patients in water to ensure that they remain conscious and that, during immersion in water, their airway does not accidentally go underwater (submersion).

Heatstroke

IDENTIFY

The key signs for heatstroke are elevated temperature and an altered mental status. Mental status changes can include irritability, agitation, confusion, combativeness, delirium, stupor, or seizures. If untreated, heatstroke

FIGURE 13-2. SEVEN Rs OF HEAT ILLNESS TREATMENT

Recognize	Know the sign and symptoms
Rest	Stop activity
Remove	Remove from heat and loosen or remove all tight clothes
Resuscitate	ABC if necessary (airway, breathing, circulation)
Reduce temperature	Evaporative cooling, ice application, wet sheet, water submersion, or cold IV fluid administration (at medical facility)
Rehydrate	Oral (if neurologically intact) or IV (at medical facility)
Rush to hospital	If unable to cool or heat stroke suspected

can lead to a coma. Additional signs include tachycardia, hypotension, and rapid respiratory rate. The climber may or may not be sweating. Previously, cessation of sweating was considered the threshold for heatstroke, but this is no longer considered to be correct. Cessation of sweating can be hard to assess in a climber with sweat-soaked clothes. Furthermore, significant changes in mental status and significant heatstroke can develop while residual sweating continues. Consequently, altered mental status is now considered the defining feature distinguishing heatstroke from milder heat exhaustion. Heatstroke can be either active or passive. Active heatstroke is more common in climbing and other rigorous outdoor sports, while passive heatstroke occurs in children, the elderly, and patients who have suppressed behavioral adjustments. They may be dehydrated, consume high-risk medications, have a cardiac history, or a respiratory infection. Heatstroke can lead to multi-organ system failure and death.

PREVENT

Prevention of heat stroke is similar to prevention of heat exhaustion. Limit physical activity, acclimatize, schedule climbing at cooler times of the day or at shaded crags, limit alcohol consumption, and hydrate with appropriate fluids. Vulnerable individuals, including those with any infections, should avoid exerting themselves in hot weather.

TREAT

Treatment should incorporate the seven Rs (Figure 13-2). The primary goal is rapid heat reduction followed by evacuation to a medical facility. The patient should be immediately moved to a cooler shaded area. Airway, breathing, and circulation must be monitored and any problems with them addressed. Rapid cooling measures should be initiated as part of the primary survey (this is the *H* in the MARCH acronym described in Chapter 1), beginning with placing the patient in a supine position with skin exposed and all restrictive clothing removed or loosened. Cold water immersion is considered the ideal method for reduction in body temperature (WMS recommendation grade 1A) (Lipman 2014). Again, vigilance must be maintained for airway protection in any patient immersed in water. Ice, if available, should be applied to the entire body, to produce rapid cooling. Alternatively, wrapping patients in a wet sheet or fanning the skin after misting it with ambient-temperature water aids in evaporative cooling. Rehydration using oral fluids should not be attempted for any climber with altered mental status, as aspiration is a risk, unless their swallowing capability can be assured. If available, hydration with normal saline via an IV would be more prudent for these patients (WMS recommendation grade of 1C).

Heat Cramps

IDENTIFY

Heat cramps are not fully understood. It is thought that the release of intracellular calcium acting on muscular filaments stimulates involuntary muscle contraction during or immediately after exercise. The skeletal muscle contractions result in brief, painful spasms most typically of the legs, arms, and abdomen. It is more common in non-acclimatized individuals and climbers with low sodium levels. Climbers who sweat profusely are more prone to developing heat cramps because of their increased fluid loss and lower sodium levels. Prolonged activity in a hot environment is a chief factor in heat cramps.

PREVENT

The best prevention for heat cramps is to maintain appropriate hydration and electrolyte balance. Climb during portions of the day when temperatures are cooler (early morning or late afternoon). Dress in light-colored, water-wicking materials to reduce heat production and optimize heat exchange.

TREAT

Rest, hydrate, and replace electrolytes with fluids and salty food. Avoid salt tablets, as they alter potassium levels and cause gastrointestinal upset. A salt-containing beverage is best. The World Health Organization Oral Rehydration Solution (ORS) can be used: It consists of 1 teaspoon salt and 6 teaspoons sugar added to 1 liter of water (WHO 2005). Other authorities, including the Rehydration Project and UNICEF, believe that a half teaspoon of salt can be used in an ORS without reduction in efficacy (Rehydration Project 2016, UNICEF 2010). Passive stretching is also helpful.

Heat Syncope

IDENTIFY

Heat syncope is characterized by dizziness, weakness, or brief and transient loss of consciousness after prolonged heat exposure. This illness is most common in individuals who have allowed blood to pool in the lower extremities from prolonged standing, sitting, or lying, causing peripheral blood vessel swelling and decreased blood vessel tone. In climbing, this most commonly happens to the belayer during a long pitch. Less blood is circulated back to the heart or to the brain from vasodilation, thus causing poor cerebral perfusion. Volume depletion from dehydration enhances this problem. Moving from a sitting or lying to a standing position can result in low blood pressure. This is more common in dehydrated, inactive, and unacclimatized individuals.

PREVENT

Avoiding long periods of inactivity in the direct heat/sunlight and ensuring proper hydration are the two keys to avoiding heat syncope. Changing positions and flexing leg muscles while at a belay are easy measures to prevent this illness.

TREAT

Move the patient out of the heat. Evaluate for any trauma if there is an associated fall. Lay flat with elevated legs, and begin cooling measures.

If the patient is dehydrated, replace fluids and electrolytes. Implement the seven Rs in Figure 13-2.

Hyponatremia

IDENTIFY

Hyponatremia (low blood levels of sodium) is often a consequence of excessive fluid replacement with plain water. It is common in competitors participating in endurance races who rehydrate while not eating. Hyponatremia that occurs in this setting is termed exercise-associated hyponatremia (EAH) and can occur in any outdoor venture in very hot environments. For example, the Grand Canyon National Park reported incidence of hyponatremia in hikers seeking care for exercise-associated collapse or exhaustion as 16% (Backer 1993); another study showed 19% of nonfatal heat-related incidents in the Grand Canyon involved hyponatremia (Noe 2013). Hyponatremia incidence in all Grand Canyon hikers is thought to be two to four per 100,000 hikers (Backer 1999). Climbers, particularly alpinists, have similar risks for hyponatremia—indeed, potentially higher risk, given the possibility of greater aerobic activity. Climbers with hyponatremia often present with stomach bloating, weakness, frequent urination, and nausea. Cerebral edema may be present and can be identified with neurological changes. Eventually the climber may collapse or become unconscious.

PREVENT

Hyponatremia usually occurs to individuals in a high heat environment who have overhydrated with water while not also eating. Avoiding overhydration is the primary strategy to prevent EAH (WMS recommendation grade 1B) (Bennett 2014). Eating and drinking moderately throughout the day and using rehydration tabs or mixes such as Nuun™ or Skratch© are good methods to prevent hyponatremia while providing the body with the needed nutrients to fuel a day of climbing. Always mix rehydration fluids as instructed by the manufacturer.

TREAT

Avoid consuming plain water and encourage consumption of salty foods as long as there is no neurological deficit or risk of aspiration.

HYPONATREMIA
Water intoxication with serum/plasma sodium level <135 mmol/L
Weakness
Anorexia
Vomiting
Muscle cramps
Altered mental state

Evacuate to a medical facility for advanced care. A treatment paradox is that EAH and dehydration may present similarly, but require opposite treatment: hydration for dehydration but fluid restriction for EAH. Because of this, the Second International Exercise-Associated Hyponatremia Consensus Development Conference concluded that "medical directors should ensure the availability of on-site serum sodium concentration analysis" for outdoor competitions (Hew-Butler 2008). However, the Wilderness Medical Society has noted, "the reality is that on-site analysis of serum sodium concentration is not widely available at organized . . . competitions, nor is it currently feasible to widely implement." Therefore, with a recommendation grade of 1A, if serum sodium testing is not available, WMS recommends fluid restriction only if EAH is suspected (Bennett 2014). This suspicion would include large volumes of free water ingested during significant exertion without significant salt or electrolyte supplementation. The sidebar above reviews EAH identification.

Miliaria Rubia (Prickly Heat)
IDENTIFY
Prickly heat is an itchy or burning rash commonly found on the waist, upper trunk, neck, underarms, and scalp that results from blocked and inflamed sweat pores during excessive perspiration. It is often more pronounced in areas where clothing is tight, restrictive, or rubs against the skin and occurs frequently along the waist and leg loop locations for climbers.

PREVENT

Prickly heat can be easily prevented by wearing loose, airy clothing and ensuring proper hygiene.

TREAT

Taking a cool shower and gently dabbing the area dry will help to resolve these rashes. Application of talcum powder or calamine lotion can also help. Antihistamines may be useful as an anti-inflammatory and as an aid to sleeping.

CHAPTER 14

SOLAR-RELATED INJURIES

Ultraviolet radiation from the sun can be our best friend, warming us after a cold overnight bivy, or our worst enemy, by melting the snow and ice and making our day in the mountains treacherous. Ultraviolet radiation can cause two conditions of note for climbers: common sunburn and photokeratitis (snow blindness).

The energy in solar radiation encompasses wavelengths measured in nanometers (nm). Ultraviolet radiation (UVR) is divided into UVA, UVB, and UVC, with wavelengths of 315 to 400 nm, 280 to 315 nm, and 100 to 280 nm, respectively. UVA and UVB rays are of the most concern, as UVC is mostly absorbed by the ozone in the Earth's atmosphere. Sixty-five percent of UVR reaches the Earth's surface in the middle of the day, between 10 a.m. and 2 p.m., when the sun is most directly overhead. UVA and UVB can result in tissue damage (Figure 14-1).

UVA penetrates deeper, damaging the dermis layer of skin, whereas UVB harms the superficial dermis. Overexposure to either leads to premature aging, wrinkling, and age spots, and increases the chance of developing basal cell carcinoma, squamous cell carcinoma, or malignant melanoma. Additionally, pterygium formation (an abnormal eye

FIGURE 14-1. UV DAMAGE

UVA (deep tissue damage)	UVB (superficial damage)
Delayed tanning	Sunburn
Skin aging	Skin aging
Carcinogenesis	Carcinogenesis
	Vitamin D synthesis

FIGURE 14-2. SKIN CHANGES WITH UV EXPOSURE

Skin changes	UVA	UVB
Immediate pigment darkening (IPD)	Presents as a bluish-gray discoloration of the skin that occurs immediately after exposure and fades within 10-20 minutes.	Apparent 2 to 6 hours after exposure and peaks in 24 to 36 hours.
Persistent pigment darkening (PPD)	Lasts 2 to 24 hours	
Delayed tanning	Due to the formation of new melanin in the epidermis and can last for days.	Peaks at 72 hours and fades rapidly.

growth), cataracts, and macular degeneration can result from UVR exposure.

UVA reaches the Earth's surface 10 to 20 times more than UVB, requiring climbers to consider protection during all daylight hours. UVB is greatest in the middle of the day, and although climbers are exposed to greater amounts of UVA, skin irritation or sunburn is more commonly due to UVB exposure. UVA is most efficient at inducing delayed tanning and is noticeable at the end of the exposure time, fading over the next 24 to 72 hours. Exposure to UVA and UVB results in three types of pigmentation changes, noted in Figure 14-2.

A guideline has been developed for UVA and UVB exposure using the minimal erythema dose (MED). The MED is defined as the lowest dose of UVR that elicits perceptible erythema (redness). This amount determines the MED that a person can receive and has been determined to be 2 to 4 MEDs of UVA and 15 MEDs of UVB daily.

Certain personal traits can make some climbers more susceptible to sunburns. These include pale skin, red hair, blue or green eyes, and freckles. Skin type has been classified into Fitzpatrick's classification of skin type (Figure 14-3). Fitzpatrick's classification can be useful for climbers to identify their personal risk. Those having skin types that fall between 1 and 3 need to be cautious and may need to limit exposure time.

There are other factors that also contribute to a climber's sensitivity to solar radiation. The most common climber-specific factors include

FIGURE 14-3. FITZPATRICK CLASSIFICATIONS

Skin type	Characteristics
I	Never tan, always burn
II	Occasionally tan, usually burn
III	Usually tan, occasionally burn
IV	Easily tan, rarely burn
V	Brown skin
VI	Black skin

medication usage, geographic location, altitude, and time of year. Common drugs that increase an individual's sun sensitivity are listed in "Drugs" sidebar on page 230.

Climbers should be aware that certain environmental factors affect UVR. At altitude, UVR increases 4% for every 300 meters due to decreased atmospheric absorption of UVR. Sunlight intensity increases near the equator and as one nears the North and South Poles. The time of the year and day affects UVR. During the winter months, with shorter daylight hours, the sun remains lower in the sky, and the UVR path through the atmosphere is relatively longer, resulting in more UVR absorption and less reaching the Earth's surface. In the summer months, with longer daylight hours, the sun remains higher in the sky for longer periods of time, and the atmosphere absorbs less UVR, transmitting more UVR to the Earth's surface. This is also the case between 10 a.m. and 4 p.m., when the sun is highest in the sky. Reflection also affects UVR exposure, especially snow, water, sand, and glass. This is particularly important for mountaineers climbing on snow or glaciers, in concave areas, or for climbers involved in deep water soloing. Protective measures should be preplanned to aid in the prevention of sunburn.

Sunburns

PREVENT

Sunburn is easier to prevent than treat. Limiting the chance of burning involves avoiding excessive UVR, especially exposure between 10 a.m.

and 4 p.m., covering up with tightly woven clothing, wearing a wide-brimmed hat, wearing sunglasses, seeking shade, and using proper sunscreen with frequent applications. Broad-spectrum sunscreen with SPF (sun protection factor) greater than 15 should be applied 20 minutes prior to sun exposure and reapplied at least every two hours when exposed to UVR.

Previously, sunscreens were divided as chemical or physical, but this is no longer common. Sunscreens can protect against UVA, UVB, or both. If they are effective against both, you will see a label indicating broad-spectrum coverage. Sunscreens are made of various products. Figure 14-4 describes different sunscreen ingredients and their characteristics.

All sunscreens have an SPF, which guides the length of time that can be spent in direct sunlight. Multiplying the MED by the SPF number determines the additional time a climber can remain protected. For example, when protected by a sunscreen with an SPF of 15, a person developing erythema after ten minutes with no protection could stay in the sun for 15 times longer (or 150 minutes) before beginning to burn. However, variables such as the time of the day, cloud coverage, time of the year, location, reflection, personal traits, and medication consumption can alter the actual protective length of time. Caution should be taken when using both sunscreen and bug spray containing

FIGURE 14-4. SUNSCREEN CHARACTERISTICS

Protection against	Sunscreen ingredients	Maximum screen %
UVA	Avobenzone	3
UVA	Benzophenones (oxyben-zone, dioxybenzone, suli-sobenzone)	3-6
UVB	Cinnamates (octylme-thoxycinnamate, cinox-ate)	3-7.5
UVA	Ecamsule	2
UVA	Methyl anthranilate	5
UVB	Octocrylene	10
UVB	Para-aminobenzoic acid (PABA)	15
	Para aminobenzoic acid ester	
	Phenylbenzimidazole sulfonic acid	4
UVB	Salicylates (homosalate, octyl salicylate)	12
UVA	Titanium dioxide	25
UVA	Zinc oxide	25

DEET, as the effectiveness of both decreases over time. Frequent applications are necessary when sweating, when in water, or when constantly wiping or brushing a protected area of skin.

Sunscreen comes in the form of lotions, gels, sprays, or sticks, and can be water-resistant or waterproof. Water-resistant sunscreens are effective for 40 minutes of water immersion and waterproof sunscreens stay effective for roughly 80 minutes. Current Food and Drug Administration (FDA) regulations prohibit waterproof labeling, and all newer sunscreen will be labeled water-resistant only. Although research is lacking, most agree that sunscreen should not be stored in areas that become hot and should be replaced annually to ensure integrity of the protection.

Clothing varies in protection and can be assessed by color and tightness of the weave of the fabric. The tightness of the weave can be determined by holding the article to a lightbulb. If light passes through and images are visible, the SPF factor for this material is less than 15. If light passes through the material but no images are visible, the SPF is considered to be between SPF 15 and SPF 50. If SPF is greater than 50, no light will be visible through the clothing during this test. Dark-colored fabrics are more protective than lighter or white fabric. Specially designed "SPF clothing" usually provides protection in the 30 to 50 SPF range. This clothing contains colorless compounds, fluorescent brighteners, or treated resins that absorb UV rays. Additionally, when clothing is wet, SPF protection is reduced. Hats are a good option—a "boonie" cap with an encompassing 3-inch brim is most protective.

IDENTIFY

Sunburn is the result of excessive UVR exposure, which can be mild to severe. Mild sunburn consists of local heat, red skin, and pain. Severe sunburn (sometimes referred to as "sun poisoning") may include swelling, itchiness, blister formation, malaise, weakness, fatigue, nausea, chills, fever, and headache.

TREAT

Once a sunburn has developed there are no effective treatments, only measures that can reduce the discomfort. Medications for pain (such as acetaminophen) and decreasing inflammation (such as NSAIDs) can help, along with cooling the area with a damp cloth or cold compresses. Application of topical anesthetics (such as Prax lotion or Neutrogena Norwegian Formula moisturizer) can alleviate some of the pain. Topical steroids (such as 1% hydrocortisone cream) can be applied to intact skin for inflammation reduction. Alternatives such as aloe vera, oatmeal, or baking soda are anecdotal and may provide some relief but have not been scientifically proven. Blisters from sunburn should drained if extremely large. Severe sunburns may need to be treated like a second-degree burn and medical attention may be required.

Photokeratitis (Snow Blindness)

PREVENT

Snow blindness, also known as photokeratitis or ultraviolet keratitis, is a sunburn of the corneal and conjunctival epithelium that can occur in as little as two hours (Figure 14-5). UVR exposure that reaches the eye and causes this condition is usually from light reflected off the ground, snow, or water; light traveling at a low angle; or sunlight from the horizon. Climbers should always protect their eyes from UVR rays by wearing glasses even on overcast days, as all UVR can penetrate cloud cover. In addition, climbers (either on snow or during waterborne approaches to a climb) should wear side shields to prevent reflected indirect light from reaching the cornea. For climbers at higher altitude, on snow, glaciers, or on concave environments, goggles are the preferred eye protection.

Backup eye protection should be carried to ensure proper eye protection in the case of loss or breakage. In the event sunglasses are not available, a pair can easily be made by cutting two slits in a piece of paper, cardboard, plastic, or fabric, and secured by string or tape to hold the eye shield in place.

FIGURE 14-5. ANATOMY OF THE EYE

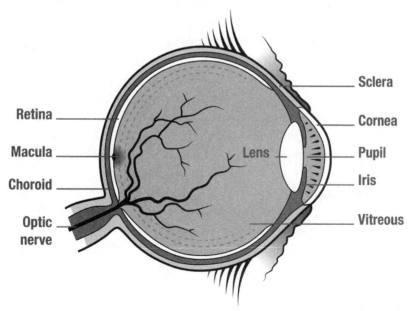

Retina — Sclera
Macula — Cornea
Choroid — Lens — Pupil
Optic nerve — Iris
— Vitreous

IDENTIFY

Unfortunately, there is no sensation that is identifiable for the onset of photokeratitis. The intensity of the light is the only warning that snow-blindness could be occurring. There is usually a six to twelve hour delay between the exposure and development of symptoms. Symptoms most often include severe pain, burning, tearing, and redness but often also include irritation, swollen eyelids, tearing, conjunctival erythema, dry/gritty feeling, *photophobia* (eye pain on exposure to light), eyelid spasms, and headache (Paterson 2014). Symptoms typically resolve in a couple of days with no permanent effects, and the retina remains undamaged. In severe cases, the epithelium may separate from the rest of the eye and the cornea may develop an ulcer leading to permanent damage. This is an emergency situation.

TREAT

Prevention is the most effective form of treatment and is best accomplished by wearing sunglasses with side shields or goggles (WMS recommendation grade 1C) (Paterson 2014). The next step of treatment is to avoid further UVR exposure. This can be accomplished by removing the person from the sun and resting in a tent or dim room. Healing will occur spontaneously over a day or two; however, steps can be implemented to decrease discomfort related to the condition. If the climber is wearing contact lenses, they should be removed. Photokeratitis is extremely painful and although there are no studies specific to this condition, experts recommend treating it similarly to a corneal abrasion. Systemic analgesia (for severe pain) and oral pain medication such as acetaminophen or NSAIDS are helpful. Topical antibiotics such as erythromycin ophthalmic 0.5% ointment (1 cm every 8 hours) and mydriatic-cycloplegic drops, which reduce ciliary muscle spasm of the pupil, should be used if available (WMS recommendation grade 1A) (Paterson 2014).The use of artificial tears and eye patches over the eyes is no longer recommended. If the condition does not subside within 72 hours, there is concern related to infection, or there is continued loss of vision, this should be treated as an emergency and the climber should be evacuated.

CHAPTER 15

LIGHTNING

Lightning is the natural electrical discharge of unequal charges between a cloud and the ground or within a cloud. These discharges are of very short duration (milliseconds) and extremely high voltage (many millions of volts). Lightning occurs nearly 50 times per second worldwide, with about 20% of those flashes becoming ground strikes.

IDENTIFY

Internationally, an estimate of 24,000 fatalities occur from lightning strikes every year. An additional quarter of a million injuries are attributed to lightning strikes, making this a common problem in the outdoors. Climbers are at particular risk for this, since their activities take place at elevated positions, often in exposed areas, and on ridgelines. However, in the United States, the incidence of lightning-related deaths has declined over the past half century. Currently, in the USA, approximately 40 deaths per year are attributed to lightning, plus approximately 400 lightning-related injuries. In the context of mountaineering, this compares to about 30 avalanche-related deaths annually. But, by definition, all avalanche-related deaths occur in mountainous terrain, whereas Florida and Texas account for fully 25% of lightning deaths, with golf courses and open fields as common locations. Therefore, epidemiologically, lightning strikes may not be among the most common sources of injury for mountaineers, and mountaineering may not be the most common activity during which a lightning strike might occur.

Regionally, thunderstorm frequency correlates with lightning strike frequency. Mountainous terrain can contribute to this pairing. For example, Central Africa has the greatest incidence of lightning strikes internationally; its mountainous terrain coupled with moist airflow from the Atlantic Ocean leads to year-round thunderstorms (Davis 2014). It is vitally important to realize that lightning can travel up to 10 to 15 miles ahead of or behind a storm cell. The familiar phrase "out of the blue" originates from lightning strikes occurring out of an apparently blue sky without storm patterns (Houghton Mifflin Harcourt 2011). Lightning is also possible in snowstorms, and graupel (snow pellets) can indicate favorable conditions for lightning formation—the pellets may generate positive and negative charges as they collide, providing an electrical gradient that promotes lightning. Cloud-to-ground lightning strikes seek the highest point to discharge, so ridgelines or high exposed points with surrounding lower ground are at high risk for lightning strikes.

When a lightning strike is imminent, many describe an "ozone smell" preceding the strike. St. Elmo's Fire is a blue haze or glowing ball of light or sparks, well known to mariners and described in writings going back to ancient times. It is a weather phenomenon due to electrical discharge preceding lightning strikes or other electrical fields such as those around volcanic eruptions. Electrical field disturbances can also make the hair on one's body stand on end ("goose bumps"), cause other static electricity sensations, or generate crackling sounds.

A lethal lightning strike may be hard to recognize as the source of death for someone coming upon the body later. Lightning does not always leave immediately apparent signs in the environment of its strike, so a body may be found without apparent cause of death.

But signs can sometimes be present. One effect of lightning strikes can be exploded clothing, due to the instantaneous vaporization of water/sweat particles on the body as the charge passes over it. This is particularly the case with socks and shoes, because of the high amount of moisture typical on feet. One's entire body can be thrown through the air due to *tetanic* (spasming) muscle contractions or simply the force of the bolt, causing blunt trauma. Somewhat later, ferning burn-like rashes called Lichtenberg figures can appear on the body. These figures are *pathognomonic* for lightning strikes, meaning that no other condition causes them and their presence alone can diagnose a lightning strike. They are not true burns, but represent the capillary rupture of liquid under the skin as a lightning current superheats tissues it momentarily passes through. They are painless and, in a patient who survives a lightning strike, eventually go away. Large Lichtenberg figures can be observed in grasses or other organic materials surrounding a lightning strike, and in some cases, deaths of unknown cause in the wilderness have been identified when, a day or two later, Lichtenberg figures appear in the grass surrounding the location where the body was found.

Direct lightning strikes are relatively rare, accounting for only about 5% of human lightning strikes. Other lightning strike injury categories include contact injury (touching an object like an ice axe that transfers electricity from a remote strike), side splash (charge "jumping" from a directly struck object like a tree, accounting for about one third of lightning strike injuries), ground current (also known as step voltage, where a charge travels through the ground until it reaches a victim; this accounts for about half of lightning injuries), and upward streamers (a current passing through the ground toward a cloud, which does not involve ground strike and usually does not become part of a completed lightning channel). In all these cases, lightning follows a predictable pattern, taking the path of least resistance. That fact, coupled with environmental features and their relative resistance, helps inform the prevention techniques as discussed above. Similarly, lightning's predictability, combined with anatomical relative resistance (nerves have least resistance and therefore better conduction, followed by blood, muscle, skin, fat, and finally bone), informs the treatment techniques discussed below.

PREVENT

The most important way to prevent lightning injury is to reduce exposure. If caught in a high, exposed environment, prevention becomes much more difficult. Lightning strikes are more common among those with certain outdoor occupations, such as farmers, and reductions in lightning strikes over generations reflects an increase in access to buildings and other reduced-risk sites. However, no place is absolutely safe from a lightning strike. Even within buildings, it is necessary to stay away from open windows and avoid using wired electrical tools such as wall-wired telephones. Consider open architecture when choosing huts or other structures in which climbers might seek shelter—more windows or open space equates to more risk. Fixed structures that might be used for lightning refuge can also benefit from structural features such as lightning rods. Cars can provide reasonable shelter, since their metal exoskeleton acts like a Faraday cage to transmit a strike to the ground. But the vehicle's metal frame must be continuous (convertibles are not effective, nor are cloth-topped cars), and tires, contrary to popular myth, do not insulate from ground strikes. Although rubber is indeed a poor conductor, the contact pad of the average tire (amount of rubber in contact with the ground) is often smaller than the contact pad of your own shoe. Then there is the relatively large amount of air within the tire—air has, of course, already conducted the lightning all the way to the ground. It is the metallic shell of the car that offers protection, so it is important to stay entirely on a (non-metallic) seat inside the car without touching metal objects in it, especially if these communicate with the car exterior. If manmade structures are not available, seek shelter inside a deep cave, far into a dense forest, or in a deep ravine. Solitary trees represent a poor choice, as they are relatively tall objects that can promote side splash or ground current (discussed below). Similarly, shallow caves or open shelters (picnic shelter, canopy, open tent, lean-to) should be avoided because the quantity of free air these contain—coupled with high positioning—can attract lightning. The lightning can then jump to an individual when it reaches the non-structural (open) portion.

If access to adequate shelter is not available, there are a number of ways to reduce the risk of lightning strike.

The United States National Weather Service recommends the maxim: "When thunder roars, go indoors." The idea is that—since lightning can travel well in advance of and behind a storm cell—if thunder is heard, one is within the potential radius of a lightning strike.

If lightning can be seen, another common maxim is to count the seconds between hearing thunder and seeing lightning to measure distance of a storm. However, this strategy depends on understanding the relative speed of light and sound. A common mistake is the notion that one second counted equates to one mile of distance. In fact, since light is faster than sound, every five seconds counted equates to one mile of distance. Therefore, the number of seconds counted must be divided by five to determine how many miles away a storm is (divide by three to determine how many kilometers away it is). Thus, people who assume seconds and mileage to be equal may think a five-second count indicates a storm five miles away, when in fact it is only 1 mile away and almost upon them!

Another numerical principle is the 30-30 rule. The first "30" in this rule (based on the calculation above) says that 30 seconds between thunder and lightning is the threshold to seek shelter. Now that you know the correct calculation, how many miles away is a storm when this threshold is reached and one should seek shelter?*

The second "30" of the 30-30 rule states that climbers should wait a minimum of 30 minutes after hearing the last thunderclap before resuming outdoor activities. Applying the calculation converting seconds to miles, the 30-30 rule predicts a ten-mile buffer between a climber and the trailing edge of a retreating storm. The Wilderness Medical Society gives these calculation-based behavioral preventions a recommendation grade of 1C (Davis 2014).

In the past, assuming the "lightning position" was the traditional standard of lightning strike prevention in wilderness activities. However, in 2014, the Wilderness Medical Society gave this technique a recommendation grade of 2C, and judged it to be only a "strategy of last resort" (Davis 2014). Other, earlier preventive measures and behaviors are far more effective. However, should climbers find themselves in the situation of an apparent impending strike (thunder, lightning strikes, or prestrike electrical phenomena described below), this position may reduce the risk of injury from lightning.

A climber taking this position squats with elbows touching knees, knees close to feet, and feet touching each other, to create a single point of contact with the ground. It is helpful to put an insulating material between the feet and ground, such as a pack (remove any metal), a rolled foam sleeping pad, or a dry coiled rope (one of the few instances in which stepping on your rope is okay in a climbing environment!). Putting palms over the ears helps prevent *tympanic membrane* (eardrum) rupture—a common consequence to a lightning strike—and maintains a positioning with one continuous line from the ground that discourages an attractive circuit completion for an electrical current. If there is more than one person assuming this position, it is recommended that individuals be positioned 20 feet apart to limit the possibility of several climbers injured by the same strike—note that lightning can jump up to 15 feet between objects. Climbing groups that know they will be traveling through lightning-prone areas—especially formally guided or institutional groups such as expeditions, camp trips, or outdoor education programs—should develop formal lightning safety plans and practice lightning drills with their clients. Examples of lightning safety plans

* 6 miles away (30 divided by 5)

are available online at the National Lightning Safety Institute* and the National Weather Service.†

Lightning detection technology is rapidly expanding, and smartphone- or PDA-based apps represent one of the most exciting ways new electronic technologies are changing wilderness safety. Many of these technologies rely on lightning detection by the National Lightning Detection Network,‡ which provides automatic notification (via email, text, or mobile phone) of lightning activity near a given location. While these technologies generally rely on mobile phone or PDA signal reception, such access is becoming increasingly common in wilderness areas. If access is not available, personal lightning detection devices can independently detect lightning as far away as 75 miles.

Finally, planning climbing, mountaineering, or trekking itineraries that acknowledge high lightning risk areas can reduce chances of lightning injury or death. Peaks and ridgelines are best avoided in the afternoon, as this is the most frequent time for thunderstorms. "Up by noon and down by two" is a common maxim among climbers that reinforces this principle of avoiding ridgelines and peaks during the afternoon. If climbers are caught in a thunderstorm, it is critically important to tie-off individually (WMS recommendation grade 1C) (Davis 2014). Wet climbing ropes make attractive electrical conductors, and strikes could pass between both belayer and climber, potentially incapacitating an entire climbing party. Also, climbers in this situation should isolate metal objects such as ski poles or ice axes to avoid contact burns or injury from lightning strike; and any direct contact with carabiners and other small metal objects should be minimized (WMS recommendation grade 1C) (Davis 2014). Additional metal objects such as watches, belt buckles, and necklaces should also be removed to avoid burn risk. If climbing involves deep-water soloing (DWS) or climbers are caught in a stream or other water while approaching or leaving a climb during a thunderstorm, they should get out of the water immediately. If the aquatic activity involves a raft or kayak, move to shore and away from the water's edge; if a boat, seek shelter belowdecks after locking off the helm.

* www.lightningsafety.com/nlsi_pls.html
† www.lightningsafety.noaa.gov/outdoors.shtml
‡ www.lightningsafety.com/nlsi_lhm/overview2002.html

TREAT

Lightning strikes can cause sudden death from simultaneous or sequential cardiac and respiratory arrest (sudden loss of heartbeat or breathing). The heart can stop either from a rhythm problem—a *fibrillatory* (irregular) rhythm that cannot sustain a pulse or blood pressure—or from loss of oxygen if breathing stops. Breathing can stop even though the pulse is normal if the lightning strike paralyzes the respiratory center in the brain, paralyzing the diaphragm and making breathing impossible, and causing cardiac arrest within minutes.

This unusual source of cardiac or respiratory arrest results in the principle of *reverse triage* for lightning strike deaths. In "mass casualty incidents"—for instance, coming upon three or more victims of a trauma—those who don't have a pulse or aren't breathing are considered definitively dead. Assuming limited resources, interventions focus on those with signs of life. In the case of lightning strikes, this is reversed, and priority is given to those without any signs of breathing or life. Unlike cases of cardiac or respiratory arrest from other causes, victims of a lightning strike often regain breathing and pulses simply from a brief period of CPR (for pulselessness) or rescue breathing (for non-breathing caused by a temporarily paralyzed respiratory center). Further discussion of CPR and rescue breathing can be found in Chapter 2. It is also important for rescuers to understand that climbers who have been struck by lightning do not carry an electrical charge, since lightning passes through the body in milliseconds, without leaving any residual electrical charge or ability to pass electricity. This is different from high-voltage injuries, which ironically have much lower voltage than lightning strikes but which continue to pass the current as long as the victim remains in contact with the source.

If an individual initially survives a lightning strike, subsequent death is very rare. Indicators for high risk of further complications or death in patients who initially survive (or are resuscitated out of cardiopulmonary arrest) include a suspected direct strike, loss of consciousness, neurological problems, chest pain or shortness of breath, major trauma, burns to the head, legs, or more than 10% of total body surface area, or pregnancy (Davis 2014). However, even if high-risk criteria are not present, all lightning strike victims deserve further medical attention and evacuation.

Neurological problems are common after lightning strikes. Nerves are by definition the best conductors of electrical current in the body and are likely to sustain the most damage from a strike. Neurological injuries can be immediate or delayed.

Immediately after a lightning strike, climbers can experience loss of consciousness, seizures, headaches, *paresthesia* (numbness or tingling), confusion, weakness, memory loss, brain injury from lack of oxygen, or stroke from bleeding in the brain. *Keraunoparalysis* is the term for temporary paralysis after a lightning strike, believed to be caused by overstimulation of the nervous system leading to the spasming of blood vessels. Legs are more often affected than arms, and symptoms may include pulselessness in the limb, discoloration, and sensation loss as well as full or partial paralysis. This condition typically resolves within hours. Needless to say, its possibility means that a central pulse (carotid artery) is more reliable than a peripheral pulse (feet or wrist) to establish pulselessness in an unconscious lightning strike patient. Keraunoparalysis can also be confused with spinal injury, with the difference being that spinal injuries rarely resolve within hours. Anyone with paralysis or weakness after a lightning strike should be presumed to have spinal injuries unless keraunoparalysis is proven by resolution of these symptoms over time, or by other testing.

Eyes are part of the nervous system and are frequently affected by lightning strikes. The lens is commonly injured: Cataracts are the most common eventual symptom. They may appear from within two days to as long as four years after a lightning strike. Retinal damage and optic nerve damage are also possible and may result in vision reduction or total loss.

Ears are also commonly affected, and eardrums rupture in as many as 60% of lightning strike victims. Such ruptures require no specific treatment, although water and ear drops should be avoided while the eardrum is healing. Any drainage from the ear may be a sign of skull fracture and warrants increased speed in evacuation and, like other head injuries, calls for close attention to level of consciousness over time (see Chapter 6). Deafness is also common and is usually temporary, but microhemorrhages and microfractures to the tiny bones and internal structures of the ear can result in permanent hearing loss.

True burns can also occur. They are typically partial thickness and involve the spontaneous vaporization of sweat and other liquids on the skin into steam. Because of this, areas of heavy sweating such as underarms, beneath the breasts, and feet tend to be most affected. Circular burns are possible where a current emerges from underlying tissue; these are generally found at the ends of the feet, where a current often exits the body. Full thickness burns are found most often in areas where skin is in contact with metal or synthetic materials that melt onto or burn the skin. True burns should not be confused with Lichtenberg figures (discussed earlier), which are painless, ferning, and disappear within hours to a day after injury. They require no treatment. Lightning burns are treated like other burns; for a more complete discussion of burns, see Chapter 9.

Psychiatric disturbances are also common after lightning strikes. These typically develop days to weeks after a strike, so they might not be part of the initial medical management of a lightning strike patient. But they can be an issue in the extended management of such patients on expeditions, long trips, or within groups that frequently climb together. These conditions include depression, sleep disturbances, emotional instability, and aggressive behavior. Lightning support networks are available (e.g., Lightning Strike and Electric Shock Survivors International, Inc.*), and psychiatric care should be sought for any symptoms of this type.

* www.lightning-strike.org

CHAPTER 16

WEATHER IDENTIFICATION

A basic understanding of weather patterns and meteorology are a must for the climber and mountaineer. Thanks to communication technology, we often have access to up-to-date weather forecasts and warnings, but this is not always the case. Batteries die and service can sometimes be nonexistent. In these cases, a rudimentary knowledge of weather can make the difference between enjoying a warm meal and a cold beer in town and eating the crumbs left in your pack in a cold, cramped improvised bivy. This chapter is a primer in identifying concerning weather patterns and preventing injury caused by changing conditions. Many of these environmentally related maladies are discussed in other chapters, including hypothermia and frostbite (Chapter 12), hyperthermia (Chapter 13), and lightning strike (Chapter 15).

The ability to understand changes in barometric pressure, to identify clouds and the weather patterns they indicate, and to make decisions based upon these and other factors is key to staying safe while in the mountains.

METEOROLOGY BASICS

So what is weather? Weather is the condition of the atmosphere on Earth at any given location during a period of time. The sun, through heat, water, atmospheric moisture, and changes to our air, creates the weather as we experience it.

Sun

The sun gives rise to all weather patterns that occur on Earth. Its heat causes water to evaporate into the air and causes air to rise. As the air rises to higher altitude, its temperature begins to cool. This cooling causes the moisture trapped within the rising air to consolidate and form droplets. As these droplets condense and grow larger, they become so heavy they can no longer be suspended within the atmosphere. This condensed moisture then falls back to Earth as rain, freezing rain, sleet, hail, or snow.

Clouds

Clouds can be used to detect coming changes in weather. There are two main types of clouds: cumulus and stratus. Cumulus clouds are tall and puffy and are associated with unstable air. Stratus clouds are usually flat and layered, and generally occur when the air is stable. Within these two broad types, clouds are subdivided based upon their location within the atmosphere (low, middle, high, and towering). Each indicates a different type of weather pattern, and thanks to this, an astute mountaineer can be forewarned of approaching bad weather (Figure 16-1).

Low clouds occur at 3,000 meters and below. They include cumulus clouds (white and fluffy) that signal good weather if they are far apart or bad weather if they are large and close together. Stratocumulus clouds are white or gray. Often seen in rolling, lumpy bands, these clouds will produce light precipitation if they are low or thick.

Low stratus clouds are gray, a color that deepens depending upon the thickness of the cloud layer. They often resemble fog and indicate that precipitation—usually in the form of drizzle or light snow—may shortly

FIGURE 16-1. DIFFERENT TYPES OF CLOUD FORMATIONS

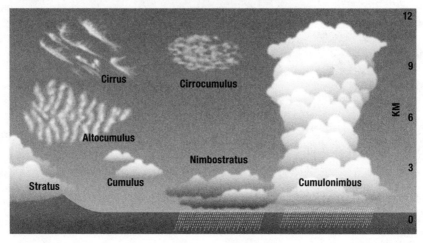

occur. If this cloud layer lifts quickly in the morning, weather during the day will often be good. Nimbostratus clouds are dark gray in color. These thick clouds, which often prevent sunlight from reaching the earth, are precursors of long and steady precipitation.

Middle clouds occur between 3,000 and 6,000 meters and are divided into two main categories, altocumulus and altostratus, together with a third cloud type distinct to mountainous regions: lenticular. Altocumulus clouds resemble waves or ripples, are white/gray in color, and are thicker than their higher cousins, cirrocumulus. Though considered good weather, they can produce rain over higher mountains. Altostratus clouds usually form a gray blanket across the sky and resemble haze. These clouds have no defined shape and are generally thin in texture. If they begin to thicken, this is a sign of coming precipitation. Lenticular clouds are lentil-shaped clouds that form around the tops of mountains. They suggest high winds of 30 mph or more at high altitude, and are among the most often-photographed weather phenomena in the mountains.

High clouds—those generally above 6,000 meters—are subdivided into three categories: cirrocumulus, cirrostratus, and cirrus. Cirrocumulus clouds indicate coming precipitation (often rain) due to instability and to their increasing moisture. These clouds resemble the rippled look of sand as the tide recedes. Cirrostratus clouds, much like their lower cousins, altostratus and nimbostratus, have no defined shape and often produce a "halo effect" around the sun or moon. These clouds often precede a warm front. Cirrus clouds are wispy and thin and indicate good weather; but if cirrostratus clouds follow closely behind cirrus clouds, expect precipitation, usually within 24 to 48 hours.

The final types of clouds are the multilayered or towering clouds called cumulus and cumulonimbus. Swelling cumulus clouds are white and puffy in nature and are a sign of unstable atmospheric conditions. These often precede cumulonimbus clouds and may form along the leading edge of a cold front. Cumulonimbus clouds are towering with dark bases and sometimes form an "anvil" shape at the top. They often bring precipitation and extreme weather and may be associated with lightning (Chapter 15).

Interpreting cloud formations and approaching weather patterns requires practice and experience. Spending time observing the sky and relating it to professional forecasts will help a climber to develop the ability to predict weather based upon cloud formations.

Thunderstorms and Lightning

Thunderstorms and the lightning associated with them are a considerable danger for climbers—so much that the entirety of Chapter 15 is dedicated to lightning injuries. Thunderstorms are caused when large air masses, warmed by the earth, rise quickly within the atmosphere. As this warm air rises, it is cooled by the upper atmosphere and large, towering clouds form. The energy created through this process is released in the form of thunder and lightning. Thunderstorms generally develop in the early to late afternoon, the warmest part of the day. Mountainous areas experience more storms than flat areas. This is due to an increase in the "lift" of warm air when moving against mountain ranges (known as orographic lift), particularly when wind encounters a mountain chain perpendicularly. Hail often accompanies thunderstorms when the storm has strong updrafts and downdrafts, and occurs more frequently in the mountains, since hail often melts before reaching lower and warmer elevations.

Winds

Wind is created when air moves from an area of high pressure to an area of low pressure. It is stronger when the pressure difference is greater. This is known as the pressure gradient. Mountain winds can be extremely volatile because of the varied terrain and topography in mountainous regions.

Winds in the higher atmosphere interest mountaineers because they directly influence weather conditions in our chosen terrain. Winds aloft move at a greater speed than those closer to the surface. An improvised method to estimate the speed of winds at altitude (1,500 to 3,000 m) is to double the wind speed forecast for a nearby low-level region.

Lee waves, a noteworthy wind event in the mountains, create the lenticular clouds mentioned above. Wind speeds of at least 30 mph are needed to form these clouds, and if they are jagged or rough, wind speeds are usually much higher. Winds that cause these conditions are generally perpendicular in relation to the mountain chain and create strong gap winds.

Gap winds, also known as channeled winds, can be dangerous. Terrain that restricts or channels wind can increase its speed dramatically. Careful assessment of terrain is important to avoid traveling unaware into an area with gap winds, especially along narrow or knife-edge ridgelines.

Mountainous terrain can also create what are known as converging and diverging winds. Like the confluence of water from two rivers, winds can gain speed when combined with other channeled winds. This usually occurs when two valleys converge to form a larger valley. The wind speed from each smaller valley increases as they meet. The opposite occurs when the wind reverses direction and flows from a main valley into two smaller branches with speeds decreasing.

Climbers should consider the effects of terrain blocking and the day/night wind changes on a mountain. Terrain blocking is the effect on wind by a mountain or land feature that diverts or disrupts its direction and speed. This occurs on the leeward side of the mountain and is like a windbreak that is often utilized by climbers. Day/night wind changes occur twice daily with wind flowing uphill from the valleys during the day and reversing direction and flowing downhill at night. The gathering of colder air in the valleys at night causes a temperature inversion, and the resulting pressure gradient then forces the air to higher altitude. As the warmth of the air increases during the day, the temperature inversion ends.

The final, and probably the most important, fact about wind is simply this: The force of wind increases exponentially as speed increases. Forty mph winds are four times stronger than 20 mph winds, not twice as strong. Consult a wind speed table to gain a better understanding of wind speed effects.

BAROMETERS, ALTIMETERS, AND THERMOMETERS

Barometers are the most useful instruments for predicting weather available to climbers except for real-time, quickly updated weather forecasts from professional meteorologists. Barometers are most useful when used in a stationary position (e.g., base camp) without a change in altitude produced by climbing. Barometer readings must be measured over time, with decreasing barometric pressure indicating worsening weather and increasing barometric pressure indicating improvement. If in transit, barometer readings will decrease with elevation gain and increase with elevation loss, and a small fluctuation in barometric pressure will occur even in a stationary position (around 0.04 mmHg). Barometers are most reliable in mid-latitudes. The equator and regions beyond 60° latitude contain areas of low pressure that are fairly constant throughout the year and can alter readings. This is of particular significance for mountaineers in Alaska, Antarctica, the Andes in Ecuador and Peru, and Mt. Kilimanjaro and Mt. Kenya in Africa.

Most altimeters work using barometric pressure readings and must be calibrated to ensure accuracy. Many wristwatches provide rough approximations of altitude as well as barometric readings. These watches often also include a thermometer, but it is frequently inaccurate due to the proximity and radiant heat of the wearer. Small and lightweight thermometers that include a windchill chart on the back are cheap and a convenient piece of equipment for a mountaineer.

A basic understanding of weather patterns and ability to recognize basic features that results in poor weather conditions is a must for all climbers and can prevent many of the environmental based injuries discussed within this book.

CHAPTER 17

AVALANCHE AWARENESS

Avalanche awareness and management of risk should begin long before crampons touch the snow, during the preparation phase of pre-trip planning. Understanding the intricacies of weather patterns and the science of avalanches requires coursework and hands-on training. There are a number of organizations that provide this information and education and include regional non-profit groups such as Northwest Avalanche Center (NWAC), the Utah Avalanche Center, and Avalanche Canada. The American Institute for Avalanche Research and Education (AIARE) offers advanced training programs to better prepare those entering terrain with avalanche potential. While it is essential that individual climbers obtain such training before entering avalanche terrain, it is equally important that their partners share the same training so they can work together to mitigate risk and make responsible decisions in the mountainous terrain. Basic elements of avalanche formation and action are shown in Figure 17-1. Despite continuing growth in training opportunities, fatality statistics show the need for continued emphasis on avalanche safety (American Avalanche Association 2016). The US national avalanche-related death toll for the 2015–2016 season was 29. Most fatal incidents are triggered by the avalanche victims or someone in their party. Despite common perceptions of this being a problem solely for backcountry skiers, the backcountry lures not only skiers and ski mountaineers, but also snowboarders, climbers, snowshoers, and snowmobilers, who share in its risk. Indeed, snowmobilers now have the highest rate of avalanche-associated mortality (Jekich 2016). The "know-before-you-go" campaign has proven helpful in increasing awareness and training.

Ninety percent of those buried for less than 15 minutes survive. This survival rate drops to a dismal 30% at 35 minutes (Johnson 2015). This

FIGURE 17-1. AVALANCHE CHARACTERISTICS

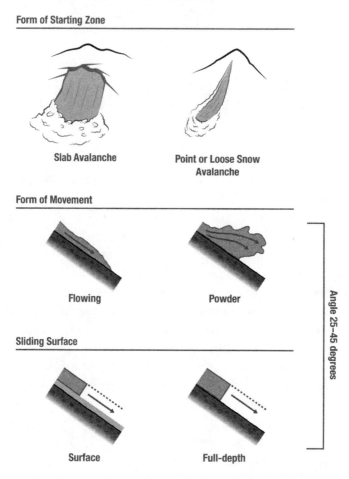

Form of Starting Zone

Slab Avalanche

Point or Loose Snow Avalanche

Form of Movement

Flowing

Powder

Angle 25–45 degrees

Sliding Surface

Surface

Full-depth

would seem to be a reasonable amount of time to find a buried mountaineer, but the actual process of identifying the burial location and retrieving the victim can be lengthy. Burial depth also affects survivability since deeper burial increases extrication time. A one-meter burial requires roughly seven to ten minutes for retrieval. This increases to 15–30 minutes for a two-meter burial (Auerbach 2013). Death typically occurs due to slow asphyxiation, but its causes may also include trauma or hypothermia if enough time elapses. Finally, snow density (increased, for example, in maritime climates) decreases survival either by the difficulty of establishing an adequate air pocket or the challenge of more difficult extrication.

When traveling in avalanche terrain, one should:

+ Never go alone, since that makes rescue challenging or impossible aside from self-rescue.
+ When crossing an avalanche-prone area of snow, travel one at a time, giving reasonable time for each person to clear before the next one enters it. Consider regrouping in areas of safety protected by natural features.
+ Develop a team travel plan through avalanche terrain, noting sun-exposed or wind-loaded slopes, utilizing safe terrain features, planning escape routes, and avoiding terrain traps such as gulleys and couloirs where burial depth could be concentrated and increased. Start early and leave early to avoid deteriorating snow conditions later in the day (due to temperature changes). Stay away from avalanched areas marked by destroyed vegetation, exposed rock, etc.
+ Teammates should inspect each other for loose items, open jackets, and items that could ensnare avalanche victims. They should also employ a "pre-departure safety check" where search beacons and other avalanche safety equipment are reviewed and found to be functional (read below). Plan ahead to jettison extraneous gear (heavy backpacks and skis), allowing team members to attempt "swimming" if caught in a slide in order to maintain body position close to the rapidly settling snow surface.
+ If a slide occurs, non-buried teammates should search for surface clues and last known position of anyone who is buried.

Each team member should be equipped with the following avalanche safety and rescue equipment: a shovel, a beacon, and a probe. All teammates should learn how to use their beacons and participate in a group beacon check confirming correct mode, battery life, and functioning transmit/receive status. Each team member should be trained and practiced in effective snow probing, utilizing the 3 probe/1 step technique (as described in standard avalanche classes), moving together in an appropriately spaced, efficient, and synchronized team probe line. A probe should remain in place to mark a positive burial finding. Everyone should be trained and practiced in efficient snow removal technique. Teammates should begin shoveling one to one-and-a-half times the suspected burial depth away and downhill from the suspected probe finding. Move snow to the sides when possible, working in tandem as a pair of shovelers or in a team conveyer belt. Practice strategic beacon searching and switching to appropriate beacon mode while searching. Division of responsibilities is important. It should include shovelers, probers, beacon searchers, and a safety supervisor to identify others entering the area, screen for additional avalanche risk, and notify authorities for more assistance. Groups should invest time, training, and equipment in acquiring pre-travel snow analysis with test pits and snowpack evaluation when traveling in avalanche-prone terrain. Individuals and teams should consider whether additional equipment investments in avalanche airbag systems (ABS), Recco reflectors, or Avalung devices are worthwhile for their activity.

Following successful identification and retrieval of the avalanche victim, climbing partners must begin patient assessment. This should not wait for complete removal from the snow burial. The International Commission for Mountain Emergency Medicine (ICAR MEDCOM) has established an evidence-based avalanche management algorithm* for the resuscitation of avalanche burial victims (Brugger 2013). It addresses the initiation and discontinuation of CPR efforts, utilizing findings at the scene (airway status and vital signs) as well as additional clinical information such as ECG (electrocardiogram—measuring electrical activity of the heart) and core temperature when available.

* www.alpine-rescue.org/ikar-cisa/documents/2013/ikar20131206001112.pdf

IV.
RESCUE

CHAPTER 18

EXTRICATION DECISIONS AND SPINAL MOTION RESTRICTION

If injured climbers are found in dangerous positions, they must be extricated, presuming such extrication does not expose rescuers to unacceptable risk. Examples of such dangerous locations include rockfall areas, avalanche areas, or swift water.

Extrication often requires technical rescue skills. Climbers expecting that they may have to deliver patient care in environments requiring technical rescue skills should enroll in a class specifically designed to prepare them for operating safely in such terrain. This includes not only high-angle technical rescue training for climbing rescues and avalanche rescue training for avalanche rescues, but also training for other environments more peripheral to the climbing world, such as swift water rescue training for swift water rescues. In the absence of such training, a risk-benefit analysis is essential, with significant weight placed on not putting rescuers in great danger. For example, a tragically high number of all drownings are actually would-be rescuers who are attempting to rescue a patient—as high as 6% of drownings in China (Zhu 2015), and 17 deaths over a five-year period in Australia (Franklin 2011).

Extrication may require short-distance carries and involve consideration of spinal immobilization. Litters and carries are discussed in more detail in Chapter 19, and spinal immobilization and motion restriction were introduced in Chapter 5, with more detail later in this chapter.

For extremely limited short-term movement, the BEAM technique is better than log rolling or ad hoc backboarding for movement. Boissy has shown the BEAM technique reduces spinal movement more than log rolling (Boissy 2011), and BEAM is now the preferred technique recommended by evidence-based Wilderness Medical Society practice

FIGURE 18-1. SPINAL TRAP TECHNIQUE

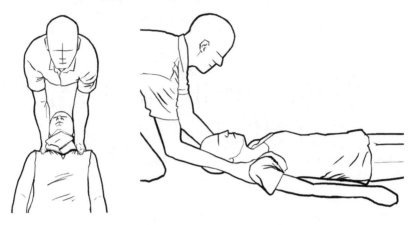

guidelines over the log roll (recommendation grade 1C) (Quinn 2014). In the BEAM technique, rescuers interlace arms underneath a patient and move the patient in a raise, lift, and lower sequence.

In addition, research from motor vehicle crashes has shown that, in cases of suspected spinal injury, patients moving themselves (walking) entails less manipulation of the spinal column than immobilization and passive movement of the patient controlled by rescuers (Shafer 2009, Dixon 2013). Thus, potential spinal cord injury patients may be able to take a more active role in their own rescue, reducing spinal movement based on their own pain rather than undergoing active spinal immobilization by a rescuer.

If immobilization or significant spinal motion restriction is desired of the cervical spine, Wilderness Medical Society practice guidelines (based on Boissy's work) also recommend a "trap" method utilizing engagement of the trapezius muscle, illustrated in Figure 18-1, over the more traditional hands-to-the-ears cervical spine immobilization method traditionally taught (recommendation grade 1C) (Boissy 2011, Quinn 2014).

DECISION TO EVACUATE

In wilderness medicine, the decision to evacuate a patient to a higher level of care is often more complex than in a frontcountry or urban environment. There may be more consequences or risks to a decision to seek higher medical care than in the frontcountry. Examples of significant consequences include abandoning an expedition already underway or splitting up a group and its resources. Examples of increased risk include the hazards to a group as they attempt to evacuate a patient, hazards to rescuers if deploying a high risk rescue resource like a helicopter, or hazards in attempting routes or environments that would not normally be engaged were an evacuation not necessary.

Medical decision-making regarding evacuation and seeking better medical care is also somewhat different in a wilderness setting. Measuring the risks and benefits of an evacuation may suggest that ailments for which healthcare would normally be sought—such as a toothache or a fever—might be managed entirely in the field, since the risks of evacuation might exceed the benefit. But other conditions that could more likely deteriorate—such as severe abdominal pain or an infected wound—might be evacuated for medical care at a lower threshold than that for which medical care would be sought in a frontcountry situation. Furthermore, climbing groups and expeditions often take medical supplies and providers with them on trips. The scope and sophistication of such supplies and providers often increase with the length or complexity of the planned expedition. Clearly, the medical supplies and training available on-site influences the decision whether or not to evacuate. See Appendix A for a more complete discussion of medical kits and equipment for various environments and trip lengths.

Whereas seeking medical care in the frontcountry is one of the simplest decisions, with minimal consequences and multiple opportunities for reconsideration, it is one of the most complex decisions in the wilderness, with significant consequences, including the potential for activating multiple additional wilderness rescuers. Individual chapters in this book discuss the thresholds for evacuation for various conditions. The remainder of this chapter will discuss how to evacuate a patient once that decision has been made.

SELECTIVE SPINAL IMMOBILIZATION AND SPINAL MOTION RESTRICTION

Historically, the decision about whether an injured patient requires spinal immobilization has been a crucial element in the medical decision-making that calculates the risks and complexity of evacuation and also the technical expertise needed to actually prepare a patient for evacuation.

Following traditional EMS instruction since the 1970s, wilderness medical providers were taught to spinally immobilize anyone with a possible back or neck injury.

In the ensuing years, two major forces began to influence emergency medical services (EMS) decisions about spinally immobilizing patients. These forces reflected growing sophistication of both hospital-based emergency medicine and wilderness medicine as medical subspecialties.

On the one hand, in hospitals, emergency medicine practitioners began to scrutinize the time, cost, and radiation exposure to the patient associated with trauma radiological studies. Seeking ways to reduce unnecessary testing, they explored protocols that might permit them to rule out spinal injury without radiological testing. The NEXUS and Canadian C-spine criteria evolved out of this effort. As discussed in Chapter 5, these guidelines can effectively rule out clinically significant spinal fractures and injuries.

On the other hand, in wilderness-based environments where patients were receiving treatment prior to traditional EMS care, providers realized that applying such rules could help to avoid unnecessary immobilization and its additional complexities and risks to a wilderness operation. Put simply, if a patient with a neck or back injury would not undergo any testing or further intervention beyond pain control in the hospital, then no immobilization is needed prior to that hospital care either. Utilizing this principle, wilderness medical practitioners have, for decades, avoided spinal immobilization of patients who would have been immobilized by traditional EMS providers. Although historically this practice was called "clearing the spine," more modern terminology is "selective spinal immobilization," acknowledging that field providers without radiological equipment cannot truly "clear" a patient of a spinal injury. They can only selectively decide when to immobilize or not.

However, the most current evidence in the emergency medicine, EMS, and wilderness medicine communities suggests that field spinal immobilization of any sort, in any patient, is likely to be not only unnecessary, but possibly even harmful. This is a dramatic and challenging change for anyone with field trauma training. Hauswald has been one of the leading authors and researchers on this topic, and has pub-

FIGURE 18-2. VERTEBRAL FRACTURES

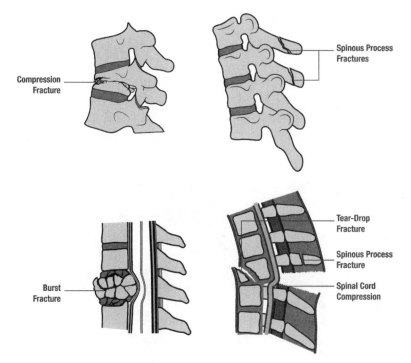

lished truly heroic works challenging the existing paradigm. In 1998 he showed that, controlling for injury severity, patients in Bangladesh who were not backboarded had lower incidents of neurological deficits than backboarded patients in Albuquerque (Hauswald 1998). However, his tour de force was the publication of "A Reconceptualisation of Acute Spinal Care" (Hauswald 2013). This work, using basic Newtonian physics and actual cadaver research, demonstrates why spinal immobilization as a goal is likely flawed in the first place. As Figure 18-2 demonstrates, most vertebral fractures are unlike long bone fractures, and his cadaver research showed movement of fractured bones was unlikely to cause additional spinal trauma unless similar forces were applied as the ones causing the injury in the first place (i.e., normal physiological movement should not be dangerous). His seminal work in these and other publications, along with that of many other researchers and EMS physicians, has led most major professional societies and many wilderness training programs—including the National Association of EMS Physicians, the American College of Surgeons Committee on Trauma, the Wilder-

FIGURE 18-3. C-SPINE FRACTURES/COLLAR PROBLEM

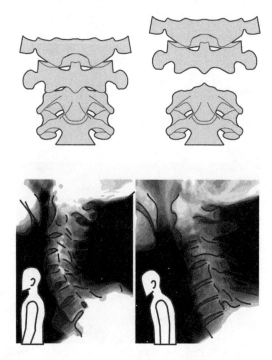

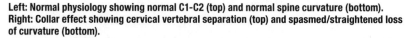

Left: Normal physiology showing normal C1-C2 (top) and normal spine curvature (bottom). Right: Collar effect showing cervical vertebral separation (top) and spasmed/straightened loss of curvature (bottom).

ness Medical Society, the American College of Emergency Physicians, and the Wilderness EMS Medical Director Course—to adopt guidelines discouraging spinal immobilization in out-of-hospital medical care. (NAEMSP/ACS 2013, Quinn 2014, ACEP 2015, WEMSMDC 2017). Many frontcountry EMS systems, including some entire American state EMS systems, have discontinued use of backboards altogether as medical tools (although they are sometimes still used as extrication tools).

Furthermore, concerns have been raised about rigid cervical collars as immobilization tools (Bledsoe 2015). First, cervical collars have been shown to be poor immobilizers of the cervical vertebrae (Hughes 1998, Perry 1999, Holla 2012, Sundstrøm 2014). Second, to the degree they do immobilize it, they replicate spasm physiology (Figure 18-3). Since it is now believed that inflammation and spasm are more responsible for secondary neurological damage than physical cord compression via move-

FIGURE 18-4. WILDERNESS MEDICAL SOCIETY RECOMMENDATIONS FOR SPINAL EVALUATION AND IMMOBILIZATION IN THE AUSTERE ENVIRONMENT

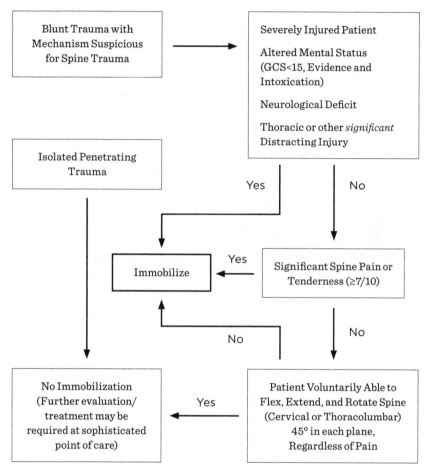

ment, any spasm or inflammation caused by unnatural neck positioning may be worse than normal physiological movement. Third, high cervical vertebral fractures (at the C1 and C2 level, often considered to be particularly dangerous neck fracture) have been shown to be pulled apart in potentially dangerous ways more significantly when cervical collars are applied (Ben-Galim 2010). These concerns are illustrated in Figure 18-3. Fourth, cervical collars can restrict breathing (Goutcher 2005) and increase brain pressure (Davies 1996, Mobbs 2002), both potentially dangerous after major trauma. Wilderness EMS (WEMS) authorities have recommended that WEMS teams deploying to climbing incidents, including mountain rescue teams, should not routinely apply rigid cervical collars, either commercial or improvised, to patients (Smith 2018).

On the basis of this evidence, it is our conviction that formal or ad hoc backboards and full "immobilization" should be used only for extrication from a technical entrapment and not for transport. We disagree with the philosophy that spinal immobilization is a desirable goal in cases of potential spinal injury, and instead believe that interventions should be taken to reduce spinal motion rather than to fully immobilize it.

In medicine, the standard of care (and medicolegal standard) sometimes lags behind medical evidence and contemporary medical science. We recognize that many certification courses, such as Advanced Wilderness Life Support and many wilderness EMS certifications (Wilderness First Responder, Wilderness EMT, etc.), still teach algorithms for selective spinal immobilization. For those who still wish to apply selective spinal immobilization, we would recommend implementing the Wilderness Medical Society's algorithm for spinal immobilization, outlined in Figure 18-4 (Quinn 2014).

CHAPTER 19

CARRIES AND LITTERS

Climbers carry resources that can be repurposed for evacuation in mountainous terrain. The litters and carries described within this chapter, though simple, require hands-on practice and often formal instruction to master.

In situations requiring evacuation, the weather, terrain, patient condition, rescuer strength, and resources dictate the type of carries or litters used. The rescuer must choose a system that accounts for all of these, ensures scene safety, and best meets the needs of the injured climber. Terrain plays a major role in determining evacuation methods and will often force the rescuers to change their methods. Steep terrain requires high-angle rescue rigging that may then transition to lower angle terrain or even single-track terrain, thus requiring flexibility in technique.

Many carry and litter techniques are well known within the rescue and wilderness medicine community. These include the fireman's carry, ground drag, and box carry (Figure 19-1). These are all efficient (albeit not entirely comfortable) ways to quickly cover short distances and remove an injured person from a dangerous environment such as rock-fall or icefall. The following techniques go beyond these basic carries and focus on techniques that allow the use of climbing gear to assist rescuers with evacuation.

ONE-PERSON ROPE LITTER (Figure 19-2)

This litter is useful for a two-person climbing team and allows the uninjured partner to evacuate the injured climber without further assistance. Coil your rope in a single-strand butterfly or backpack coil starting with

FIGURE 19-1. THE BOX CARRY

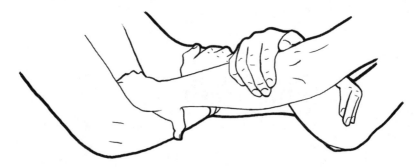

FIGURE 19-2.
1-PERSON ROPE LITTER

FIGURE 19-3.
2-PERSON ROPE LITTER

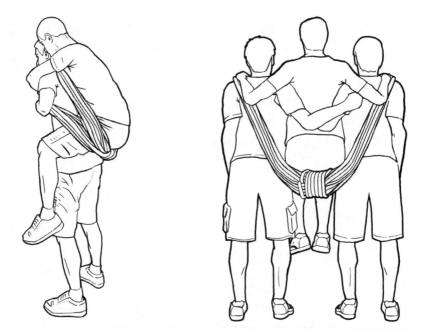

one end of the rope running over your shoulder and touching the ground. Coil the remainder of the rope in a single strand, taking care to make each coil as uniform in length as possible (ideally just slightly shorter than the full wingspan of the rescuer). The length of the loops is important due to the nature of stretch present in a dynamic rope. Keeping the lengths shorter will allow this stretch that will occur due to the patient's weight and will prevent the readjustment of the litter later in the rescue. Continue coiling until there is between one and two meters of rope left. Carefully lay the rope on the ground. Loop the initial portion of the rope back to the center of the coil. Loop the last portion of the rope to the middle of the coil, and complete the butterfly coil by completing a tight finishing wrap several times around the center of the coils and tucking the tail back through these wraps to tighten and secure the end of the rope. This wrap will become the patient's "seat." It is important to make each strand of the coil as equal as possible in order to distribute the patient's weight evenly along all portions of the rope and onto the rescuer's shoulders. If this is not done properly, the patient's weight will be distributed on only a few coils and the carry will be much more uncomfortable for the rescuer.

The rescuer should position the coiled rope so that the wrapped "seat" is under the injured climber's buttocks. Injured patients can usually assist the rescuer in getting themselves into the litter. If it is possible, the patient should be positioned upon a rock, stump, against a tree, or any other object that will allow easier threading of the coil below the buttocks. The rescuer then slips their arms through each set of loops so one end of the coil is wrapped around each shoulder. Pad the coils around the shoulders for comfort with whatever clothing or gear is available. Rescuers can also use a sling and carabiner or a quickdraw to secure the two sets of coils at their chest. Pull the sling beneath the coils at the chest, wrap it around each set of coils, and clip the ends with the carabiner. This acts like the chest strap of a backpack, taking some of the weight off of the rescuer's shoulders and better securing the patient within the system. The patient's legs go to each side of the rescuer, with the patient's inner thighs directly against the rescuer's flanks, as if being carried piggyback.

TWO-PERSON ROPE LITTER (SPLIT COIL SEAT CARRY)
(Figure 19-3)

This carry employs the same method as above, but with two rescuers. Again, arrange the rope in a single-strand butterfly or backpack coil, but this time with larger loops in the rope. One way to do this is to place two rocks at the desired length and start coiling around them. The wrap in the middle is again the patient's "seat." Throw a loop over the head and on top of the outside shoulder of each person. Padding the coils that are on the shoulder with any soft material available will increase the comfort for the two rescuers who are carrying the injured climber. The rescuers stand side-by-side, with each set of coils slung over each person's outside shoulder and head, leaving the "seat" hanging between them. The patient sits in the middle of the rope while the rescuers extend their inside arms and grasp each other's elbows to form a seatback for the patient. Remember, a dynamic climbing rope will stretch with time. Do not make the split coil too long, in order to protect the patient's lower extremities from touching the ground.

ROPE LITTER AND HYPOTHERMIA WRAP (Figures 19-4 and 19-5)

This technique is best utilized when there are a number of rescuers and the patient is severely injured. Begin by laying a climbing rope on the ground in a serpentine fashion creating large, slender "U" bends on the ground (Figure 19-4). Create a tail at each end and tie an overhand or figure-8 on a bight. Lay out even spaced and equal-length bends of the rope on the ground. The length of each bend should be roughly twice the girth of the victim at the point they will be laid onto it. For example, the width of the rope bends located at the shoulder will likely be wider than the length of the bends at the waist, knees, and ankles. Too long is better than too

FIGURE 19-4. ROPE LITTER + HYPOTHERMIA WRAP

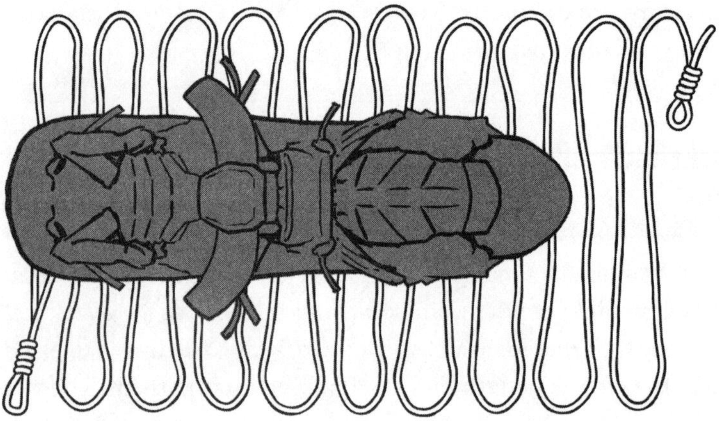

FIGURE 19-5. BIGHTS/DAISY CHAIN FOR 19-4

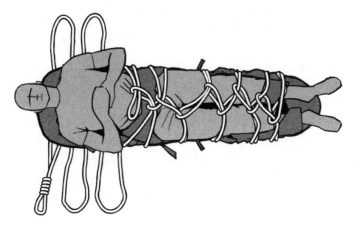

short, as extra rope can be managed more easily when completing the litter. After the rope is properly dressed, lay a tarp or tent fly on top of it, followed by adequate padding over the central portion of the rope bed. Depending on the climate and needs of the patient, multiple insulating layers can be added to allow for patient warmth and padding of the anticipated "voids" beneath the patient (e.g., the small of the back and behind the knees). While the rescuing climbers will be working quite hard in the evacuation, the injured climber will be lying relatively still—sometimes on snow—and not exerting energy or creating warmth. If available, an upside down backpack (hip belt on the top) will serve as additional padding behind the upper torso/head/neck, and can be adjusted to provide additional support for the cervical spine. This does not constitute rigid spinal immobilization, but it provides some protection and comfort. Finally, a hat, helmet, eye protection, pee bottle, or diaper (trash bag with leg cut-outs) may be fitted to the patient to provided added safety and comfort during transport.

As the patient is placed into position for packaging, Nalgene-type water bottles (filled with warm water in a cold environment) may be placed around the neck, groin, and armpits to assist in warming. The previously formed bends in the rope can then be daisy chained, beginning at the overhand or figure-8 on a bight, and then proceeding to the opposite end of the patient (Figure 19-5). Some authorities recommend starting at the feet and terminating at the chest (AdventureMed 2013, Simon 2015), which permits rapid access to the patient's torso if needed in transport without undoing the entire daisy chain. This technique also allows the use of any excess rope at the head to be used to assist and even belay the litter down steep terrain. Other instructors recommend starting at the chest and terminating at the feet, which provides an "accordion" configuration that prevents the patient from sliding headward during transport, potentially rubbing the rope against the neck. If one starts at the foot, this headward movement can be prevented by creating a bight of rope in the chain at the collarbone location on either side of the patient and tying off anchors. With either approach, putting a tether at both ends for single-track terrain litter management is helpful, especially when less attendants can stand at each side. For additional comfort, rescuers can use full-length runners, slings, or accessory cord to fashion over the shoulder loops by girth hitching these items into the daisy chained loops and padding the sling at the opposite shoulder.

The rope litter with hypothermia wrap is a useful evacuation method that can prevent heat loss and provide protection from the elements for the injured climber. Building a rope litter is a difficult technique to master and several attempts may be needed to create a usable litter. The rope litter itself can be used on snow or ice to provide a friction barrier that will help act as a brake on a gentle, low-angle slope. However, it should not be used as the sole protection when more formal lowering is required.

CHAPTER 20

RESCUE COMMUNICATION

Communication technology in the wilderness has advanced considerably in recent years, with many options available to the climber and mountaineer. Planning for any climbing trip, especially to remote areas or mountain ranges, should include detailed consideration of communication within the climbing party as well as the potential need to communicate with rescue personnel. This chapter discusses the technology currently available, preparation and selection criteria, and tips and techniques for such communication.

PRE-TRIP PREPARATION AND SELECTION

An important factor in determining what communication devices to carry with you while climbing is the geographical destination. Within the United States, many popular climbing areas will have cellular service available. Consult local guidebooks or the Mountain Project app to learn more about coverage at your destination. This may also be true of popular climbing areas in developed regions overseas. For remote locations, the selection process changes from cell phone coverage to the types of satellite phones, personal locator beacons, or messenger devices that are optimal for you and your climbing partners.

No matter what your destination will be, a key component in your planning is to leave a detailed itinerary with at least two reliable people who can notify search and rescue personnel if you do not check in or return as planned. This information should include members of your party, dates, destinations, cell phone numbers, what satellite-enabled devices (with registration information) you might be carrying, and any radio frequencies that you might monitor during the trip.

Additionally, for more remote crags in North America and Europe it is also often helpful to leave a note in your car's front windshield with destination and timing. Parking areas, especially in national parks and forests, are frequented by rangers who take note of vehicles and could act as your lifeline in case of an emergency.

COMMUNICATION METHODS AND TECHNOLOGY

Communication methods range from the simple, such as a visual SOS, to the most advanced, such as satellite-enabled phones and messaging devices. Regardless what type is used, remember that calm, clear communication with search and rescue personnel is the single most important factor in a quick evacuation.

Visual Distress Signals

The SOS sign is an internationally recognized symbol for extreme distress. Whether stomped into snow or spelled out with rope or drink powder or rocks or branches, this signal denotes the need for assistance. Remember, what looks large on the ground may still look very small from an aircraft. Make sure to build your SOS as large as possible. A good general rule of thumb is for the letters to be one foot in width and between eight and twelve feet in height.

In addition to the SOS, you can also spell out *HELP* or use the letter *V*, which denotes assistance needed, or an *X*, which signifies the need for medical help.

Whistle

The whistle is as low-tech as it gets, but can be very useful for climbers to communicate in high noise or wind situations or during rescue. It is best to select a pealess whistle so that a pea does not become jammed, water-damaged, or iced over, rendering the whistle less audible or entirely useless. The chief advantage of carrying such a whistle is that it always works and the battery never dies! The chief disadvantage is the limited audible range. The international distress signal using a whistle is three blasts. A whistle should be considered for all climbing first aid kits, as it is lightweight and occupies minimal space.

Signal Mirror

A mirror can also act as a signaling device in the mountains to alert passing aircraft or to attempt to signal other parties. Among the chief advantages of the mirror is its light weight, while the main disadvantages are that it is only useful on a sunny day and within line of sight. To sight a mirror and reflection to an aircraft, extend your arm and ensure that the reflection falls between your thumb and forefinger. Carefully move your extended arm until the aircraft is between these fingers and move the mirror slightly back and forth to aim the reflection in that direction.

Fire

Having fire-starting materials can be very useful for signaling, and even for survival. An important element of starting a fire for signaling is to ensure that the fuel gathered will create smoke that is in contrast to the surroundings. Adding green flora to a fire will create white smoke, while adding plastics and nylon (from tents or packs) or rubber (from climbing shoes) creates darker smoke.

Radio Services/Handheld Radios

There are multiple types of radios that can be used by climbing parties and expeditions, including Family Radio Service (FRS), General Mobile Radio Service (GMRS), citizens band (CB), and the Amateur Radio Service (ham radio). The most commonly used radios for climbing are the FRS service type that utilize 14 UHF frequencies and are not regulated by the Federal Communications Commission (FCC). These radios are inexpensive and have an effective range of up to one mile. GMRS radios are regulated by the FCC and require a license to operate. Their effective range is often published as 20 to 35 miles, but five miles (with a direct line of sight) is a better estimate. FRS and GMRS are used for climbing parties to communicate both in a multi-pitch environment and to keep separate climbing teams in contact with one another and with expedition base camp managers.

CB and ham radios are not as commonly used in climbing expeditions. The CB is another unregulated system and is common among commercial truck drivers. This type of radio might be considered when climbing near major transportation corridors, due to the large numbers of units

FIGURE 20-1. EMERGENCY CHANNEL/FREQUENCY FOR RADIO SERVICES

Radio	Channel	Frequency
Family Radio Service (FRS)	Channel 1	None
General Mobile Radio Service (GMRS)	None	462.675 MHz
Citizens Band (CB)	Channel 9	None
Amateur Radio Service (HAM)*	None	146.520 MHz

*Monitored for first 5 minutes, every three hours (i.e. 0700-0705, 1000-1005 etc.)

monitoring this band. Handheld units are manageable in size and have a range of one to five miles. In order to utilize ham radios, an operator must pass a test to acquire a license. When traveling internationally, it is recommended to check the appropriate regulations governing use of radios. Marine band radios are also available for vehicle mounting and have wide reception but may not be legal outside of marine operations. See Figure 20-1 for emergency channels and frequencies for various radio services.

Cell Phones

Advances in cellular technology and the supporting tower network within the United States has expanded rapidly over the past fifteen years, making many formerly uncovered areas accessible by mobile phone. The usefulness of phones for rescue communications is directly related to coverage area and battery life. When heading into remote areas for climbing, power down phones to save energy. Otherwise many will search for service and drain much of the remaining battery life if left fully on.

Satellite Telephones

Satellite phone technology has changed dramatically in recent years, resulting in better coverage, smaller and lighter handsets, and cheaper units and plans. Satellite phones operate off one of two systems: either the fixed equator system (geostationary) or low Earth orbit system (LEO). This sector is rapidly changing, and a thorough review of each system should be conducted prior to purchase (or rental), with an emphasis on the following criteria: destination, costs for units and airtime, and contract costs related to subscription services.

Currently, there are four satellite networks: Iridium, Globalstar, Inmarsat, and Thuraya. Iridium has a robust system of 66 satellites and works well in canyons and mountain ranges. It is the only network that functions at the North and South Poles and covers the majority of the globe.

Globalstar has 48 satellites in orbit and offers audio nearly as good as a cellular phone. This network has gaps in coverage in sub-Saharan Africa, both the North and South Poles, portions of Central America, and southern Asia, including the entire Himalayas.

Inmarsat, based in Great Britain, operates 11 satellites and has overall better coverage than Globalstar. The Inmarsat network has gaps in coverage for the two poles, Greenland, Siberia, and—most notable for climbers—Alaska.

Thuraya is based in the United Arab Emirates (UAE) and currently has two satellites in orbit that work with the existing Global System for Mobile Communications (GSM) ground network. The coverage area for this system is limited to Europe, Africa, Asia, and Australia. It has recently developed a device called a SatSleeve that allows the use of an iPhone or Android device as a satellite phone.

Personal Locator Beacons (PLB)

The concept of personal locator beacons, or PLBs for short, originated with emergency beacons mandated for ocean-going vessels (emergency position-indication radio beacons, or EPIRBs) and for aircraft (emergency locator transmitters, or ELTs). PLBs are one-way communication devices that digitally communicate via the Cospas-Sarsat satellite system on the 406 MHz frequency. This satellite system was first developed and deployed in the late 1970s and early 1980s through the cooperation of Canada, France, the United States, and the former USSR. These devices must be registered with national authorities; for the United States this is the National Oceanic and Atmospheric Administration (NOAA). Registration is free at www.beaconregistration.noaa.gov or www.406registration.com. There are no subscription fees related to these devices. This registration allows the climber to enter their identity as well as emergency contact information. Not only is this useful to assist in rescue, but it also allows the authorities to authenticate a call-and-abort initiation of rescue resources in the case of a false alarm. When considering PLBs for purchase, newer models can also include GPS coordinates with the transmission. This greatly increases the accuracy for search and rescue personnel from the standard three-mile radius of a normal unit. ACR and McMurdo are the two most common PLBs available on the commercial market.

Satellite Emergency Notification Devices (SENDs)

The final type of communication device available for climbers is also the most recent to the marketplace. SEND messenger devices operate on private satellite networks and allow users to send and receive messages via text message. The two most common SEND devices are the SPOT family of devices (Globalstar) and devices built by DeLorme (Garmin) that operate on the Iridium satellite network. There are multiple units with different capabilities, but all of these devices can send and receive information, distress or "all okay" messages, and GPS coordinates. Some more advanced devices sync via Bluetooth to a smartphone to allow for easier typing, longer messages, and more detailed GPS mapping.

Avalanche Transceiver/Beacon

An avalanche transceiver is an essential piece of gear when traveling in avalanche prone terrain. These devices work by transmitting a pulsed radio signal that can be picked up by other units in the area. They are not traditional communication devices, rather they are purely used for emergency situations. These units have two modes, transmit and receive. When traveling in terrain with a risk of avalanche, all units should be in transmit. If a person is buried by an avalanche, other uninjured climbers can then switch to receive mode in order to search for the person buried. See Chapter 17 for additional information regarding travel and search techniques in potential avalanche terrain.

COMMUNICATING WITH RESCUE PERSONNEL

The three most important rules to remember when attempting to communicate with search and rescue personnel are: 1) stay calm, 2) use all forms of communication available, and 3) communicate the situation as clearly as possible. See Chapter 1 for details about assessment and Appendix H for a sample SOAP note to communicate the situation and patient injuries. At a minimum, the first information given to rescue personnel should be your location, condition, and the type of rescue that is required (ground, air, high-angle). In some situations, the use of a phonetic alphabet may be helpful to communicate your needs clearly (Figure 20-2). Additional information related to calling for and communicating with helicopters can be found in Appendix B.

FIGURE 20-2. PHONETIC ALPHABET

The US Military along with many other agencies utilize a phonetic alphabet to minimize confusion when relaying important information while using radio communication. The standard phonetic alphabet is included below:

A – Alpha	B – Bravo	C – Charlie	D – Delta
E – Echo	F – Foxtrot	G – Golf	H – Hotel
I – India	J – Juliet	K – Kilo	L – Lima
M – Mike	N – November	O – Oscar	P – Papa
Q – Quebec	R – Romeo	S – Sierra	T – Tango
U – Uniform	V – Victor	W – Whiskey	X – X-ray
Y – Yankee	Z – Zulu		

V.
APPENDICES

APPENDIX A: FIRST AID KIT CONTENTS FOR MOUNTAIN TRAVEL

When building a first aid kit, there are many variables that must be considered in order to adequately cover emergency contingencies while at the crag or during the course of an expedition. Retail kits are often a good start, but every first aid kit should be individualized based upon a number of factors.

CONSIDERATIONS

1. *Medical Knowledge of Climbing Team*
   Consider the knowledge base of you and your climbing partners. Members of the climbing team or group must have knowledge sufficient to use items included within the kit, otherwise they are of little value and add unnecessary weight.
2. *Size of Climbing Group*
   The number of climbers on the trip must also be considered, as this influences the amount of each item that might be needed. This is of specific importance when determining the amount of medication and wound management materials to include within the kit. These high-use items need special consideration. Something as small as a blister will use an enormous amount of dressing material in the course of a weeklong trip.
3. *Climbing Environment*
   Environmental factors related to climbing destination determine much of the specialty medications and equipment that will be needed. High-altitude environments require additional medications and equipment to address the potential for altitude illness (Figure A-1).

FIGURE A-1. SPECIAL MEDICATION AND EQUIPMENT CONSIDERATIONS FOR HIGH ALTITUDE

Medications

Acetazolamide (Diamox®)

Dexamethasone (Decadron®)

Nifedipine (Procardia®)

Equipment

Pulse oximeter

Hyperbaric Bag (Gamow Bag)

Oxygen tanks and delivery systems

Variation in temperatures can also affect medications. Tablets can often melt and liquid medications can freeze. Protection of kit contents is essential. Moisture from humidity, rain, or snow can destroy the usefulness of both medications and wound management materials.

Consideration must be given to the terrain and common incidents that occur in the mountain range destination. Reviewing *Accidents in North American Climbing* is recommended prior to climbing in a new area within the United States, as this publication analyzes prior accidents and may indicate common hazards such as rockfall or avalanche-prone areas.

4. *Destination and Diseases/Illnesses Common to the Region*
What diseases are endemic to the region where you are climbing? Early preparation through vaccinations and the addition of medications to avoid or treat illness are a must. Will you be traveling or transiting through areas in which malaria is endemic? If so, prophylactic antimalarials are a necessity.

Consider antibiotics that are effective within a country or destination. A great example of the need for prior planning is Nepal. While ciprofloxacin is very effective across a broad spectrum of bacteria, up to 20% of bacterial diarrhea in Nepal is caused by *Campylobacter*, which is often resistant to ciprofloxacin and other fluoroquinolones. In this case, azithromycin is a good choice and should be included in any Nepal-bound first aid kit.

5. *Medical History of Team Members*

   Understanding medical conditions of climbing partners and having the knowledge to respond and treat these are essential to caring for each other, and in the event that your climbing partner is unconscious, prior medical history is important during rescue operations. Each member of a climbing party should know of other members' allergies and essential medications.

6. *Duration of Climbing Trip*

   Often, the length of the trip will determine the amount of individual items taken, again with emphasis on wound management materials and medications.

7. *Distance from Definitive Medical Care and Availability of Rescue Assets*

   A review of medical facilities in the area will assist in planning kit contents. Readily available medical care with shorter evacuation distances may allow for a less comprehensive kit. The inverse is true for areas without proper medical facilities or long evacuation distances. Plan accordingly and be prepared for the worst case scenario. Evacuation insurance should be considered.

8. *Availability of Communications*

   Many expeditions carry satellite phones or messengers in remote areas. The ability to connect with medical providers while in remote areas is helpful for identification and treatment.

9. *Space and Weight Considerations*

   All climbers are concerned with space and weight, whether they are at a local multi-pitch crag or a faraway alpine ridge. Identification of items that can serve multiple purposes is helpful in keeping weight to a minimum.

ORGANIZATION, DESIGN, AND CONTAINERS

Organization of a kit is important both while constructing the kit and when storing items within. The acronym PAWS is a helpful guideline to organize the creation of a first aid kit.

Prevention/**P**rocedures
Analgesics/**A**ntibiotics/**A**naphylaxis

Wound Care
Survival

Packaging like items together, such as wound management materials, allows the user to identify and access the needed items quickly.

We recommend the use of durable and waterproof containers and small plastic sealable bags for storage in first aid kits. A durable outer container made of nylon or Cordura® is optimal and protects contents. Vinyl or plastic compartments within, especially when paired with small plastic bags, create a double barrier against dirt or moisture. Small hard-shell containers within the outer kit should be used to protect breakables (e.g., ampules). Another technique, though not as durable, is the use of quart- or gallon-size sealable plastic bags reinforced at the seams with duct tape. Any holes or tears that develop can be patched with additional duct tape. This material is not as durable as the nylon-encased kit and should be kept separate from climbing gear such as crampons.

SAMPLE KIT CONTENTS

The kit below is included as an example of what a person or team might take for a day at a single-pitch crag, on a minimalist multi-pitch route, or during an alpine ascent. An expedition medical kit includes many more items and should be developed by the medical provider of the group. Inclusion of items is a personal preference based upon the factors listed above. The following list should not be considered the "approved solution," but merely an example of a well-designed and thoroughly considered kit. The kit contents below do not include any prescription medications. Consult your physician for these medications based upon your individual and team health history.

Crag or Multi-Pitch Climbing Medical Kit—The Vertical Aid Kit (aka Oh S#!T Kit)

This kit, designed by Vertical Medicine Resources, is a climbing-specific first aid/bail kit that can be used as a daily crag outing first aid kit or as a lightweight kit used for small alpine teams. The following items come standard within the kit with additional room to allow for customization and are organized using the PAWS acronym. Note that this kit includes multiple climbing-specific "bail" items for use if needed.

PREVENTION/PROCEDURES

Trango Piranha Alpine Accessory Knife
NUUN hydration tabs
Aquatab water purification tablets
1/2" roll athletic tape
SPF 15 lip balm
SPF 30 sunscreen (PABA-free)
Chemical hand warmer

ANALGESICS/ANTIBIOTICS/ANAPHYLAXIS

Ibuprofen
Acetaminophen
Diphenhydramine
Loperamide
Antacid
Bacitracin ointment
Sting relief pad (topical lidocaine)

WOUND CARE

Curad Bloodstop Hemostatic Gauze
Nexcare Blister Care pads
3" x 3" gauze sponges
2" x 2" gauze sponges
3" Conform gauze
Latex-free examination gloves
Bandages (assorted sizes)
Sterile alcohol prep pads
Antiseptic towelettes

SURVIVAL

VMR emergency whistle
6 mm cord (2 m long)
Aluminum SMC rappel ring
Survival blanket (84" x 52")

APPENDIX B: HOW TO COMMUNICATE WITH HELICOPTERS, AND PREPARATIONS FOR HELICOPTER EVACUATION

Helicopter evacuation in the mountains is a complex and highly dangerous operation for pilots and their crews as well as for climbers in need of assistance on the ground or mountainside. ICAR (the International Commission for Alpine Rescue) is increasingly concerned about deaths of rescuers during helicopter operations, with one study showing that 29% of all rescuer fatalities occur during these types of evacuations (Tomazin 2003). Calling for helicopter assets is a decision not to be made lightly, but on the other hand, can certainly be instrumental in saving lives.

Evacuation by helicopter should be considered only when other forms of evacuation are unavailable or in case of extreme injury. Some examples of injuries that may require helicopter evacuation for climbers include acute emergencies involving neurologic, vascular, surgical, or cardiac injuries; any compromised respiratory or hemodynamic function; altitude illness; severe burns requiring treatment in a burn center; or any injury that threatens life, limb, or loss of eyesight. Critical questions to consider when deciding whether to call for helicopter evacuation include:

+ Is the patient's condition time-critical?
+ Can the patient receive adequate treatment in their current location?
+ Where can this patient receive definitive care? (Local facility, repatriation?)
+ What is the capacity, availability, and suitability of local trans-

portation? Do air services offer a different scope of care than local ground transportation?

+ Can the patient survive a road/water journey or is air evacuation necessary?
+ Is medical supervision available for the evacuation?

COMMUNICATION

There are a great variety of techniques to communicate with rescuers, from rudimentary SOS markers arranged on the ground to satellite phones that can communicate across the globe. Chapter 20 offers a more complete discussion of this topic.

The most important aspect of communication in any rescue is clarity of the situation, both with respect to the injured climber and to the geographic location. Establishing communication early is helpful to transmit critical information to the aircrew prior to arrival. Use of the 9-Line MEDEVAC (Figure B-1 and Figure B-2) and use of cardinal directions (north, south, east, and west) are helpful to organize and direct aircraft.

Once visual contact has been made, the use of hand and arm signals to ground-guide the aircraft to the appropriate landing zone (LZ) should be used if an LZ has not been properly marked. See Figure B-3 for basic hand and arm signals.

When handing off the injured climber, be sure to give the aircrew or accompanying medical provider a written accident report and SOAP note that describes the incident, relays information about the patient, and details the care provided (see Appendix H).

SELECTION AND PREPARATION OF LANDING ZONE (LZ)

When selecting a landing zone, ground personnel should consider security, slope, surface, and scatter, better known as the 4 S's.

Security involves keeping the scene safe for the injured climber, the aircrew, and any bystanders in the area. Minimizing the number of people near the landing zone increases safety and reduces potential injury from flying objects scattered by the downwash of the rotors.

FIGURE B-1. 9-LINE MEDEVAC

The United States military and NATO forces utilize the 9 Line MEDEVAC form to communicate with helicopters during evacuation. Within the US and some areas overseas air rescue is conducted by military aviation units and most helicopter pilots for civilian firms are familiar with this report structure.

Line 1. Location of the pick-up site

Line 2. Radio frequency, call sign, and suffix

Line 3. Number of patients by precedence:
  A: Urgent
  B: Urgent Surgical
  C: Priority
  D: Routine
  E: Convenience

Line 4. Special equipment required:
  A: None
  B: Hoist
  C: Extraction equipment
  D: Ventilator

Line 5. Number of patients:
  A: Litter
  B: Ambulatory

Line 6. Security at pick-up site:
  N: No enemy troops in area
  P: Possible enemy troops in area
    (approach with caution)
  E: Enemy troops in area (approach
    with caution)
  X: Enemy troops in area (armed
    escort required)

*In peacetime—number and types of wounds, injuries, and illnesses

Line 7. Method of marking pick-up site:
  A: Panels
  B: Pyrotechnic signal
  C: Smoke signal
  D: None
  E: Other

Line 8. Patient nationality and status:
  A: US Military
  B: US Civilian
  C: Non-US Military
  D: Non-US Civilian
  E: EPW

Line 9. NBC Contamination:
  N: Nuclear
  B: Biological
  C: Chemical

*In peacetime—terrain description of pick-up site

Slopes of less than 10% are ideal for an LZ. Any slope with greater than a 15% grade is considered extremely unsafe. The surface of the landing zone is ideally a wide, flat area that is clear of any obstacles. Different airframes require different sizes of LZ, so identifying the largest flat area is key.

A chief consideration of the *surface* for LZ selection is what is known

**FIGURE B-2. EXAMPLE OF COMMUNICATION USING
9-LINE MEDEVAC FORMAT**

"Helo, this is Ground, over"

"Ground, this is Helo, send over"

"This is Ground, request MEDEVAC, over"

"Roger Ground, send your request, over"

"Line One—LZ location (GPS Coord.)—Break"

"Line Two—HF-231.45, UHF-114.1 Ground—Break"

"Line Three—2A, 3C—Break"

"Line Four—A—Break"

"Line Five—2L, 3A—Break"

"Line Six—2 head injuries, 3 lacerations—Break"

"Line Seven—A, red jackets—Break"

"Line Eight—B—Break"

"Line Nine—Rocky, all debris removed, flat—Break"

"How Copy my last, Over"

"Roger Ground, solid copy, stand-by MEDEVAC—over"

"Ground standing-by, over"

as a "run out." A run out allows a helicopter to approach on a smooth downward angle rather than lowering directly down to an LZ while in a hover. The use of a run out gives the pilot the ability to adjust their approach and is especially useful in high altitude or in windy conditions. Additionally, climbers must identify an LZ that has no standing trees, poles, or power lines that might inhibit the helicopter landing.

The final S of the four is *scatter*. Prior to the arrival of a helicopter, climbers on the ground should gather any debris, secure any loose articles of clothing or gear, and compact snow to prevent these items from becoming airborne due to the rotor wash of the aircraft. Loose snow will quickly deteriorate visibility, and the air turbulence caused by the helicopter blades can pick up large pieces of clothing and gear, causing them to become projectiles or potentially tangle in the rotors.

If there is time, marking the landing zone with heavy stones in an

FIGURE B-3. AIRCRAFT HAND SIGNALS

Land here
DAY

LZ unsafe
DAY

Land here
NIGHT

LZ unsafe
NIGHT

"H" pattern or using drink mix powder on snow is helpful. Improvising a windsock using a plastic bag helps the pilot anticipate wind direction on the ground.

APPROACHING THE AIRCRAFT

Once the helicopter is safely in the landing zone, there are a few important rules to maintain a safe environment. The most important is to *always* follow the instructions and guidance of the aircrew. Other rules include:

+ Approach only when cleared by the aircrew or after visual contact and approval by the pilot.
+ Always approach in a crouched position (wind gusts and turbulence can cause rotors to dip downward without warning).
+ Always approach from the front or sides.
+ Never go near the rear of the aircraft.

If the helicopter is unable to land and instead must hover over the terrain, take special care in approaching and take all directions from the aircrew. Approach and depart in a crouch from the downhill side of the aircraft and be prepared for heavy rotor wash. Never approach from the uphill side of the aircraft.

Steep terrain may dictate the use of a cable-and-winch system. Usually, a member of the aircrew will accompany the winch, basket, or seat. If not, make sure that the cable touches the ground or rock before touching it to allow for a discharge of static electricity. You may need to fashion a chest harness using a sling and attach the injured climber from both the climbing harness and improvised chest harness to keep them upright once secured to the cable hook. The pilot and crew are well-trained professionals and will direct and control the situation.

APPENDIX C: CONVERSION TABLES

Our convention in this book is to express temperature in Celsius, distance in miles, and height in meters. We recognize, however, that this is an international text and may be used by readers more familiar with different units. Below is a table to help facilitate conversion.

LENGTH

When you know	Multiply by	To find
Millimeters	0.04	Inches
Centimeters	0.39	Inches
Meters	3.28	Feet
Meters	1.09	Yards
Kilometers	0.62	Miles
Inches	25.40	Millimeters
Inches	2.54	Centimeters
Feet	30.48	Centimeters
Yards	0.91	Meters
Miles	1.61	Kilometers

MASS

When you know	Multiply by	To find
Grams	0.035	Ounces
Kilograms	2.20	Pounds
Ounces	28.35	Grams
Pounds	0.45	Kilograms

TEMPERATURE

Degrees Fahrenheit	(F-32) x 1.8	Degrees Celsius
Degrees Celsius	(C x 1.8) + 32	Degrees Fahrenheit

APPENDIX D: FROSTBITE AND WINDCHILL TABLE

The windchill temperature index provides a measure of how wind can speed up the rate of heat loss from exposed skin. Wind speed that is equal to or less than three miles per hour is considered calm. Only exposed skin is affected by windchill, and it is of greater significance when it is cooler. Windchill effect can be negated if the climber is properly dressed and prepared for the weather conditions.

WIND (MPH)	TEMPERATURE (FAHRENHEIT)																	
Calm	40	35	30	25	20	15	10	5	0	-5	-10	-15	-20	-25	-30	-35	-40	-45
5	36	31	25	19	13	7	1	-5	-11	-16	-22	-28	-34	-40	-46	-52	-57	-63
10	34	27	21	15	9	3	-4	-10	-16	-22	-28	-35	-41	-47	-53	-59	-66	-72
15	32	25	19	13	6	0	-7	-13	-19	-26	-32	-39	-45	-51	-58	-64	-71	-77
20	30	24	17	11	4	-2	-9	-15	-22	-29	-35	-42	-48	-55	-61	-68	-74	-81
25	29	23	16	9	3	-4	-11	-17	-24	-31	-37	-44	-51	-58	-64	-71	-78	-84
30	28	22	15	8	1	-5	-12	-19	-26	-33	-39	-46	-53	-60	-67	-73	-80	-87
35	28	21	14	7	0	-7	-14	-21	-27	-34	-41	-48	-55	-62	-69	-76	-82	-89
40	27	20	13	6	-1	-8	-15	-22	-29	-36	-43	-50	-57	-64	-71	-78	-84	-91
45	26	19	12	5	-2	-9	-16	-23	-30	-37	-44	-51	-58	-65	-72	-79	-86	-93
50	26	19	12	4	-3	-10	-17	-24	-31	-38	-45	-52	-60	-67	-74	-81	-88	-95
55	25	18	11	4	-3	-11	-18	-25	-32	-39	-46	-54	-61	-68	-75	-82	-89	-97
60	25	17	10	3	-4	-11	-19	-26	-33	-40	-48	-55	-62	-69	-76	-84	-91	-98

Adapted from *Wilderness Medicine* by Paul Auerbach

Light Gray = Frostbite within 30 minutes at this temperature and wind
Dark Gray = Frostbite within 10 minutes at this temperature and wind
Black = Frostbite within 5 minutes at this temperature and wind

APPENDIX E:
WATER PURIFICATION METHODS

Safe water is essential for adequate hydration. Destruction and removal of harmful organisms through disinfection produces safe drinking water. Bacteria, viruses, and protozoa are the most common causes of water contamination for climbers. The risk of illness from contaminated water depends on the concentration of organisms, volume of water consumed, and the treatment method used. Killing all life forms, called sterilization, is not necessary for safe drinking water. Instead, the desired outcome of water disinfection is to reduce the number of infectious organisms to an acceptably low number, thus eliminating the possibility of gastrointestinal illness. Figure E-1 illustrates the four major waterborne pathogen types, with examples of each within the corresponding column.

Cloudy water indicates a higher risk of contamination, yet even clear water should be assumed to be contaminated. Appearance, odor, color, and taste are not reliable indicators of tainted water. Water sources that are near human or animal activity are commonly contaminated with fecal pollution containing enteric pathogens that trigger gastrointestinal illnesses.

Water should always be pretreated to remove large and small debris, which can interfere with the disinfection process. This can be accomplished by allowing the water to stand (sedimentation), by screening for larger particles, or by using the coagulation-flocculation method for smaller particles or cloudy water. Sedimentation occurs by leaving water unmoved for a number of hours and allowing gravity to pull large particles to the bottom of a container. The surface water can then be decanted or filtered from the top. Screening removes the largest particles from water and can be accomplished by pouring water through clothing or a coffee filter. Coagulation-flocculation is necessary for

FIGURE E-1. WATER PATHOGENS

Bacteria	Viruses	Protozoa	Parasites
Escherichia coli	Hepatitis A, E	Giardia lamblia	Ascaris lumbricoides
Shigella	Norovirus	Entamoeba histolytica	Hookworm
Campylobacter	Poliovirus	Cryptosporidia	Tapeworm
Vibrio cholerae	Rotavorus	Blastocystis hominis	Sheep liver fluke
Salmonellae		Isospora belli	Dracunculus medinensis
Yersinia enterocolitica		Balantidium coli	Pinworm
Aeromonas		Ancanthamoeba	Whipworm
		Cyclospora	Oriental liver fluke
			Lung fluke
			Fish tapeworm
			Hydatid disease

Source: Backer HD. Field Water Disinfection. In: Auerbach PS, ed. Wilderness Medicine. *7th ed. Philadelphia, PA: Mosby Elsevier; 2017.*

particles that are not large enough for gravity or filtration to be effective. This is accomplished by adding a nontoxic powder such as alum, iron, lime, white ash from burned wood, or baking powder to the water. These substances cause particles in the water to agglomerate into small particulates. Following coagulation, larger particulates are formed through gentle agitation in the flocculation step. After a 30-minute settling period, these larger clusters are removed through screening, sedimentation, and/or decanting. Charcoal may also be incorporated to remove any chemical contaminants in water, though this can be difficult in a wilderness setting. The easiest pretreatment method for climbers is usually the screening method, though the other methods are useful in a base camp situation. Figure E-2 outlines advantages and disadvantages of different techniques.

Pre-treatment technique	Process	Advantage/Disadvantage
Sedimentation	Large particles settle by gravity	Improves water aesthetics Takes a long time
Screening	Large particles are removed	Removes large particles Easy Improves water quality, efficacy of filtration, and chemical disinfection
Coagulation-flocculation	Suspended particles are removed	Removes smaller particles Easy Improves water quality, efficacy of filtration, and chemical disinfection
Activated charcoal	Removes chemicals	Removes pesticides and chemical disinfectants Improves taste

Climbing destination is an important factor in determining potential contaminants and identifying the best methods for safe water collection. Methods of treatment include heat, filtration, chemical treatment, and irradiation. These methods, along with the common contaminants that are neutralized using each, are illustrated in Figure E-3.

BOILING

Heat is the surest method to kill all enteric pathogens. Many organisms are killed at temperatures lower than the boiling point of 100°C (212°F). Lower temperatures can be effective if the contact time is longer (pasteurization), but without a thermometer it is too difficult to accurately gauge the temperature. Boiling is the most certain method to eradicate all pathogens, ensuring the appropriate temperature has been reached.

FIGURE E-3. TREATMENT EFFECT

Disinfection techniques	Heat	Filtration	Halogens	Chlorine dioxide
Bacteria	good	good	good	good
Viruses	good	fair	good	good
Protozoa-Giardia	good	good	good	good
Protozoa-Cryptosporidium	good	good	poor	good
Parasites	good	good	fair	fair

Sources: Backer HD. Field Water Disinfection. In: Auerbach PS, ed. Wilderness Medicine. 7th ed. Philadelphia, PA: Mosby Elsevier; 2017.
Johnson C, Anderson S, Dallimore J, Winser S, Warrell DA. Oxford Handbook of Expedition and Wilderness Medicine. 2nd ed. Oxford University Press, Oxford, UK 2015.

According to the World Health Organization (WHO) and the Centers for Disease Control and Prevention (CDC), bringing water to a boil at sea level is sufficient, and the Environmental Protection Agency (EPA) suggests an extra one to three minutes for an added margin of safety (Backer 2012). For alpine climbers, altitude must be considered, as it decreases the boiling point. Figure E-4 indicates the boiling temperatures at various altitudes.

The CDC recommends boiling water for three minutes when higher than 2,000 meters (Backer 2012). Prior to boiling water, the removal of

FIGURE E-4. BOILING TEMPERATURE AT VARIOUS ALTITUDES

Altitude (M)	Altitude (ft)	Boiling point °Celsius	Boiling point °Fahrenheit
1,500	4,921	95°	203°
3,050	10,006	90°	194°
4,250	13,944	86°	186.8°
5,800	19,028	81°	177.8°

Sources: Backer HD. Field Water Disinfection. In: Auerbach PS, ed. Wilderness Medicine. 7th ed. Philadelphia, PA: Mosby Elsevier; 2017.
Johnson C, Anderson S, Dallimore J, Winser S, Warrell DA. Oxford Handbook of Expedition and Wilderness Medicine. 2nd ed. Oxford University Press, Oxford, UK 2015.

debris (pretreatment) should be completed, but is not completely necessary, as heat kills all enteric pathogens regardless, and there are no alterations in the taste. The limitation of using heat is the fuel source and amount required. It generally takes one kilogram (2.2 lb.) of wood to boil 1 liter of water. Be aware of local and national rules and regulations regarding the use of wood, and be environmentally friendly.

FILTRATION

Filters remove cysts and bacteria, but are not reliable for complete removal of viruses. Viruses can be as small as 0.1 micron in diameter, and filters are unable to reliably remove items that small. Filters are simple, do not alter the taste, and require no curing time. The downfalls of filters are cost, weight, size, and reliability, as they can malfunction due to clogging. All models require pressure to drive the water through the filter, and the smaller the pore size the more pressure is required. Filters require additional pressure once congested with contaminants, which can force organisms through the filter, yielding contaminated water. All filters require cleaning, and the ability to easily service the unit in the field is a plus. Back flushing and surface cleaning usually clears the filter.

Filters can be divided into microfilters, ultrafilters, and nanofilters, which have pores as small as 0.1, 0.01, and 0.001 or less microns, respectively. This attribute defines their abilities. Ultrafiltration is considered sufficient to remove viruses from water while nanofiltration can filter even smaller particles (e.g., chemicals). The surest method for safe drinking water that may have viral contaminants is a combined treatment of filtering and one other method (heat, halogens, chlorine dioxide, or ultraviolet light) to eradicate viruses. Filters can be utilized without the addition of another disinfection method in areas where human or animal contact is limited.

Some filters come with integrated charcoal or iodine elements. Charcoal is the optimal technique to remove toxic chemicals and radioactive contaminants, with the added bonus of improved taste and odor. Unpleasant taste and odor can be the initial sign of ineffective charcoal. Iodine is impregnated into some filters in an attempt to destroy viruses as water passes through the filter.

Reverse osmosis filtering units are available but unrealistic for climbers, as this type of filter is used for desalinating water and is more applicable for recreation near the ocean or saltwater lakes.

HALOGEN DISINFECTION

Halogens eliminate bacteria, but their effectiveness against protozoa is not guaranteed. Halogens include iodine and chlorine, and their effectiveness depends on the concentration, time, water temperature, contaminants, and pH of the water. In cold water, the contact time or overall dose should be increased. For areas where giardia is common, the contact time must be at least three to four times longer in cold water. The optimal pH for halogen disinfection is 6.5 to 7.5, and when the pH is more alkaline and closer to 8.0, a larger dose of halogen is required. Certain desert water is very alkaline and not palatable. Equipment to test water pH is not a common tool taken by most climbers, and compensating for the pH is not necessary as most halogens have some buffering capacity for minor pH differences.

Most climbers find that halogens have an unpleasant taste that requires a second step to neutralize. For treatment times and information, the product label should always be referred to prior to use.

IODINE

Iodine is effective for killing bacteria, viruses, and some protozoa. Iodine use should be limited to one month and should not be used by pregnant women, iodine-sensitive individuals, or climbers with thyroid disease, a family history of thyroid disease, or who suffers from chronic iodine deficiency (Figure E-5).

After adequate disinfection, flavoring can be added to improve the taste, such as ascorbic acid (vitamin C) in drink mixes or sodium thiosulfate.

CHLORINE

Chlorine, such as household bleach (5% sodium hypochlorite), is sufficient to inactivate bacteria, viruses, and some protozoa (Figure E–5).

FIGURE E-5. USE OF IODINE AND CHLORINE FOR WATER PURIFICATION

Iodine techniques	Clear surface x 15-30 mins in warm + 45-60 mins in cold	Cloudy water x 15-30 mins in warm + 45-60 mins in cold
Iodine tabs	1 tab	2 tab
2% iodine solution	1 mL	2 mL
10% Povidone-iodine	4 mL	8 mL
Iodine crystals in water (4-8g of iodine in 1-2oz bottle filled with water)	13 mL	26 mL
Iodine crystals in alcohol (8g iodine to 100ml of 95% ethanol)	1 mL	1 mL
Chlorination techniques		
Household bleach 5% (Sodium hypochlorite)	1-2 mL	2-4 mL
Calcium hypochlorite (Redi Chlor)	¼ tab	⅛ tab
Sodium dichloroisocyanurate (AquaTab)	½ tab	1 tab
Chlorine plus flocculating agent (Chlor-Floc)	½ tab	1 tab

It is more sensitive and less suitable in cold contaminated water. Acute toxicity or irritation is extremely rare and only occurs if solutions are highly concentrated. It does become less potent when exposed to heat, air, or moisture, and to extend the shelf life, the manufacturer packages chlorine tabs individually in foil.

To reduce the taste and smell of chlorine, several drops of 30% hydrogen peroxide solution can be added, forming calcium chloride, a common food additive. Again, this requires a second step, as the peroxide should not be added until at least ten to fifteen minutes after the chlorine tab.

Flavored drink mixes containing ascorbic acid can also mask the unpalatable halogen taste of chlorine.

Halogens can be used independently unless water sources are contaminated with protozoa. Giardia requires longer contact time with higher concentrations and cryptosporidium cysts are resistant to certain halogens. Halogens can be combined with chlorine dioxide or ultraviolet light to eradicate the protozoa.

CHLORINE DIOXIDE

This agent is effective against all microorganisms, including cryptosporidium. It has no taste and is very portable in small doses. Chlorine dioxide is sensitive to sunlight and should be kept in a shaded bottle during treatment. Aquatabs® are a common brand of chlorine dioxide. This is the single most effective and weight-conscious solution for water disinfection, and a good choice for most climbers and alpinists.

MIOX PURIFIER

The Miox purifier uses a current passed through a brine solution that generates free chlorine as well as other mixed disinfectants. This creates an environment that is effective against bacteria, viruses, and sometimes cryptosporidium. The battery life for this device creates an element of uncertainty for this method. Climbers in the alpine setting should keep a spare set of batteries close to their body not only for a backup but also to prolong the battery life when not in use. These purifiers can be difficult to use. They are listed here to be comprehensive, but in the opinion of the authors would not be a preferred water treatment tool.

SILVER

This method is used in Europe. The EPA in the United States has not approved it for use and therefore it is limited to purchase and use at overseas climbing destinations. Silver can be used to treat water contaminated with bacteria and for the prevention of growth in previously treated or stored water. Some filters are silver-impregnated to inactivate bacteria during filtration, and this element decreases the growth of bacteria on the inside of the filter. Silver will need to be combined with another method if there is a chance of the presence of viruses or protozoa in the water being treated. Note that long-term ingestion of large volumes of silver has been implicated in the development of argyria, a condition causing blue skin (James 2006).

ULTRAVIOLET LIGHT

Ultraviolet light is an effective method to kill bacteria, viruses, and protozoa. This method works rapidly and does not alter the taste. It is important for the user to remember that there is no residual effect and water may become recontaminated. In other words, if you add additional water to the container, you must activate the ultraviolet light again to disinfect. While some units have solar panels integrated into the unit, most require batteries, which are sensitive to temperature and can become ineffective when climbing in cold environments. As with the Miox purifier, extra batteries are essential, and keeping them warm in cold climates is helpful. These are effective against cryptosporidium. This method can be used as a single method against all contaminants. The most common example of this water disinfectant method is the SteriPEN.

Solar irradiation (sunlight) is used with a SolarBag and can disinfect up to three liters of water. The bag has a mesh insert coated with titanium dioxide. The unit is placed in direct sunlight for one to two hours or two to four hours on a cloudy day. A dye can be used to indicate when the water is safe to consume. This method should be combined with other methods if viruses and protozoa are a possibility.

Another form of solar irradiation can be conducted using clear water bottles, preferably made of polyethylene terephthalate (PET), which have the least amount of additives. Irradiation occurs if the bottle is placed upon a reflective metal surface in the sun for up to four hours, or if the water is cold, for up to six hours. Glass should not be used, as it inhibits the UV from penetrating the contained water with as much effectiveness as clear plastic. For cloudy water, the time of exposure to UV rays should

FIGURE E-6. CHOOSING THE APPROPRIATE DISINFECTION TECHNIQUE IN THE VARIOUS ENVIRONMENTS

Effective methods for various concerns	Wilderness water with little human or domestic animal activity	Tap water in 2nd or 3rd world country	Clear water near human and animal activity	Cloudy water near human and animal activity
Primary concern	bacteria, giardia	bacteria, giardia, viruses	All pathogens	All pathogens
Disinfection method	Any method	Heat, or filtration plus halogen, chlorine dioxide, or ultraviolet method	Heat, or filtration plus halogen, chlorine dioxide, or ultraviolet method	Pretreat with coagulation, flocculation plus heat, or filtration plus halogen, chlorine dioxide, or ultraviolet method

Sources: Backer HD. Field Water Disinfection. In: Auerbach PS, ed. Wilderness Medicine. 7th ed. Philadelphia, PA: Mosby Elsevier; 2017.
Johnson C, Anderson S, Dallimore J, Winser S, Warrell DA. Oxford Handbook of Expedition and Wilderness Medicine. 2nd ed. Oxford University Press, Oxford, UK 2015.

be extended for at least two days. While this can be a low-cost treatment method against bacteria, viruses, and protozoa, the large amount of time needed for disinfection makes this method unsuitable for climbers. This method should be combined with another to ensure cleanliness.

HOW TO CHOOSE A WATER PURIFICATION METHOD

There are multiple options for water treatment and the best method should take into account likely infective organisms, personal taste, group size, location, and available fuel. As a general guideline, pristine watershed areas can be considered free of viral agents; however, it can be very difficult to determine who or what has been in the area. With increasing human and animal contact, viral contamination becomes more of a risk. The prudent action would be to adhere to the principle that all wilderness water sources are contaminated and treat accordingly. Boiling will eliminate all pathogens but may not be feasible. Overseas, the use of Aquatabs®, which are effective against all contaminants, even cryptosporidium, is recommended. There is a time delay with this method, and the manufacturer's recommendation must be precisely followed. SteriPENs are a great method for all contaminates as long as the water is not extremely cloudy or full of large particles. Batteries can be a challenge, and in certain climbing destinations other methods may be more advantageous. Water treatment, strict personal hygiene, and proper waste management methods are the best practices to remain free of illness. Figure E-6 summarizes safe water disinfection strategies.

APPENDIX F: RECOMMENDED MEDICATIONS FOR MOUNTAIN TRAVEL

All travelers should be up-to-date on routine vaccinations and inquire about region-specific vaccinations as soon as possible after deciding upon an expedition location. Climbers should acquire needed medications prior to departure. Prescription medications should stay in their original packaging to prove they are prescribed by a physician for the person carrying them during customs and border checks. Despite this, be prepared for a routine practice of confiscation in some countries, whether legal or illegal. While medications can be cheaper in the developing world, they may also be substandard in quality. All personal medications should be carried onto airlines, and once in-country separated into two different bags in case of loss or damage of baggage.

DRUGS FOR A BASIC FIELD KIT

Basic field kits should include elements of the following drug groups:

Analgesic/Antipyretic

Analgesics relieve pain and antipyretics reduce fever. Drugs that relieve pain can be classified as mild, moderate, or strong. Strong analgesics and codeine are controlled substances in the United States, and a prescription is needed to obtain them. Strong analgesics should only be given when required for severe pain and for no longer than two weeks. A less potent analgesic should be started once the pain has been reduced.

Antiallergic Medications

Epinephrine is used for anaphylaxis. For non-anaphylactic reactions, antihistamines are usually used.

Antacids

Antacids are drugs that neutralize acids in the stomach for the treatment of indigestion, peptic ulcers, heartburn, and GERD. For long-term maintenance, a proton pump inhibitor, such as omeprazole, Prevacid®, Protonix®, Nexium®, or Zantac® are good choices.

Antifungal

A broad-spectrum antifungal agent can be used topically for fungal skin infections. There are multiple over-the-counter (OTC) brands available.

Antihistamines

These agents block histamine, which is a substance that is released in the body during an allergic or inflammatory reaction. These medications are also used to reduce motion sickness. An example of this drug class is Benadryl®.

Antimicrobial

Antimicrobials kill or reduce the spread of microorganisms that include bacteria, viruses, protozoa, and parasites that can cause infection. Note that the specific term "antibiotic" only refers to antimicrobials that kill bacteria (and sometimes protozoa and parasites). Antibiotics are not effective against viruses.

Antimalarials

Climbers traveling to malaria-endemic regions must get the most current recommendations, as effective drugs change frequently. For self-treatment of malaria, a therapeutic dose of the appropriate antimalarial drug should be given, but only when a significant fever accompanied by systemic illness occurs. This is a last resort and the goal is to prevent death. Medical attention should be sought within twenty-four hours.

Antimotility/Antiemetics

Antimotility drugs are used to control diarrhea through reduction of intestinal motility. The most commonly used example of this type of drug is loperamide (Imodium®). These agents should be used sparingly, if at all, in individuals with dysentery or fever (see Chapter 7). Antiemetic medications are used to reduce vomiting. A common example of this type of drug is ondansetron (Zofran®), which comes in a convenient oral dissolving tablet (ODT). This means that the medication need not be swallowed, in case of severe vomiting.

Antiseptics

Antiseptics are used to kill microorganisms on contact, and are useful for cleaning a wound or disinfecting contaminated water. Alcohol swabs are lightweight and easy to carry.

Cough Suppressants or Expectorants/Throat Lozenges

Better known as cough drops, these drugs help minimize coughing and aid in the relief of a sore throat.

Decongestants

Decongestants aid with congestion in the upper respiratory tract. This class of drugs functions by causing the blood vessels in the nasal mucosa to contract, thus promoting sinus drainage related to a cold, hay fever, or sinusitis.

Mild Laxatives

These medications are used for constipation, which can occur from dehydration or as a side effect from the taking of pain medications.

Motion Sickness Medications

Antihistamines are the most commonly used medications for motion sickness. Sedation is a common side effect of these medications. There are non-sedating medications available or non-pharmacological interventions that can help manage motion sickness. Nonmedical solutions to motion sickness include: driving a vehicle instead of riding, sitting in the front seat of a vehicle rather than the back, sitting over the wing of an aircraft, or sitting in the central cabin on a ship. Lying prone with eyes closed or sitting and focusing on the horizon also works for some individuals.

Rehydration Packs

These solutions can be used for travelers suffering from dehydration occurring due to strenuous activity, vomiting, and/or diarrhea. See Chapter 13.

Sedating Medications

Sedation or sleeping medications are used for insomnia or anxiety. These drugs should not be taken above 3,000 meters (10,000 feet) because respirations are decreased, which can lead to hypoxemia and an increased risk of AMS. Certain sedating medications such as benzodiazepines may cause persistent drowsiness and should only be given if there is adequate time for the drug to wear off. These medications should not be given to individuals with head injuries or central nervous system diseases. Alcohol should not be consumed, as the depressive effects of the medication are enhanced. Some antihistamines that are sold over the counter have a sedating effect and can be utilized to assist in sedation.

VACCINATIONS AND PREVENTIVE MEDICATIONS

The following list of vaccinations and preventive medications/measures should be considered for overseas travel in addition to the basic field kit. Consult a physician to receive the latest guidance on needed vaccinations and preventive medications as disease locales can change rapidly (e.g., Zika virus in 2015–2016).

Argentina/Brazil

Yellow fever vaccine and antimalarial medications should be considered. As of the summer of 2016, Zika virus is a growing concern in Brazil, although no vaccination is currently available.

Belize/Guatemala

Hepatitis A, B, and typhoid vaccinations, and for some travelers, the rabies vaccination should be included. Antimalarial drugs should be taken. Mosquito precautions should be taken, as dengue fever could be a concern. Cutaneous leishmaniasis can be a concern when walking barefoot on contaminated beaches.

Bolivia/Ecuador/Peru

Antimalarial medications should be considered.

Caribbean

Hepatitis A, B, typhoid, and possibly rabies vaccinations should be acquired prior to travel. Mosquito precautions should be taken, as dengue and Zika virus are a risk. Vaccination against yellow fever is recommended for certain areas.

China

Consider vaccines for hepatitis A, B, typhoid, Japanese encephalitis (JE), and rabies vaccinations prior to travel. Antimalarial medications should be considered.

East/South Africa

Hepatitis A, B, typhoid, and yellow fever vaccinations should be given prior to travel. Antimalarial drugs should be considered depending on the time of travel. Tick bites caused by rickettsial species can be fatal, and measures should be taken to avoid exposure ("Tick Bite" sidebar on pages 180–181). HIV is a concern in this region, and appropriate caution is advised. Ebola is generally only seen in certain West African countries, not in Southern or East African regions, but preventive measures should be taken to avoid exposure if traveling in those countries.

India

Hepatitis A, B, rabies, and typhoid vaccinations are recommended. Japanese encephalitis (JE) vaccine should be considered for climbers traveling for extended periods in certain locations. Antimalarial medications should also be considered. Mosquito precautions should be taken, as dengue fever and chikungunya are an issue, particularly at the end of the monsoon season.

Mexico

Hepatitis A, B, rabies, and typhoid vaccinations are recommended. Mosquito precautions should be taken, as dengue fever is a concern. Antimalarial medications should be considered depending on the location of travel. Flea and tick bites should be avoided, as rickettsial disease, including Rocky Mountain spotted fever and flea-borne typhus, can occur ("Tick Bite" sidebar on pages 180–181).

Nepal/Himalayas

Hepatitis A, B, rabies, typhoid, and Japanese encephalitis vaccinations are recommended. Antimalarial medications should be considered depending on the location of travel.

Tanzania/Kenya

Hepatitis A, B, and typhoid vaccinations are recommended. Antimalarial medications should be taken.

APPENDIX G: IMPROVISED SHELTERS

Rarely do all trips go as planned and sometimes the difficulties encountered on a multi-pitch climb or on a mountaineering trip require an unexpected night in the mountains. Whether due to poor planning, an injury, or becoming lost, being mentally, intellectually, and physically prepared for these possibilities can mean the difference between life and death. Often, the best solution is to stay put rather than attempt navigation to or from the objective in limited visibility or poor conditions. When faced with these circumstances, construction of a well-built shelter can increase the likelihood of survival. All climbers should consider the worst case scenario when planning trips into the mountains, and many carry a bivy sack for just that eventuality.

In addition to carrying a bivy sack and other emergency gear, climbers should commit to memory the acronym STOP.

S = **S**TOP
T = **T**HINK
O = **O**BSERVE
P = **P**LAN

STOP
Consider all elements of the current situation prior to making any decision or beginning any preparations.

THINK
Consider scene safety (e.g., rockfall or icefall) and the purpose of the shelter (living space for two, cooking space, construction integrity, mitigation of heat loss in cold environments).

OBSERVE
Mountainous terrain is constantly changing and presenting challenges.

Consider all environmental factors (nearby food/water/fuel sources) and resources available for construction.

PLAN

Based upon the situation, develop an adequate shelter with available resources to create the safest and most comfortable shelter possible.

Terrain often dictates what shelters can be built or used. If lucky, the environment may include fallen trees, brush piles, natural terrain trenches, snow tree wells, boulders, and mountain cave formations that can form the foundation of a suitable shelter and help protect the stranded climber from the weather. If terrain features such as those listed are not available, climbers can craft shelters from their carried gear. These include everything from portaledges, tarps, and bivy bags to basecamp shelter tents. The only limitation to the utilization of these items is the climbers imagination. Hybrid shelters combine natural shelters and features with improvised gear. Any combination that results in a shelter that optimizes safety and warmth is the goal as conditions deteriorate in the mountains. These shelters are described in Figure G-1.

FIGURE G-1. TYPES OF SHELTER

One-pole parachute tepee

One-man shelter

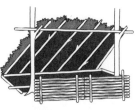

Field-expedient lean-to and fire reflector

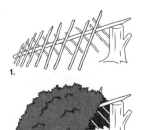

Debris hut

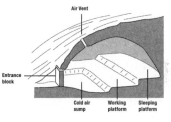

Snow cave

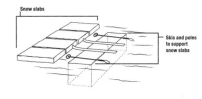

Tree-pit snow shelter

Snow trench

1. *Tarp Trench*

   Built in snow or dirt, this design creates a vapor barrier that mitigates heat loss. Further insulation can be placed in the trench outside the tarp wall to limit conduction of warmth to the ground below. In the absence of a tarp, a bough or tree branch may be used for the bottom, top, and sides of the trench.

2. *Shielded Tree Wall*

   Built upon the same concept, the snow of a tree well is lined both with ground insulation followed by a tarp by which heat loss is mitigated. In the absence of a tarp, a bough or tree branch may be used for the bottom, top, and sides of the tree well.

3. *Single Pole Tarp Tent (snow)*

   Making maximal use of a small tarp, snow anchors stake the tarp in place at its perimeter, while a buffered trekking/ski pole maintains the erect center of the tarp. Thereafter, the floor of the tent is then excavated by the climbers to create a suitable living space. Excavated snow is deposited outside the tents and used for structural reinforcement and closing of air gaps.

4. *Snow shelter*

   From the same model as above (minus the tarp): Snow is accumulated into a large single mound and allowed to cure (time is variable based on humidity and temperature). Following appropriate timing for "snow to set" into a firm mound, excavation begins at base of mound and is best accomplished between multiple climbing partners to create a suitable internal dwelling within the mound. Care should be made for appropriate ventilation if cooking is to be pursued and outside of mount should be marked so as to not be disturbed or trampled upon.

5. *Lean-to*

   Multiple design configurations exist whereby a single or double wall configuration is erected by leaning tree branches and boughs against a standing beam. This horizontal beam may be naturally occurring or repurposed from natural material nearby. Customization of this design allows for a three-sided shelter which may also serve for a heat reflector back to the inhabitants.

APPENDIX H: VERTICAL MEDICINE RESOURCES ASSESSMENT SHEET

Date: _____

Route: _____

Weather: _____

Patient Demographics

_____

_____

_____

_____

SOAP NOTE

S = SUBJECTIVE

Signs/symptoms (PQRST: Pain, Quality, Radiation, Severity, Timing)

_____

_____

Allergies

_____

_____

Medications

_____

_____

Past medical history

_____

_____

_____

Last oral intake

_____

Event (incident history)

_____

_____

_____

O = OBJECTIVE

Physical Exam Findings

_____

_____

_____

Primary Survey (ABCs)

_____

_____

_____

Secondary Survey

_____

_____

_____

Progression of Patient Condition

_____

_____

A = ASSESSMENT

Suspected areas of injury/illness

1) _____

2) _____

3) _____

P = PLAN

Evacuation method and timing

_____

_____

_____

GLOSSARY

AAC: American Alpine Club

abduction: movement away from the torso

acidemia: acidity of blood

ACL: anterior cruciate ligament

acromion: the point of the shoulder, a portion of the scapula (shoulder blade) where it articulates with the clavicle (collarbone)

acromioclavicular: the joint connecting the acromion (point of the shoulder)

ACS: acute coronary syndrome, or heart attack

adduction: movement towards the torso

ad libitum hydration: drinking based on thirst or desire to drink

amenorrhea: absence of menstruation

AMGA: American Mountain Guide Association

analgesia: pain control

anaphylactic shock (see also shock): low blood pressure due to anaphylaxis (life-threatening allergic reaction)

angina: chest pain caused by insufficient oxygen supply to heart

anisocoria: unequal pupils; present in about 15% of the population

anterior: front of the body

appendectomy: surgical removal of the appendix

ataxia: absence of coordination, especially when walking

atherosclerosis: deposits in arterial walls

auscultation: listening for internal sounds within the body

avulsion, avulsed: tissue torn away from its base; in dental terms, a tooth completely displaced from its socket

axial: related to or along an axis

axilla, axillary: underarm region

bradycardia: low heart rate (in adults, generally defined as less than 60 beats per minute)

bursa: sac filled with fluid (synovial fluid) within connective tissue of joints

bursitis: inflammation of the bursa

calcaneus: heel bone

capillary: tiniest of blood vessels connecting the smallest veins (venules) with the smallest arteries (arterioles)

capillary refill: the speed at which color returns to a fingernail or toenail after pressure is applied and then quickly released, a measure of blood flow to extremities; in normal capillary refill, color returns within 2 seconds or less

cardiac arrest: complete termination of heart function

CAT: Combat Application Tourniquet

cerebral edema: brain swelling or excess fluid in the brain

cerebrospinal fluid: fluid around the brain and spinal cord

clavicle: "collar bone"; the long bone connecting the sternum (breast bone) with the shoulder

clinical diagnosis: a diagnosis made solely based on exam without any testing

coccyx: "tail bone"; the bone at the base of the spinal column

concussion: a clinical syndrome marked by immediate and time-limited alteration in brain function resulting from mechanical trauma

contracture: connective tissue constriction preventing normal mobility

COPD: chronic obstructive pulmonary disease

coronary: heart-related

crepitus: crackling or rattling sound of a specific body part

CT: computed tomography

degloving: large section of skin pulled off from its underlying tissue

deltoid: muscle forming the rounded side of the shoulder

DIC: disseminated intravascular coagulation; a syndrome where excessive clotting results in small blood clots throughout the body, ultimately causing organ damage and severe bleeding

dislocation: displacement of a bone from its normal position in a joint

distal: further from the trunk on an extremity

diverticulitis: inflammation or infection of diverticula

diverticulum: pouches within the intestinal wall; plural is diverticula

dorsal: anatomically related to the back side of a two-sided body part, such as back of the hand

dysentery: bloody diarrhea

dysrhythmia: abnormal heart rate or rhythm

eccentric strengthening exercises: slow release of lengthening muscles while under load ecchymosis: "bruising"; bleeding underneath the skin

ECG: electrocardiogram; measurement of the electrical pattern of the heart

ED: emergency department

epiphyseal: growth plate of a bone

EPOC: excess post-exercise oxygen consumption

ER: extended release (note that "ER" contracted to mean "emergency room" is outdated terminology; more modern terminology is "ED," meaning "emergency department")

erythema: red color to the skin; adjective is erythematous

evacuation: movement of a patient out of a field environment into the front country or to a medical center

extrication: movement of a patient from a dangerous, confined or restraining situation

extension: movement pulling ends of a joint into or towards a straight position

external rotation: rotation away from the midline

fartlek: Swedish for "speed play"; blend of continuous training with interval training

fecal: adjective of feces (body waste discharged from the anus or "stool")

femur: "thigh bone"; long bone connecting hip and knee

fibula: the outer, smaller bone of the two long bones connecting the knee to the ankle

flapper: a piece of loose skin due to injury; a climbing-specific term

flatulence: rectal gas; "fart"

flexion: movement pulling a joint into or towards a bent position

FTF: fast twitch fibers in muscles used for rapid movements

GERD: gastroesophageal reflux disease

glenohumeral joint: shoulder joint

hamstring: three muscles in the posterior thigh responsible for flexing the leg

hemostasis: bleeding control

herniation: bulging of tissue inappropriately out of the space it should normally occupy, usually through a hole not meant to allow such movement

HIIT: high-intensity interval training

histotoxic: poisonous to tissue

HIV: human immunodeficiency virus

humerus: the bone of the upper arm

hyperlipidemia: increased fat levels in the blood

hypertension: high blood pressure

hyponatremia: low levels of sodium (salt) in the blood

hypotension: low blood pressure

hypovolemic shock (see also shock): shock due to reduced blood volume, usually due to either dehydration or blood lost from bleeding

ICAR: International Commission for Alpine Rescue

ICH: intracranial hemorrhage; bleeding in brain

iliac crest: highest and widest part of the hip

IM: intramuscular (into a muscle)

incarcerated: imprisoned or confined

inferior: lower position

inspection: visual examination

internal rotation: rotating towards the midline

intertrochanteric: between the greater and lesser trochanters (bulges) in the superior femur

intra-abdominal hemorrhage: bleeding in the abdominal cavity

IUD: intrauterine contraceptive device, also known as IUCD

IV: intravenous (into a vein)

keraunoparalysis: transient weakness in the limbs after a lightning strike

labrum: rim around the margin of the shoulder joint

lateral malleolus (ankle): the bulging portion of bone on the lateral (outside) portion of the ankle

LCL: lateral cruciate ligament in the knee

ligament, ligamentous: fibrous tissue connecting bone to bone

malaise: sense of weakness or fatigue

MCL: medial cruciate ligament in the knee

medial malleolus (ankle): the bulging portion of bone on the medial (inside) portion of the ankle

metatarsal: bones in the midfoot connecting proximal foot bones with toe (5th metatarsal is the one used in the Ottawa Ankle Rules)

MHR: maximum heart rate

MRI: magnetic resonance imaging

MTBI: mild traumatic brain injury (see TBI)

myocardial infarction: cell death in the heart due to insufficient oxygen; "heart attack"

myocardial ischemia: cell stress in the heart due to insufficient oxygen

navicular: a bone in the wrist and the ankle

neurological deficit: problems with nerve conduction, i.e., numbness or paralysis or weakness in one body part

neuromuscular: related to both nerves and muscles

normothermia: normal body temperature

NSAID: non-steroidal anti-inflammatory, such as ibuprofen (Advil®)

occult: hidden

ODT: oral dissolving tablet

opioid: medications that act on receptors to produce morphine-like effects

ORS: oral rehydration solution

orthopedic: related to bones

ossification: formation of bone tissue

palmar: on the palm side of the hand

palpation, palpable: examination by touch or appreciable by touch

patella: "knee cap"

pathognomonic: a finding that is characteristic, defining, or exclusive to a certain disease

PCL: posterior cruciate ligament, a ligament in the knee

PCP: primary care provider

periodization: breaking training into segments, altering intensity, volume, rest, and frequency over weeks, months, and year

peritonitis: inflammation of the thin surrounding layer of the abdominal cavity

photophobia: pain on exposure to light

PID: pelvic inflammatory disease

pneumothorax: an inappropriate collection of air or gas in the chest cavity outside the lungs

postconcussive syndrome: collection of symptoms following a concussion

posterior: back of the body or a body part

pronation: turning the hand so the palm faces downward

proton pump inhibitors (PPIs): drugs that inhibit the enzyme producing hydrogen ions and gastric acids

proximal: closer to the trunk on an extremity

radial: related to the radius bone (the long bone connecting the elbow to the thumb side of the hand) or the radial nerve in the arm

regimental patch area: side of shoulder over deltoid muscle

reduce, reduction: realigning a dislocation or a deviated, displaced fracture

RHR: resting heart rate

sacrum: a large triangular bone that intersects with the hip bones to form the pelvis

SBP: systolic blood pressure, the measure of the blood pressure when the heart is contracting

SCD (sudden cardiac death): sudden cessation of heart activity

sepsis: a system-wide inflammatory reaction to an infection with evidence of inadequate blood flow to body tissues

sesamoid (foot): a bone in the foot

shock (see also hypovolemic shock, anaphylactic shock): systemically, a low blood pressure, and specifically, inadequate oxygen supply to a particular body tissue or region

SOF-T: Special Operations Forces Tourniquet

SPI: Single Pitch Instructor: certification from AMGA

spinal immobilization: the restriction of any movement of the spine; especially the use of a commercial or improvised cervical collar and/or backboard to immobilize the spinal column; recently being challenged in favor of spinal motion restriction (see Chaps 5 and 18)

spinal motion restriction: reducing motion, usually using pain as a threshold, in a body part that may be injured, without specific or complete attempt at immobilization; contrast with spinal immobilization (see Chaps 5 and 18)

STBI: Severe Traumatic Brain Injury (see TBI)

sternum: breastbone

STF: slow twitch fibers in muscles that can function for a long time; used for endurance

stratum corneum: outer layer of epidermis

subluxation: partial or incomplete dislocation

substernal: midline in the chest, under the sternum (breastbone)

subtrochanteric: distal to the lesser trochanter (a bone bulge) on the femur

subungual hematoma: pooled blood beneath a toenail or fingernail, often dark red or black in color

superior: above or higher

supination: in the hand, turning the hand so the palm is facing upward

supraspinatus: a muscle in the upper back

systolic blood pressure: see SBP

tachycardia: rapid heart rate (in adults, generally defined as more than 100 beats per minute)

talus: the large bone at the top portion of the ankle connecting to the tibia and fibula

TBI (traumatic brain injury): "closed head injury"; condition when a head blow results in injury to the brain; see also divisions into MTBI and STBI

TBSA: total body surface area of a burn

tendon: fibrous tissue connecting muscle to bone

tibia: the larger, medial bone of the two long bones connecting the knee to the ankle; "shin" bone

toe box: part of a shoe covering the toes

trachea: breathing tube in the neck connecting the mouth with the lungs

tympanic membrane: eardrum

UIAA: Union Internationale des Associations d'Alpinisme, or the International Climbing and Mountaineering Federation

ulnar: related to the ulna (the long bone connecting the elbow to the little finger) or the ulnar nerve in the arm

UTI: urinary tract infection; "bladder infection"

valgus: outward movement or pressure

vascular: blood vessel-related

vasoconstriction: constriction (narrowing) of blood vessels

ventricular fibrillation: a heart condition consisting of uncontrolled muscular activity ("fibrillation") of the bottom part of the heart responsible for pumping blood to the body or lungs ("ventricle")

vertebra, vertebrae: cube-like bones making up the spine; "backbones"

virus: a small infectious organism that only replicates inside other organisms' cells, responsible for many infections in human beings

WBGT: wet bulb globe temperature
WMS: Wilderness Medical Society

MNEMONIC ACRONYM GLOSSARY

AVPU: Alert, Verbal, Painful, Unresponsive
CAMS: Chest, Abdomen, Meat, Skin/Slab/Snow
CSM: Circulation, Sensation, Motor
IPA: Inspection, Palpation, Auscultation
MARCH: Massive Hemorrhage, Airway, Respiratory, Circulation, Hypothermia/Hyperthermia/Hanging, Helo/Hike/Hunker Down
PAWS: Prevention/Procedures, Analgesics/Antibiotics/Anaphylaxis, Wound Care, Survival
RICE: Rest, Ice, Compression, Elevation
STOP: Stop, Think, Observe, Plan

REFERENCES AND ADDITIONAL RESOURCES

CHAPTER 1

Della-Giustina D, Ingebretsen R. *Advanced Wilderness Life Support.* Utah: AdventureMed, 2013.

Gill DS, Mitra B, Reeves F, et al. Can Initial Clinical Assessment Exclude Thoracolumbar Vertebral Injury? *Emerg Med J.* 2013 Aug;30(8):679-82.

Quinn RH, Williams J, Bennett BL, Stiller G, Islas A, McCord S. Wilderness Medical Society Practice Guidelines for Spine Immobilization in the Austere Environment: 2014 Update. *Wilderness Environ Med.* 2014;25(4):S105-S117.

Radecki R. The Trauma Log Roll is Dead. *Emergency Medicine Literature of Note.* Published November 4, 2013. http://www.emlitofnote.com/2013/11/the-trauma-log-roll-is-dead.html. Accessed May 3, 2016.

Simon RB. Essentials: Basic Injury Assessment: How to Help Before Help Arrives. *Accidents in North American Climbing.* Golden, CO: American Alpine Club, 2016, p. 23-4.

Singh T, Singh E, Olaussen A, Liew S, Fitzgerald MC, Mitra B. What is the purpose of log roll examination in the unconscious trauma patient during trauma reception? *Emerg Med J.* 2016 Jun;33(9):632-5.

CHAPTER 2

Adisesh A, Lee C, Porter K. Harness suspension and first aid management: development of an evidence-based guideline. *Emerg Med J.* 2011;28(4):265-8.

Adisesh A, Robinson L, Codling A, Harris-Roberts J, Lee C, Porter K. Evidence-based review of the current guidance on first aid measures for suspension trauma. Norwich, UK: Health & Safety Executive, 2009.

Curtis R. Epinephrine: medical & ethical necessity or legal nightmare? *OutdoorEd. com: The Outdoor Professional's Resource.* March 25, 2015. Available at https://www.outdoored.com/articles/epinephrine-medical-ethical-necessity-or-legal-nightmare#. Accessed October 2, 2016.

Elsenohn F, Agazzi G, Syme D, et al. The use of automated external defibrillators and public access defibrillators in the mountains: official guidelines of the International Commission for Mountain Emergency Medicine. ICAR-MEDCOM. *Wilderness Environ Med.* 2006;17:64-6.

Elsensohn F, Soteras I, Resiten O, Ellerton J, Brugger H, Paal P. Equipment of medical backpacks in mountain rescue: official recommendations of the International Commission for Mountain Emergency Medicine. *High Alt Med Biol.* 2011;12(4):343-8.

Gaudio FG, Lemery J, Johnson DE, Wilderness Medical Society. Wilderness Medical Society practice guidelines for the use of epinephrine in outdoor education and wilderness settings: 2014 update. *Wilderness Environ Med.* 2014;25(4 Suppl):S15-18.

Golden DBK. Insect sting anaphylaxis. *Immunol Allergy Clin.* 2007;27(2):261-272.

Hawkins SC, Weil C, Baty F, Fitzpatrick D, Rowell B. Retrieval of additional epinephrine from auto-injectors. *Wilderness Environ Med.* 2013;24(4):434-44.

Hawkins SC. Wet & Wild: Submersion Injuries: Submerged Vehicles. *Wilderness Medicine.* February 26, 2015. Available at http://wildernessmedicinemagazine.com/1137/drowning-submerged-vehicles. Accessed October 2, 2016.

International Life Saving Federation. Medical Position Statements: MPS 01: The Use of Abdominal Thrusts in Near Drowning. Belgium: International Life Saving Federation. Sept 26, 1998. Available at http://www.ilsf.org/sites/ilsf.org/files/filefield/MPS-01%20Abdominal%20Thrust.pdf. Accessed July 2, 2016.

International Life Saving Federation. Medical Position Statement: MPS 08: In Water Resuscitation. Belgium: International Life Saving Federation. September 4, 2001. Available at http://www.ilsf.org/about/position-statements. Accessed July 2, 2016.

International Life Saving Federation. Medical Position Statement: MPS 15: Compression-Only CPR and Drowning. Belgium: International Life Saving Federation, 2008. Available at http://www.ilsf.org/about/position-statements. Accessed July 2, 2016.

International Life Saving Federation. Lifesaving Position Statement: LPS 17: Definition of Drowning. Belgium: International Life Saving Federation, Sept 16, 2014. Available at http://www.ilsf.org/about/position-statements. Accessed July 2, 2016.

Kolb JJ, Smith E. Suspension Shock: Redefining the Diagnosis and Treatment. *J Emerg Med* 2015;40(6):48-51.

Landmark Learning. Wilderness Starguard. Available at https://landmarklearning.edu/courses/starfish-aquatics-institute/wilderness-starguard®. Accessed July 2, 2016.

McDonald GK, Giesbrecht GG. Vehicle submersion: a review of the problem, associated risks, and survival information. *Aviat Space Environ Med.* 2013;84:498-510.

Nolan JP, Hazinski MF, Billi JE, et al. International Consensus on Cardiopulmonary Resuscitation and Emergency Cardiovascular Care Science with Treatment Recommendations. *Resuscitation.* 2010 Oct;81(1):e1-e332.

Mortimer RB. Risks and Management of Prolonged Suspension in an Alpine Harness. *Wilderness Environ Med.* 2011;22(1):77-86.

Nardo R. Fall Rescue plan: The Often-Overlooked Factor. *Fall-Proof Newsletter.* March 21, 2014. Available at https://www.fallproof.com/blog/fall-rescue-plan-the-often-overlooked-factor/. Accessed July 2, 2016.

Nolan JP, Soar J, Zideman DA, et al. European Resuscitation Council Guidelines for Resuscitation 2010. *Resuscitation.* 2010;81:1219-76.

Occupational Health and Safety Administration. Safety and Health Information Bulletin: Suspension Trauma/Orthostatic Intolerance (SHIB 03-24-2004). US Dept. of Labor, Occupational Safety and Health Administration, Directorate of Science, Technology and Medicine, Office of Science and Technology Assessment. Washington, DC: 2011. Available at https://www.osha.gov/dts/shib/shib032404.pdf. Accessed July 2, 2016.

Penney K, Balram B, Trevisonno J, Ben-Shoshan M. Incidence of Biphasic Anaphylactic Reactions: A Systematic Review and Meta-Analysis. *J Aller Clin Immun.* 2015;135(2):AB204.

Raynovich W, Al Rwaili FT, Bishop P. Dangerous Suspension: Understanding suspension syndrome & prehospital treatment for those at risk. *J Emerg Med.* 2009 Aug;34(8):44-51.

Roco Rescue. Preparing for the Forgotten Hazard: Rescue from Fall Protection. Rescue Talk: November 29, 2011. Available at http://www.rocorescue.com

/roco-rescue-blog/19_preparing_for_the_forgotten_hazard-rescue_from_fall_protection#.V3iAn1dg6WU. Accessed July 2, 2016.

Sampson HA, Muñoz-Furlong A, Campbell RL, et al. Second symposium on the definition and management of anaphylaxis: Summary Report. *J Allergy Clin Immunol.* 2006;117(2):391-7.

Schmidt AC, Sempsrott JR, Hawkins SC, et al. Wilderness Medical Society Practice Guidelines for the Prevention and Treatment of Drowning. *Wilderness Environmental Medicine* 2016;27(2):236-51.

Sempsrott J, Hawkins SC. Starfish Aquatics Institute Position Statement 15-1: Use of the Terms Near, Dry, Delayed, and Secondary Drowning. Lincolnshire, IL: Starfish Aquatics Institute, 2015. Available at http://starfishaquaticsinstitute.blogspot.com/2015/04/defining-drowning.html.

Simons FE, Gu X, Simons KJ. Epinephrine absorption in adults: intramuscular versus subcutaneous injection. *J Allergy Clin Immunol.* 2001;108(5):871-3.

Thomassen O, Skaiaa SC, Brattebo G, et al. Does the horizontal position increase risk of rescue death following suspension trauma? *Emerg Med J.* 2009;26(12):896-8.

United States Lifeguard Standards Coalition. United States Lifeguard Standards: An evidence-based review and report by the United States Lifeguard Standards Coalition. January 2011. Available at http://www.lifeguardstandards.org/pdf/USLSC_FINAL_APPROVAL_1-31-11.pdf. Accessed July 2, 2016.

Van Beeck E, Branche C. "Definition of drowning: a progress report." In Bierens JJLM. Drowning: prevention, rescue treatment, 2e. New York: Springer, 2014.

Vanden Hoek TL, Morrison LJ, Shuster M, et al. Guidelines for Cardiopulmonary Resuscitation and Emergency Cardiovascular. Part 12: Cardiac Arrest in Special Situations: 2010 American Heart Association. *Circulation* 2010;122;S829-S61.

CHAPTER 3

Anderson ML, Anderson ML. *The Rock Climber's Training Manual: A Guide to Continuous Improvement.* Boulder, CO: Fixed Pin Publishing; 2014.

Bennett BL, Hew-Butler T, Hoffman MD, Rogers IR, Rosner MH. Wilderness Medical Society practice guidelines for treatment of exercise-associated hyponatremia. *Wilderness Environ Med.* 2014 Sep;25(4 Suppl):S30-42.

Butt MS, Sultan MT. Coffee and its consumption: Benefits and Risks. *Crit Rev Food Sci.* 51(4)2011:363-73.

Dietary supplementation with n-3 polyunsaturated fatty acids and vitamin E after myocardial infarction: results of the GISSI-Prevenzione trial. Gruppo Italiano per lo Studio della Sopravvivenza nell'Infarto miocardico. *Lancet.* 1999;354:447-55.

Fitzgerald M. *Racing Weight: How to Get Lean For Peak Performance.* 2nd ed. Boulder, CO: Velo Press; 2012.

Giles LV. The physiology of rock climbing. *Sports Med.* 2006;36(6):529-45.

Hak PT, Hodzovic E, Hickey B. The nature and prevalence of injury during CrossFit training. *J Strength Cond Res.* 2013;3159-72.

Hochholzer T, Schöffl V. *One Move too Many . . . How to Understand the Injuries and Overuse Syndromes of Rock Climbing.* Ebenhausen, Germany: Lochner-Verlag; 2006.

Horst E. *Conditioning for Climbers: The Complete Exercise Guide.* Guilford, CT: Morris Book Publishing; 2008.

House S, Johnston S. *Training for the New Alpinism: A Manual for the Climber as Athlete.* Ventura, CA: Patagonia Books; 2014.

Koralek DO, Peters U, Andriole G, et al. A prospective study of dietary alpha-linolenic acid and the risk of prostate cancer. *Cancer Causes Control.* 2006 Aug;17(6):783-91.

Kris-Etherton PM, Pearson TA, Wan Y, et al. High-monounsaturated fatty acid diets lower both plasma cholesterol and triacylglycerol concentrations. *Am J Clin Nutr.* 1999;70(6):1009-15.

Layton M. *Climbing Stronger, Faster, Healthier: Beyond the Basics.* Salt Lake City, UT: CreateSpace Publishing; 2009.

Leaf A. Prevention of sudden cardiac death by n-3 polyunsaturated fatty acids. *J Cardiovasc Med.* (Hagerstown). 2007; 8 Suppl 1:S27-9.

MacLeod D. *Make or Break: Don't let climbing injuries dictate your success.* Inverness-shire, Scotland: Rare Breed Productions; 2015.

Page P. Current concepts in muscle stretching for exercise and rehabilitation. *Int J Sports Phys Ther.* 2012 Feb;7(1):109–19.

Sheel AW. Physiology of sport rock climbing. *Br J Sports Med.* 2004;38:355-359.

Soles C. *Climbing: Training for Peak Performance.* 2nd ed. Seattle, WA: The Mountaineers Books; 2008.

Valenzuela PL, de la Villa P, Ferragut C. Effect of Two Types of Active Recovery on Fatigue and Climbing Performance. *J Sport Sci Med.* 2015;14:769-75.

Watts PB. The physiology of difficult rock climbing. *Eur J Appl Physiol.* 2004 Apr;91(4):361-72.

Weisenthal BM, Beck CA, Maloney MD. Injury Rate and Patterns Among CrossFit Athletes *Orthop J Sports Med.* 2014 Apr; 2(4):1-7.

CHAPTER 4

Addiss DG, Baker SP. Mountaineering and Rock-Climbing Injuries in US National Parks. *Annals of Emerg Med.* 1989;18(9):975-79.

Ali M, Asim M, Danish SH, et al. Frequency of DeQuervain's tenosynovitis and its association with SMS texting. *Muscles Ligaments Tendons J.* 2014:4(1)74.

American Red Cross (ARC). *Wilderness and Remote First Aid Emergency Reference Guide.* Krames StayWell Strategic Partnerships Division: 2014.

Auerbach PS, Constance BB, Freer L. Field guide to wilderness medicine, 4e. Philadelphia: Elsevier, 2013.

Bledsoe B, Barnes D. Traction splint: an EMS relic? *JEMS* 2004;(29);64-69.

Boy Scouts of America (BSA). *2010 Boy Scouts of America (BSA) Wilderness First Aid Curriculum and Doctrine Guidelines.*

Caselli MA. Managing hallux rigidus in the athlete. *Podiatry Today.* 2004;17(4).

Crowley TP. The flexor tendon pulley system and rock climbing. *J Hand Microsurg.* 2012 Jun; 4(1):25–9.

De Palma AF, Callery C, Bennett GA. Variational anatomy and degenerative lesions of the shoulder joint. AAOS Instructional Course Lectures. 1949;6:255-81.

Dean DB. Field Management of Displaced Ankle Fractures: Techniques for Successful Reduction. *Wilderness Environ Med.* 2009;20:57-60.

Ditty J, Chisholm D, Davis M, Estelle-Schmidt M. Safety and efficacy of attempts to reduce shoulder dislocations by non-medical personnel in the wilderness setting. *Wilderness Environ Med.* 2010;21(4):357-61.

El-Sheikh Y. Diagnosis of finger flexor pulley injury in rock climbers: A systematic review. *Can J Plast Surg.* 2006 Winter;14(4):227–31.

Gandy WE, Grayson S. Sacred cow slaughterhouse: the traction splint. *EMS World.* July

31, 2014. Available at http://www.emsworld.com/article/11542786/traction
-splint-evidence-and-efficacy. Accessed July 6, 2016.

Gentile D, Morris J, Schimelpfenig T, Bass SM, Auerbach PS. Wilderness injuries and illnesses. *Annals of Emerg Med.* 1992;21(7):853-61.

Gerdes E, Hafner J, Aldag J. Injury patterns and safety practices of rock climbers. *J Trauma.* 2006;61:1517-1525.

Gilpin D. Injectable collagenase Clostridium histolyticum: a new nonsurgical treatment for Dupuytren's disease. *J Hand Surg Am.* 2010 Dec;35(12):2027-38.

Gnecchi S, Moutet F. *Hand and Finger Injuries in Rock Climbers.* New York, NY: Springer; 2015.

Heit EJ, Bouche RT. How to treat sesamoid injuries in athletes. *Podiatry Today.* 2004;17(4).

Hochholzer T, Schöffl V. *One Move too Many . . . How to Understand the Injuries and Overuse Syndromes of Rock Climbing.* Ebenhausen, Germany: Lochner-Verlag; 2006.

Humphries D. Injury rates in rock climbers. *J Wilderness Med.* 1993;4:281-5.

Jindal N, Gaury Y, Banshiwal RC, Lomoria R, Bacchal V. Comparison of short term results of single injection of autologous blood and steroid injection in tennis elbow: a prospective study. *J Orthop Surg Res.* 2013;8:10.

Johnson D. Traction splints in wilderness medicine. Wilderness Medical Associates, 2011. Available at https://www.wildmed.com/blog/tractions-splints-in
-wilderness-medicine/. Accessed July 10, 2016.

Josephsen G, Shinneman S, Tamayo-Sarver J, et al. Injuries in bouldering: A prospective study. *Wilderness and Environ Med.* 2007;18:271-80.

Klauser A, Frauscher F, Bodner G, et al. Finger pulley injuries in extreme rock climbers: Depiction with dynamic US. *Radiology.* 2002;222(3):755-61.

Krzyzaniak MJ, Nunez TC, Miller RS. Wilderness Trauma and Surgical Emergencies. In Auerbach PS, ed. *Auerbach's Wilderness Medicine, 7ᵗʰ edition.* Philadelphia, PA: 2017.

Lack D, Sheets A, Entin J, Christenson D. Rock climbing rescues: Causes, injuries, and trends in Boulder County, Colorado. *Wilderness Environ Med.* 2012;23:223-30.

Leeman D, Schimelpfenig T. Wilderness injury, illness, and evacuation: National Outdoor Leadership School's incident profiles, 1999-2002. *Wilderness Environ Med.* 2003;14:174-82.

Lipman GS, Krabak BJ. Foot Problems and Care. In: Auerbach PS, ed. *Wilderness Medicine.* 6ᵗʰ ed. Philadelphia, PA: Mosby Elsevier; 2012.

Logan AJ, Mason G, Dias J, Makwana N. Can rock climbing lead to Dupuytren's Disease? *Br J Sports Med.* 2005,39:639-44.

MacLeod D. *Make or Break: Don't let climbing injuries dictate your success.* Inverness, Scotland: Rare Breed Productions; 2015.

Marco RA, Sharkey NA, Smith TS, Zissimos AG. Pathomechanics of closed rupture of the flexor tendon pulleys in rock climbers. *J Bone Joint Surg Am.* 1998 Jul;80(7):1012-19.

Montalvo R, Wingard DL, Bracker M, Davidson TM. Morbidity and mortality in the wilderness. *West J Med.* 1998;168:248-54.

Nelson N, McKenzie L. Rock climbing injuries treated in emergency departments in the U.S., 1990-2007. *Am J Prev Med.* 2009; 37:195-200.

O'Donovan P. Dupuytren's Contracture—A Climber's Condition? UKClimbing.com. July 2010. http://www.ukclimbing.com/articles/page.php?id=1312. Accessed March 8, 2016.

Ootes D, Lambers K, Ring D. The epidemiology of upper extremity injuries presenting to the emergency department in the United States. *Hand*. 2012;7(1):18-22.

Paige T, Fiore D, Houston J. Injury in traditional and sport rock climbing. *Wilderness Environ Med*. 1998;9:2-7.

Pasquier M, Yersin B, Valloton L, Carron PN. Clinical update: suspension trauma. *Wilderness Environ Med*. 2011;22(2):167-71.

Pegoli L. Hand Injury in Rock Climbing. *IFSSH Ezine* 2015; 5(3):16-20. http://www.ifssh.info/pdf/ISSUE2_August_2015.pdf. Accessed March 8, 2016.

Peters P. Orthopedic problems in sport climbing. *Wilderness Environ Med*. 2001;12:100-10.

Robinson AH, Limbers JP. Modern concepts in the treatment of hallux valgus. *J Bone Joint Surg Br*. 2005;87(8):1038-45.

Saunders J. Rock Climbing Injury: Left Hand: Hook of the Hamate Fracture. *Rock and Ice*. April 2015:225.

Schöffl I, Einwag F, Strecker W, Hennig F, Schöffl V. The impact of taping after finger flexor tendon pulley ruptures in rock climbing. *J Appl Biomech*. 2007;23(1):52-62.

Schöffl V, Einwag F, Strecker W, Schöffl I. Strength measurement and clinical outcome after pulley ruptures in climbers. *Med Sci Sports Exerc*. 2006;38(4):637-43. (2006a)

Schöffl V, Hochholzer T, Winkelmann HP, Strecker W. Pulley injuries in rock climbers. *Wilderness Environ Med*. 2003;14(2):94-100.

Schöffl V, Hoffmann G, Küpper T. Acute Injury Risk and Severity in Indoor Climbing—A Prospective Analysis of 515,337 Indoor Climbing Wall Visits in 5 years. *Wilderness Environ Med*. 2013;24:187-94. (2013a)

Schöffl V, Küpper T. Feet injuries in rock climbers. *World J Orthop*. 2013; 4(4):218-28. (2013b)

Schöffl V, Lutter C, Popp D. The "Heel Hook"—A Climbing Specific Technique to Injure the Leg. *Wilderness Environ Med*. 2016;27:294-301.

Schöffl V, Morrison A, Hefti U, Ullrich S, Küpper T. The UIAA Medical Commission Injury Classification for Mountaineering and Climbing Sports. *Wilderness Environ Med*. 2011;22:46-51.

Schöffl V, Morrison A, Schwarz U, Schöffl I, Küpper T. Evaluation of Injury and Fatality Risk in Rock and Ice Climbing. *Sports Med*. 2010;40(8):657-79.

Schöffl V, Popp D, Küpper T, Schöffl I. Injury trends in rock climbers: Evaluation of a case series in 911 injuries between 2009 and 2012. *Wilderness Environ Med*. 2015;26:62-7.

Schöffl V, Schöffl I. Injuries to the finger flexor pulley system in rock climbers: Current concepts. *J Hand Surg*. 2006;31(4):647-54. (2006b)

Schöffl V, Schöffl I. Isolated cruciate pulley injuries in rock climbers. *J Hand Surg Eur*. 2010;35(3):245-6.

Schussman LC, Lutz LJ, Shaw RR, Bohnn CR. The epidemiology of mountaineering and rock climbing accidents. *J Wilderness Med*. 1990;1:235-48.

Shiri R, Eira VJ, Varonen H, Heliövara M. Prevalence and Determinants of Lateral and Medial Epicondylitis: A Population Study. *Am J Epidemiol*. 2006; 164:1065-74.

Simon D. Sport climber perceptions of stick clip use for the prevention of lead ground falls. Master's Thesis, University of Leicester, 2016.

Simon R, Koenigsknecht S. *Emergency Orthopedics—the Extremities*. 4th ed. McGraw-Hill New York, 2001.

Simon RB. Ropes to the Rescue: Climber Evacuation Techniques. *Wilderness Medicine*.

March 2015. http://wildernessmedicinemagazine.com/1141/Climbing
-Ropes-to-the-Rescue.

Simon RB. The Coolest Trick I Know: The Rope Litter. *Climbing*. 2012; Issue 309, October 2012: 77. http://www.climbing.com/skill/the-rope-litter/. Accessed February 11, 2016.

Simon RB. Treat an Injured Ankle. *Climbing*. 2013; Issue 313, March 2013: 76-7. http://www.climbing.com/skill/treat-an-injured-ankle/. Accessed February 11, 2016.

Smith B, Bledsoe B, Nicolazzo P. Trauma Management in WEMS. In Hawkins SC, ed. *Wilderness EMS*. Philadelphia, PA: Wolters Kluwer, 2018.

Smith W. Technical Rescue Interface Introduction: Principles of Basic Rigging, Packaging, and Rope Skills. In Hawkins SC, ed. *Wilderness EMS*. Philadelphia, PA: Wolters Kluwer, 2018.

Tashjian RZ. Epidemiology, natural history, and indications for treatment of rotator cuff tears *Clin Sports Med*. 2012 Oct;31(4):589-604.

Tempelhof S, Rupp S, Seil R. Age-related prevalence of rotator cuff tears in asymptomatic shoulders. *J Shoulder Elbow Surg*. 1999 Jul-Aug;8(4):296-9.

Thompson RN, Hanratty B, Corry IS. "Heel Hook" Rock-Climbing Maneuver: A Specific Pattern of Knee Injury. *Clin J Sport Med*. 2011;21:365-8.

Warme WJ, Brooks D. The effect of circumferential taping on flexor tendon pulley failure in rock climbers. *Am J Sports Med*. 2000;28(5):674-78.

Wilk K, Macrina L, Cain E, Dugas JR, Andrews JR. The recognition and treatment of superior labral (SLAP) lesions in the overhead athlete. *Int J Sports Phys Ther*. 2013; 8(5):579-600.

Williamson JE, ed. *Accidents in North American Mountaineering*. Golden, CO: The American Alpine Club; 2014.

CHAPTER 5

Canadian CT Head & C-Spin (CCC) Study Group. Canadian C-Spine Rule study for alert and stable trauma patients: I. Background and rationale. *Can J Emerg Med Care*. 2004;4 (2): 84-90.

Chin LS. Spinal Cord Injuries Treatment & Management: Steroid Therapy in SCI and Controversies. Medscape. Published May 12, 2016. Available at http://emedicine.medscape.com/article/793582-treatment#d11. Accessed July 4, 2016.

Epstein N. A review article on the benefits of early mobilization following spinal surgery and other medical/surgical procedures. *Surg Neurol Int*. 2014;5(Suppl 3):S66-S73.

Hadley MN, Walters BC. Guidelines for the Management of Acute Cervical Spine and Spinal Cord Injuries. *Neurosurgery*. Mar 2013;72(Suppl 2):1-259.

Hawkins SC. Wilderness EMS. In: Aehlert B, ed. *Paramedic Practice Today: Above and Beyond*. St. Louis: Mosby-JEMS Elsevier; 2010.

Hoffman JR, Wolfson AB, Todd K, Mower WR. Selective cervical spine radiography in blunt trauma: methodology of the National Emergency X-Radiography Utilization Study (NEXUS). *Ann Emerg Med*. 1998;32(4):461-9.

Hoffman JR, Mower WR, Wolfson AB, Todd KH, Zucker MI, for the National Emergency X-Radiography Utilization Study Group. Validity of a Set of Clinical Criteria to Rule Out Injury to the Cervical Spine in Patients with Blunt Trauma. *N Engl J Med*. 2000;343:94-9.

Schwartz SEB. *JFK's Secret Doctor: The Remarkable Life of Medical Pioneer and Legendary Rock Climber Hans Kraus*. Foreword, Chouinard Y. Skyhorse Publishing, 2015.

Vaillancourt C, Stiell IG, Beaudoin T, et al. The out-of-hospital validation of the Canadian C-Spine Rule by paramedics. *Ann Emerg Med.* 2009;54:663-71.

Weingart S. EMCrit: Podcast 63—A Pain in the Neck—Part I. Published December 25, 2011. Available at http://emcrit.org/podcasts/cervical-spine-injuries-i/. Accessed July 6, 2016.

Zafren K, Giesbrecht GG, Danzl DF, et al. Wilderness Medical Society practice guidelines for the out-of-hospital evaluation and treatment of accidental hypothermia: 2014 update. *Wilderness Environ Med.* 2014;25(4 Suppl):S66-85.

CHAPTER 6

American Association of Neurological Surgeons. Patient Information: Concussion. Available at http://www.aans.org/patient%20information/conditions%20and%20treatments/concussion.aspx. Accessed June 26, 2016.

Attarian A. Rock climbers' self perceptions of first aid, safety, and rescue skills. *Wilderness Environ Med.* 2002:13;238-44.

Gerdes EM, Hafner JW, Aldag JC. Injury Patterns and Safety Practices of Rock Climbers. *J Trauma.* 2006;61(6):1517-25.

MacDonald D. No-Brainer? Why Do So Many Climbers Not Wear Helmets? *Climbing.* July 30, 2013. No 317, p. 40. Available at http://www.climbing.com/news/no-brainer-helmet/. Accessed June 26, 2016.

Nelson N, McKenzie L. Rock climbing injuries treated in emergency departments in the U.S., 1990–2007. *Am J Prev Med.* 2009:37(3):195-200.

Simon RB. Level of wilderness first aid training and knowledge retention of climbers in the United States. Master's Thesis, University of Leicester, UK 2017.

Simon RB. Essentials: Head Injuries. *Accidents in North American Mountaineering.* Golden, CO: American Alpine Club; 2015: p. 93-4.

Simon RB. Essentials: Head Injuries. American Alpine Club, 2015. Available at http://publications.americanalpineclub.org/articles/13201213544/Essentials-Head-Injuries. Accessed June 26, 2016.

Smith B, Bledsoe B, Nicolazzo P. Trauma Management in WEMS. In Hawkins, SC. *Wilderness EMS.* Philadelphia, PA: Wolters Kluwer, 2018.

Soleil KHH. Helmet Use Among Outdoor Recreational Rock Climbers Across Disciplines: Factors of Use and Non-use. Master's Thesis, University of Tennessee, 2012. Available at http://trace.tennessee.edu/utk_gradthes/1263

Williamson JE, ed. *Accidents in North American Mountaineering.* Golden, CO: American Alpine Club; 2014.

CHAPTER 7

ACEP Clinical Policies Committee. Clinical Policies Subcommittee on Acute Blunt Abdominal Trauma: clinical policy: critical issues in the evaluation of adult patients presenting to the emergency department with acute blunt abdominal trauma. *Ann Emerg Med.* 2004; 43:278-90.

Adachi JA, Backer HD, Dupont HL. Infectious Diarrhea from Wilderness and Foreign Travel. In: Auerbach PS, ed. *Auerbach's Wilderness Medicine, 7th edition.* Philadelphia, PA: Mosby Elsevier; 2017.

Auerbach PS, Constance BB, Freer L. *Field Guide to Wilderness Medicine.* 4th ed. Philadelphia, PA: Mosby Elsevier; 2013.

Biffl W, Kaups K, Cothren CC. Management of patients with anterior abdominal stab wounds: A Western Trauma Association Multicenter Trial. *J Trauma*. 2009; 66:721-33.

Bowen A, Schilling KA, Mintz E. Shigellosis. In: Burnette GW, ed. *The Yellow Book: CDC Health Information for International Travel*. Oxford, UK: Oxford University Press; 2014.

Davis AC, Mell H. Management of General Infectious Diseases in the Wilderness Environment. In Hawkins SC, ed. *Wilderness EMS*. Philadelphia, PA: Wolters Kluwer, 2018.

Date K, Mintz E. Cholera. In: Burnette GW, ed. *The Yellow Book: CDC Health Information for International Travel*. Oxford, UK: Oxford University Press; 2014.

Delany HM, Jason RS. *Abdominal Trauma: Surgical and Radiologic Diagnosis*. New York, NY: Springer-Verlag; 2011.

Di Saverio S, Sibilio A, Giorgini E, et al. The NOTA Study (Non Operative Treatment for Acute Appendicitis): prospective study on the efficacy and safety of antibiotics (amoxicillin and clavulanic acid) for treating patients with right lower quadrant abdominal pain and long-term follow-up of conservatively treated suspected appendicitis. *Ann Surg*. 2014;260(1):109-17.

Glass RI, Parashar UD, Estes MK. Norovirus gastroenteritis. *N Engl J Med*. 2009; 361(18): 1776-85.

Greenwood Z, Black J, Weld L, et al. Gastrointestinal infection among international travelers globally. *J Travel Med*. 2008 Jul-Aug;15(4):221-8.

Hall AJ, Lopman B. Norovirus. In: Burnette GW, editor. *The Yellow Book: CDC Health Information for International Travel*. Oxford, UK: Oxford University Press; 2014.

Hawker J, Begg N, Blair I, Reintjes R, Weinberg J, Ekdahl K. *Communicable Disease Control and Health Protection Handbook*. 3rd ed. Chicester, UK: Wiley-Blackwell; 2012.

Jacoby L, Cushing T. General Management of Medical Conditions in the Wilderness Environment. In: Hawkins SC, ed. *Wilderness EMS*. Philadelphia, PA; Wolters Kluwer; 2018.

Johnson C, Anderson S, Dallimore J, Winser S, Warrell DA. *Oxford Handbook of Expedition and Wilderness Medicine*. 2nd ed. Oxford, UK: Oxford University Press; 2015.

Krzyzaniak MJ, Nunez TC, Miller RS. Wilderness Trauma and Surgical Emergencies. In Auerbach PS, ed. *Auerbach's Wilderness Medicine, 7th edition*. Philadelphia, PA: 2017.

Kumar A, Sharma A, Khullar R, Soni V, Baijal M, Chowbey PK. Stump Appendicitis: A Rare Clinical Entity. *J Minim Access Surg*. 2013;9(4):173-6.

MacDonald D, ed. *Accidents in North American Mountaineering*. Golden, CO: American Alpine Club; 2015.

McLaughlin JB, Gessner BD, Bailey AM. Gastroenteritis Outbreak Among Mountaineers Climbing the West Buttress Route of Denali—Denali National Park, Alaska, June 2002. *Wilderness Environ Med*. 2005;16:92-6.

Meunier YA. *Tropical Diseases: A Practical Guide for Medical Practitioners and Students*. Oxford, UK: Oxford University Press; 2014.

Nemethy M, Pressman AB, Freer L, McIntosh SE. Mt Everest Base Camp Medical Clinic "Everest ER": Epidemiology of Medical Events During the First 10 Years of Operation. *Wilderness Environ Med*. 2015;26:4-10.

Okhuysen PC. Traveler's diarrhea due to intestinal protozoa. *Clin Infect Dis*. 2001; 33(1):110-14.

Rosen CL, Legome EL, Wolfe RE. Chapter 79: Blunt Abdominal Trauma. In: Adams JG, ed. *Emergency Medicine: Clinical Essentials*. 2nd ed. Philadelphia, PA: Elsevier Saunders; 2012.

Rosen CL, Legome EL, Wolfe RE. Chapter 80: Penetrating Abdominal Trauma. In: Adams JG, ed. *Emergency Medicine: Clinical Essentials*. 2nd ed. Philadelphia, PA: Elsevier Saunders; 2012.

Roy SL. Amebiasis. In: Burnette GW, ed. *The Yellow Book: CDC Health Information for International Travel*. Oxford, UK: Oxford University Press; 2014.

Roy SL, Hlavsa MC. Cryptosporidiosis. In: Burnette GW, editor. *The Yellow Book: CDC Health Information for International Travel*. Oxford, UK: Oxford University Press; 2014.

Roy SL, Hlavsa MC. Giardiasis. In: Burnette GW, editor. *The Yellow Book: CDC Health Information for International Travel*. Oxford, UK: Oxford University Press; 2014.

Shandera WX. Travel-related diseases: injury and infectious disease. *J Wilderness Med*. 1993;4:40-61.

Stout K, Hendler C, Bartelmo J, eds. *Lippincott's Guide to Infectious Diseases*. Ambler, PA: Lippincott Williams and Wilkins; 2011.

Viray M, Lynch M. *Campylobacter* Enteritis. In: Burnette GW, ed. *The Yellow Book: CDC Health Information for International Travel*. Oxford, UK: Oxford University Press; 2014.

CHAPTER 8

Forgey W, ed. *Wilderness Medical Society Practice Guidelines for Wilderness Emergency Care*. 5th ed. Falcon Guide—Morris Book Publishing, LLC, 2006. p. 6-12.

Johnson C, Anderson S, Dallimore J, Winser S, Warrell DA. *Oxford Handbook of Expedition and Wilderness Medicine*. 2nd ed. Oxford, UK: Oxford University Press; 2015.

Jones TE, Yamamoto K, Hayashi U, Jones NR. Summer climbing incidents occurring on Fujisan's north face from 1989 to 2008. *Wilderness Environ Med*. 2014;25(4):378-83.

Lazcano A, Doughterty J, Kruger M. Use of rib belts in acute rib fractures. *Am J of Emerg Med*. 1989;7(1):97-100.

MacDonald D, ed. *Accidents in North American Mountaineering*, Golden, CO: The American Alpine Club; 2015.

Mannino, David. Changing the burden of COPD mortality. *Int J Chron Obst Pulm Dis*. 2006: Sep 1(3):219-33.

Mozaffarian D, Benjamin EJ, Go AS, et al. Heart disease and stroke statistics—2015 update: a report from the American Heart Association. *Circulation*. 2015; 131:e29-e322.

Némethy M, Pressman AB, Freer L, McIntosh SE. Mt Everest Base Camp Medical Clinic "Everest ER": epidemiology of medical events during the first 10 years of operation. *Wilderness Environ Med*. 2015;26(1):4-10.

National Park Service. Fatalities at Mt Rainer National Park (1897–present), National Park Service—Department of the Interior, http://www.mountrainierclimbing.us /sar/fatalities.php. Accessed June 27, 2016.

CHAPTER 9

American Academy of Pediatrics. Committee on Infectious Diseases. Prevention of Lyme disease. *Pediatrics*. 2000;205:142-47.

ANZCOR (Australian Research Council, New Zealand Resuscitation Council). ANZCOR Guideline 9.4.3: Envenomation from Tick Bites and Bee, Wasp and Stings. ANZCOR Guidelines 9.4.3, January 2016.

ASCI (Australasian Society of Clinical Immunology and Allergy). Tick Allergy, June

2016 Update. ASCI: 2016. Available at http://www.allergy.org.au/images/pcc /ASCIA_PCC_Tick_allergy_2016.pdf. Accessed July 6, 2016.

Bissinger BW, Zhu J, Apperson CS, Sonenshine DE, Watson DW, Roe RM. Comparitive Efficacy of BioUD to Other Commercially Available Arthropod Repellents against Ticks *Ablyomma americanum* and *Dermacentor variablis* on Cotton Cloth. *Am J Trop Med Hyg*. 2009;81(4):685-90.

Bradford JE, Freer L. Bites and Injuries by Wild and Domestic Animals. In: Auerbach PS, ed. *Wilderness Medicine*. 6th ed. Philadelphia, PA: Mosby Elsevier; 2012.

Burnette GW, ed. *The Yellow Book: CDC Health Information for International Travel*. Oxford, UK: Oxford University Press; 2017.

Davis KP, Derlet RW. Cyanoacrylate glues for wilderness and remote travel medical care. *Wilderness Environ Med*. 2013;24:67-74.

Della-Giustina D, Ingebretsen R. Advanced Wilderness Life Support, Edition 8.1. Utah: AdventureMed; 2013.

Diehr S, Hamp A, Jamieson B. Do topical antibiotics improve wound healing? *J Fam Practice*. 2007;56(2):140.

Doyle G, Taillac P. Tourniquets: a review of current use with proposals for expanded prehospital use. *Prehosp Emerg Care*. 2008;12(2):241-56.

Draelos ZD, Rizer RL, Trookman NS. A comparison of postprocedural wound care treatments: do antibiotic-based ointments improve outcomes? *J Am Acad Dermatol*. 2011;64(3Suppl):S23-9.

Drew BD, Bennett BL, Littlejohn L. Application of Current Hemorrhage Control Techniques for Backcountry Care: Part One, Tourniquets and Hemorrhage Control Adjuncts. *Wilderness Environ Med*. 2015;26:236-45.

Forgey W. *Wilderness Medicine: Beyond First Aid*, 7th ed. Guilford, CT: Falcon Guides; 2017.

Gautret P, Parola P. Rabies vaccination for international travelers. *Vaccine*. 2012;30:126-33.

Gentile D, Morris J, Schimelpfenig T, Bass SM, Auerbach PS. Wilderness injuries and illnesses. *Annals of Emerg Med*. 1992;21(7):853-61.

Gerdes E, Hafner J, Aldag J. Injury patterns and safety practices of rock climbers. *J Trauma*. 2006; 61:1517-25.

Griffiths R, Fernandez R, Ussia C. Is tap water a safe alternative to normal saline for wound irrigation in the community setting? *J Wound Care*. 2001;10:407-11.

Gunduz A, Turkmen S, Turedi S, Nuhoglu I, Topgas M. Tick Attachment Sites. *Wilderness Environ Med*. 2008; 19:4-6.

Hubbell F, Frizzell L. Infectious Diseases Associated with Wilderness Environments. In: Hawkins SC, ed. *Wilderness EMS*. Philadelphia, PA: Wolters Kluwer; 2018.

Immunization Action Coalition. *Ask The Experts: Diseases & Vaccinations*. Updated Aug 1, 2013. Available at http://www.immunize.org/askexperts/experts_rab.asp. Accessed February 3, 2017.

Jackson A. Current and future approaches to the therapy of human rabies. *Antivir Res*. 2013;99:61-7.

Jamshidi R. Wound Management. In: Auerbach PS, ed. *Auerbach's Wilderness Medicine*. 7th ed. Philadelphia, PA: Mosby Elsevier; 2017.

Lanteri CA, Nguyen K, Gibbons RV. Rabies. In: Auerbach PS, ed. *Auerbach's Wilderness Medicine*. 7th ed. Philadelphia, PA: Mosby Elsevier; 2017.

Leeman D, Schimelpfenig T. Wilderness injury, illness, and evacuation: National Outdoor Leadership School's Incident Profiles, 1999-2002. *Wilderness Environ Med.* 2003;14:174-82.

Linscott AJ. Rabies. *Clin Microbiol News.* 2012; 34(22):177-80.

Manning SE, Rupprecht CE, Fishbein D, et al. Advisory Committee on Immunization Practices, Centers for Disease Control and Prevention (CDC). Human rabies prevention—United States, 2008: recommendations of the Advisory Committee on Immunization Practices. *MMWR Recomm Rep.* 2008;57:1-28.

MacDonald D, ed. *Accidents in North American Mountaineering.* Golden, CO: American Alpine Club; 2015.

Mosier M, Sheridan RL, Heimbach D. Emergency care of the burned victim. In: Auerbach PS, ed. *Auerbach's Wilderness Medicine.* 7th ed. Philadelphia, PA: Mosby Elsevier; 2017.

Nelson N, McKenzie L. Rock climbing injuries treated in emergency departments in the U.S., 1990-2007. *Am J Prev Med.* 2009;37:195-200.

Novak RT, Thomas CG. Tetanus. In: Burnette GW, ed. *The Yellow Book: CDC Health Information for International Travel.* Oxford, UK: Oxford University Press; 2014.

Oragui E, Parsons A, White T, Longo, UG, Khan WS. Tourniquet use in upper limb surgery. *Hand.* 2011; 6(2):165-73.

Presutti RJ. Prevention and treatment of dog bites. *Am Fam Physician.* 2001;63(8):1567-1573.

Quinn R, Wedmore I, Johnson E, et al. Wilderness Medical Society practice guidelines for basic wound management in the austere environment: 2014 update. *Wilderness Environ Med.* 25:2014;118-33.

Renz EM, Cancio LC. Acute Burn Care. In: Savitsky E, Eastridge B, eds. *Combat Casualty Care: Lessons Learned from OEF and OIF.* Falls Church, VA: Office of the Surgeon General, Department of the US Army; 2012.

Richards G. Taping and Bandaging. In: Auerbach PS, ed. *Auerbach's Wilderness Medicine.* 7th ed. Philadelphia, PA: Mosby Elsevier; 2017.

Rupprecht CE, Shlim DR. Rabies. In: Burnette GW, ed. *The Yellow Book: CDC Health Information for International Travel.* Oxford, UK: Oxford University Press; 2014.

Schöffl V, Popp D, Küpper T, Schöffl I. Injury trends in rock climbers: Evaluation of a case series in 911 injuries between 2009 and 2012. *Wilderness Environ Med.* 2015;26:62-7.

Shreck CE, Fish D, McGovern TP. Activity of repellents applied to skin for protection against *Amblyomma americanum* and *Ixodes scapularis* ticks. *J Am Mosq Control Assoc.* 1995;11:136-40.

Simon D. Sport climber perceptions of stick clip use for the prevention of lead ground falls. Master's Thesis, University of Leicester, UK 2016.

Simon RB. West Virginia: Animal Bite, Bozoo. *Accidents in North American Mountaineering.* Golden, CO: American Alpine Club; 2015. p. 108-9.

Simon RB. Oregon: Animal Bite, Smith Rock State Park. *Accidents in North American Climbing.* Golden, CO: American Alpine Club; 2016. p. 92-93.Simon RB. Hidden danger: Non-Lyme tick-borne diseases. *Nursing.* 2013;43(9):48-55.

Staub D, Debrunner M, Amsler L, Steffen R. Effectiveness of a Repellent Containing DEET and EBAAP for Preventing Tick Bites. *Wilderness Environ Med.* 2002;13:12-20.

Steel, G. UIAA standard 105/harnesses: recommendation for inspection and retirement. Union Internationale des Association d'Alpinisme (UIAA). 2014. http://www.theuiaa.org/safety-standards.html.

Stewart S, Duchesne J, Khan, M. Improvised tourniquets: Obsolete or obligatory? *J Trauma Acute Care Surg.* 2015;78(1):178-83.

Suzuki M, et al. Antimicrobial ointments and methicillin-resistant Staphylococcus aureus USA300. *Emerg Infect Dis.* 2011;17(10):1917-20.

US Environmental Protection Agency, 2013. Insect Repellents: Use and Effectiveness. Available at: http://cfpub.epa.gov/oppref/insect/. Accessed Mar 12, 2016.

Valente J, Forte R, Fruendlich J, Zandieh SO, Crain EF. Wound irrigation in children: saline solution or tap water? *Ann Emerg Med.* 2003;41;609-16.

Watson KR. Structure of the Skin. In: Hall BJ, Hall JC, eds. *Sauer's Manual of Skin Diseases. 10th ed.* Philadelphia, PA: Wolters Kluwer/Lippincott Williams & Wilkins; 2010.

Williamson JE, ed. *Accidents in North American Mountaineering.* Golden, CO: The American Alpine Club; 2014.

CHAPTER 10

Anderson ML, Anderson M. *The Rock Climber's Training Manual: A Guide to Continuous Improvement.* Boulder, CO: Fixed Pin Publishing; 2014.

Basler R. Sports Medicine Dermatology. In: Hall BJ, Hall JC, eds. *Sauer's Manual of Skin Diseases.* 10th ed. Philadelphia, PA: Wolters Kluwer/Lippincott Williams & Wilkins; 2010.

Brennan FH Jr., Jackson CR, Olsen C, Wilson C. Blisters on the battlefield: the prevalence of and factors associated with foot friction blisters during Operation Iraqi Freedom 1. *Mil Med.* 2012;177:157-62.

Davis KP, Derlet RW. Cyanoacrylate glues for wilderness and remote travel medical care. *Wilderness Environ Med.* 2013;24:67-74.

Flanagan D. Friction science. *Climbing.* 2014 Oct: p. 50-1.

Jamshidi R. Wound Management. In: Auerbach PS, ed. *Wilderness Medicine.* 7th ed. Philadelphia, PA: Mosby Elsevier; 2017.

Kyle P, Davis, Derlet RW. Cyanoacrylate glues for wilderness and remote travel medical care. *Wilderness Environ Med.* 2013;24(1):67-74.

Lipman GS, Krabak BJ. Foot Problems and Care. In: Auerbach PS, ed. *Wilderness Medicine.* 7th ed. Philadelphia, PA: Mosby Elsevier; 2017.

Lipman GS, Scheer BV. Blisters: the enemy of the feet. *Wilderness Environ Med.* 2015;26:275-6.

Polliack AA, Scheinberg S. A new technology for reducing shear and friction forces on the skin: implications for blister care in the wilderness setting. *Wilderness Environ Med.* 2006;17:109-19.

Quinn R, Wedmore I, Johnson E, et al. Wilderness Medical Society practice guidelines for basic wound management in the austere environment: 2014 update. *Wilderness Environ Med.* 2014;25:118-33.

Richards G. Taping and Bandaging. In: Auerbach PS, ed. *Auerbach's Wilderness Medicine.* 7th ed. Philadelphia, PA: Mosby Elsevier; 2017.

Schulte C. Ultimate skin care handbook. *Climbing.* 2015 May: p. 42-3.

Van Tiggelen D, Wickes S, Coorevits P, Dumalin M, Witvrouw E. Sock systems to prevent foot blisters and the impact of overuse injuries of the knee joint. *Mil Med.* 2009;174:183-89.

Watson KR. Structure of the Skin. In: Hall BJ, Hall JC. *Sauer's Manual of Skin Diseases.* 10th ed. Philadelphia, PA: Wolters Kluwer/Lippincott Williams & Wilkins; 2010.

CHAPTER 11

Aldashev A, Naeije R. eds. *Problems of High Altitude Medicine and Biology*. Netherlands: Springer; 2008. p. 221-9.

Auerbach PS, Constance BB, Freer L. *Field Guide to Wilderness Medicine*. 4th ed. Philadelphia, PA: Elsevier Mosby; 2013. p. 1-12.

Bachman J, Beatty T, Levene DE. Oxygen Saturation in High-Altitude Pulmonary Edema. *J Am Board Fam Med*. 1992;5(4):429-31.

Bärtsch P, Swenson E. Acute High-Altitude Illnesses. *New Engl J Med*. 2013;368 (24):2294-302.

Bärtsch P, Haefeli WE, Gasse C, et al. Lack of association of high altitude pulmonary edema and polymorphisms of the NO pathway. *High Alt Med Biol*. 2002;3:105 (abstr).

Basnyat B, Murdoch D. High-altitude illness. *The Lancet*, 2003;1967-74.

Basnyat B, Gertsch JH, Holck PS, et al. Acetazolamide 125 mg BD is not significantly different from 375 mg BD in the prevention of acute mountain sickness: the prophylactic acetazolamide dosage comparison for efficacy (PACE) trial. *High Alt Med Biol*. 2006;7:17–27.

Basnyat B. High Altitude Cerebral and Pulmonary Edema. *Travel Med Infect. Dis*. 2005 Nov;3(4):199-211.

Beidleman BA, Fulco CS, Muza SR, et al. Effect of six days of staging on physiologic adjustments and acute mountain sickness during ascent to 4300 meters. *High Alt Med Biol*. 2009;10:253-60.

Doherty MJ. James Glaisher's 1862 account of balloon sickness: altitude, decompression injury, and hypoxemia. *Neurology*. 2003;60(6):1016-8.

Dorma Y, Hanaoka M, Ota M, et al. Positive association of the endothelial nitric oxide synthase gene polymorphisms with high-altitude pulmonary edema. *Circulation*. 2002;106:826-30.

Donegani E, Paal P, Küpper T, et al. Drug Use and Misuse in the Mountains: A UIAA MedCom Consensus Guide for Medical Professionals. *High Alt Med Biol*. 2016;17(3):157-84.

Fagenholz PJ, Gutman JA, Murray AF, Harris NS. Treatment of high altitude pulmonary edema at 4240 m in Nepal. *High Alt Med Biol*. 2007;8:139-46.

Forwand SA, Landowne M, Follansbee JN, Hansen JE. Effect of acetazolamide on acute mountain sickness. *N Engl J Med*. 1968;279:839-45.

Gilbert DL. The first documented report of mountain sickness: the China or headache story. *Resp Physiol*. 1983;52(3):315-26.

Hackett PH, Luks AM, Lawley JS, Roach RC. High-Altitude Medicine and Pathophysiology. In: Auerbach PS, ed. *Auerbach's Wilderness Medicine*. 7th ed. Philadelphia, PA: Mosby Elsevier; 2017.

Hackett P, Shlim D. The Pre-travel Consulatation. In: Brunette GW, ed. *CDC Health Information for International Travel: The Yellow Book 2014*. New York, NY: Oxford University Press; 2014.

Harris M. High Altitude Medicine. *Am Fam Physician*. 1998 Apr;57(8):1907-1914.

Hultgren HN, Honigman B, Theis K, Nicholas D. High-altitude pulmonary edema at a ski resort. *Western J. Med*. 1996;164:222-7.

International Society for Mountain Medicine. Normal acclimatization. Available at: http://ismm.org/index.php/normal-acclimatization.html. Accessed July 9, 2016.

Johnson C, Anderson S, Dallimore J, Winser S, Warrell DA. *Oxford Handbook of Expedition and Wilderness Medicine*. 2nd ed. Oxford University Press, Oxford, UK 2015.

Jones BE, Stokes S, McKenzie S, Nilles E, Stoddard GJ. Management of High Altitude Pulmonary Edema in the Himalaya: A Review of 56 Cases Presenting at Pheriche Medical Aid Post (4240 m). *Wilderness Environ Med*. 2013;24:32-6.

Kelly TE, Hackett PH. Acetazolamide and sulfonamide allergy: a not so simple story. *High Alt Med Biol*. 2010;11(4):319-23.

Low EV, Avery AJ, Gupta V, Schedlbauer A, Grocott MPW. Identifying the lowest effective dose of acetazolamide for the prophylaxis of acute mountain sickness: systematic review and meta-analysis. *Brit Med J*. 2012; 345:e6779.

Luks AM, McIntosh SE, Grissom CK, et al. Wilderness Medical Society Consensus Guidelines for the Prevention and Treatment of Acute Altitude Illness: 2014 Update. *Wilderness Environ Med*. 2014;25(4S):S4-S14.

Maggiorini M, Brunner-La Rocca HP, Peth S, et al. Both tadalafil and dexamethasone may reduce the incidence of high-altitude pulmonary edema: a randomized trial. *Ann Intern Med*. 2006;145:497-506.

Man-kam H, Yuet-chung S. High Altitude Medicine. *Hong Kong Medical Diary*. 2010;15(6):32-4.

Platt D, Griggs RC. Use of acetazolamide in sulfonamide-allergic patients with neurologic channelopathies. *Arch Neurol-Chicago*. 2012;69(4):527-9.

Schoene RB. Illnesses at high altitude. *Chest*. 2008;134:402-16.

Simon DA, Simon RB. Preparing for Travel to High Altitude Locations. *Nursing*. 2012;42(9):66-7.

Simon RB, Simon DA. Illness at high altitudes. *Nursing*. 2014;45(7):36-41.

Stream JO, Grissom CK. Update on high-altitude pulmonary edema: pathogenesis, prevention, and treatment. *Wilderness Environ Med*. 2008;19:293-303.

West J. *High Life: A History of High-Altitude Physiology and Medicine*. New York: Springer, 1998, pp. 4-9.

West JB, Schoene RB, Milledge JS, Luks AM. *High Altitude Medicine and Physiology*. 5th ed. London, UK: CRC Press; 2012.

Zafren K. Does Ibuprofen Prevent Acute Mountain Sickness? *Wilderness Environ Med*. 2012;23:297-9.

Zafren K. Management of High Altitude Injuries. In Hawkins SC, ed. Wilderness EMS. Philadelphia, PA: Wolters Kluwer, 2018.

CHAPTER 12

Auerbach PS, Constance BB, Freer L. Field Guide to Wilderness Medicine 4th ed. Philadelphia, PA: Elsevier Mosby; 2013.

Cauchy EC, Davis CB, Pasquier M, Meyer EF, Hackett PH. A New Proposal for Management of Severe Frostbite in the Austere Environment. *Wilderness Environ Med*. 2016;27:92-9.

Charkoudian N, Crawshaw LI. Thermoregulation. In: Auerbach PS, ed. *Auerbach's Wilderness Medicine*. 7th ed. Philadelphia, PA: Mosby Elsevier; 2017.

Danzl D, Huecker MR. Accidental hypothermia. in: Auerbach PS (Ed.) Wilderness Medicine 7th ed. Philadelphia: Elsevier; 2017.

Geisbrecht GG. Emergency treatment of hypothermia. *Emerg Med (Fremantle)*. 2001; 13:9-16.

Geisbrecht GG, Arnett JL, Vela E, Bristow GK. Effect on task complexity on mental performance during immersion hypothermia. *Aviat Space Environ Med*. 1993;64:206-11.

Henriksson O, Lundgren P, Kuklane K, Holmer I, Bjornstig U. Protection against cold in prehospital care—thermal insulation properties of blankets and rescue bags in different conditions. *Prehosp Disaster Med.* 2009;24:408-415.

Iserson KV. *Improvised Medicine.* New York, NY: McGraw Hill Medical; 2012.

Johnson C, Anderson S, Dallimore J, Winser S, Warrell DA. *Oxford Handbook of Expedition and Wilderness Medicine.* 2nd ed. Oxford University Press, Oxford, UK 2015.

Kleinman ME, Brennan EE, Goldberger ZD, et al. Part 5: adult basic life support and cardiopulmonary resuscitation; 2015 American Heart Association Guidelines update for cardiopulmonary resuscitation and emergency cardiovascular care. Circulation. 2015;132(18):S2.

Laskowski-Jones L, Jones L. Management of Cold Injuries. In: Hawkins SC, ed. *Wilderness EMS.* Philadelphia, PA: Mosby Elsevier; 2018.

Luks AM, Grissom CK, Jean D, Swenson ER. Can People with Raynaud's Phenomenon Travel to High Altitude? *Wilderness Environ Med.* 2009;20:129-38.

Lundgren JP, Henriksson O, Pretorius T, et al. Field torso-warming modalities: a comparative study using a human model. *Prehosp Emerg Care.* 2009;13:371-78.

McIntosh SE, Opacic M, Freer L, et al. Wilderness Medical Society Practice Guidelines for the Prevention and Treatment of Frostbite: 2014 update. *Wilderness Environ Med.* 2014;25(4):S43-S54.

Paal P, Milani M, Brown D, Boyd J, Ellerton J. Termination of cardiopulmonary resuscitation in mountain rescue. *High Alt Med Biol.* 2012;13:200-8.

Thomassen O, Faerevik H, Osteras O, et al. Comparison of three different prehospital wrapping methods for preventing hypothermia—a crossover study in humans. *Scand J Trauma Resusc Emerg Med.* 2011;19:41.

Weiss, EA. *Adventure Medical Kits Wilderness & Travel Medicine.* 4th ed. Seattle, WA: The Mountaineers Books; 2012.

Wilkerson J, Moore E, Zafren K. *Medicine for Mountaineering and Other Wilderness Activities.* Seattle, WA: The Mountaineers Books; 2010.

Zafren K, Giesbrecht GG, Danzl DF, et al. Wilderness Medical Society practice guidelines for the out-of-hospital evaluation and treatment of hypothermia: 2014 Update. *Wilderness Environ Med.* 2014;25(4):S66-S85.

CHAPTER 13

Auerbach PS, Constance BB, Freer L. *Field Guide to Wilderness Medicine.* 4th ed. Philadelphia, PA: Elsevier Mosby; 2013.

Backer HD, Shopes E, Collins, SL, Barkan H. Exertional heat illness and hyponatremia in hikers. *Am J Emerg Med.* 1999;17:532.

Backer HD, Shopes E, and Collins SL. Hyponatremia in recreational hikers in Grand Canyon National Park. *J Wilderness Med.* 1993;4(4):391-406.

Bennett BL, Hew-Bulter T, Hoffman MD, Rogers IR, Rosner MH. Wilderness Medical Society Practice Guidelines for Treatment of Exercise-Associated Hyponatremia: 2014 Update. *Wilderness Environ Med.* 2014;25(4S):S30-S42.

Charkoudian N, Crawshaw LI. Thermoregulation. In: Auerbach PS, ed. *Wilderness Medicine.* 6th ed. Philadelphia, PA: Mosby Elsevier; 2017.

Hew-Butler T, Ayus JC, Kipps C, et al. Statement of the Second International Exercise-Associated Hyponatremia Consensus Development Conference, New Zealand, 2007. *Clin J Sport Med.* 2008 Mar;18(2):111-21.

Iserson KV. *Improvised Medicine.* New York, NY: McGraw Hill Medical; 2012.

Johnson C, Anderson S, Dallimore J, Winser S, Warrell DA. *Oxford Handbook of Expedition and Wilderness Medicine*. 2nd ed. Oxford University Press, Oxford, UK 2015.

Leon LR, Kenefick RW. Pathology of Heat-Related Illness. In: Auerbach PS, ed. *Wilderness Medicine*. 6th ed. Philadelphia, PA: Mosby Elsevier; 2012.

Lipman GS, Eifllng KP, Ellis MA, et al. Wilderness Medical Society Practice Guidelines for the Prevention and Treatment of Heat-Related Illness: 2014 Update. *Wilderness Environ Med*. 2014;25:S55-S65.

Noe RS, Choudhary E, Cheng-Dobson J, Wolkin AF, Newman SB. Exertional heat-related illnesses at the Grand Canyon National Park, 2004-2009. *Wilderness Environ Med*. 2013;24:422-28.

Rehydration Project. Oral Rehydration Solutions. Available at http://www.rehydrate.org/solutions/homemade.htm. Accessed June 29, 2016.

Schimelpfenig G, Tarter S, Richards G. Management of Heat Illnesses. In: Hawkins SC, ed. *Wilderness EMS*. Philadelphia, PA: Wolters Kluwer, 2018.

UNICEF, et al. Facts for Life. 4th ed. New York: United Nationsolutions/homemade.htm-homeAvailable at http://factsforlifeglobal.org/resources/factsforlife-en-full.pdf. Accessed January 19, 2016.

Weiss, EA. *Adventure Medical Kits Wilderness & Travel Medicine*. 4th ed. Seattle, WA: The Mountaineers Books; 2012.

World Health Organization. The treatment of diarrhoea: a manual for physicians and other senior health workers.—4th Rev. Geneva: WHO Press, 2005. Available at http://apps.who.int/iris/bitstream/10665/43209/1/9241593180.pdf. Accessed Jan 16, 2016.

CHAPTER 14

Auerbach PS, Constance BB, Freer L. *Field Guide to Wilderness Medicine 4th ed*. Philadelphia, PA: Elsevier Mosby; 2013.

Brunello A, Walliser M, Hefti U. *Outdoor and Mountain Medicine*. Bern, Switzerland: SAC Verlag; 2014.

Brunette G. *CDC Health Information for International Travel The Yellow Book 2012*. New York, NY: Oxford University Press; 2012.

Drake B, Paterson R, Tabin G, Butler FK Jr, Cushing T. Wilderness Medical Society Practice Guidelines for Treatment of Eye Injuries and Illnesses in the Wilderness. *Wilderness Environ Med*. 2012;23:325-36.

Ellerton J, Zuljan I, Agazzi G, Boyd JJ. Eye Problems in Mountain and Remote Areas: Prevention and Onsite Treatment - Official Recommendations of the International Commission for Mountain Emergency Medicine (ICAR MEDCOM). *Wilderness Environ Med*. 2009;20:169-75.

Eng C, Van Pelt J. *Freedom of the Hills*. 8th ed. Seattle, WA; 2012.

Hall B, Hall J. *Sauer's Manual of Skin Diseases*. 10th ed. Philadelphia, PA: Lippincott Williams & Wilkins; 2010.

Iserson KV. *Improvised Medicine*. New York, NY: McGraw Hill Medical; 2012.

Johnson C, Anderson S, Dallimore J, Winser S, Warrell DA. *Oxford Handbook of Expedition and Wilderness Medicine*. 2nd ed. Oxford University Press, Oxford, UK 2015.

Krakowski A, Goldenberg A. Exposure to Radiation from the Sun. In: Auerbach PS, ed. *Wilderness Medicine*. 7th ed. Philadelphia, PA: Mosby Elsevier; 2017.

McIntosh S, Guercio B, Tabin GC, Leemon D, Schimelpfenig T. Ultraviolet Keratitis

Among Mountaineers and Outdoor Recreationalists. *Wilderness Environ Med.* 2011;22:144-7.

Paterson R, Drake B, Tabin G, Butler FK Jr, Cushing T. Wilderness Medical Society Practice Guidelines for Treatment of Eye Injuries and Illnesses in the Wilderness: 2014 Update. *Wilderness Environ Med.* 2014;25:S19-S29.

Weiss EA. *Wilderness & Travel Medicine.* 4th ed. Seattle, WA: The Mountaineers Books; 2012.

Wilkerson J, Moore E, Zafren K. *Medicine for Mountaineering and Other Wilderness Activities.* Seattle, WA: The Mountaineers Books; 2010.

CHAPTER 15

Davis C, Engeln A, Johnson EL, et al. Wilderness Medical Society Practice Guidelines for the Prevention and Treatment of Lightning Injuries: 2014 Update. *Wilderness Environ Med.* 2014;25(4):S86-S95.

Houghton Mifflin Harcourt. "bolt from the blue." *American Heritage® Dictionary of the English Language, Fifth Edition.* 2011. Houghton Mifflin Harcourt Publishing Company. Available at http://idioms.thefreedictionary.com/bolt+from+the+blue. Accessed Oct 5, 2016.

Nelson D, McGinnis H. Management of Lightning Injuries & Storms. In: Hawkins SC, ed. *Wilderness EMS.* Philadelphia, PA: Wolters Kluwer; 2018.

CHAPTER 16

Auerbach PS, Constance BB, Freer L. *Field Guide to Wilderness Medicine.* 4th ed. Philadelphia, PA: Mosby Elsevier; 2013.

Mioduszewski J, Fernando DN. Principles of Meteorology and Weather Predication. In: Auerbach PS, ed. *Wilderness Medicine.* 7th ed. Philadelphia, PA: Mosby Elsevier; 2017.

Renner J. *Mountain Weather.* Seattle, WA: The Mountaineers; 2007.

Wilkerson JA, Moore EE, Zafren K. Medicine for *Mountaineering & Other Wilderness Activities.* 6th ed. Seattle, WA: The Mountaineers; 2010.

Woodmencey J. *Reading Weather.* Guilford CT: Morris Book Publishing; 2012.

CHAPTER 17

American Avalanche Center. US Avalanche Accidents Report. Available at http://www.avalanche.org/accidents.php. Accessed June 29, 2016.

Auerbach PS, Constance BB, Freer L. *Field Guide to Wilderness Medicine.* 4th ed. Philadelphia, PA: Mosby Elsevier; 2013. p. 13-6.

Beissinger JP, Millin M. Technical Rescue Interface: Ski Patrols and Mountaineering Rescue in the Snow or Glaciated Environment. In: Hawkins, SC. *Wilderness EMS.* Philadelphia, PA: Wolters Kluwer; 2018.

Brugger H, Durrer B, Elsensohn F, et al. Resuscitation of avalanche victims: Evidence-based guidelines of the international commission for mountain emergency medicine (ICAR MEDCOM). *Resuscitation.* 2013;84(5):539-46.

Jekich B. Avalanche Fatalities in the United States: A Change in Demographics, *Wilderness Environ Med* 2016;27(1):46-52.

Johnson C, Anderson S, Dallimore J, Winser S, Warrell DA. *Oxford Handbook of Expedition and Wilderness Medicine.* 2nd ed. Oxford University Press, Oxford, UK 2015. p. 642-3.

CHAPTER 18

American College of Emergency Physicians. Policy Statement: EMS Management of Patients with Potential Spinal Injury. American College of Emergency Physicians: 2015. Available at https://www.acep.org/clinical---practice-management/ems-management-of-patients-with-potential-spinal-injury/. Accessed July 4, 2016.

Ben-Galim P, Dreiangel N, Mattox KL, et al. Extrication collars can result in abnormal separation between vertebrae in the presence of a dissociative injury. J Trauma. 2010;69(2):447-50.

Bledsoe B. Why EMS should limit the use of rigid cervical collars : making the case for soft collars & alternative methods of spinal stabilization. Journal of EMS. 2015;40(2).

Boissy P, Shrier I, Brière S, et al. Effectiveness of cervical spine stabilization techniques. *Clin J Sport Med.* 2011;21:80-8.

Davies G, Deakin C, Wilson A. The effect of a rigid collar on intracranial pressure. Injury. 1996;27(9):647-9.

Dixon M, O'Halloran J, Cummins NM. Biomechanical Analysis of Spinal Immobilization during Prehospital Extrication: A Proof of Concept Study. *Emerg Med J.* Published online 28 June 2013.

Franklin RC, Pearn JH. Drowning for love: the aquatic victim-instead-of-rescuer syndrome: drowning fatalities involving those attempting to rescue a child. *J Paediatr Child Health.* 2011;47(1-2):44-7.

Goutcher CM, Lochhead V. Reduction in mouth opening with semi-rigid cervical collars. Br J Anaesth. 2005;95(3):344-8.

Hauswald M, Ong G, Tandberg D, Omar Z. Out-of-hospital spinal immobilization: its effect on neurologic injury. *Acad Emerg Med.* 1998;5(3):214-9.

Hauswald M. A re-conceptualisation of acute spinal care. *Emerg Med J.* 2013;30(9):720-3.

Holla M. Value of a rigid collar in addition to head blocks: A proof of principle study. Emerg Med J. 2012;29(2):104-7.

Hughes SJ. How effective is the Newport/Aspen collar? A prospective radiographic evaluation in healthy adult volunteers. J Trauma. 1998;45(2):374-8.

Mobbs RJ, Stoodley MA, Fuller J. Effect of cervical hard collar on intracranial pressure after head injury. ANZ J Surg. 2002;72(6):389-91.

National Association of EMS Physicians, American College of Surgeons Committee on Trauma. EMS spinal precautions and the use of the long backboard. *Prehosp Emerg Care* 2013;17:392-3.

Perry SD, McLellan B, McIlroy WE. The efficacy of head immobilization techniques during simulated vehicle motion. Spine. 1999;24(17):1839-44.

Quinn RH, Williams J, Bennett BL, Stiller G, Islas A, McCord S. Wilderness Medical Society Practice Guidelines for Spine Immobilization in the Austere Environment: 2014 Update. *Wilderness Environ Med* 2014;25(4):S105-S17.

Shafer JS, Naunheim RS. Cervical Spine Motion During Extrication: A Pilot Study. *West J Emerg Med.* 2009;10(2):74-8.

Smith B, Bledsoe B, Nicolazzo P. Trauma Management in WEMS. In Hawkins, SC. *Wilderness EMS.* Philadelphia, PA: Wolters Kluwer, 2018.

Smith W. Technical Rescue Interface Introduction: Principles of Basic Rigging, Packaging, and Rope Skills. In Hawkins SC, ed. *Wilderness EMS.* Philadelphia, PA: Wolters Kluwer, 2018.

Sundstrøm T, Asbjørnsen H, Habiba S, et al. Prehospital use of cervical collars in trauma patients: A critical review. J Neurotrauma. 2014;31(6):531-40.

Wilderness EMS Medical Director Course. WEMSMDC Curriculum, delivered January 2017, National Association of EMS Physicians Annual Scientific Meeting Preconference. Available at www.wemsmdcourse.com. Accessed Jan 30, 2017.

Zhu Y, Jiang X, Li H, Li F, Chen J. Mortality among drowning rescuers in China, 2013: a review of 225 rescue incidents from the press. *BMC Pub Health*. 2015 Jul;15:631.

CHAPTER 19

AdventureMed. Advanced Wilderness Life Support Instructor Guide v8.3. Utah: AdventureMed, 2013.

Simon RB. Ropes to the Rescue: Climber Evacuation Techniques. *Wilderness Medicine Magazine*. March 15, 2015. Available at http://wildernessmedicinemagazine.com/1141/Climbing-Ropes-to-the-Rescue. Accessed December 4, 2016.

Simon RB. Technical Rescue Interface: High Angle and Low Angle Rescue. In: Hawkins SC, ed. *Wilderness EMS*. Philadelphia, PA: Wolters Kluwer; 2018.

Simon RB. The Coolest Trick I Know: The Rope Litter. *Climbing*. 2012; Issue 309, October 2012.

Smith W. Technical Rescue Interface Introduction: Principles of Basic Rigging, Packaging, and Rope Skills. In Hawkins SC, ed. *Wilderness EMS*. Philadelphia, PA: Wolters Kluwer, 2018.

CHAPTER 20

Auerbach PS, Constance BB, Freer L. *Field Guide to Wilderness Medicine*. 4th ed. Philadelphia, PA: Mosby Elsevier; 2013.

Carleton SC. Wilderness Navigation Techniques. In: Auerbach PS, ed. *Wilderness Medicine*. 7th ed. Philadelphia, PA: Mosby Elsevier; 2017.

Sholl M, George D. The Interface of Wilderness EMS, Professional Organizations/Guides, and Other EMS Agencies. In: Hawkins SC, ed. *Wilderness EMS*. Philadelphia, PA: Wolters Kluwer; 2018.

Simon RB. Technical Rescue Interface: High Angle and Low Angle Rescue. In: Hawkins SC, ed. *Wilderness EMS*. Philadelphia, PA: Wolters Kluwer; 2018.

APPENDIX A

Auerbach PS, Constance BB, Freer L. *Field Guide to Wilderness Medicine*. 4th ed. Philadelphia, PA: Mosby Elsevier; 2013.

Johnson C, Anderson S, Dallimore J, Winser S, Warrell DA. *Oxford Handbook of Expedition and Wilderness Medicine*. 2nd ed. Oxford University Press, Oxford, UK 2015.

Lipnick MS, Lewin MR. Wilderness Preparation, Equipment, and Medical Supplies. In: Auerbach PS, ed. *Auerbach's Wilderness Medicine*. 7th ed. Philadelphia, PA: Mosby Elsevier; 2017.

Shlim DR. Nepal. In: Brunette GW, ed. *CDC Health Information for International Travel: The Yellow Book 2014*. New York, NY: Oxford University Press; 2014.

Weiss EA. *Wilderness and Travel Medicine*. 4th ed. Seattle, WA: The Mountaineers; 2012.

Wilkerson JA, Moore EE, Zafren K. Medicine for *Mountaineering & Other Wilderness Activities*. 6th ed. Seattle, WA: The Mountaineers; 2010.

APPENDIX B

Auerbach PS, Constance BB, Freer L. *Field Guide to Wilderness Medicine.* 4th ed. Philadelphia, PA: Mosby Elsevier; 2013.

Ellerton J. ed. *Casualty Care in Mountain Rescue.* 2nd ed. Penrith, Cumbria, UK: Mountain Rescue Council; 2006.

Eng, RC. *Mountaineering: The Freedom of the Hills.* 8th ed. Seattle, WA: The Mountaineers; 2010.

Scheele B. Technical Rescue Interface: All-Terrain Vehicle, Off-road Vehicle, and Helicopter Rescue. In: Hawkins SC, ed. *Wilderness EMS.* Philadelphia, PA: Wolters Kluwer; 2018.

Teichman PG, Donchin Y, Kot RJ. International aeromedical evacuation. *N Engl J Med.* 2007; 356:262.

Thomas SH, Koller K, Maeder MB. Helicopter Rescue and Air Medical Transport. In: Auerbach PS, ed. *Auerbach's Wilderness Medicine.* 7th ed. Philadelphia, PA: Mosby Elsevier; 2017.

Tomazin I, Kovacs T. International Commission for Mountain Emergency Medicine: Medical considerations in the use of helicopters in mountain rescue. *High Alt Med Biol.* 2003;4:479-83.

Tyson A, Loomis M. *Climbing Self-Rescue: Improvising Solutions for Serious Situations.* Seattle, WA: The Mountaineers; 2006.

Wilkerson JA, Moore EE, Zafren K. *Medicine for Mountaineering & Other Wilderness Activities.* 6th ed. Seattle, WA: The Mountaineers; 2010.

Worley GH. Wilderness Communication. *Wilderness Environ Med.* 2011;22:262-9.

APPENDIX E

Auerbach PS, Constance BB, Freer L, *et al.* Field Guide to Wilderness Medicine 4th ed. Philadelphia, PA: Elsevier Mosby; 2013.

Backer HD. Field Water Disinfection. In: Auerbach PS, ed. *Wilderness Medicine.* 7th ed. Philadelphia, PA: Mosby Elsevier; 2017.

Iserson KV. *Improvised Medicine.* New York, NY: McGraw Hill Medical; 2012.

James WD, Berger TB, Elston D. *Andrews' Diseases of the Skin: Clinical Dermatology.* Saunders Elsevier, 2006. p. 858.

Johnson C, Anderson S, Dallimore J, Winser S, Warrell DA. *Oxford Handbook of Expedition and Wilderness Medicine.* 2nd ed. Oxford University Press, Oxford, UK 2015.

Weiss, EA. *Adventure Medical Kits Wilderness & Travel Medicine.* 4th ed. Seattle, WA: The Mountaineers Books; 2012.

APPENDIX F

Auerbach PS, Constance BB, Freer L. *Field Guide to Wilderness Medicine.* 4th ed. Philadelphia, PA: Elsevier Mosby; 2013.

Backer HD. Field Water Disinfection. In: Auerbach PS, ed. *Wilderness Medicine.* 7th ed. Philadelphia, PA: Mosby Elsevier; 2017.

Brunello A, Walliser M, Hefti U. *Outdoor and Mountain Medicine.* Bern, Switzerland: SAC Verlag; 2014.

Brunette, GW. ed. *CDC Health Information for International Travel: The Yellow Book 2012.* New York, NY: Oxford University Press; 2012.

Ellerton J. ed. *Casualty Care in Mountain Rescue*. 2nd ed. Penrith, Cumbria, UK: Mountain Rescue Council; 2006.

Griffith HW. *Complete Guide to Prescription and Nonprescription Drugs 2016-2017*. New York, NY: Perigee/Penguin Random House; 2015.

Iserson KV. *Improvised Medicine*. New York, NY: McGraw Hill Medical; 2012.

Johnson C, Anderson S, Dallimore J, Winser S, Warrell DA. *Oxford Handbook of Expedition and Wilderness Medicine*. 2nd ed. Oxford University Press, Oxford, UK 2015.

Luks AM, McIntosh SE, Grissom CK, et al. Wilderness Medical Society Practice Guidelines for the Prevention and Treatment of Acute Altitude Illness: 2014 Update. *Wilderness Environ Med*. 2014;25:S4-S14.

Pietroski N. Pharmacology. In: Hawkins SC, ed. *Wilderness EMS*. Philadelphia, PA: Wolters Kluwer, 2018.

Russell KW, Scaife CL, Weber DC, et al. Wilderness Medical Society practice guidelines for the treatment of acute pain in remote environments. *Wilderness Environ Med*. 2014;25:41-9.

Shandera WX. Travel-related diseases: injury and infectious disease prevention. *J Wilderness Med*. 1993;4:40-61.

Wedmore IS, Johnson T, Czarnik J, Hendrix S. Pain management in the wilderness and operational setting. *Emerg Med Clin North Am*. 2005;23:583-601.

Weiss, EA. *Adventure Medical Kits Wilderness & Travel Medicine*. 4th ed. Seattle, WA: The Mountaineers Books; 2012.

Wilkerson J, Moore E, Zafren K. *Medicine for Mountaineering and Other Wilderness Activities*. Seattle, WA: The Mountaineers Books; 2010.

INDEX

*Italics indicate illustrations.

A

ABC mnemonic, 4

Abdomen, 14–15

anterior compartments of, *14*

constipation and, 140

distention of, 14

fecal impaction and, 140

GI bleeding and, 140–141

hemorrhoids and, 141

lower pain in, 134

appendicitis, 135–136

diverticulitis, 136

ectopic pregnancy, 136–137

GI obstruction, 137–138

hernia, 138

pelvic inflammatory disease, 138–139

urinary tract infection, 139

pain in, 131

trauma in, 141–143

blunt, 142–143

penetrating, 149

upper pain in, 132

gallstone-related disease/cholecystitis,

132–133

gastroesophageal reflux disease,

133–134

peptic/stomach ulcer, 134

Abdominal compressions, 22

Abduction, xii

Abrasions, 163–164, 171–172

Accidental hypothermia, 202

Accidents in North American Climbing, 282

*Accidents in North American Mountaineer-

ing,* 149, 173

Acclimatization, 194, 199, 218

AccuWeather "RealFeel" Temperature, 218

Acetaminophen, 79, 83, 86, 146

Acetazolamide (Diamox®)

in preventing acute mountain sickness, 19

in treating high-altitude cerebral edema,

199

Achilles tendinitis, 107–109, 108

Achilles tendon, rupture/tear of, 107

Acid reflux, 131, 133–134

Acromioclavicular (AC) joint, separation of,

63–64

Acromion, 63

Activated charcoal, *298*

Acute amebic dysentery, 150

Acute coronary syndrome (ACS), 154–157

Acute mountain sickness (AMS), 194,

195–198

HACE as progression of, 198–199

preventive measures for, 196–197

Acute pancreatitis, 132–133

Adduction, xii

Adhesive bandages, 185

Ad hoc backboarding, 257

Ad libitum hydration, 219

Advanced life support (ALS) drugs, 19

Advanced Wilderness Life Support curricu-

lum, 5, 16

Aerobic conditioning and fitness, 45, 46, 48

AIDS, 147

Airway with cervical spine assessment, 8

Alcohol, 37

Allergens, 24

Alpine environment, climbing in, 43

Altimeters, 249–250

Altitude illness, 193–201

Alveolar hypoxia, 200

Alzheimer's disease, 37

Amateur Radio Service, 273, *274*

Amebiasis, 160–161

Amenorrhea, 136

American Alpine Club, 5

American Association of Neurological Sur-

geons, 121, 126

American College of Chest Physicians, grading recommendations of, x–xi
American College of Emergency Physicians, 262
American College of Surgeons, 121
    Committee on Trauma, 261
American Heart Association, guidelines on hypothermia, 202–203
American Institute for Avalanche Research and Education (AIARE), 251
American Red Cross (ARC), 66
Amputation of finger, 87
Anaerobic metabolism, 48, 49
Anaerobic thresholds, 46
Anal fissure, 140
Analgesia, 121, 307
Anaphylaxis, 24–28, *26,* 158, 179
adjunct medications in, 27–28
    defined, *26*
    motion sickness, 309
    sedating, 310
    sources of, 25
    treating, 25, 28–29
        epinephrine in, 25, 28–29
Anatomical terminology, xii
Angina, 155–156
Animal bites and stings, 25, 164, 178–179
Anisocoria, 128
Ankle. *See also* Foot
    achilles tendinitis, 107–109
    achilles tendon rupture/tear, 107
    ankle/foot fracture, 109–111
    fracture of, 109–111
    Ottawa rules, 109–110, *111*
    splinting, 113
    sprain of, 111–112
Antacids, 133, 308
Anterior, xii
Anterior cruciate ligament (ACL), sprain/tear of, 102
Anterior elbow pain, 74–77
Antiallergics, 307
Antibiotics, 132–133, 135, 149, 151, 185, 188, 308
    triple ointment, 169
Antiemetics, 308–309
Antifungal agents, 308
Antihistamines, 28–29, 226, 308

Antihydral cream, 189
Antimalarials, 308
Antimicrobials, 308
Antimotility drugs, 308–309
Antioxidant, caffeine as known, 37
Antiseptics, 309
Antivenin, 179
Appendicitis, 135–136
    stump, 135
Aquatabs®, 303, 305
Aristotle, 193
Arm. *See also* Forearm
    cutaneous nerves of, *71*
Artificial sweeteners, 36
Asphyxiation, 20, 30, 252
Assessment, 3–17
    circulation, sensation and movement (CSM), 72, 86, 100, 101, 105, 110, *111*
    communication as element of, 17
    expanded efforts in, 16–17
        physical exam in, 11–12
        primary survey, 4–7
            airway with cervical spine, 8
        hanging, 8–9
        helicopter out, 9
        hike out, 9
        hunker down, 9
        hyperthermia, 8
        hypothermia, 8
        massive hemorrhage, 5–6
        respiration and circulation, 8
        secondary survey, 4, 7–15
            abdomen, *14,* 14–15
            chest, 13–14
            meat, 15
            skin, slab, snow, 15
            shock in, 13
            smartphones in, 9
Asthma, 157–158, 200
Atherosclerosis, 154
Athlete's foot, preventing, 184
Athletic tape, 185
Atipyretics, 307
ATP creatine phosphate system, 49
Auscultation, 14
Automated external defibrillators (AEDs), 19–20, 155
Auvulsed tissue, 87

Avalanche airbag systems (ABS), 254
Avalanche Canada, 251
Avalanches, 251–254
    burial in, 20
    characteristics of, *252*
    deaths related to, 235
Avalanche transceiver/beacon, 278
Avalung devices, 254
Avascular necrosis, 83
AVPU responsiveness survey, 8–9, 126
Avulsed tissue, 87
Axilla, 187
Azetazolamide, 195
Azithromycin, 153

B
Bacitracin, 169
Back-packer's disease, 148
Badger Balm, *184*
Baitracin/polymyxin B, 169
Balance, 54
Balance boards, 54
Ball and socket joint, 64
Bandages, 169–170
    adhesive, 185
    hemostatic, 166
    liquid, 186
Barometers, 249
Barrier gloves, 164
Basal cell carcinoma, 227
Battle's sign, 128
BEAM technique, 15, 257–258
Beaver fever, 148
Bee strings, 179
Belayer's neck, 62
Belay glasses, 62
Benzoin, compound tincture of, 185
Beta Balm, *184*
Biceps tendinitis, 75
Bleeding. *See also* Hemorrhage
    shock from, 29
    from wounds, 165
Blindness. *See also* Eyes
    snow, 201, *233*, 233–234
Blisters, 186–187
    in frostbite, 210–211
    preventing, 187
    from sunburn, 232

    unroofed, 186, 187
Blood-borne pathogens, 22
Blunt abdominal trauma, 141, 142–143
Body composition, 39–41, *41*
Body fat, calculation of, 40
Body Glide®, 188
Body mass index (BMI) scale, 39, *39*
    adaption for climbers, *39*
Boiling in water purification, 298–300, *299*, 305
Boots, drying soaked, 184
Bowstringing, 91
Box carry, 265
Boy Scouts of America, 66
Brachial artery, injuries to, 71
Brachialis, 75
Brain
    intracranial hemorrhage in, 123, 127–128, 130
    traumatic, injury in, 123, 125
Brain rest, 129
Branched chain amino acids (BCAAs), 38
Breakfast, carbohydrates in, 42
Bupuytren's cords, 94
Burns, 15, 164, 174–178
    assessing, *175*, 175–176
    chemical, 175
    deep partial thickness, 178–179
    electrical, 175
    first degree, 178
    fourth degree, 177
    full thickness, 177
    superficial partial thickness, 178
    types of, 174
Bursa, 69
Bursitis, 69
Burt's Bees® Hand Salve, 183, *184*

C
Cable-and-winch system, 291
CAB mnemonic, 4–5
Caffeine, 37
Calcaneus, 109
Calluses, 187
CamelBak®, 167
Campylobacter eteritis (campylobacteriosis), 152
CAMS mnemonic, 13–15

Canadian Association of Emergency Physicians, 121
Canadian C-spine study, 119, 120, 260
Cancer, 37, 227
Carabiner tourniquet, 23, *24*
Carbohydrates, 35–36
    complex, 35–36, 42
    consuming before exercise, 42
    consuming protein with, 43
    diet low in, 35
    limiting consumption of, 40
    non-processed, 43
    simple, 35
Carcinoma, 227
Cardiac arrest, 18
Cardiac tamponade, 162
Cardiopulmonary arrest, 18, 20
Cardiopulmonary resuscitation (CPR),
        18–19, 28, 156, 241
    changes in techniques, 19
    compression-only, 20, 21
    rotation of rescue breathing and chest
        compressions in, 20
    training in, 18–19
Carotid pulse, 12
Carpal bones, 82
Carpal tunnel syndrome, 94–95
Carries, 257
Casein, 38
Cataracts, 228, 242
Cefixime, 153
Cell phones, 274
Celox®, 166
Cerebral edema, 216
Cerebrospinal fluid, 128
Certification, importance of recurring, 19
Cervical collars, 262
Cervical spine assessment, airway with, 8
Cervical vertebra, 5, 117, *118*
Chafing, 187–188
Chalk, use of, in climbing, 189
Charcoal, 297, *298*
Chemical burns, 175
Chemical heat packs, 208–209, 214
Chest, 13–14. *See also* Respiratory issues
    flail, 160–161
    inspection of wall, 14
Chest compressions, 28

Chlamydia, 138
Chlorine dioxide in water purification, 303
Chlorine in water purification, 301–303, *302*
Choking, 22, 28, *29*
    Heimlich maneuver for, 28, *29*
    in infants, 28
Cholangitis, 132
Cholecystitis, 132–133
    acute, 132
Cholera, 149–150
Chondroitin, 38
Ciprofloxacin, 151
Circulation, sensation and movement (CSM)
        assessment, *72*, 86, 100, 101, 105, 110,
        111
Circumferential burns, 175
Citizens band (CB), 273, *274*
Clavicle, 63
    fracture of, 63–64
Clearing the spine, 260
Climbers
    adaptation of body mass index for, *39*
    calorie requirements for, *41*
    healthy diet for, 33
    sport, 33
Climber's elbow, 74–77
Climbing
    alpine, 43
    crack, 116
    range of activities in, ix
    training for rock, 50–51
    urban centers for, ix
    use of chalk in, 189
Climbing harness, as tourniquet for lower
        limb hemorrhage, 168
ClimbingWeather.com, 249
Climb On®, 183, *184*
Clinical diagnosis, 125
Clinically significant, 120
Clothing
    heat illnesses and, 219–220
    in preventing hypothermia, 207–208, *208*
    SPF, 232
Clouds, 245–247
    altocumulus, 246
    altostratus, 246
    cirrocumulus, 246
    cirrostratus, 246

cirrus, 24
cumulonimbus, 245
cumulus, 245
lenticular, 246
nimbostratus, 246
stratocumulus, 245
stratus, 245–246
Cloud-to-ground lightning, 236
Coagulation-flocculation, 296–297, *298*
Coccyx, 117
COLDER mnemonic, 16
Cold fronts, 247
Cold injuries, 85, 202–214
frostbite as, 210–213
frostnip as, 214
hypothermia as, 202–210
mechanisms of heat exchange, 202, *203*
preventing, *207*
Raynaud's phenomenon as, 213–214
Collagen, 182
Collagenase clostridium histolyticum (Xiaf-lex®), 94
Colles' fracture, 79, 80
Combat Application Tourniquet (C-A-T®), 166–167
Communication, 271–279
avalanche transceiver/beacon in, 278
cell phones in, 274
as element of assessment, 17
fire in, 273
helicopters in, 286–291
personal locator beacons in, 275–276
pre-trip preparation and selection in, 271–272
radio services/handheld radios in, 273–274, *274*
rescue personnel in, 278–279
satellite emergency notification devices in, 278
satellite telephones in, 274–275
signal mirrors in, 273
visual distress signals in, 272
whistles in, 272
Compartment syndrome, 60, 85
signs of, 60–61
Complex carbohydrates, 35–36, 42
Compression, 61
Compression-only CPR, 21

Concussions, 123, 125–128, 129
symptoms of, 126–127
Conduction, *203,* 217
Congress of Neurological Surgeons, 121
Constipation, 140
Contact burns, 175
Contact lenses, 234
Contamination, goals of managing, 164
Convection, *203,* 217
Conversion tables, 292–293
Core homeostasis, 215
Core training, 50
Coronary artery disease (CAD), 154–157
Cospas-Sarsat satellite system, 275
Cough suppressants, 309
CPR. *See* Cardiopulmonary resuscitation (CPR)
Crack climbing, 116
Creatine, 37
Creatine phosphate, 49
Crepitus, 65
Crimping tear, *90*
CrossFit programs, 51
Cross-training, 54
Crush injuries, 31
Cryptosporidiosis, 147
Cubital tunnel syndrome, 78
Cullen sign, *142*
Curad BloodStop®, 166
Cysts, ganglion, 95–96

D
Davis, Steph, 35, 102
Deafness, 242
Deaths
avalanche-related, 235
rescue, 30–31
reverse triage for lightning, 241
sudden cardiac, 154–157
Decongestants, 309
Deep tissue massage, 116
Deep-water soloing, 21, 240
Degloving, 89
Dehydration
hypothermia and, 206
signs and symptoms of, *145*
volume depletion from, 223
Dengue fever, 179

DeQuervain's tenosynovitis, 96–97

Dermabond, 130

Dermis, 182

Desitin®, 188

Dexamethasone (Decadron®)
    in preventing acute mountain sickness, 197, 198
    in treating high-altitude cerebral edema, 199
    in treating high-altitude pulmonary edema, 201

Diabetes, 37

Diagnosis, differential, 11

Diarrhea, 131, 135, 136, 145–147
    organisms that cause, *144*
    rice water, 150
    traveler's, 146–147

Differential diagnosis, 11

Digits, 117

Direct pressure, 23, 165

Dislocation
    of elbow, 70–72
    glenohumeral, 64–67
    hip, 98
    patella, 104–105

Disseminated intravascular coagulation (DIC), 216

Distal, xii

Distal radius, fracture of, 79–81

Distracting injuries, 142

Diverticulitis, 136

Dorsal, xii

Drop knee, 103

Drowning, 20, 21–22
    submerging vehicles and, 21–22

Dupuytren, Baron Guillaume, 93

Dupuytren's contracture, 93–94

Dynamic stretching, 53

Dysentery, 145–147
    acute amebic, 150

Dyspepsia, 132

Dysrhythmias, 20, 154–157

E

Ears, lighting strikes and, 242

Eccentric strengthening exercises, 109

Ectopic pregnancy, 136

Ehlers-Danlos syndrome, 65

Elastin, 182

Elbow, 70–79
    anterior pain in, 74–77
    climber's, 74–75
    dislocation of, 70–72, *71, 72*
    golfer's, 77
    improvised splint for, 80
    lateral epicondylitis in, 72–74, *73*
    medial epicondylitis in, 77
    snapping, syndrome, 78
    stability of, 70
    tennis, 72–74
    ulnar collateral ligament stress, 78

Electrical burns, 175, 178

Electrolyte balance, in preventing heat cramps, 222

Emergency locator transmitters, 275

Emergency position-indication radio beacons, 275

Emery boards, 187, 188

Emphysema, subcutaneous, 14

Empty calories, 34

Energy bars or gels, 42

Energy expenditure, reduction in, in preventing acute mountain sickness, 196

Enteric fever, 152

Envenomation, 179

Epicondylitis
    lateral, 72–74
    medial, 77

Epidermis, 182

Epinephrine
    intramuscular injection of, 26–27
    need for multiple doses of, 27
    subcutaneous injection of, 27
    in treating anaphylaxis, 25, 28–29

EpiPen®, 27

Epiphyseal fracture, 91

Erythema, 186

Erythropoiesis, 195

Eschar, 211

Ethyl chloride, 122

European Committee for Standardization, 124

Evacuation. *See also* Extraction
    need for, 7
    preparations for helicopter, 286–291

Evaporation, *203*, 217

Evidence-based medicine, ix, 30

Excess post-exercise oxygen consumption (EPOC), 47
Exercise
  aerobic, 45, 46, 48
  consuming carbohydrates before, 42
  eccentric strengthening, 109
  high-intensity, 41
  low-intensity, 41–42
Exercise-associated hyponatremia, 43, 219, 224
Expectorants, 309
Extension, xii
Extensor carpi radialis brevis (ECRB), 73
External rotation, xii
Extraction. *See also* Evacuation
  decision-making on, 258–259
  selective spinal immobilization and spinal motion restriction, 259–264
Extrication, 257–259
Eyes
  backup protection for, 233
  cataracts and, 228, 242
  lighting strikes and, 242
  macular degeneration and, 228
  raccoon, 128
  snow blindness and, 201, *233*, 233–234

F
Family Radio Service (FRS), 273
Fartleks, 48
Fast twitch fibers (FTF), 49, *49*
Fats, 36
Fecal impaction, 140
Federal Communications Commission (FCC), 273
Femoral neck fractures, 98
Femoral pulse, 12
Femur, 117
  fracture of, 100–101
Fiber, 35
Fibula, fracture of, 105–106
Fiction, skin and, 183
Field Guide to Wilderness (Auerbach), 60
Filtration in water purification, 300
Fingers
  amputation of, 87
  isometric strength in, 51
  Raynaud's phenomenon and, 213
  trigger, 92–93

Finkelstein test, 96
Fire, 273
Fireman's carry, 265
First aid kits
  contents for mountain travel, 281–286
  epinephrine in, 26, 27
Fitness tests, 45
Fitzpatrick's classification of skin type, 228, *229*
Flail chest, 160–161
Flame burns, 175
Flappers, 188
Flash burns, 175
Flexion, xii
Flexor pulley, injuries to, 90–92
Flexor tendon, injuries to, 89–90
Flexor tenosynovitis, 92–93
Foot. *See also* Ankle
  athlete's, 184
  fracture of, 109–111
  hallux rigidus, 112, 114
  hallux valgus, 114–115
  Morton's neuroma, 116
  plantar fasciitis, 116–117
  sesamoid injury in, 116
Forearm
  anatomy of, 73
  cutaneous nerves of, *71*
Foreign bodies in choking, 22
Fractures
  ankle, 109–111
  clavicle, 63–64
  Colles', 79, 80
  distal radius, 79–81
  femur, 100–101
  fibula, 105–106
  foot, 109–111
  hamate, 84–86
  lunate, 83–84
  metacarpal, 86–87
  patella, 104–105
  pelvis, 98–100
  phalangeal, 86–87
  proximal humerus, 64–67
  rib, 160
  scaphoid, 81–83
  tibia, 105–106
  ulna, 79–81
Frog position, 103

Frostbite, 46, 214
  preventing, 211–212
  stages of, *211*
  treating, 212–213
Frostnip, 46, 214
Fungus, preventing foot, 184

G
Gallstone-related disease, 132–133
Gamow bag, in preventing acute mountain
  sickness, 198, 199
Ganglion cyst, 95–96
Gastroenteritis, 131
Gastroesophageal reflux disease (GERD),
  133–134
Gastrointestinal system
  bleeding in, 140–141
  infectious diseases affecting, *144,*
    144–153
    amebiasis, 160–161
    campylobacter eteritis (campylobacte-
      riosis), 152
    cholera, 149–150
    cryptosporiodiosis, 147
    dehydration and, *145*
    diarrhea, 145–147
    dysentery, 145–147
    giardiasis, 148–149
    norovirus, 148
    salmonellosis, 149
    shigellosis, 151–152
    traveler's diarrhea, 146–147
    typhoid, 152–153
  obstruction in, 137–138
  preventing issues, 131
General Mobile Radio Service (GMRS), 273,
  274
Get Giddy, *184*
Ginkgo biloba
  in preventing acute mountain sickness,
    198
  for Raynaud's phenomenon, 214
GI obstruction, 137–138
Glenohumeral joint, 62
  dislocation of, 64–67
Glissading accident, 81
Globalstar satellite network, 275
Glucosamine, 38

Glycogen, 35, 41
Glycolysis, 35, 49
Gobies, 171
Golfer's elbow, 77
Grading recommendations, x–xi
Grand Canyon National Park, hyponatremia
  in, 224
Graupel, 236
Ground current, 237
Ground drag, 265
Gunshot wounds, 143
Gutter splint, 64, *66,* 84
  improvised, 72, 84

H
H2 blockers, 133
HACE (high-altitude cerebral edema),
  198–199
  evacuation and, 198
Hail, 247
Hair follicles, 182
Hallux rigidus, 112, 114
Hallux valgus, 114–115
Halogen disinfection in water purification,
  301
Hamate, fracture of, 84–86
Ham radio, 273, *274*
Handheld radios, 273–274, *274*
Hands. *See also* Wrist and hands
  creams/salves for, 183–184
  split/cracked tips on, 188–189
  washing of, 183
HAPE (high-altitude pulmonary edema),
  194, 199–201
Hazard mitigation in mountainous terrain, 3
Head injuries, 123–130
  as concern for climbers, 123
  concussions as, 125–128
  intracranial hemorrhage as, 127–128
  lacerations and fractures, 128–129, 130
  preventing, 123–125
  severe traumatic brain injuries as,
    127–128
Heart attack, 20, 155
Heart disease, 37
Heat injuries, 85, 215–226
  heat cramps as, 222–223
  heat exhaustion as, 219–220

heatstroke as, 220–222
heat syncope as, 223–224
hyponatremia as, 224–225
miliaria rubia as, 225–226
predisposing risk factors and, *216,*
    216–217
seven Rs of treating, 220, *221, 222, 223*
Heatstroke, 220–222
Heat syncope, 223–224
Heel-bow type sleeve, 78
Heel hook, 103
Heimlich maneuver, 22, 28, *29*
Helicobacter pylori infection, 133
Helicopters
    communication with, 286–291
    in evacuation, 7
Helmets in preventing head injuries, 123–125
Hematoma, visualization of, 14
HemCon®, 166
Hemoglobin, 37
    concentration, 195
Hemorrhage, 98
    controlling, 22–24, *24,* 87, 165–167
    intraabdominal, 142
    intracranial, 123, 127–128, 130
    intraperitoneal, clinical indicators of, *142*
    massive, 5–6
    micro, 242
    use of climbing harness as tourniquet for
        lower limb, 168
Hemorrhoids, 140, 141
    prolapsed, 141
    thrombosed, 141
Hemostatic agents, 22
Hemostatic gauze and bandages, 166
Hemostatis, 165
Hepatitis, 164
Hernia
    incarcerated, 138
    inguinal, 138
    symptoms of, 138
Herniation, 128
High altitude, effects of, 193
High-carbohydrate diet, in preventing acute
    mountain sickness, 196
High-intensity exercise, 41
High-intensity interval training (HIIT),
    40–41, 47

Hiking out, 7
Himalayan Karakoram Pass, 193
Hip. *See also* Pelvis
    dislocation of, 98
History, 9–10
Homeostasis, core, 215
Honnold, Alex, 35
Hook of the hamate, 84
House, Steve, 45
Human Immunodeficiency Virus (HIV), 164
Humerus, 64, 117
Hunkering down, 7
Hydration, 183
    in injury prevention, 43–44
    in preventing acute mountain sickness,
        196
    in preventing heat cramps, 222
    skin and, 183
Hypertension, 156
Hypoglycemia, 10, 35
Hyponatremia, 44, 196, 224–225
    exercise-associated, 43, 219, 224, 225
Hypotension, 12, 99, 156
Hypothalamus, heat injuries and, 215
Hypothermia, 202–210, 252
    accidental, 202
    mild, 202, *204,* 210
    moderate, 202, *204–205*
    preventing, 206–208
    rope litter and wrap, *268,* 268–270, *269*
    severe, 202, *205*
    treating, 208–210
Hypovolemia, 150
Hypoxia, 195
Hypoxic ventilator response (HVR), 194

I
Ibuprofen, in preventing acute mountain
    sickness, 197
Ice, 69
    cups, 76
    reusable packs, 76
Immarsat satellite network, 275
Immunizations, 149, 170–171, 310–312]
    rabies, 170–171
    tetanus, 170
Immunocompromise, 147
Impingement syndrome, 69–70

INDIAN mnemonic, 119, 120
Indoor climbing gyms, 54
Infants, choking in, 28
Infectious diseases affecting gastrointesti-
    nal system
    amebiasis, 160–161
    campylobacter eteritis (campylobacterio-
        sis), 152
    cholera, 149–150
    cryptosporiodiosis, 147
    dehydration and, 145
    diarrhea, 145–147
    dysentery, 145–147
    giardiasis, 148–149
    norovirus, 148
    salmonellosis, 149
    shigellosis, 151–152
    thyroid, 152–153
    traveler's diarrhea, 146–147
    typhoid, 152–153
Inferior, xii
Injury prevention, 33–54
    hydration in, 43–44
    nutrition in, 33–43
    planning in, 54
    training in, 44–54, 45
Insulin, 41
Internal rotation, xii
International Commission for Alpine Rescue
    (ICAR), 296
International Commission for Mountain
    Emergency Medicine (ICAR MEDOM),
    254
International Hypoxia Symposium, 195–196
International Mountaineering and Climbing
    Federation, 124
Interval training, 48
Intraabdominal hemorrhage, 142
Intracranial hemorrhage (ICH), 123, 127–
    128, 130
Intraperitoneal bleed, clinical indicators of,
    142
Intrauterine contraceptive device (IUD), 138
Intubation, 19
Iodine in water purification, 301, 302
IPA mnemonic, 11–12
Iridium satellite network, 275, 276
Iron, 37–38

deficiency of, 37
    overconsumption of, 38
Irrigation, 167, 169
Ischemia, 85
Isometric finger strength, 51

J
Jaundice, obstructive, 132, 133
Johnston, Scott, 45
Joshua Tree Skin Care, 183, 184
Junk foods, 34

K
Kehl, Jason, 102
Kehr sign, 142
Kennedy, John F., 121, 122
Keratin, 182
Keraunoparalysis, 242
Kerlix™, 173
Ketosis, 35
Knees. See also Patella
    anterior cruciate ligament (ACL) and
        medial collateral ligament (MCL)
        sprains/tears, 102
    lateral collateral ligament (LCL) and pos-
        terior cruciate ligament (PCL) injuries,
        103
    meniscal tears, 103–104
    patella dislocation, 104–105
    patella fracture, 104
"Know-before-you-go" campaign, 251
Kraus, Hans, 121

L
Labral derangement, 67
Labrum, tears in, 67–68
Lacerations, 128–129, 163–164, 172–173
Lake Louis Consensus Committee on acute
    mountain sickness, 196
Lateral, xii
Lateral collateral ligament (LCL), injuries
    to, 103
Lateral epicondylitis, 72–74
Laxatives, 309
Lean-to, 316
Lichtenberg figures, 236–237, 243
Life-threatening emergencies, 18–32
    anaphylaxis as, 24–28, 26

cardiac and respiratory arrest as, 18–20

choking as, 28, *29*

drowning as, 21–22

hemorrhage control as, 22–24, *24*

suspension syndrome as, 28–32

Ligaments, 48

injuries to lateral collateral, 103

injuries to posterior cruciate, 103

scapholunate, 83

sprains/tears of anterior cruciate, 102

sprains/tears of medial collateral, 102

ulnar collateral stress, 78

Lightning, 20, 175, 235–243

cloud-to-ground, 236

contact injury from, 237

detection technology and, 240

direct strikes of, 237

ground current, 237

lethal strikes of, 236

Lichtenberg figures and, 236–237, 243

preventing injuries from, 237–240

reverse triage for deaths, 241

snowstorms and, 236

30-30 rule and, 238–239

thunderstorms and, 24, 235

treating strikes from, 241–243

upward streaming, 237

Lipolysis, 49

Liquid bandages, 186

Litters, 257

one-person rope, 265–267, *266*

rope, and wrap, *268*, 268–270, *269*

two-person rope, *266*, 267–268

Log rolling, 15, 129, 257, 258

Loperamide, 146

Low-intensity exercise, 41–42

Lumbar vertebra, 117, *118*

Lunate, fracture of, 83–84

Lyme disease, 179

M

Macular degeneration, 228

Malaria, 179

Malignant melanoma, 227

MARCH mnemonic, 5, 8, 12, 17, 177, 222

Marine band radios, 274

Massage, deep tissue, 116

Maximum heart rate (MHR), 46–47

Medial, xii

Medial collateral ligament (MCL), sprain/ tear of, 102

Medial epicondylitis, 75, 77

Median nerve, injury to, 79

Medications. *See also specific*

adjunct, in anaphylaxis, 27–28

advanced life support, 19

antiallergic, 307

antibiotics, 132–133, 135, 149, 169, 185, 188, 308

antimotility, 308–309

in increasing sensitivity to the sun, *230*

for mountain travel, 307–312

preventive, 310–312

Men

alcohol consumption in, 37

sweating by, 44

Meniscus, tears of, 103–104

Metacarpal fractures, 86–87

Metolius, *184*

Metronidazole, 151

Microfractures, 242

Microhemorrhages, 242

Mild hypothermia, 202, *204*, 210

Mild traumatic brain injury, 125, 129, 130

Miliaria, 182

Miliaria rubia, 225–226

Minimal erythema dose (MED), 228, 230

Miox purifier in Water purification, 303

Mnemonics

ABC, 4

CAB, 4–5

CAMS, 13–15

COLDER, 16

INDIAN, 119, 120

IPA, 11–12

MARCH, 5, 8, 12, 17, 177, 222

PAWS, 283–284

RICE, 61, 75, 76, 96, 102, 103, 106, 107, 108, 112

SAMPLE, 9

Moderate hypothermia, 202, *204–205*

Monistat® Chaing Relief Powder Gel®, 188

Monounsaturated fats, 36

Morton's neuroma, 116

Mosquitos, bites from, 179

Motion sickness medications, 309

Mountain-Forecast.com, 249
Mountainous terrain, hazard mitigation in, 3
Mountain Project, 271
Mountain travel
    first aid kit contents for, 281–286
    medications for, 307–312
Muscle fibers
    fast twitch, 49
    slow twitch, 49
    training for, *49*
Muscle pump, 45
Myocardial infarction, 155
Myocardial ischemia, 155
Myositis ossificans, 75

N
National Association of EMS Physicians, 261
National Collegiate Athletic Association, 127
National Lightning Detection Network, 240
National Lightning Safety Institute, 240
National Outdoor Leadership School
    (NOLS), 163
National Weather Service, 240
Neck, 62
    belayer's, 62
Needles
    in blister care, 185
    sterilizing, in the backcountry, 186–187
Neosporin®, 169
Neurological injuries, 8
Neuroma, Morton's, 116
Neutrogena Norwegian Formula moistur-
    izer, 232
New-Skin®, 186
NEXUS (National Emergency X-Radiogra-
    phy Utilization Study), 118–119, 120,
    260
Nifedipine
    for high altitude pulmonary edema, 201
    for Raynaud's phenomenon, 214
NOLS Wilderness Medicine, 9
Non-processed carbohydrates, 43
Norovirus, 148
Northwest Avalanche Center, 251
NSAIDs, 69, 75, 79, 103, 108, 115, 134, 153,
    160
Nunn™, 224
Nutrition, 33–43, 183

alcohol in, 37
body composition and, 39–41, *41*
caffeine in, 37
carbohydrates in, 35–36
fats in, 36
protein in, 34–35
supplements in, 37–38
tips for performance, 41–43

O
Obstructive jaundice, 132, 133
O'Keeffe's Working Hands, 183–184, *184*
Olecranon, 70–71
Ondansetron, 146
One-person rope litter, 265–267, *266*
Oral rehydration solutions (ORS), 145–146,
    151, 153
Orographic lift
Orthopedics, 59–116
    general muscle/tendon injuries, 106–116
    muscle/tendon strains and tears, 106–107
    lower body, 59, 97–106
        ankle
            achilles tendinitis, 107–109
            achilles tendon rupture/tear, 107
            ankle/foot fracture, 109–111
            ankle sprain, 111–112
            splinting techniques for, 113
        foot
            foot sesamoid injury, 116
            hallux rigidus, 112, 114
            hallux valgus, 114–115
            Morton's neuroma, 116
            plantar fasciitis, 116–117
        knee
            anterior cruciate ligament (ACL) and
                medial collateral ligament (MCL)
                sprains/tears, 102
            lateral collateral ligament (LCL) and
                posterior cruciate ligament (PCL)
                injuries, 103
            meniscal tears, 103–104
            patella dislocation, 104–105
            patella fracture, 104
        pelvis/hip, 98–100
            hip dislocation, 98
            pelvis fracture, 98–100
            thigh/femur, 100–101

fracture, 100–101
  tibia/fibula, 105–106
  fracture, 105–106
upper body, 59, 62–97
  elbow, 70–79
    anterior elbow pain or climber's
      elbow, 74–77
    elbow dislocations, 70–72, *71, 72*
    lateral epicondylitis or tennis elbow,
      72–74, *73*
    medial epicondylitis or golfer's elbow,
      77
    ulnar collateral ligament stress, 78
  neck, 62
    belayer's, 62
  shoulder, 62–70
    glenohumeral dislocation and proxi-
      mal humerus fractures, 64–67
    impingement syndrome and rotator
      cuff tears, 69–70, *70*
    SLAP lesion, 67–68, *68*
  wrist and hand, 79–97
    carpal tunnel syndrome, 94–95
    DeQuerain's tenosynovitis, 96–97
    distal radius/ulna fracture, 79–81, *80,*
      81
    Dupuytren's contracture, 93–94
    flexor pulley injuries, 90–92
    ganglion cyst, 95–96
    hamate fracture, 84–86
    isolated flexor tendon injuries, 89–90
    lunate fracture, 83–84
    metacarpal and phalangeal fractures,
      86–87
    other fractures, 81, *82*
    scaphoid fracture, 81–83
    tendon and pulley ruptures, 87–89, *88*
    trigger finger or flexor tenosynovitis,
      92–93
Orthotic arch supports, 116
Ossification, 75
Ottawa Ankle Rules, 109–110, *111*
Overhydration, 196
Overtraining, 54
  preventing, 54
  symptoms of, 54
Overuse injuries, 59
Oxidative metabolism, 48–49

Oximetry test, 200
Oxygenation, 18
  in preventing acute mountain sickness,
    198, 199

P
Palmar, xii
Palm method, 175
Pancreatitis, acute, 132–133
Paresthesia, 242
Parkinson's disease, 37
Patella, 104. *See also* Knees
  dislocation of, 104–105
  fracture of, 104
Pathognomonic, 236
Pelvic binder, 99
Pelvic inflammatory disease (PID),
  138–139
Pelvis. *See also* Hip
  fracture of, 98–100
Penetrating abdominal trauma, 143
Peptic ulcers, 133
Performance, nutrition tips for, 41–43
Periodization, 51–52
Peritonitis, 73, 135
  signs of, 136
Personal locator beacons, 275–276
Phalangeal fractures, 86–87
Pharmaceutical prophylaxis, in preventing
  acute mountain sickness, 196–197
Phones
  cell, 274
  satellite, 274–275
  smart, 9
Phonetic alphabet, 277, *277*
Phonic obstructive pulmonary disease
  (COPD), 157
Phosphodiesterase inhibitors, in treating
  HAPE, 201
Photokeratitis, 201, 233–234
Photophobia, 234
Planning in injury prevention, 54
Plantar fasciitis, 116–117
Plyometric training, 51
Pneumonia, 157, 158–159, 200
  bacterial, 158
  fungal, 158
  viral, 158

Pneumothorax, 63, 161–162
    open, 161
    signs of, 63
Polyethylene terephthalate (PET), 304
Polyunsaturated fatty acids, 36
Postconcussive syndrome, 129
Posterior, xii
Posterior cruciate ligament, injuries to, 103
Post-exposure prophylaxis (PEP), 170–171
Post-traumatic arthritis, 80
Prax lotion, 232
Pressure breathing, 160
Pressure sores, 85
Preventive medications, 310–312
Prickly heat, 225–226
Primary survey, 4–7
    airway with cervical spine assessment, 8
    hanging, 8–9
    hasty assessment, 8
    helicopter out, 9
    hike out, 9
    hunker down, 9
    hyperthermia, 8
    hypothermia, 8
    massive hemorrhage, 5–6
    respiration and circulation, 8
Progressive overload, 50
Pronation, xii
Prone, xii
Protein, 34–35
    consuming carbohydrates and, 43
    free-range sources of, 33
    for vegetarians/vegans, 34–35
Protein powder, 38
Proton pump inhibitors (PPIs), 133, 134
Provider, trained, 66
Proximal, xii
Proximal humerus, fracture of, 64–67
Psychiatric disturbances, lighting strikes
    and, 243
Psychological shock, 12
Pterygium, 227
Puccio, Alex, 102
Pulley injury, 90, 90
Pulley ruptures, 87–89
Pulmonary embolism, 201
Pulse
    carotid, 12, 13

femoral, 12
    radial, 12
Punctures, 163–164

Q
QuikClot®, 166

R
Rabies, 170–171, 178–179
Raccoon eyes, 128
Radial pulse, 12
Radiation, 203, 217
Radio services, 273–274, 274
Raynaud's phenomenon, 212, 213–214
Recco reflectors, 254
Regimental patch area, 65
Rehydration, 145–146, 150
    packs for, 309
Rehydration Project, 223
Rescue breathing, 21
Rescue communication, pre-trip preparation
    and selection, 271–272
Rescue death, 30–31
Resistance training, 41, 50
Respiratory alkalois, 194
Respiratory arrest, 18
Respiratory issues, 154–162. See also Chest
    acute coronary syndrome, 154–157
    asthma, 157–158
    atherosclerosis, 154
    coronary artery disease, 154–157
    dysrhythmias, 154–157
    pneumonia, 157, 158–159
    sonic obstructive pulmonary disease, 157
    sudden cardiac death, 154–157
    traumatic conditions, 159–162
        cardiac tamponade, 162
        flail chest, 160–161
        pneumothorax, 161–162
        rib fractures, 160
Rest, 54
Resting heart rate (RHR), 46
Resting metabolic rate (RMR), 40, 41
Reusable ice packs, 76
Reverse osmosis filtering, 300
Reverse triage, for lighting strike deaths,
    241
Rib fractures, 160

RICE (rest, ice, compression, elevation), 61, 75, 76, 96, 102, 103, 106, 107, 108, 112
Risk
    mitigating, 3
    situational, 3–4
Rock and Ice, 84
Rock climbers, training for, 50–51
Rocket Pure, *184*
Rocky Mountain spotted fever, 179
Rope litters
    building, 270
    with hypothermia wrap, 268, *268,* 269
    one-person, 265–267, *266*
    two-person, *266,* 267–268
Rotation
    external, xii
    internal, xii
Rotator cuff, tears of, 69–70
Rule of nines, 175, *175*
Ruptures, achilles tendon, 107

S
Safety pins in blister care, 185
St. Augustine, 193
St. Elmo's Fire, 236
Salmonellosis, 149
SAMPLE history, 9
Sanding blocks, 185–186, 187, 188
Sandpaper, 187
Satellite emergency notification devices, 278
Satellite telephones, 274–275
SatSleeve, 275
Saturated fats, 36
Scald burns, 175
Scalp, lacerations to, 128, 173
Scaphoid, fracture of, 81–83
Scapholunate ligament, 83
SCAT3, 126
Scene safety check, 3–4
Sciatic nerve, 98
Scorpion bites, 179
Screening, 296, *298*
Sebaceous glands, 182
Secondary survey, 4, 7–15
    abdomen in, *14,* 14–15
    chest in, 13–14
    meat in, 15
    skin, slab, snow in, 15

Sedating medications, 310
Sedimentation, 296, *298*
Seizures, 65
Sepsis, 139
Sesamoiditis, 116
Severe hypothermia, 202, *205*
Severe traumatic brain injury (STBI), 127–128, 129
    signs of, 128
Sharma, Chris, 102
Shelters, improvised, 313–316
Shielded tree wall, 315
Shigellosis, 151–152
Shock, 12, 24
    assessment of, 13
    from bleeding, 29
    consequences of, 30
    hanging in harness and, 28
    psychological, 12
    recognizing, 12
    source of, 13
Shoulder, 62–70
    anterior, 67, *68*
    dislocation and proximal humerus fractures, 64–67
    impingement syndrome and rotator cuff tears, 69–70, *70*
    posterior, 69, *70*
SLAP lesion, 67–68, *68*
Side splash, from lightning strike, 237
Signal mirrors, 273
Sildenafil in treating HAPE, 201
Silver in water purification, 303–304
Simple carbohydrates, 35
Single pole tarp tent, 315–316
Situational awareness, 3
Situational risk, 3–4
Skin, 182
    care of, 183–184
    fiction and, 183
    Fitzpatrick's classification of type, 228, *229*
    injuries to, 186–189
        blisters, 186–187
        calluses, 187
        chafing, 187–188
        flappers, 188
        split/cracked tips, 188–189

Skin, injuries to, (*continued*)
    subungual hematoma, 189
    worn/smooth tips, 189
  kit for caring for, 185–186
  layers of, 182–183
  use of chalk and, 189
    Skin glue, 186, 188
Skratch®, 224
Skull fracture, 123
Slackline, 54
SLAP lesion, 67–68
Sleep, 54
Slings
  gutter, 64, *66*
  improvised, with shirt, 63, *64*
  webbing, 64, *65*
Slow twitch fibers (STF), 49
Smartphones in assessment, 9
Snakebites, 179
Snapping elbow syndrome, 78
Snow blindness, 201, *233*, 233–234
Snow shelter, 316
Snowstorms, lightning strikes and, 236
SOF® Tactical Tourniquet (SOF®-T), 166–167
Solar irradiation, 304
Solar-related injuries, 227–234
  photokeratitis as, *233*, 233–234
  sunburns as, 229–232
  UBA and, 227, *227*, 228, *228*
  UVA and, *227*, 227–228
  UVC and, 227
Soy protein isolate, 38
Spenco 2nd skin, 187
Sphygmomanometer, 12
Spider bites, 179
Spinal immobilization, 120–121, 129*n*
Spinal trap, 258, *258*
Spine, 117, *118*
  injuries to, 117–122
  selective immobilization and motion
    restriction, 259–264
Splints
  ankle, 113
  gutter, 66, 84
  improvised, 72, *72*, 84
  improvised elbow, 80
  sugar tong, *81*, 84
  tape, 113

U-, 113
  ulnar/spica, 82
  wrist, 85
Split/cracked tips on hands, 188–189
Sport climbers, 33
Sports drinks, 42
SPOT family of devices, 278
Sprains, ankle, 111–112
Squamous cell carcinoma, 227
Stabbings, 143
Staged ascent in preventing acute mountain
    sickness, 196
Static stretching, 52–53
Step-off deformity, 63
Step voltage, 237
SteriPEN, 304, 306
Steri-Strips™, 172–173
Steroids, 28–29, 121
Stratum corneum, 187, 189
Strength training, 45, 48, 50
Stretching
  dynamic, 53
  static, 52–53
Stump appendicitis, 135
Subcutaneous emphysema, 14
Subcutaneous tissue, 182, 183
Submerging vehicles, drowning in, 21–22
Subungual hematoma, 189
  prevention of, 184
Sucking chest wound, 161
Sudden cardiac death (SCD), 154–157
Sugar tong splint, *81*, 84
Sun, 244–245
  drugs in increasing sensitivity to the, *230*
Sunburn, blisters from, 232
Sun poisoning, 232
Sunscreens, 230–233
  characteristics of, *231*
  water-resistant, 231
Superior, xii
Super-setting, 51
Supination, xii
Supine, xii
Supplements, 37–38
Suspension syndrome, 8–9, 28–32, 121
Suspension trauma, 31–32
Sweat, water loss from, 44
Sweat glands, 182

Sypeland Climber's Balm, *184*
Systemic inflammatory response syndrome
    (SIRS), 216
Systolic blood pressure, 12, 165

T
Tadalafil, in treating HAPE, 201
Talus, 109
Tarp trench, 315
Tears
    achilles tendon, 107
    anterior cruciate, 102
    labrum, 67–68
    medial collateral, 102
    meniscal, 103–104
    rotator cuff, 69–70
Tendons, 48
    flexor, 88, *88*
    ruptures of, 87–89
    strains and tears of, 106–107
Tennis elbow, 72–74
Terrain blocking, 248
Tetanic muscle contractions, 236
Tetanus, 170, 174
    frostbite and, 213
Thermal chemical packets, 209
Thermometers, 249–250
Thigh, fracture of, 100–101
    fracture, 100–101
30-30 rule, 238–239
Thoracic vertebrae, 117, *118*
Throat lozenges, 309
Throwing athletes, 67
Thunderstorms, lightning and, 24, 235
Thuraya satellite network, 275
Tibia, fracture of, 105–106
Ticks
    bite prevention and removal guides,
      180–181
    bites from, 179
Tip Juice, *184*
Toenails, cutting of, 184
Toes, Raynaud's phenomenon and, 213
Too Kin, 193
Total body surface area (TBSA), 175, 177,
    178
Tourniquets, 5, 23, 166
    carabiner, *24*

Combat Application, 166–167
    field expedient, 168
    placement of, 5, 23
    SOF® Tactical, 166–167
    traditional, 23
    use of climbing harness as, for lower limb
      hemorrhage, 168
Trained provider, 66
Training, 44–54, *45*
    alternate regimes for specific results,
      52–53
    basic fitness test in, *45*
    controlling level of intensity during,
      48–49
    core, 50
    cross, 54
    interval, 48
    for muscle fibers, *49*
    plyometric, 51
    resistance, 50
    strength, 48, 50
    zones in, 47, *47*
Training for the New Alpinism (House and
    Johnson), 45
Training log, keeping, 45
Trans fatty acids, 36
Trauma, abdominal, 141–143
    blunt, 141, 142–143
    penetrating, 143
Traumatic brain injury (TBI), 123, 125
    mild, 125, 129, 130
    severe, 127–128, 129
Traveler's diarrhea, 146–147
Trigger finger, 92–93
Trimethoprim-sulfamethoxazole, 151
Triple antibiotic ointments, 169
Turf toe, 116
Turner sign, *142*
Two-person rope litter, *266*, 267–268
Tympanic membrane, 239
Typhoid, 152–153

U
Ulcers, peptic, 133
Ulna, fracture of, 79–81
Ulna nerve
    entrapment of, 78
    injuries to, 71

Ulnar collateral ligament, stress to, 78
Ulnar neuritis, 78
Ulnar/spica splint, 82
Ultrafiltration, 300
Ultraviolet keratitis, 201, 233
Ultraviolet light in water purification,
    304–305
Ultraviolet radiation (UVR), 227, *227*
    skin changes with exposure to, *228*
UNICEF, 223
Union Internationale des Associations d'Al-
    pinisme (UIAA)
    criteria for diagnosing HAPE, 200
    Medical Commission, 201
United States National Weather Service, 238
United States Pharmacopeia, 37
Unroofed blisters, 186, 187
Upward streamers, 237
Urban climbing centers, ix
Urinary tract infection, 139
Urine, color of, 43
Urochrome, 43
U-splint, 113
Utah Avalanche Center, 251
UV keratitis, 201

V
Vaccinations. *See* Immunizations
Valgus stressors, 78
Vasoconstriction, 206
Vegetarians/vegans
    iron deficiency in, 37
    protein for, 34–35
Venous pumps, 28–29
Ventilation, 18
Ventral, xii
Ventricular fibrillation, 209
Vertebrae, 117
    cervical, 5, 117, *118*
    lumbar, 117, *118*
    thoracic, 117, *118*
Vertical Medicine Resources, xiii
    assessment sheet, 317–318
    Crag or Multi-Pitch Climbing Medical
        Kit, 284
    High & Dry medical kit of, 27n, 158
Visual distress signals, 272
Vital signs, changes in, 4

Vitamin A, 35, 36
Vitamin B-12, 35
Vitamin C, 35, 37
Vitamin D, 36
Vitamin E, 36, 37
Vitamin K, 36

W
Warming up, 54
Water loss from sweat, 44
Water pathogens, *297*
Water purification, 296–306
    advantages/disadvantages of different
        techniques, *298*
    boiling in, 298–300, *299*
    chlorine dioxide in, 303
    chlorine in, 301–303, *302*
    choosing method in, 305–306
    filtration in, 300
    halogen disinfection in, 301
    iodine in, 301, *302*
    Miox purifier in, 303
    silver in, 303–304
    ultraviolet light in, 304–305
Weather identification, 244–250
    altimeters and, 249–250
    barometers and, 249
    clouds and, 245–247
    lightning and, 247
    sun and, 244–245
    thermometers and, 249–250
    thunderstorms and, 247
    winds and, 247–250
Webbing sling, 64, *65*
Weight-to-strength ratio, 51
Wet bulb globe temperature (WBGT),
    217–218
Whey protein, 38
Whistles, 272
Wilderness, CPR in the, 19
Wilderness EMS, 263
    Medical Director Course, 262
Wilderness & Environmental Medicine, 31
Wilderness Medical Society, 5, 43–44, 258,
    261–262
    on altitude illness, 193
    on behavioral preventions, 239
    on exercise-associated hyponatremia, 225

on HAPE, 201
on hypothermia, 202, 205, 212
proposal of *ad libitum* hydration strategy
    by, 219
on spinal immobilization, *263*, 264
on wound care, 166
Windchill, 217
    chart on, 250, 284
Winds, 247–250
    channeled, 248
    converging, 248
    diverging, 248
    estimating speed of, 248
    gap, 248
    lee, 248
Wobble boards, 54
Women
    alcohol consumption in, 37
    iron deficiency in, 37
    sweating by, 44
World Health Organization Oral Rehydra-
    tion Solution, 223
Worn/smooth tips, 189
Wounds
    bandaging and closure of, 169–170
    basic care of, *164*
    bleeding, 165
    clean, 164
    contaminated, 164, 173
    dirty, 164

gunshot, 143
irrigation and cleaning of, 167, 169
puncture, 173–174
Wrist and hands, 79–97
    carpal tunnel syndrome, 94–95
    DeQuerain's tenosynovitis, 96–97
    distal radius/ulna fracture, 79–81, *80,*
        81
    Dupuytren's contracture, 93–94
    flexor pulley injuries, 90–92
    ganglion cyst, 95–96
    hamate fracture, 84–86
    isolated flexor tendon injuries, 89–90
    lunate fracture, 83–84
    metacarpal and phalangeal fractures,
        86–87
    other fractures, 81, *82*
    scaphoid fracture, 81–83
    splinting, 85
    tendon and pulley ruptures, 87–89, *88*
    trigger finger or flexor tenosynovitis,
        92–93

Y
Yellow fever, 179

Z
Zika, 179
Zinc, 35
Z-plasty incisions, 94

AUTHOR BIOGRAPHIES

Seth Collings Hawkins, MD, FACEP, FAEMS, MFAWM

Seth began rocking climbing in Vermont in the 1980s, where he worked as a climbing instructor at Farm & Wilderness. He went on to become an emergency physician specializing in EMS and wilderness medicine. He is one of only a few American physicians holding dual board certification in both emergency medicine and EMS, and has worked for over twenty years in wilderness medicine and out-of-hospital emergency medical care. He is the executive editor of *Wilderness Medicine* magazine and the founder of the Appalachian Center for Wilderness Medicine (ACWM), the first non-profit wilderness medicine organization of its kind. He is the medical director for Burke EMS (which provides emergency response to climbing areas in Linville Gorge, the deepest gorge in the eastern United States), Landmark Learning, Western Piedmont Community College, and the NC State Park system. He is the medical advisor for the North Carolina Outdoor Bound School and REI. He is also the co-founder and course director of the Wilderness EMS Medical Director Course and founder and course director of the Carolina Wilderness EMS Externship. He is the founder and current Chief of the Appalachian Mountain Rescue Team, currently in application to become the first fully Mountain Rescue Association-credentialed team in the southeastern USA. Seth was in the first cohort of providers awarded Fellowship in the Academy of Wilderness Medicine in 2007, and in 2014, he became the first physician ever awarded the degree of Master Fellow by this Academy. He has been awarded numerous medical and technical rescue awards, including the Society of Academic Emergency Medicine's *Excellence in Emergency Medicine Award*, Orange Technical Rescue Team's *Technical Excellence Award*, the *University of Pittsburgh Ron Stewart Excellence in Teaching Award*, the *WMS-BALL Wilderness Medicine Award*, Hurst's *Green Cross*, and ACWM's lifetime achievement *Mountain Laurel Award*. He has been named a *Hero of Emergency Medicine* by the American College of Emergency Physicians and was named one of the Top Ten EMS Innovators of 2011 by the *Journal of EMS*. He is a co-founder and co-owner of Vertical Medicine Resources. When indoors, Dr. Hawkins is a full-time clinical emergency physician at Catawba Valley Medical Center in North Carolina and an assistant professor of emergency medicine at Wake Forest University.

R. Bryan Simon, RN, DiMM, FAWM

R. Bryan Simon, a contract registered nurse, is a graduate of the United States Military Academy at West Point, a former U.S. Army infantry officer, and graduate of the US Army Ranger School. After an injury in 2003, he left the military to pursue other goals. He is also an AMGA Certified Single Pitch Instructor (SPI), a Fellow in the Academy of Wilderness Medicine, and holds a Diploma in Mountain Medicine from the International Mountaineering and Climbing Federation (UIAA). Bryan serves on the editorial board for the journal *Nursing*, is an associate editor for the American Alpine Club's *Accidents in North American Climbing*, and is the climbing medicine columnist for *Wilderness Medicine*. He writes on a variety of subjects related to wilderness/climbing medicine, nursing, and adventure sports and his work has been featured in outdoor and climbing industry magazines such as *Climbing* and *Dead Point Magazine (DPM)*. Bryan is also the author of *Hiking and Biking in the New River Gorge: A Trail User's Guide*. Bryan has climbed and trekked around the world and has participated in rescues both here and abroad. He is a co-founder and co-owner of Vertical Medicine Resources, a founding member of the board of directors for the non-profit Appalachian Mountain Rescue Team (AMRT), a board member for the New River Alliance of Climbers (NRAC), and serves on the membership committee of the Wilderness Medical Society (WMS). Bryan is also the recipient of the Wilderness Medical Society's 2014 *Warren D. Bowman Award* presented for contributions in service to wilderness medicine.

J. Pearce Beissinger, MS, PA-C, FAWM

Pearce is a California native who mainly grew up along the East Coast. His first experiences "going vertical" were in the hills of western North Carolina and in New England. Along the way, he became a board certified physician assistant in orthopaedics and eventually transitioned his career into cardiothoracic surgery. His adventures continued and he is now an accomplished climber and alpinist with successful summits both within the United States and abroad. Whether in a gorge, gym, or on a Cascade volcano, he continues to explore climbing in the Pacific Northwest. Pearce is a Fellow in the Academy of Wilderness Medicine (WMS) and an AMGA Certified Single Pitch Instructor (SPI). In his early years, he served as a guide for L.L. Bean and on the board of directors for the Appalachian Center for Wilderness Medicine (ACWM), a non-profit organization promoting quality health care in limited resource environments. Pearce has dedicated many years of service to search and rescue teams and has participated in numerous mountain rescues both on the east and west coast. He is currently president of Portland Mountain Rescue (PMR) and co-chairman of their medical committee. Pearce also participates in mountain missionary work. He was a team member with Climbing for Christ (C4C) during their Mission-Nepal Expedition 2012 and most recently served as a medical guide with the 2014 and 2015 Equipping Saints for Ministry (ES4M) team during their Nepal mission trips. He is a co-founder and co-owner of Vertical Medicine Resources.

Deb Simon, RN, DiMM, CPT, FAWM

Deb Simon, originally from Ontario, Canada, is a registered nurse and avid climber and mountaineer, having summited peaks on five continents. She is certified as a Single Pitch Instructor (SPI) by the American Mountain Guides Association (AMGA) and guides regularly in the New River Gorge, WV. She is a Fellow in the Wilderness Medical Society's Academy of Wilderness Medicine, holds a Diploma in Mountain Medicine (DiMM) through the International Mountaineering and Climbing Federation (UIAA), and she has submitted her thesis for the award of a master's degree in Mountain Medicine through the University of Leicester in the United Kingdom. Deb is a member of the American Alpine Club, Medical Expeditions, and the Wilderness Medical Society. She is also a co-founder, co-owner, and trainer-in-chief at Vertical Medicine Resources. She has published multiple articles on wilderness medicine and altitude illness in peer-reviewed journals, and has worked in a variety of nursing specialties to include the Trauma and Cardiovascular ICU and the Cardiovascular Operating Room. She has been certified as a critical care registered nurse (CCRN) and is currently a certified Operating Room nurse (CNOR).